(NOTES)

Language and Television Series

This book offers a comprehensive linguistic analysis of contemporary US television series. Adopting an interdisciplinary and multi-methodological approach, Monika Bednarek brings together linguistic analysis of the Sydney Corpus of Television Dialogue with analysis of scriptwriting manuals, interviews with Hollywood scriptwriters, and a survey undertaken with university students about their consumption of TV series. In so doing, she presents five new and original empirical studies. The focus on language use in a professional context (the television industry), on scriptwriting pedagogy, and on learning and teaching provides an applied linguistic lens on TV series. This is complemented by perspectives taken from media linguistics, corpus linguistics, and sociocultural linguistics/sociolinguistics. Throughout the book, multiple dialogue extracts are presented from a wide variety of well-known fictional television series including *The Big Bang Theory*, *Grey's Anatomy*, and *Bones*. Researchers in applied linguistics, discourse analysis, critical discourse analysis, corpus linguistics, sociolinguistics, and media linguistics will find the book both stimulating and unique in its approach. The companion website (www.syd-tv.com) contains a wealth of additional material.

Monika Bednarek is Associate Professor in Linguistics at The University of Sydney, Australia. She is the author of five books including *The Discourse of New Values* (2017) and *The Language of Fictional Television* (2010). She is co-editor of the international, peer-reviewed journal *Functions of Language*.

THE CAMBRIDGE APPLIED LINGUISTICS SERIES

The authority on cutting-edge Applied Linguistics research

Series Editors   2007–present: Carol A. Chapelle and Susan Hunston
                   1988–2007: Michael H. Long and Jack C. Richards

For a complete list of titles please visit: www.cambridge.org

Recent titles in this series:

Intelligibility, Oral Communication, and the Teaching of Pronunciation
John M. Levis

Multilingual Education
Between Language Learning and Translanguaging
Edited by Jasone Cenoz and Durk Gorter

Learning Vocabulary in Another Language
2nd Edition *I. S. P. Nation*

Narrative Research in Applied Linguistics
Edited by Gary Barkhuizen

Teacher Research in Language Teaching
A Critical Analysis
Simon Borg

Figurative Language, Genre and Register
Alice Deignan, Jeannette Littlemore and Elena Semino

Exploring ELF
Academic English Shaped by Non-native Speakers
Anna Mauranen

Genres across the Disciplines
Student Writing in Higher Education
Hilary Nesi and Sheena Gardner

Disciplinary Identities
Individuality and Community in Academic Discourse
Ken Hyland

Replication Research in Applied Linguistics
Edited by Graeme Porte

The Language of Business Meetings
Michael Handford

Reading in a Second Language
Moving from Theory to Practice
William Grabe

Modelling and Assessing Vocabulary Knowledge
Edited by Helmut Daller, James Milton and Jeanine Treffers-Daller

Practice in a Second Language
Perspectives from Applied Linguistics and Cognitive Psychology
Edited by Robert M. DeKeyser

Feedback in Second Language Writing
Edited by Ken Hyland and Fiona Hyland

Task-Based Language Education
From Theory to Practice
Edited by Kris van den Branden

Second Language Needs Analysis
Edited by Michael H. Long

Insights into Second Language Reading
A Cross-Linguistic Approach
Keiko Koda

Research Genres
Exploration and Applications
John M. Swales

Critical Pedagogies and Language Learning
Edited by Bonny Norton and Kelleen Toohey

Exploring the Dynamics of Second Language Writing
Edited by Barbara Kroll

Understanding Expertise in Teaching
Case Studies of Second Language Teachers
Amy B. M. Tsui

Criterion-Referenced Language Testing
James Dean Brown and Thom Hudson

Corpora in Applied Linguistics
Susan Hunston

Pragmatics in Language Teaching
Edited by Kenneth R. Rose and Gabriele Kasper

Cognition and Second Language Instruction
Edited by Peter Robinson

Research Perspectives on English for Academic Purposes
Edited by John Flowerdew and Matthew Peacock

Computer Applications in Second Language Acquisition
Foundations for Teaching, Testing and Research
Carol A. Chapelle

Language and Television Series

A Linguistic Approach to TV Dialogue

Monika Bednarek

The University of Sydney
and
Freiburg Institute for Advanced Studies,
University of Freiburg

CAMBRIDGE
UNIVERSITY PRESS

CAMBRIDGE
UNIVERSITY PRESS

University Printing House, Cambridge CB2 8BS, United Kingdom

One Liberty Plaza, 20th Floor, New York, NY 10006, USA

477 Williamstown Road, Port Melbourne, VIC 3207, Australia

314–321, 3rd Floor, Plot 3, Splendor Forum, Jasola District Centre, New Delhi – 110025, India

79 Anson Road, #06–04/06, Singapore 079906

Cambridge University Press is part of the University of Cambridge.

It furthers the University's mission by disseminating knowledge in the pursuit of education, learning, and research at the highest international levels of excellence.

www.cambridge.org
Information on this title: www.cambridge.org/9781108472227
DOI: 10.1017/9781108559553

First published 2018

Printed in the United Kingdom by TJ International Ltd. Padstow Cornwall

A catalogue record for this publication is available from the British Library.

Library of Congress Cataloging-in-Publication Data
Names: Bednarek, Monika, 1977- author.
Title: Language and television series : a linguistic approach to
   TV dialogue / Monika Bednarek.
Description: Cambridge ; New York, NY : Cambridge University
   Press, 2018. | Series: The Cambridge applied linguistics series | Includes
   bibliographical references and index.
Identifiers: LCCN 2018022338 | ISBN 9781108472227 (hardback : alk. paper) |
   ISBN 9781108459150 (paperback : alk. paper)
Subjects: LCSH: Television broadcasting–Language. | Dialogue in television
   programs. | Dialogue analysis. | Discourse analysis.
Classification: LCC PN1992.8.L35 B42 2018 | DDC 808.2/25014–dc23
   LC record available at https://lccn.loc.gov/2018022338

ISBN 978-1-108-47222-7 Hardback
ISBN 978-1-108-45915-0 Paperback

Contents

Figures

Tables

Series Editors' Preface

Television series made in the United States are sold around the world and constitute a major influence on how English is used. Monika Bednarek's book is a fascinating study of dialogue from a corpus of programmes from sixty-six US series ranging from gritty drama to light comedy. Most readers of this book will be familiar with at least some of these programmes. TV series of this type have been the subject of academic research from perspectives such as media studies, but this is one of the few books to investigate the language of such series.

The book examines dialogue in TV series from a number of angles. Bednarek offers a detailed categorisation of the functions of such dialogue, including narrative-related functions such as progressing the plot or filling out character, and medium-related functions such as endorsing products or engaging audience emotions. The discussion and illustration of these functions reminds us that TV dialogue is an important part of a carefully crafted artefact designed to inform, entertain, and influence. The book then addresses the issue of how similar TV dialogue is to naturally occurring language, taking a corpus linguistics approach. TV dialogue needs to sound convincingly real without necessarily replicating actual features of natural interaction. An investigation of how this is done is supported by studies of key words and phraseology. Bednarek also presents a close study of what she calls non-codified language. The analysis reveals words and phrases that are invented for individual series, as well as neologisms that are at the leading edge of language change, existing in the community but not yet codified in any dictionary. The role of TV dialogue in supporting such change is fascinating.

Bednarek goes beyond the study of the dialogues as text or corpus (the dialogue as product) by conducting interviews with writers and producers to investigate how scripts are written and produced. This analysis gives an insight into the degree of intentionality and awareness on the part of the producers that lies behind the artefact of TV dialogue. In the final section of the book she also considers the role of TV dialogue in two pedagogical situations: the training of scriptwriters and the learning of English as a foreign or additional language. The latter is based on questionnaires completed by students of English in Germany. The value, and limitations, of TV dialogue as a pedagogic resource is explored in this chapter. In addressing the production

---

(by writers) of dialogue and its consumption (by viewers), Bednarek closes the circle around the dialogue itself.

This book has much to say to researchers into language education who are interested in the influence of television on language learning and its potential as a pedagogic resource. Researchers into the role of dialogue in narrative will also find much of interest here. The book also informs researchers who take an applied linguistics approach to the media or who wish to extend their research in that direction. A key feature is that the methodologies used are described in detail, allowing the studies to be replicated on other data. The book offers unique insight into a topic that is popular in every sense, and is a welcome addition to our series.

Acknowledgements

There are many people and institutions that have been instrumental in assisting me with the production of this book. I would like to acknowledge and thank them all most sincerely here. I am grateful to Susan Hunston and Carol Chapelle for commissioning the book for the Cambridge Applied Linguistics series and to the whole Cambridge University Press production team for seeing the manuscript through to publication. I would also like to thank the anonymous reviewers who provided feedback on earlier draft chapters of the manuscript, and Susan Hunston, who reviewed the final manuscript. Thanks also go to the participants for feedback and suggestions at various research seminars and conferences where parts of the research have been presented over the last few years.

The corpus that I analyse in this book – the Sydney Corpus of Television Dialogue (SydTV) could not have been built without school and faculty funding provided by The University of Sydney. I want to thank the research assistants who helped with building the corpus over several years: Cassandra Liardét (née Fawcett), David Lesslie, Samuel Luke, Ganna Veselovska, and Charlie Revett. I am also grateful to Georgia Carr for assisting with the transcription of interviews and editing the book manuscript. Throughout this project, Mike Scott provided help on WordSmith, implemented features, and fixed bugs – I am incredibly grateful for his support. Thanks are also due to the Sketch Engine team for assistance in exploiting SydTV with Sketch Engine, and to Joel Nothman for advice on Excel. Oral historian Tina Wright provided helpful information on the transcription of the data for the Charlotte project.

The research leading to these results has received funding from the People Programme (Marie Curie Actions) of the European Union's Seventh Framework Programme (FP7/2007–2013) under REA grant agreement no. 609305. I wish to express my thanks to the Freiburg Institute for Advanced Studies (FRIAS), University of Freiburg, Germany, for awarding me an FCFP External Senior Fellowship. Much of the groundwork and writing for this book was undertaken in late 2015 and early 2016 during my fellowship. I am immensely grateful for this opportunity and would like to thank Bernd Kortmann and Cristian Mair for fruitful discussions around standardness and corpus linguistics. A big thank you is also due to Roland Muntschick for general research assistance and analysis of questionnaire results.

The remainder of the writing was mostly done during my sabbatical in the first half of 2017 at the University of California, Santa Barbara. I would like to thank the Department of Linguistics for inviting me to come to UCSB as a Visiting Scholar and Mary Bucholtz for being my faculty sponsor, discussing language use in TV series, and commenting on earlier draft sections of this book. I am extremely grateful to John Du Bois for giving me access to the Longman Spoken American Corpus, for information on the corpus contents, and advice on transcription. I would also like to thank Stefan Gries for a helpful conversation about corpus statistics, and the participants at the SocioCult research seminar for their advice on dialogue lines in African American Vernacular English. The University of Sydney provided institutional and financial support during my sabbatical, for which I am very grateful.

I also wish to thank the university lecturers in Germany who helped me with undertaking questionnaires at the Universität Mannheim (Ira Gawlitzek, Rosemarie Tracy); Universität Augsburg (Christian Hoffmann); Universität Heidelberg (Beatrix Busse, Sandra Mollin); Ludwig-Maximilians-Universität, Munich (Renate Bauer, Susanne Handl, Jennifer Arendholz); Albert-Ludwigs-Universität, Freiburg (Christian Mair, Brigitte Halford); Rheinisch-Westfälische Technische Universität, Aachen (Stella Neumann); and Friedrich-Alexander-Universität Erlangen-Nürnberg (Brigitta Mittmann, Cordula Glass, Michael Klotz).

I am extremely thankful, too, to the five Hollywood scriptwriters/showrunners whom I interviewed for this book: Jane Espenson, David Mandel, Doris Egan, Bob Berens, and one writer who preferred to remain unidentified. Special thanks are due to Jane Espenson, who was so generous with her time and assistance. I also appreciate the help from Javier Barrios and Hilary Swett regarding access to official final scripts archived in the Writers Guild foundation's Shavelson-Webb library in Los Angeles. Copyright for all material analysed in this book remains with the original authors/creators and is used exclusively for criticism and scholarship.

Most of all I want to thank Helen Caple, who acted as a sounding board for ideas, read draft chapters as well as the final manuscript, and always gave me valuable feedback. She also had to endure countless hours of television watching, and the fact that I could never turn off my analytical media brain. Without her love and support in all ways, writing this book would have been so much more difficult!

Spoiler Alert

In this book I discuss and analyse examples from many US television series. Readers should be aware that in this process plot elements from some series may be revealed.

Part I

Introduction

1 *Television Dialogue*

1 Introduction

Many of us have a favourite line of dialogue from a TV series. It might be 'to boldly go where no one has gone before' (*Star Trek*), 'Winter is coming' (*Game of Thrones*), 'I am the one who knocks' (*Breaking Bad*), 'Treat Yo'self' (*Parks and Recreation*), 'Clear eyes, full hearts, can't lose' (*Friday Night Lights*), or perhaps something more nerdy like 'She's an assistant professor in the Linguistics department ... They're wild!' (*Friends*). It is unquestionable that television dialogue has given us many such memorable lines, but it also fulfils important functions in its more mundane incarnations, in the lines we do not consciously remember. As part of the mass media, television is one of the 'agents of socialisation' (Lippi-Green 2012: 101) and significantly shapes our sociolinguistic environment (Coupland 2007: 185). We can speak of a culture–media dialectic, where TV dialogue both constructs and reflects cultures and their ideologies. Dialogue is hence an important source of information about language and society, in addition to being fundamental to how televisual narratives work (Queen 2015).

Undoubtedly, television series are a significant social and psychological phenomenon; they have an immense cultural impact and often demonstrate artistic sophistication. They are popular cultural products, consumed by millions of viewers world-wide: 'even a moderately successful series, if it continues for enough years to go into syndication, is seen by hundreds of millions' (Douglas 2011: 21).[1] Highly popular US TV series such as *Lost* are licensed to more than 180 international territories (Pearson 2007b: 255–6). English-language TV dialogue is thus consumed by many viewers who do not speak English as a first language. When consumed in the original (rather than dubbed) version, television dialogue can be a key way in which learners encounter English-language conversations, and it may constitute an influential model for such viewers (Mittmann 2006: 575). Indeed, Bleichenbacher

(2008: 2) quotes a European Union survey in which interviewees stated that watching films and television was the second most frequent situation for the use of English as a second language. Clearly, from an applied linguistic perspective it is a worthwhile endeavour to analyse the kind of language such learners of English encounter.

This book offers just such an investigation of the language used in contemporary US television series. In particular, its aims are:

- to develop a new categorisation of the multiple functions of TV dialogue
- to identify and explain the salient linguistic characteristics of TV dialogue
- to examine non-codified language phenomena in TV dialogue[2]
- to provide new insights into production and consumption aspects of TV series, and to connect these to the linguistic analysis.

In analysing TV dialogue, this book uses a new, carefully designed dataset of TV dialogue, the Sydney Corpus of Television Dialogue (SydTV). The name derives from the fact that this corpus was designed and built at the University of Sydney, with funding provided by the university. SydTV is a small, specialised corpus (~275,000 words), representative of the language variety of contemporary US TV dialogue. In total, it contains dialogue from one episode each from sixty-six different TV series (first season). About half of the corpus comes from comedy genres and the other half from drama genres, since this is one of the major distinctions made in the TV industry.[3] Based on the rise and importance of so-called quality television, about half of the corpus comes from Emmy- or Golden Globe-winning or -nominated series, and the other half does not. The corpus design and construction is described in more detail in Chapter 5, and a list of all included episodes is available in the Appendix (Table A.1). When citing examples from SydTV in this book I will simply provide the name of the TV series, as additional information can easily be retrieved from the Appendix. For example, a dialogue line will be attributed to 'SydTV, *Pushing Daisies*' rather than 'SydTV, *Pushing Daisies*, season 1, episode 7, "Smell of success"'. Season and episode number are specified only for dialogue from episodes that do *not* come from SydTV, on which I will occasionally draw.

More precisely, SydTV will be analysed using corpus linguistic and computer-assisted approaches to identify the linguistic characteristics of TV dialogue. Given that US TV series are consumed by so many viewers worldwide, it is important to discover what this language looks like. From an applied linguistic perspective it is vital to know the input that learners are exposed to. Insights into TV dialogue can inform the use of TV series in language learning and teaching as well as the teaching of televisual literacy in the university curriculum. All of these aspects are explored in this book. Further, a special focus of the analyses of SydTV is on non-codified language, including non-standard language use and linguistic innovation.[4] These analyses aim to contribute to the emerging body of sociocultural linguistic research on contemporary television narratives (e.g. Lopez & Bucholtz 2017).

These linguistic analyses of SydTV examine TV dialogue from a 'product' perspective. However, this book has a more ambitious aim, which is to connect these analyses to aspects of production and consumption. I therefore also draw on ethnographic research. To do so, I undertook a survey of pedagogic scriptwriting material as well as interviews with five Hollywood scriptwriters. I also report on my findings from a questionnaire with almost 600 German university students about their consumption of English-language TV series. I therefore bring together the three perspectives from which TV series can be approached (Bednarek 2015d): that of the process of creation/production, that of the outcome/product, and that of consumption. This allows a richer contextualisation of TV dialogue in terms of how it is produced and consumed (see also Richardson 2010a). The focus on language use in a professional context (the television industry), on scriptwriting pedagogy, and on learning and teaching provides an applied linguistic lens on TV series. This is complemented by perspectives taken from media linguistics and sociocultural linguistics.

I do not want to repeat here what I and others have written about the value and significance of media in general and TV series in particular. I assume that readers who have decided to read this book do not need any further convincing that linguistic analysis of such media texts is a worthwhile endeavour. Interested readers can consult the justifications for analysing language in the media in Coupland et al. (2016), and in films and TV series in Bednarek (2010a: 7–11; 2012b: 199–202; in press a), Androutsopoulos (2012), and Queen (2015). Suffice it to say that many linguists agree that fictional mass media require more attention, including 'much more analysis of the structural characteristics of media representation of language, of different genres, formats' (Stuart-Smith 2011: 235). In the midst of a 'golden' age of television, we need a comprehensive investigation of language use in televisual narratives. This book contributes to this endeavour, and explores three main themes about TV dialogue. Put simply, they can be paraphrased as follows:

- TV dialogue fulfils a range of functions relating to the audience.
- TV dialogue is both similar and different to spontaneous speech.

- TV dialogue is innovative and contains non-codified language, which is essential to its character.

In this first chapter I provide an introduction to television dialogue (Section 2), televisual narratives (Section 3), how TV dialogue is produced (Section 4), and its participation framework (Section 5).

2 What Is *Television Dialogue*? Clarification of Terms

So far, I have used the term *television dialogue* without explicitly defining it. Put simply, I use the term to refer to dialogue from television series. In contrast, the term *film* or *movie dialogue* refers to dialogue from films/movies. I borrow Piazza et al.'s (2011: 1) term *telecinematic discourse* as a cover term for both kinds of dialogue. I also use Queen's (2015) label *narrative mass media* to refer to both films and TV series. It is important to emphasise at this point that there are both similarities and differences between television series and films. Both feature fictional, audiovisual narratives that address an external audience (see Section 5) and both include scripted and poly-functional dialogue with some similar storytelling techniques (Thompson 2003; Piazza et al. 2011; Androutsopoulos 2012; Bednarek 2015a).

On the other hand, there are manifold differences between TV series and films (Thompson 2003; Douglas 2011; Redvall 2013; Bednarek 2015a; Mittell 2015): this includes the serial nature of an often long-running TV narrative – as Richardson (2010a: 136) puts it, 'much television drama operates on presumptions of continuity'. And unlike films, traditional network TV series are structured around ad breaks and feature dispersed exposition (Thompson 2003). In addition, the stability and consistency of televisual characters (see Section 3) leads to significant depth of audience involvement.

These two cultural products are also differentiated by their business models, target audiences, rules and regulations, and production processes (including differences in the role of directors and writers; amount of content per year; time frames; budgets, etc.). Thompson (2003: xi) concludes that '[f]ilm and television are [...] two different (if overlapping) media'. The industry recognises these differences by offering special courses and manuals on writing *for television* (see Chapter 10). Such differences can impact on language – for example, changed funding models affect the use of language variation (Queen 2015: 19). In sum, my assumption is that we cannot automatically assume that film and television dialogue are identical, and further, that it is crucial to have specific terms that allow us to distinguish them from each other where relevant. The term *television dialogue* permits us to do so. However, both components of the term *television dialogue* – (1) television series and (2) dialogue – require further explanation.

First, by *television series* I essentially refer to scripted, fictional (imaginative) narratives,[5] with characters and plot strand(s), and include series and serials that are intended to run over several seasons.[6] The label covers both scripted narrative series that are produced by television networks and those that are produced by companies such as Amazon or Netflix, for instance *House of Cards* (sometimes referred to as *web series* or *web television series* or *internet drama series*). There are well-known differences between such outlets (network, cable, subscription, etc.), which impact on language use, especially in relation to the use of particular swear/taboo words, which are censored only in network/broadcast television. Technically speaking, shows such as *House of Cards* are not *television series*, as they are not produced by TV networks and not originally broadcast on TV. They may nevertheless be broadcast on television in certain countries, in the same way in which an HBO subscription programme may end up on free-to-air television through processes of syndication and export. Rather than using Bednarek's (2015a) term *digital series* (DS), I will employ the term *television series* as a cover term for both; and the same broad reference applies to *television dialogue*. Further, TV series are nowadays consumed via a range of platforms or mediums (television, tablet, laptop, mobile phone, etc.), but I will refer to them as *TV series* regardless of how they are experienced.

Second, I use the term *dialogue* as shorthand for all character or narrator speech, whether this speech is by one speaker (monologues, asides, voice-over narration, etc.), between two speakers (dyadic interactions), or between several speakers (multiparty interactions). As such, dialogue is differentiated from screen directions, which may refer to elements such as location and time, angle, special effects, transition, sounds, setting, clothing, name/age, mental state, actions, pauses, and voice source. Some instances of TV dialogue are represented in examples 1 (voice-over by a narrator), 2 (voice-over by a character), 3 (dyadic interaction), and 4 (multiparty interaction).

(1)

TV dialogue instantiated as voice-over by a narrator (VOICE)

VOICE: At this very moment at the Longborough School for Boys, young Ned was nine years, forty-one weeks, fourteen hours and three minutes old and exhausted. For despite the endless waking hours spent assuring himself that his heart was on the mend, Ned discovered the truth in his sleep. Sadly, not a single night had passed since the death of his mother that he didn't dream of her coming back to him. Realizing he couldn't rush his heart into healing, he concocted a plan, to reconnect with his mother in a way that only he could. For young Ned wasn't like the other children, or the other adults for that matter, which, in this case, delighted him, briefly. Although young Ned knew he couldn't taste the pie lest the fruit rot again, he didn't care. The mere smell of it made him feel, if only for an hour, exactly like he wanted to feel, safe and warm and loved. Which is why he became the pie maker, who at this very moment, was planting flowers to make Chuck feel as safe and warm and loved as he once did.   (SydTV, *Pushing Daisies*)

(2)

TV dialogue instantiated as voice-over (V) by a character

EARL (V):   Me and Jessie had a good thing goin', and it was all happenin' pretty fast, but not as fast as it happened later that night with Joy. In just seven hours, I went from having a semi-serious three-week girlfriend to bein' the husband of a pregnant woman whose name I kept forgettin'. I thought about callin' Jessie to talk to her and tell her what I had done, but then I realized I'd have to talk to her and tell her what I had done.   (SydTV, *My Name is Earl*)

(3)

TV dialogue instantiated as dyadic interaction

ANN: Andy. Andy, we need to talk.
ANDY: Hey, uh, we're just about to start. Could you grab me a triple whiskey and water?
ANN: You would like that wouldn't you.
ANDY: Yep.
ANN: You have two perfectly good legs, get it yourself.
    (SydTV, *Parks and Recreation*)

(4)

TV dialogue instantiated as multiparty conversation

PENNY: Hey, guys, guys, some of the other waitresses wanted me to ask you something.
LEONARD: Oh, it's called trestling.
HOWARD: It combines the physical strength of arm wrestling with the mental agility of tetris into the ultimate sport.
PENNY: Yeah, that's terrific, but what they wanted me to ask you was to cut it the hell out.   (SydTV, *The Big Bang Theory*)

As audiences (and researchers) we can engage with such dialogue in various forms, for instance by reading official and unofficial scripts, transcripts or subtitles, or by experiencing the audiovisual performance (dubbed or not, on television or via other mediums). In this book I am interested in on-screen dialogue – the dialogue that the audience encounters when watching a TV episode. In terms of mode, such dialogue can be characterised as 'THE SPEAKING OF WHAT IS WRITTEN TO BE SPOKEN AS IF NOT WRITTEN' (Gregory 1967: 191, original capitalisation). But as a whole, the television narrative is a multimodal and multisemiotic text, and it must be acknowledged here that a focus on dialogue does not capture all elements of meaning-making (Bednarek 2010a, 2015a; Richardson 2010b; Valentini 2013; Toolan 2014).

3 Televisual Stories and Characters

Dialogue contributes significantly to the fundamental goal of TV series, namely 'the telling of a narrative, one which might absorb, entertain, inspire, and move the viewer' (Toolan 2011: 181). To better understand such narratives, I provide a brief overview of televisual stories and characters in this section. Since studies in narratology and stylistics mainly focus on prose fiction or literary drama (e.g. Pfister 1988; Bal 1997; Rimmon-Kenan 2002; Prince 2003), with some also commenting on film (e.g. Chatman 1978; Culpeper 2001; Toolan 2001, 2014; Fludernik 2009), my overview instead comes from TV scriptwriting manuals (e.g. Finer & Pearlman 2004; Priggé 2005; Douglas 2011), and research in television studies (Thompson 2003; Pearson 2007a; Mittell 2015).

In such work, televisual stories are considered to consist of a succession of events, typically with a trajectory and involving one or several participants. Structurally, they are broken down into acts and scenes or beats (story points). The structure of particular TV series varies, as does the number of acts. Comedies tend to have two or three acts, but dramas have four or more. Landau (2014: 184) gives a breakdown of almost fifty series, including several included in SydTV. In TV series that have a title sequence (opening credits, intro, credit sequence – see Bednarek 2014b, c) this can be preceded by a recap ('previously on') or new dramatic material in a so-called teaser/cold opening (Douglas 2011: 91).

Stories are typically talked about in terms of an Aristotelian structure with a beginning, middle, and end, including turning points/twists or, potentially, cliff-hangers, with the latter story elements structured around commercial breaks in traditional network series. Comedic scenes can have a distinct structure, for example in sitcoms where punchlines are often included at the end of an exchange (Smith 2009: KL 995–6).[7] In a single TV episode, we can find multiple storylines (A, B, C stories), which are distinct, complementary, parallel, or interwoven. These storylines can be 'open' (with plot and character arcs continuing across episodes or seasons) or 'closed' (achieving closure or resolution, for example within an episode). Many series that resolve storylines within an episode also have ongoing stories.

The desires or goals of characters are seen as central to many storylines, to the extent that it is argued by some that 'story *is* character' (Finer & Pearlman 2004, emphasis in original). Many emphasise that televisual characters need to be distinct from each other (i.e. not sound alike) as well as stable entities so that viewers can develop relationships with them. In Mittell's (2015: 141–2) words:

The desire for stable characters with consistent traits and personalities is a major draw for serial storytelling, as we want to feel connected to such characters through parasocial relationships and might be quite disappointed if they changed in ways that violate their initial connections and appeals.

Most television characters are thus stable figures who accumulate life events, experiences, and relationships but do not change from them (Pearson 2007a). Generally, TV characters are hence described in terms of depth, complexity, and dimension rather than change and transformation. Douglas (2011: 14) speaks of vertical instead of horizontal development.[8]

In addition, I have suggested that aspects of emotion, attitude, and ideology are particularly important in televisual characters and have introduced the concept of *expressive character identity* for relevant character traits (Bednarek 2010a, 2011c). Other aspects of character relate to a range of social and personal variables, and include the relationships between characters, as further discussed in Chapter 3.

How are TV characters built? Mittell (2015: 130–1) suggests that audience members infer characters' interior states through explicit exterior marks (dialogue, actions, appearance), the dramatic context, and their knowledge of characters. This is more or less in line with cognitive stylistic models of characterisation (Culpeper 2001). While dialogue 'cues' (Culpeper 2001: 35) are thus not the only means of constructing character, they are one way in which characters are built. Such cues function to indicate character directly/explicitly (naming the trait) or indirectly/implicitly (displaying the trait) (Culpeper 2001: 163–229), and may be reiterated throughout the TV narrative (Thompson 2003: 27). Importantly, television characters are collaboratively created by writers, producers, and actors, who 'have varying degrees of creative authority and collaborative ownership of their ongoing characters' (Mittell 2015: 119). In addition, cognitive models of televisual characterisation assume that the interpretation of character draws on the prior knowledge of viewers (e.g. Richardson 2010a: 127–50).

According to Culpeper (2001), a wide range of linguistic features can contribute to characterisation in drama, including conversational structure, affective language, lexical richness/diversity, terms of address, syntactic structure, accent/dialect, impoliteness strategies, and (non-)adherence to conversational maxims. While Culpeper's examples come from literary drama and film, his inventory would seem to at least partially apply to televisual characterisation.[9] A wide range of dialogue cues have indeed been examined in relation to the traits of television characters, and many aspects of character identity have been examined, including expressive character identity, gender, sexuality, impoliteness, nerdiness, national identity, affluence, character relationships, and so on (see survey in Bednarek 2017b).

This overview has of necessity been somewhat simplified, since there are various differences between genres and types of TV series as well as individual series. Television series pursue different modes of storytelling, from the more conventional to the more sophisticated, with 'narrative complexity' (Mittell 2015: 17) emerging since the 1990s, enabled by a range of technological, industrial, and reception shifts (Mittell 2015).[10] However, such complex storytelling has not replaced conventional sitcoms and dramas; both exist side by side. While storytelling techniques, story structure, and characterisation are not the focus of this book, the communication of the narrative (characters, happenings, setting) is one of the many functions that TV dialogue fulfils and will be taken up again in Chapter 3.

4 Producing Dialogue for US Television Series

The features and functions of dialogue in US TV series also need to be understood in relation to the production process. Because this book is not located within a political economy framework, I will not discuss aspects such as industrial conditions, business models, ownership, vertical integration, etc. here. Two general points are nevertheless important to keep in mind. First, business models differ between platforms (e.g. traditional network television versus subscription cable or digital distributors), and second, TV series are both creative and *commercial* products – 'hot properties, which enable the extraction of maximum profits in minimum time through simultaneous distribution across multiple platforms and across the globe' (Pearson 2007b: 252).

Many of the manuals that teach aspiring writers how to write for TV series also explain the production process in the United States, as does some of the research from television studies. In this section I provide a brief summary based primarily on Douglas (2011) and Mittell (2015: 86–92). I focus on what happens during production as far as the writing process is concerned, but am not going to talk about the process of developing *new* TV series (from the pitching of ideas to the production of pilots; see Douglas 2011: 45–77).

The overall managerial responsibility in TV series lies with the executive producer or 'showrunner' (who is also the head writer) rather than the director as in films. It is therefore frequently asserted that 'television is a writer's medium' (e.g. Finer & Pearlman 2004: 5). Indeed, authorship is often assigned to the showrunner and an 'author brand' has emerged (Pearson 2007b: 243), especially in relation to 'quality' television (e.g. Hassler-Forest 2014) This means that showrunners are promoted as 'creators' or 'auteurs' by networks/studios. Staff writers write their own episodes but also workshop and rewrite other writers' drafts. Their goal is to create a script that 'mimic[s] the showrunner's voice in an effort for stylistic consistency' (Mittell 2015: 91). As Landau (2014: 41) emphasises, 'It's important that the scripts have a singular voice.'

However, except for rare cases with singular writers, a team of six to twelve writers or writer-producers work *collaboratively* in the famous 'writers' room' (although not all series use one), a space that has attracted much attention and scrutiny:

> the writers' room, the place where the drama begins and ends, has become the subject of intense curiosity and scrutiny [...] Inevitably there are websites and blogs and memes devoted to gossip about these sacred and profane spaces, places to get a fix of favourite dramas before the next series is uploaded. Some shows – *Orange Is the New Black* and *The Good Wife* pioneered the practice – provide the backstory to the genesis and creation scenes in live Twitter feeds, with whiteboards and interview links and photos.
>
> (Adams 2017)

While there are differences between drama and comedy as well as individual series, this collaborative process may include all or some of the following steps. First, writers sometimes collaboratively map out story arcs and the narrative structure of the whole season. Together or individually they then map out the structure, plots, and scenes for an episode. This process is called 'breaking' stories and tends to happens in the writers' room, typically using a whiteboard (see Figure 1.1).

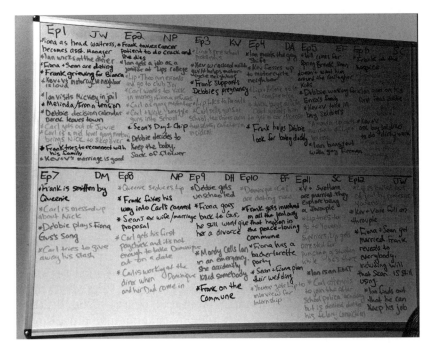

Figure 1.1 What a whiteboard in the writers' room might look like (author's own photo of a whiteboard for Shameless, *hanging in the room dedicated to screenwriting at the Warner Bros. Studio Tour Hollywood)*

This is the basis for an outline (a list of scenes); if an individual writer is assigned to produce the outline, the writing team (or just the show-runner) reviews it, providing notes to the writer for revision.

In any case, a specific writer is responsible for creating the episode script on the basis of an approved outline. The writing credits for that episode will identify this person (a staff writer or a freelance writer). The writing team (or just the showrunner) provides feedback on the episode scripts produced by that writer, often two drafts. Consultants may also provide input (e.g. in medical or legal shows). The show-runner ensures that the script fits the standards, style, and arcs of the series and may do major rewrites before finalising the script. In fact, he or she has the opportunity to rewrite every line of dialogue, but does not necessarily do so. Network and studio executives also provide notes during the whole process, including on the outline and script (for example on structure, style, characterisation, offensiveness). The amount and type of notes vary, but executives do need to give their approval.

Once the script has been finalised, rewriting may occur in rehearsals (if they are used) or as late as during the filming, but the extent to which this happens again varies. Thus, some showrunners do not allow actors to make any changes to the dialogue in scripts, while others permit or even encourage it. Interestingly, the script may also be influenced by aspects of production such as budgetary constraints. For instance, dialogue between two people is easier and cheaper than multiparty conversations (Epstein 2006: 97)

In sum, the process moves from pitching the story to breaking the story to writing the story outline to writing and revising script drafts. As far as dialogue is concerned, some lines may be suggested in the writers' room during the process of breaking stories, and some lines may already be included in the outline, but the bulk of the dialogue is written when script drafts are produced and revised. During post-production further changes can be made, for instance editing or cutting certain lines of dialogue in the edit room.

In conclusion, even though showrunners have the final responsibility; provide consistency of the dialogue, plot, and characters; and are regarded as 'the primary authorial figures' (Mittell 2015: 92), the writing of TV dialogue is a highly collaborative process with multiple authors. In linguistics, this multiple authorship has been discussed in relation to the participation framework, the subject of the next section.

5 The Participation Framework of TV Dialogue

Television dialogue is an example of 'screen-to-face discourse' (Bubel 2006: 46), which is similar to other kinds of fictional and mediated discourse in featuring different communicative layers or levels: the communication within the diegesis (interaction among on-screen characters in the fictional world), and the communication with the narrative's external audience. Most research on TV series draws on relevant work in literary and media studies (e.g. Short 1981; Pfister 1988; Scannell 1991) in recognising this 'double' communicative interaction plane, although different terms are used to label and conceptualise the layers. A relevant review is provided in Bubel (2008).

The production process of TV series is not usually described in much detail in linguistic research (but see Richardson 2010a: 66–8); however, its multiple authorship is clearly recognised (e.g. Bubel 2006; Dynel 2011). TV series are thus seen to derive from the efforts of the production crew (producers, directors, writers, camera operators, actors, editors, and so on). Dynel (2011: 313) uses the term *collective sender* for this 'author'.

But in general, linguists have shown more interest in the audience, drawing on Goffman's (1976, 1979) model of participation structure (e.g. Bubel 2006, 2008; Dynel 2011, 2012; Brock 2015). There is general agreement that the viewer is an overhearing but ratified participant for whom the dialogue is ultimately designed, but there is some debate about how to best conceptualise and label this role. For example, Bubel (2006, 2008, 2011; Bubel & Spitz 2006) uses the term *overhearer*; Richardson (2010a) employs *eavesdropper*, while Dynel (e.g. 2011) prefers the term *recipient*. Brock (2015: 28) suggests that these approaches can be reconciled by taking into account the different communicative layers: the television viewer is ultimately the intended recipient of television dialogue, but can also be assigned different listener roles at the level of the fictional world (most frequently that of the overhearer, sometimes that of the eavesdropper or speaker). Much research on the participation framework in TV series explores how participation-based strategies create pragmatic effects such as humour or impoliteness (e.g. Brock 2011, 2015, 2016; Dynel 2011, 2012, 2016; Messerli 2016).

In this book, I am not so much concerned with the different listener roles of the audience, but I proceed from the assumption that characters talk both to each other and to viewers. I also assume that TV dialogue is designed to fulfil a range of functions for its audience. Like film (Kozloff 2000: 121), the defining characteristic of TV dialogue is that it is designed for 'us', the viewers – what is variously called *audience, recipient,* or *overhearer design*. After all, the overarching purpose of TV dialogue is to attract and retain an audience: a TV series must 'be entertaining to people, they have to be engaged and curious and wanting to come back next week' (Terence Winter, cited in Bennett 2014: KL 1264–6).

In other words, the participation framework of TV dialogue necessitates an examination of the functions of language use that differs from how we analyse the functions of utterances in 'real' life. For example, if a TV character invites another TV character to a party, we might ask what functions this dialogue performs for the audience. Depending on the narrative, such an invitation might propel the plot, inform viewers about the relationship between the two characters, elicit an emotional reaction from the audience to the fact that this character has summoned up the courage to invite the other character, create realism by using a conventionalised phrase to express the invitation, and so on. These specific functions would not normally play a role in analysing spontaneous conversation between people in non-fictional contexts, but they are crucial for the analysis of television dialogue. In later chapters, I provide an extended explanation of relevant functions with the help of many examples from contemporary TV series.

6 Conclusion and Overview of the Book

In this chapter I have introduced aspects of TV dialogue and TV series that are pertinent to this book. The chapter has provided an introduction to (US) TV dialogue, including its participation framework and how it is produced, as well as the narratives and characters found in TV series. Other important aspects, such as television genres and multimodality, are discussed in Bednarek (2010a, 2015a) and briefly mentioned in later chapters where they are relevant.

In sum, this book proceeds from the following key assumptions:

- US TV dialogue has no single author, but multiple authors – most importantly, the writing team who produces the shooting script, but also others who contribute to the on-screen dialogue.
- Television dialogue creates a fictional world for viewers, a narrative with characters and plot (strands) – a world where characters communicate with each other.
- We can assume that characters simultaneously talk to each other within the fictional world and to the audience who is entertained by this fictional world.
- Ultimately, TV dialogue is therefore designed to fulfil a range of different functions for its audience; its characteristics and functions can be associated with this design.

As I have argued above, the time is ripe for a comprehensive investigation of language use in televisual narratives. The following chapters of this book aim to contribute to this endeavour. In the next chapter I review linguistic approaches to telecinematic discourse. Since my interest is in English-language series, especially those from the United States, the book does not refer to research on TV series (and films) in other languages. This is not to deny the importance of such work; however, comparative or cross-cultural analysis is beyond the remit of this book.

In Part II (Chapters 3 and 4) I introduce a new functional approach to television series (FATS), illustrating the functions of TV dialogue with multiple examples from different series. Part III (Chapters 5 and 6) describes the Sydney Corpus of Television Dialogue in more detail and explains the approaches used in this book. Part IV presents analyses of this corpus: Chapters 7 and 8 use corpus linguistic methods to explore the salient linguistic characteristics of TV dialogue, while Chapter 9 examines non-codified language features in SydTV. Together, the chapters in Part IV unpack the characteristics of TV dialogue in a way that I hope will be both insightful and entertaining. Part V then shifts the perspective to aspects of production and consumption. It examines what scriptwriting manuals and scriptwriters say about TV dialogue (Chapter 10) and shows how advanced learners of English consume such dialogue, including their linguistic awareness (Chapter 11). Note that I use *scriptwriter* in this book as a cover term for staff writers, freelance writers, creators, and showrunners.

The vast majority of linguistic research focuses on TV dialogue as an 'outcome' or 'product', by analysing dialogue in scripts or transcripts. Linguists less often analyse scriptwriting processes/pedagogy or hone in on the audience. An innovative and hopefully useful contribution of this book is that it brings the three perspectives together in moving linguistic research 'beyond the product' and making connections between product, production, and consumption. I therefore complement analysis of SydTV with ethnographic research. In so doing, this book brings together several linguistic approaches:

- *Applied linguistics*: it examines language use in a professional context (the television industry) and investigates scriptwriting pedagogy and language learners.
- *Corpus linguistics*: it applies corpus linguistic tools and techniques.
- *Media linguistics*: it looks at media language *as* media language (especially in relation to the functions of TV dialogue).
- *Sociocultural linguistics*: it pays attention to the relationship between language and society (for instance, with respect to nonstandard language and linguistic innovation).

While the primary audience of this book is thus linguists from different disciplines, it may also be of interest to other researchers fascinated by the creative achievement that is contemporary television dialogue.

2 Linguistic Approaches to Telecinematic Discourse

1 Introduction

For a long time, television series were neglected and deemed unworthy of linguistic study, although this has changed in recent years. It is interesting that even in television studies, TV series were often treated as evidence of negative aspects of society rather than examined from an aesthetic perspective. This lack of close textual analysis, as explained by Thompson (2003: 3), speaks to scholars' 'lingering prejudice against taking television seriously as an art form', which has also been true of linguists. However, in the last decade or so many relevant linguistic studies have emerged. The analysis of telecinematic discourse is now a trend, even in sociolinguistics, which has long rejected such data as inauthentic, artificial, or irrelevant, but which now exploits such data for analysis of linguistic ideologies, indexicality, and stylisation (Queen 2013: 220). Some sociolinguists have even argued that the 'mass media are changing the terms of our engagement with language and social semiosis in late-modernity [...]. TV in particular has put mediated linguistic diversity in front of the viewing public far more pervasively and with much richer and more saturated indexical loading than face-to-face social reality can achieve' (Coupland 2010: 69). This emerging interest in the narrative mass media contrasts starkly with the situation when I first started working on US TV series a decade ago, with only a handful of linguistic studies and no broader engagement at conferences.

Extensive reviews of the state-of-the-art in linguistics are provided in Bednarek (2015d, 2017b) and – with a specific focus on corpus linguistics – in Bednarek (2015a). From a sociolinguistic perspective, Richardson (2010a) provides a more detailed discussion of some relevant early research. A 21-page bibliography is also available (Bednarek & Zago 2018). In contrast, the overview in this chapter focuses only on those areas that are most pertinent to this book: research on the characteristics of TV dialogue and the extent to which it is similar to unscripted spoken language (Section 2), and research on non-standard language, linguistic innovation, and language change (Sections 3 and 4). In addition, Chapter 10 will review linguistic research on scriptwriting pedagogy, while Chapter 11 deals with applied linguistic research on the usefulness of TV dialogue for language learning. My discussion is limited to research on English-language products (mainly from the United States) and does not touch upon multimodal discourse analysis (e.g. Bateman & Schmidt 2012; Wildfeuer 2014) or audiovisual translation (e.g. Queen 2004; Valdeón 2011; Baños 2013; Bonsignori & Bruti 2014; Bruti & Vignozzi 2016a).

2 TV Dialogue versus Unscripted Spoken Language

Much linguistic research focuses on investigating the extent to which telecinematic discourse is similar or different to unscripted spoken language, i.e. in how far it is 'naturalistic' or 'realistic'. In so doing, such studies also provide insight into the linguistic characteristics of film or television dialogue. In line with the topic of this book, I will focus on the latter here. Readers interested in the linguistic features of *film* dialogue can refer to the many relevant entries in Bednarek and Zago (2018).

Clearly, as dialogue that is designed to be spoken as if not written, TV dialogue is scripted in advance and addresses the audience. At the most general level, the fact that much TV dialogue features short and equal exchanges between characters, rather than long monologues by one character, can be tied to the need to entertain the audience (Bednarek 2010a: 65). From a historical perspective, the pace of dialogue has increased over time (Epstein 2006: 79).

TV dialogue must also be intelligible, accessible, and comprehensible, which means that words are often enunciated relatively clearly and unfamiliar words may be unpacked through dialogue. It has been described as 'clean – every word can be heard' (Richardson 2010a: 19). Repetition and multimodal strategies compensate for 'incomprehensible' dialogue in series such as *The Wire* (Toolan 2011). In general, 'much of television storytelling aims to make comprehension easy, invisible, and automatic', although some types of television are more open to the possibility of viewer confusion (Mittell 2015: 164). Richardson (2010a: 6) talks about 'easy listening' as a design goal.

Compared with naturally occurring interaction, typically there is less overlap and abrupt topic shift, fewer interruptions, repair sequences, and speech errors, false starts, hesitation phenomena, and minimal responses (Bubel 2006; Quaglio 2009: 148; Richardson 2010a; Toolan 2011; Dose 2013). TV dialogue is thus both fluent and '"unnaturally" coherent and focussed' (Toolan 2011: 181). As commonly observed, when such features occur they fulfil important narrative functions like signalling a character's emotional response or personality traits (e.g. Bubel 2006: 262; Quaglio 2009: 119, Richardson 2010a; Bednarek 2012a; Dose 2013).

In addition, TV dialogue contributes to 'performance which is linguistically "stylized" – that is planned, rehearsed, self-aware, stagey, and at times exaggerated' (Gibson & Bell 2010: 235). Section 3 describes in more detail the exaggerated or stereotypical use of language. In some series, a large amount of intertextuality and witty exchanges/jokes differentiate TV dialogue from spontaneous conversation. Higher levels of impoliteness and interpersonal discord may also occur (Richardson 2010a: 110; Dynel 2015: 158).

Some TV series use devices that foreground the 'constructedness' of the dialogue, such as voice-over narration (e.g. *Pushing Daisies*, *Desperate Housewives*), musical interludes or special musical episodes (e.g. *Glee*; *Buffy the Vampire Slayer*), metafictional comments (e.g. the line *I thought I was doing a voice-over* from *Glee*),[1] or direct audience address (e.g. asides in *House of Cards* or voice-overs in *Mr. Robot*). In 'quality' dramas, devices such as visual metaphors, symbolism, and salient self-referential devices are threats to viewer immersion (Dynel 2016: 71). However, audiences in the twenty-first century are by now familiar with such and similar techniques and do not seem to be radically prevented from losing themselves in such narratives and from caring about their characters. Rather, they seem able to enjoy 'the operational aesthetic of narrative mechanics' (Mittell 2015: 108). These aesthetic devices also fulfil important functions: for example, voice-over can make a story more accessible to its audience (Landau 2014: 79) or it can convey a character's attitude or perspective, provide novel information, remind viewers of events that have happened, and so on (Mittell 2015).

All this does not mean that TV dialogue is completely non-naturalistic – there is general agreement that TV dialogue has to be naturalistic enough not to alienate viewers or prevent suspension of disbelief. Indeed, the creation of 'realistic', 'authentic', or 'naturalistic' dialogue is one of the functions of TV dialogue, just as it is for film (Kozloff 2000: 47; Quaglio 2009: 120; Bednarek 2012a: 43). Gibson and Bell (2010: 249) argue that contemporary TV series can mirror everyday language features at least qualitatively, if not quantitatively. TV series also portray character relations such as friendship in ways that are 'socially and linguistically realistic' (Mandala 2007: 66; see also Bubel 2006, 2011). TV dialogue uses the same resources and relies on the same principles available to language users more generally (Richardson 2010a: 106, 169; Dynel 2015). Deviations from linguistic realism and the principles of everyday conversational organisation are often thematically motivated (Mandala 2007) or create humour (Stokoe 2008; Richardson 2010a: 121; Walshe 2011: 144).

Particular TV series, like *Friends*, indeed share many language features with natural conversation (Tagliamonte & Roberts 2005; Quaglio 2009; Heyd 2010; Al-Surmi 2012), even if there is less variation in the sitcom (Quaglio 2008: 197). For instance, Quaglio's (2008, 2009) analysis has shown that the language of *Friends* closely resembles natural conversation if we consider lexicogrammatical features associated with involved production, i.e. 'the core linguistic features that typify conversation' (Quaglio 2009: 68). Quaglio goes as far as arguing that 'the use of television dialogue as a surrogate for natural conversation for the analysis of *certain* linguistic features seems perfectly appropriate' (Quaglio 2009: 148–9, emphasis added).

More generally, several linguists have compared corpora that contain US TV dialogue with corpora of unscripted conversation. These studies are distinguished by the different methods they use: multidimensional analysis (Rey 2001; Quaglio 2008, 2009; Al-Surmi 2012; Berber Sardinha & Veirano Pinto 2017), keyness or word list analysis (Mittmann 2006; Bednarek 2010a, 2011b, 2012a) or analysis of the frequencies of particular linguistic features such as intensifiers (Tagliamonte & Roberts 2005), hesitation phenomena and discourse markers (Dose 2013), or the address term *you guys* (Heyd 2010). Together, this body of research suggests that TV dialogue contains more routine formulae (e.g. *please, sorry, hi, nice to meet you*) and is more abstract as well as more emotional/emphatic than the comparison corpora of unscripted spoken English. Sitcoms such as *Friends* may also be more informal/colloquial (Quaglio 2009; Heyd 2010) – as further discussed in Section 4. In contrast, TV dialogue appears to be less narrative and less vague than unscripted language and includes fewer performance phenomena, interactive features, and situation-dependent references. The differences in particular dimensions (i.e., clusters of co-occurring features that are interpreted functionally) may not be large, however, as far as lexicogrammar is concerned (see Berber Sardinha & Veirano Pinto 2017).[2]

Some of the identified differences have to do with the nature of the comparative corpora. For example, the high frequency of greetings and leave-takings in TV dialogue is partially due to the fact that unscripted conversation corpora do not include all situations when speakers meet, arrive, and leave (Quaglio 2009: 148). Similarly, highly emotional and intimate settings may not be included as often in natural conversation corpora (Dose 2013). The occurrence of swear/ taboo words in conversation corpora may not be indicative of actual usage, since speakers may suppress their use because they know they are being recorded (McEnery et al. 2000: 50). In other words, some linguistic features are over-represented in TV dialogue not necessarily 'because they are rare in "the real world", but because of the principles of authentic data collection' (Dose 2013). Other over-represented features reflect the avoidance of incomprehensibility, the closeness of character relationships, or the dramatic nature of TV series (Quaglio 2008, 2009). Indeed, many features can reasonably be tied to the communicative context of television dialogue, i.e. its need to fulfil particular functions for the audience:

> television discourse needs to be comprehensible to the audience (avoiding unintelligible and vague language); entertain the audience (including emotional and aesthetic language; avoiding repetition, long monologues or narratives); create characters that the audience finds realistic (featuring informal language); and attract a large audience (featuring conventions of stage dialogue, stock lines; less linguistic variation).
> (Bednarek 2010a: 65–6; see also Bednarek 2011b, 2012a).

It is somewhat problematic that existing research examines only a limited number of TV series, as series and genres exhibit linguistic variation: Al-Surmi's (2012) and Berber Sardinha and Veirano Pinto's (in press) studies of register variation identified both similarities and differences between sitcoms, drama series, and soap operas. TV series/ genres differ in the use of most frequent words and n-grams (Bednarek 2011b), vocabulary coverage (Webb & Rodgers 2009), overlapping speech (Richardson 2010a: 45), dysfluencies (Valdeón 2011), filled pauses and discourse markers (Dose 2013), routine formulae (Bonsignori & Bruti 2014; Bruti & Vignozzi 2016b), and vocatives (Bruti & Vignozzi 2016b). In SydTV, some of the series feature more overlap and interruption than others, as evident from the transcription process. On the whole, it is clear that there are linguistic differences between TV series, including but not limited to the extent to which they resemble unscripted spoken English. Individual showrunners may also favour particular linguistic styles. All this means that corpora that contain only one or a few series are not necessarily representative of TV dialogue as a language variety. In Chapter 7, I will therefore compare a corpus that contains dialogue from sixty-six different TV series (SydTV) with a corpus of unscripted spoken American English, while Chapter 8 will explore variation in the data.

Summing up this section, most TV dialogue artfully but selectively simulates naturalistic speech (Richardson 2010a: 71; Toolan 2011). TV dialogue draws on many of the same resources and principles as everyday language, but it needs to fulfil particular functions for the audience. In a general sense, the main differences to unscripted conversation appear to be that TV dialogue typically:

- favours comprehensibility/intelligibility (e.g. is more clearly enunciated, is less vague)
- tends towards focus, coherence, fluency (e.g. is less narrative, has different turn lengths and organisation, has fewer interactive and performance features)
- has a focus on emotionality and entertainment (e.g. is more emotional, may focus on conflict or humour, may feature exaggerated/stereotypical language use)
- permits the use of devices that foreground the 'constructedness' of the dialogue.

These differences result in the overuse of particular linguistic features and the underuse of others, when TV dialogue is compared with non-fictional conversation. A corpus of TV dialogue is therefore not representative of unscripted, spontaneous spoken language, although it will feature many examples of linguistic features associated with the latter.[3]

3 Non-Standard Language Use in Films and TV Series

The study of language variation is a key area in sociolinguistic research on telecinematic discourse. This section reviews relevant research on non-standard language (e.g. regional, vernacular, and stigmatised varieties). The notion of 'standardness' is in itself problematic, as explained in Chapter 6. Further, linguistic innovations may also be considered non-standard but are discussed separately in Section 4.

A series of important questions can be asked about non-standard language use in the narrative mass media: is such language present or absent, frequent or rare? If present, is it used to construct and reflect linguistic stereotypes, language ideologies, or negative images with respect to its speakers? Such questions are important to ask, because for many viewers films and television series will be an important channel for experiencing the use of non-standard language varieties, especially if they do not interact with speakers of such varieties in their everyday lives. This would be the case for many L1 users and even more LX users of English.[4] TV series construct particular images of social groups and non-standard varieties and present them to viewers who may be unfamiliar with these groups or varieties (Bell 2016: 254); TV dialogue puts such varieties on display and infuses them with values (Coupland et al. 2016: 36). Historically, the broadcast media have promoted standardisation (Wolfram & Schilling Estes 2006: 184, 314; Lippi-Green 2012: 131, 230; Squires & Iorio 2014: 331), but this is not always the case, and the media can also represent, promote, and raise awareness of linguistic diversity (Coupland et al. 2016: 27).

Most linguistic research on non-standard English in telecinematic discourse focuses on *linguicism* (linguistic discrimination), linguistic stereotypes, and the extent to which representations perpetuate or challenge standard language ideology. The latter is defined as:

a bias toward an abstracted, idealized, homogenous spoken language which is imposed and maintained by dominant bloc institutions and which names as its model the written language, but which is drawn primarily from the spoken language of the upper middle class.   (Lippi-Green 2012: 67)

From a linguistic point of view, fictional non-standard varieties are problematic if they have (much) higher frequencies of features, exaggerate the linguistic form of a feature, select some features but not others and mis-realise features (Gibson & Bell 2010: 236–7). In sociolinguistic terms, stereotyped and exaggerated realisations of non-standard varieties are examples of 'stylisation' (Androutsopoulos 2012: 151).

The most famous critical sociolinguistic study of the narrative mass media is Lippi-Green's (2012) investigation of animated children's Disney movies, with a focus on accented English (including LX accents) and other markers of language variation associated with geographical area, race/ethnicity, or economic group. One of her findings is that 40 per cent of 'evil' characters are non-native speakers but only 20 per cent are US English speakers. She also identifies a number of ideology-laden stereotypes, such as the African American jokester/trickster or the evil British genius. According to Lippi-Green (1997, 2012) these films thus socialise children into the standard language ideology. Others have also argued that the mass media introduce and reinforce stereotypes about minorities, socialising viewers into dominant values (e.g. Penfield and Ornstein-Galicia 1985: 74). Negative representations and stereotypes have been identified in relation to LX users (Bleichenbacher 2008, 2012), African Americans (Green 2002), Native Americans (Meek 2006; Buscombe 2013), Asians (Lippi-Green 2012: 287; Chung 2013), Latinx (Penfield and Ornstein-Galicia 1985), Irish (Walshe 2011), and Southern

Americans (Mitchell 2015), or identities that are seen as problematic such as the *wigger* (white hip hop fan; see Bucholtz 2011; Bucholtz & Lopez 2011). Indeed, Hollywood films have long been criticised for the stereotypical representation of ethnic minorities and foreign nationalities (Kozloff 2000: 82; Bleichenbacher 2008: 32).[5]

Negative or at least problematic findings by the above-mentioned linguists and others (Queen 2012, 2013, 2015; Zago 2016) about non-standard language use in the narrative mass media include the following:

- With the exception of accents, non-standard language use is comparatively rare.
- Non-standard language features mark speakers as different, as 'Other'.
- Non-standard varieties are represented through linguistic stereotypes or 'mock' varieties; they are characterised by a few marked linguistic features that are easily recognisable and ideologically salient or iconic, without the variation found in 'real' life. To give just one example, a TV character from the American South often draws on linguistic features such as *ain't*, multiple negation, the alveolar [In] instead of [Ing] in words ending in <ing> (e.g. *doin'*), vowel raising and lengthening, non-standard lexis, and metaphorical or florid language (Mitchell 2015: 300; Queen 2015: 165).
- Such styles may never have existed as a real variety and can convey racist and other negative ideologies; they are also drawn upon in performances by 'outsiders' (e.g. white speakers playing 'Indian' or performing 'blackness').
- The use of non-standard language is associated with negative, minor, humorous, weak characters or characters that represent cultural stereotypes (while 'standard' English may be associated with heroes or desirable qualities).
- Non-standard (LX English) speakers may be represented as having an inferior language proficiency compared with L1 (English) speakers.

The participation framework helps to explain some of these findings. If telecinematic discourse is designed to fulfil a range of functions for its audience, it is crucial that non-standard language use be both familiar and comprehensible to viewers. The representation of non-standard language in films and TV series thus often tempers the creation of realism in favour of the comprehensibility of the dialogue and the familiarity of linguistic cues. As scriptwriter Jane Espenson put it when I interviewed her: 'language can do a similar thing [as casting to the stereotype] where you're just like "oh I'll give them [viewers] exactly what they expect this guy to talk like"'. The use of focused (concentrated) cues means that viewers can easily and quickly assess and categorise characters, whereas the incorporation of actual variation might make this too difficult (Queen 2015: 165, 200). In addition, using such salient cues might make it easier for the scriptwriting team to construct stable, consistent characters. Unfamiliarity with a particular dialect can also play a role (see further Chapter 10). This also means that particular dialectal features are at times used incorrectly – as when the uninflected form *be* is used to signify 'blackness' in the narrative mass media even when its use does not follow the rules of African American Vernacular English (AAVE) (Green 2002: 205, 207, 214).[6]

Metalinguistic comments are also interesting for the study of language ideology in telecinematic discourse (Bleichenbacher 2012: 161–5). Example (1) comes from SydTV:

(1)

HUSBAND:	We're in New York on vacation. We're not from here.
JACKIE:	I gathered.
HUSBAND:	How could you tell?
JACKIE:	I'm gonna guess midwest?
PATIENT:	Ohio, how'd you know?
JACKIE:	Because you're in pain and you're apologizing.
PATIENT:	Oh, sorry.
HUSBAND:	Sorry. (SydTV, *Nurse Jackie*)

In this example, the dialogue itself draws attention to the US stereotype of Midwestern politeness, an iconic pragmatic feature. The metalanguage and ensuing utterances create humour (the Midwestern couple not being able to keep themselves from apologising despite prior reference to the stereotype), but it also communicates this stereotype to LX viewers, who were likely not previously familiar with it. In other examples of metalanguage, characters may correct the grammar of non-standard speakers, evaluating their language use as substandard (Mitchell 2015).

The construction of cultural (stereo-)types is not limited to non-standard English (Bednarek 2012b), nor is the exploitation of marked or iconic features limited to scripted dialogue (Wolfram & Schilling Estes 2006: 284–5). But the narrative mass media depend on the indexical relationship between bundles of linguistic features and particular meanings, associations that may have a long history in the narrative mass media and that viewers will hence be familiar with (Queen 2015: 129).

The above list of 'problematic' findings is not meant to imply that such negative representation can be generalised to all narrative mass media, that all representations are equally common, or that this representation is immune to change. After analysing twenty-eight Hollywood movies released between 1984 and 2003, Bleichenbacher (2008: 220) goes as far as stating that 'it is very tricky – if not impossible – to make generalizations about how Hollywood depicts members of specific linguistic communities, because there are important exceptions to every perceived ethnolinguistic stereotype'. Further, media watchdogs and audiences can resist such representations, including both 'ordinary' viewers and pressure groups (Bleichenbacher 2012; Chung 2013; Mitchell 2015; Queen 2015).

There are two issues with this body of research as far as its relevance to this book is concerned. First, most of it is based on analysis of films rather than TV series. But because films differ from TV series in numerous aspects (see Chapter 1), we cannot assume that results from films hold for contemporary television narratives. For instance, many TV series do clearly feature non-standard language use (e.g. Latinx/Hispanic English and AAVE in *Orange Is the New Black*). A program like *The Wire* chooses to present realistic but sometimes incomprehensible everyday speech (Toolan 2011), and its dialogue has been assessed as high-fidelity representation of AAVE (Trotta & Blyahher 2011, cited in Lopez & Bucholtz 2017).

Second, in the rare cases when linguists make observations on television series, these observations often are not based on comprehensive empirical research projects or they relate to TV series that are not contemporary, or both. For instance, Queen (2015) is more of an introduction to the sociolinguistics of the narrative mass media, while Lippi-Green (2012: 225) comments on Southern American accents in TV series from the 1960s. Queen (2012) is a comprehensive linguistic investigation, but of soap opera broadcasts from 1999. Those that have examined contemporary US TV series tend to examine only one series and/or make use of limited data. However, such studies do seem to suggest that contemporary TV series may continue stereotypical or negative representations, but that there are also exceptions – with storylines and dialogue that criticise linguistic prejudice (Mitchell 2015), TV series that feature 'incomprehensible' dialogue (Toolan 2011), that select appropriate linguistic variables and represent variations within non-standard varieties (Gibson and Bell 2010), or that expose, destabilise, or challenge language ideologies, linguistic stereotypes, and linguistic dominance (Bell 2016; Coupland 2016). Some contemporary series, such as *The Wire*, simultaneously challenge stereotypical representations of blackness (and queerness) while also relying on familiar stereotypes to do so, for example by ideologically linking non-standard varieties to masculinity and toughness (Lopez & Bucholtz 2017).

This book contributes to this emerging area of sociolinguistic research but does so through a corpus linguistic approach. SydTV is used as the empirical basis for analysing non-standard language features. This means that this investigation of contemporary US TV narratives is not limited to one particular series. A specific aspect of non-standard language that will be analysed in depth is the use of the stigmatised word form *ain't* (Chapter 8).

4 Linguistic Innovation and Change

Another emerging trend within sociolinguistics concerns the study of linguistic innovation and change in relation to the narrative mass media. Classic sociolinguistic theories reject the analysis of media talk on the basis that it has no influence on (systematic, structural, enduring) language change. To give just one example, a recent introduction to language change (Bybee 2015), which 'offers a guide to the types of change at all levels of linguistic structure, as well as the mechanisms behind each type' (blurb), has no index entries for *media, mass media, social media/network, radio, film, television,* or *print.* But other sociolinguists have pointed out that the media are crucial for *sociolinguistic change* – a concept that refers to 'changing relationships between language and society, and [. . .] changes that are socially consequential in one way or another for language users' (Coupland et al. 2016: 37). In fact, the media impact on a range of linguistic processes and practices.

As already discussed above, the narrative mass media play a significant role in establishing, reflecting, recycling, and changing language ideologies, language attitudes, and sociocultural values and norms, including processes of standardisation and de-standardisation (e.g. Elliott 2000; Wolfram & Schilling Estes 2006; Queen 2015; Coupland et al. 2016). They may even raise awareness of language ideologies, allowing viewers to reflect and reconsider them; in so doing, they may temporarily challenge, destabilise, and reconstrue linguistic realities and categories, an effect that has the potential to endure (Bell 2016; Coupland 2016). Media representations of social values and ideologies create manifold additional dialogue (such as media and public debates); that is, they have a clear '*discursive* impact' (Bednarek 2010a: 219, emphasis in original). Media representations also trigger (transnational) discourses by fans and other audience members (e.g. Richardson 2010a; Bleichenbacher 2012; Gregoriou 2012; Bednarek 2017a, c).

The narrative mass media have also helped spread (varieties of) English worldwide and have influenced contemporary English registers as well as other languages (Kozloff 2000: 27; Mittmann 2006; Bleichenbacher 2008: 2; Díaz-Cintas 2009). In addition, they have been shown to spread, accelerate, and enhance existing sociolinguistic variation and ongoing language change, including innovative phonetic variants, grammatical and lexical changes, pragmatic formulae, slang, and discourse markers (Eble 2004; Quaglio 2009: 117; Heyd 2010; Gramley 2012: 446; Stuart-Smith 2016), while lexical innovation may also be *generated* by the media (Oxford Dictionaries 2012a; Curzan 2014). The use of metalanguage by characters, producers, or viewers in relation to media dialogue contributes to enregisterment, i.e. 'the process of how [linguistic] systems emerge as recognizable wholes' (Queen 2015: 236). Finally, the narrative mass media offer reference points and resources for speakers and their identities; speakers take up, recirculate, appropriate, and play with language chunks and styles, for various social purposes (e.g. Coupland 2007; Richardson 2010a; Coupland et al. 2016; Stuart-Smith 2016).

Only a few of the studies on linguistic innovation and change have focused on English-language TV series, and all focus on individual programmes: the British soap opera *EastEnders* (Stuart-Smith 2011, 2016), and the US TV series *Buffy the Vampire Slayer* (Mandala 2007) and *Friends* (Tagliamonte & Roberts 2005; Quaglio 2009; Heyd 2010). Stuart-Smith's research on the potential influence of London-based *EastEnders* on Glaswegian speakers shows that such research is methodologically complex and that there are no clear and direct links. There is no 'blanket imprinting, displacing local features and bleaching local dialects' (Stuart-Smith 2011: 234), but her research suggests, for instance, that watching *and liking* the soap opera corresponds with Glaswegians pronouncing consonants in ways that are associated with London.

In a different vein, the use of linguistic innovation for characterisation is briefly explored by Queen (2015: 6–8) in relation to *be like* as quotative. Her example shows how language change can be an explicit focus of a scene and how this innovation iconically characterises a shallow teenage girl in the sitcom *Modern Family*. Similarly, Mandala's (2007) study of *Buffy the Vampire Slayer* examines the use of innovative marked -*y* suffix adjectives (e.g. *Halloween-y*) as markers of character relationships and in-group identity. *Buffy the Vampire Slayer* has more generally been recognised for its inventions, slang, and innovative use and play with language (e.g. Adams 2003; Oxford Dictionaries 2012b). While Mandala notes that her findings are consistent with sociolinguistic theories of social networks, she does not directly compare *Buffy* dialogue with unscripted dialogue.

In contrast, the three studies on *Friends* (1994–2004) compare dialogue from the sitcom with unscripted English, focusing on different aspects of linguistic innovation: Tagliamonte & Roberts (2005) examine the intensifiers *very*, *really*, and *so* (when modifying adjectives), including an in-depth study of *so*. Heyd (2010) explores the use of *you guys*, and Quaglio (2008, 2009) briefly investigates a range of innovations (*all* + adj/gerund; innovative uses of *totally* and *so*; *hey* as greeting; *in* + negative present perfect + time). Whatever their focus, the studies of *Friends* demonstrate that TV series that feature characters that are relatively young adults, constitute a community of friends (equal and familiar), and communicate most often in informal contexts are likely to feature a high degree of linguistic innovation. This is also consistent with Mandala's (2007) study of *Buffy*. In terms of genre, it is often sitcoms that revolve around such characters and situations. *The Big Bang Theory* is a contemporary example and also features the use of the innovative -*y* adjective noted by Mandala – in example (2) the suffix is attached to the proper noun *Sheldon*:

(2)

LEONARD: When did my idea become our idea?
SHELDON: When I mixed it with **Sheldony** goodness and cooked it in the
           Easy-Bake oven of my mind.   (*The Big Bang Theory*,
                                                          season 8, episode 14)

The extent of linguistic innovation thus depends on TV characters, their relationships, and their interactions: given that TV dialogue selectively imitates unscripted conversation (Section 2), we would expect the use of innovations by young, urban speakers (Heyd 2010: 44) and their use in extremely casual conversations among close friends (Quaglio 2009: 120).

The studies that include comparison with other corpora seem to suggest that there is more innovation in certain TV series than in other types of American English, including spoken broadcast media. The problem is that none of the studies compares like with like, as it were: Tagliamonte and Roberts (2005) compare the American English *Friends* data with research on British English and Canadian English. Heyd (2010) compares results from the sitcom corpus with a corpus of email hoaxes, written corpora, and the spoken part of the Corpus of Contemporary American English (COCA), which consists of transcripts from radio and TV programmes. Quaglio (2009) uses the most comparable corpus, namely a subset of the American conversation section of the Longman Grammar corpus that includes casual face-to-face and phone conversations, but also task-related/service encounters and work-related interactions (all collected 1995–6). As Quaglio (2008: 207; 2009: 117, 144) acknowledges, the higher frequency of innovations in the *Friends* data may stem from the fact that the conversation corpus is older and does not feature as many casual and intimate exchanges.

While still in its infancy, existing research on TV series does seem to suggest that the language used in such series may indeed impact on or reflect ongoing language change (possibly to an enhanced degree) but needs to be considered in relation to the specificity of the data, as these features would be chosen for particular purposes. What is clear is that language change is complex and multidimensional, influenced by both language-external and language-internal factors, and it would be rash to dismiss television series and other media language entirely from its investigation. However, we need better resources for such investigations, including freely available comparable corpora of spontaneous, casual spoken American English. For this reason, Chapter 9 focuses first and foremost on categorising the different kinds of non-codified language that can be found in SydTV, although I will include some comparisons with other corpora. Further details on my approach will be provided in Part III.

5 Concluding Remarks

This chapter has reviewed key areas in the emerging body of research that examines television and film dialogue from a linguistic perspective. My focus was on research on the characteristics of TV dialogue and the extent to which it is similar to unscripted spoken language, as well as research on non-standard language and linguistic innovation in telecinematic discourse. It has become apparent that researchers have uncovered interesting linguistic and sociolinguistic phenomena but that the data they have relied on are limited in their amount and variety. For example, corpus linguistic studies examine only a few series, and there is very little research on non-standard language use or linguistic innovation in contemporary US TV series – most of the latter is solely based on analysis of the classic sitcom *Friends*. Thus, in relation to his own work, Quaglio (2009: 14) explicitly states: 'the results of this study should not be (and are not meant to be) generalized to television dialogue overall'.

In general, much linguistic research focuses on specific TV narratives rather than analysing a wide range of series, and much work has been done on 'classic' or 'cult' shows. Such studies provide useful understanding of these specific cultural products but are somewhat limited in the insights they can offer into TV dialogue as a type of language, because they are not based on representative datasets. There is thus scope for linguistic research that focuses on television dialogue as a language variety, examining a wider range of TV series. In this book I build on my previous work in this area to offer three new empirical studies of US TV dialogue using SydTV. However, to better interpret findings it is necessary to consider television dialogue as an instance of media language. This means taking seriously its participation framework (especially its audience/recipient/overhearer design) and drawing on its recognisable *functions*. To do so, the following chapters present a new categorisation of the functions of TV dialogue, illustrating these with multiple examples.

Part II

A Functional Approach to Television Series (FATS)

3 Functions Relating to the Communication of the Narrative

1 Introduction

In Chapter 1, I stated that televisual dialogue fulfils a range of functions that are ultimately aimed at the audience. This part of the book delves deeper into what these functions might be, introducing and discussing a new functional approach to television series (FATS). It first provides a brief overview of previous research on the functions of dialogue in telecinematic discourse before introducing the new model using multiple examples, mainly from SydTV. The framework will be used in this book in later chapters, and I hope that other researchers will also find it useful for their own subsequent explorations.

2 Functions of Telecinematic Discourse

There is relatively little research that focuses specifically and explicitly on categorising the different functions of telecinematic discourse. Linguists have mainly commented on the functions of particular phenomena, for instance multilingualism (Bleichenbacher 2008), accent/dialect (Bruti & Vignozzi 2016a), terms of address/referring expressions (Bubel 2006; Quaglio 2009; Bednarek 2011a; Zago 2015; Bruti & Vignozzi 2016b), or linguistic variation (Queen 2015). As the overview in Bednarek (2017b) shows, much research has explored televisual characterisation – the important function of TV dialogue to create characters and relationships between them, while plot development has seen less attention. The creation of realism and humour are two other functions that have attracted some attention from linguistics.

In the field of narratology, Pfister (1988: 105–18) draws on Jakobson (1960) to delineate the different communicative functions of language in drama. Most relevant to this book, however, is Kozloff's (2000) work on film dialogue. While the disciplinary origin of her research is film studies, her influence is most apparent in linguistics

(Jaeckle 2013: 14), and her categorisation does provide a useful starting point for considering the functions of dialogue in TV series. Richardson (2010a) argues that it is relevant to television drama and applies it in her analysis of TV dialogue.

Kozloff (2000: 33–4) distinguishes between functions relating to the communication of the narrative and those relating to 'aesthetic effect, ideological persuasion, and commercial appeal' (Kozloff 2000: 33). The first category contains six functions:

(1) anchorage of the diegesis (the fictional world) and of the characters
(2) communication of narrative causality
(3) enactment of narrative events
(4) character revelation
(5) adherence to the code of realism
(6) control of viewer evaluation and emotions.

The second category contains three functions:

(1) exploitation of the resources of language (with four subcategories: poetic use of language, jokes and humour, dramatic irony, on-screen verbal storytelling)
(2) thematic messages, authorial commentary, allegory
(3) opportunities for star turns.

In past research I have applied this categorisation to the analysis of *wh*-questions in TV dialogue (Bednarek 2014a), and more recently have added new (sub-)categories (Bednarek 2017b). I build on these studies here to propose a new analytical framework, which significantly extends Kozloff's categorisation. My interest is in the potential functions or effects of television dialogue (its meaning *potential*) rather than scriptwriters' intentions or *actual* audience effects. An overview of the new functional approach to television series (FATS) is provided in Table 3.1, but this chapter and the next will discuss it in more detail. This approach is called *functional* because it emphasises that TV dialogue is designed to fulfil a range of functions for its audience (cf. Chapter 1). In other words, the particular aspect of TV series that is the focus of this functional analysis is the dialogue.

As Table 3.1 indicates, the functions of TV dialogue can relate to the communication of the narrative, to aesthetic and interpersonal effect and commercial appeal, to thematic messages and ideology, to realism, and to the serial nature of TV narratives. Each of these major categories has several subcategories, discussed in the following sections with relevant examples. In this chapter I focus on functions relating to the

Table 3.1 A new functional approach to television series (FATS)

Functions relating to the communication of the narrative
  Settings and happenings: Anchorage of time and space, clarification of
    modality, enactment of narrative events, communication of narrative
    causality, scene structure and scene changes
  Characters: Anchorage of the characters, character biographies, social and
    individual character traits, relationships between characters, narrative roles
Functions relating to aesthetic and interpersonal effect and commercial appeal
  Control of viewer evaluation and emotions
  Exploitation of the resources of language: Poetic use of language, jokes/
    humour, dramatic irony, on-screen verbal storytelling, linguistic
    innovation, intertextuality, metafictionality
  Opportunities for star turns
Functions relating to thematic messages and ideology
  Explicit or implicit thematic messages
  Promotion of real-life products, 'verbal' product placement
  Ideological representations
Functions relating to realism
  Imitating 'real' spoken and written language
  References to the 'real' world
Functions relating to the serial nature of TV narratives
  Creation of consistency
  Creation of continuity

communication of the narrative, while the next chapter discusses the
remaining functions.

Examples in both chapters are mostly taken from episodes included
in the Sydney Corpus of Television Dialogue – these examples are
labelled *SydTV* and were transcribed according to specific conventions
(cf. Chapter 5), although I have added other information to the
transcripts where relevant to the discussion. Other examples come
from additional episodes, mainly from US TV series and very occasionally from UK series. These examples were mainly transcribed
orthographically. For the sake of clarity, I mostly discuss each example
with respect to only *one* function, even though a piece of dialogue
frequently has several functions at the same time. In addition,
I sometimes refer to the characters only by their name, rather than
prefacing the name with *the character* or *the protagonist*. This strategy
is used as a shorthand, and it should not be forgotten that these are
not real people but rather constructed characters (whose dialogue is
produced by multiple authors; cf. Chapter 1).

3 Functions Relating to the Communication of the Narrative

Functions relating to the communication of the narrative concern the use of dialogue for constructing a fictional world populated by characters who participate in actions, happenings, or events in space and time. This includes the construction of settings and happenings as well as characters.

3.1 Settings and Happenings

The construction of settings and happenings involves anchorage of time and space, clarification of modality, enactment of narrative events, communication of narrative causality, and management of scene structure and scene changes.

3.1.1 ANCHORAGE OF TIME AND SPACE

Kozloff posits a function called 'anchorage of the diegesis and characters', defined as the use of dialogue to create and identify aspects of the diegetic world, that is, to orient viewers as regards character movement in space and time and to name characters (Kozloff 2000: 34–7). I include anchorage of time and space under 'settings and happenings', while anchorage of the characters is included under 'characters' in Section 3.2.

In traditional narrative texts (novel, short story), space and time can be constructed linguistically through descriptions, deixis, tense, adverbials of place, time, or conjunctions (Fludernik 2009: 42). In TV series, shots often show the location, but dialogue also plays a role. In example (1), from the crime series *Bones*, the camera shows the three protagonists (Angela, Booth, Brennan) walking along what viewers would recognise as a hospital corridor, while one of the character's turns identifies the location very specifically as a paediatric cancer floor.

(1)

[Shot of characters walking along a hospital corridor]

ANGELA: Uh, Agent Booth?
BOOTH: Yes, Angela?
ANGELA: **This is the pediatric cancer floor of the hospital**.
BOOTH: Mm-hmmm. Yeah.
ANGELA: Right. Well, uh, what I'm about to show deputy director Cullen is kinda gruesome.
BRENNAN: Why are we meeting Cullen here?   (SydTV, *Bones*)

In this way, dialogue works in conjunction with camera shots to locate the narrative in space, specifying the location for the audience at home. While the camera can *show* viewers the physical world, the dialogue *identifies* it (Kozloff 2000: 35). This can also work prospectively, using what Bordwell calls 'dialogue hooks' (cited in Kozloff 2000: 35). For instance, a character in the comedy-drama *The Big C* mentions in one scene that she has an appointment with a dermatologist, which identifies the setting for the next scene as occurring in said dermatologist's office (see example (7b) below).

Technical or specialised vocabulary, for instance relating to forensic or medical procedures, can also be considered as an indirect way of establishing the setting as a lab, a hospital, and so on. Settings can also be indicated through the presence of particular languages, accents, or dialects (Bleichenbacher 2008; Lippi-Green 2012; Bruti & Vignozzi 2016a).

In addition to space, dialogue can orient and reorient viewers in relation to the characters' movement in time (Kozloff 2000: 35–6). I will provide just two short examples here. In example (2) the voice-over narration by the main character, Earl, specifies to viewers that what will be shown next actually happened at the same time as what they have just seen:

(2)

EARL (V):   **Meanwhile** Darnell was busy tryin' to stall Jessie.

(SydTV, *My Name Is Earl*)

Also included are instances of dialogue that explicitly introduce flashbacks or flashforwards, as in example (3), where the protagonist's dialogue introduces the following scenes as yesterday's happenings:

(3)

VERONICA (V):   So how does a girl end up surrounded by a motorcycle gang at four in the morning on the wrong side of town? For that answer, **we'll have to rewind to yesterday**.

(*Veronica Mars*, season 1, pilot (DVD version), as cited in Mittell 2015: 75, emphasis added)

3.1.2 CLARIFICATION OF MODALITY

As I have argued in Bednarek (2017b), it is also important to clarify the modality of happenings to the audience. *Modality* is used here in the sense of the credibility or reliability of messages: 'Is what we see or hear true, factual, real, or is it a lie, a fiction, something outside reality?' (Kress & van Leeuwen 2006: 154). In other words, is what viewers experience on the screen marked as a happening that 'really' happened in the fictional world in the past, present, or future, or is it identified as a dream, fantasy, desire, hallucination, etc.? Admittedly, it is often visual cues that identify something as 'non-real', for instance shot sequencing, use of dissolve, distorted images, slow motion, high contrast, and so on (van Leeuwen 1996). But dialogue can contribute to the anchorage of modality, as evident in example (4) from the dramedy (drama-comedy hybrid) *Desperate Housewives*. In this example, the dialogue is in the form of voice-over narration by a (dead) character (VOICE), which is a recurring feature of this TV series. This narration accompanies shots that show another character, Lynette Skavo (one of the eponymous housewives), and the contents of one of her daydreams:

(4)

VOICE: Every morning as she went to take out her trash, **Lynette Skavo would indulge in a little daydream, the details of which were always the same**. [Camera switches from showing Lynette to showing what the voice-over narration describes.] One day, her nasty neighbor Karen McClusky would keel over and die, and her home would be bought by a lovely Swedish family, with two adorable twin daughters. The families would form an everlasting friendship, culminating in their daughters marrying her sons at an elaborate wedding [camera switches back to showing Lynette] the Skavos wouldn't have to pay for. Yes, **Lynette enjoyed her little daydream**, but Mrs McClusky always had a way of **pulling her back to reality**.   (SydTV, *Desperate Housewives*)

In example (4) the voice-over narration explicitly marks the accompanying visuals (which show the Swedish family) as a fantasy (*daydream*) and therefore 'non-real' (*pulling her back to reality*) as far as the diegetic world is concerned. In this case, the modality of the visuals seems unmarked, and the dialogue – in conjunction with the shot sequencing – clearly contributes to identifying their content as a character's daydream.

3.1.3 ENACTMENT OF NARRATIVE EVENTS

The category 'enactment of narrative events' concerns 'verbal events' (Kozloff 2000: 41), i.e. speech acts that constitute major narrative events. The extent to which such narrative events include verbalisation varies – for instance, a car chase does not necessarily involve dialogue, but a confession does (Richardson 2010a: 54). Queen (2015) provides examples for how performative verbs such as *apologise* can be used to perform actions that are important for particular scenes. An interesting example from SydTV is provided in example (5) from the sitcom *Community*.

(5)

JEFF: You've just stopped being a study group. You have become something unstoppable. **I hereby pronounce you a community.**

(SydTV, *Community*)

In this example, one of the main characters (failed lawyer Jeff) performs the action of turning the members of his study group at a community college into the 'community' implied by the TV series' title. He does this by using the performative construction *I hereby pronounce X y*. This may lead viewers to re-evaluate the sitcom title itself and recognise its double meaning, referring both to the setting (community college) and to the bonds developing between the protagonists. It is also noteworthy that this narrative event happens in the pilot episode.

Examples for verbal events provided by Kozloff (2000: 41–3) include disclosure of (secret) information, declaration of love, closing arguments, verdicts, witness breakdowns, prayer, absolution, and exorcism. It is a matter of interpretation which actions are identified as pivotal to the narrative, although some speech acts appear to be particularly salient in certain film genres, e.g. commanding in Westerns, threatening in gangster films, teasing in screwball comedies (Kozloff 2000: 209).

In example (6), from the fantasy action comedy-drama *Teen Wolf*, sheriff Stilinski discloses an important piece of information to his son Stiles. The example shows how the question–answer sequence between father and son works to communicate several crucial details: that the relevant arson case important to this narrative was organised by a woman who is now in her late twenties and who has a distinctive pendant.

(6)

STILINSKI: You know what, that girl in there has got nothin' to do with a six-year-old arson case.
STILES: When did you decide it was definitely arson?

STILINSKI:	Well we got a key witness, and no I'm not telling you who it is, but yeah, yeah we know it's arson, and it was probably organized by a young woman.
STILES:	What young woman?
STILINSKI:	If I knew that she'd be in jail.
STILES:	Was she young then or is she young now?
STILINSKI:	She's probably in her late twenties. Damn! I gotta grab this call.
STILES:	You don't know her name?
STILINSKI:	No, I don't, what is it, twenty questions? All we know is that she had a very distinctive uh, what do you call it, a pendant.
STILES:	What the hell's a pendant?
STILINSKI:	Stiles do you go to school? A pendant, a pendant, it's a it's a necklace, now can I answer the phone?
STILES:	Yes.
STILINSKI:	Thank you. (SydTV, *Teen Wolf*)

In sum, this function is concerned with how TV dialogue contributes to the enactment of events that are important to the narrative. This can be achieved through the use of performative constructions but also more indirectly, including through longer stretches of talk.

3.1.4 COMMUNICATION OF NARRATIVE CAUSALITY

For Kozloff, the function labelled 'communication of narrative causality' relates to the use of dialogue 'to communicate "why" and "how" and "what next?"' (Kozloff 2000: 38). This includes providing background information, clarifying connections between events, creating causal chains, or anticipating a narrative development. Richardson (2010a: 53) explains the difference between enactment of narrative events and communication of narrative causality as follows:

in the first case, audiences see and hear narrative events as they happen to the characters, whereas in the second, characters learn from one another about what has happened, what might have happened, and what might happen in their future – and audiences, thereby, learn this too.

Example (7a) comes from *The Big C* and features a conversation between two of the protagonists, husband Paul and wife Cathy. The exchange functions both to provide background information about a prior event (that Paul has been kicked out of the house) and to anticipate later events (Cathy's appointment with the dermatologist, and that Paul and Cathy will have dinner) – as well as to identify later settings (see Section 3.1.1 on dialogue hooks).

(7a)

PAUL: [. . .] Is that your new lover? **Is that why I'm sleepin' on my sister's couch?**

CATHY: I'm gonna bump out the deck and put in a hot-tub.

[Five turns]

CATHY: I'm sorry Paul, I have to go. **I have an appointment with the dermatologist.**

PAUL: **Well can we just have dinner or something?** Can we at the very least figure out what we're gonna tell Adam tomorrow because right now my story is, "Adam, your mom's a meanie!"

CATHY: **Okay. Dinner.**   (SydTV, *The Big C*)

In her conversation with the dermatologist (7b), Cathy provides further background information about her argument with Paul to the audience:

(7b)

CATHY: I was going to tell him [that she has cancer], and then when I got home, there were fifteen men in my house playing video games. Paul was drunk and peeing in the front yard. I found myself saying, "I think I need to be alone for a while."   (SydTV, *The Big C*)

This is a good example of how TV dialogue can communicate information on 'events that took place before the time period pictured on screen' (Kozloff 2000: 39). Just as such information may be frequent in the beginnings of films (Kozloff 2000: 37), it may be frequent in the beginning of TV series. For instance, the pilot of the comedy-drama *Weeds* gives a succinct explanation of the main character's situation. The subordinate clause in bold occurs in the sixth turn of this episode:

(8)

MOTHER 2:   She probably treated herself, poor thing. **If my husband dropped dead**, I'd suck out, lift up and inject anything that moved.   (SydTV, *Weeds*)

Voice-over narration may also fulfil this function, as in example (9), which occurs at the beginning of the pilot episode of the fantasy action drama *Birds of Prey*:

(9)

ALFRED (V):   My name is Alfred Pennyworth, and I have a story to tell. For many years in the city of New Gotham, a secret war raged by night. Unknown to the everyday world, a battle for the very heart of the city was waged between Batman and Joker. One night, the final battle was fought, and Joker lost. Joker's revenge was taken not on Batman himself, but on the ones he loved. Helena Kyle didn't know that her father was Batman, nor did she know that her mother had once been Catwoman.   (SydTV, *Birds of Prey*)

Alfred's narration and the interspersed flashbacks that follow provide viewers with the TV series' premise and relevant backstory the very first time they encounter the televisual narrative.

In contrast, example (10) shows how TV dialogue can be used to set up a *non-actual* happening that needs to be prevented by the protagonists. This extract is taken from the action/adventure drama series *Human Target*, which revolves around the main character Chance protecting various clients in each episode – in this case the client is Victoria, a fictional Princess of Wales.

(10)

CHANCE: What I know is that in an hour and a half, your security detail's gonna put you in a car which is gonna bring you to a museum uptown to meet the queen, your husband, Prince What's-his-name, and the rest of the gang. At thirty-eighth and first, your motorcade is gonna be obstructed. Now usual security protocol is to go faster, maybe even turn around, do anything to avoid being boxed in, but in this particular instance, your detail has different orders. They're there to serve you up. So while you're stopped, your men watching, you'll be assassinated. Luckily, Gerard got wind of the plot while we still have time to do something about it.
VICTORIA: Lucky, is that the word you'd use?
CHANCE: Well, we're lowering the bar today. So we have the who, the what, the where, all we need is a why.
VICTORIA: Because I'm in love with a man who isn't my husband.
CHANCE: That generally will do it.   (SydTV, *Human Target*)

This exchange between Victoria and Chance explains the plot to assassinate the princess and attempts to construct a motivation for such a plot. It hence provides information about the 'what next' as well as the 'why'. Again, it occurs at the beginning of the episode.

Example (11) is a good example for how visuals and dialogue co-construct causality, when dialogue helps viewers to understand and interpret the visuals (Kozloff 2000: 39). It represents a conversation between four characters from the crime drama *Bones* – Brennan (a forensic anthropologist), Zack (a PhD student/intern), Angela (a forensic artist), and Booth (an FBI agent). During the exchange, the camera shows the characters standing around and interacting with two computer screens featuring a scan and microscope report.

(11)

BRENNAN: This is a cross section from Amy's bone graft. Zack, what's the ratio of primary to secondary osteons?

ZACK: I only see secondary. Exactly what you'd expect to see in a, older decedent.

BRENNAN: And accompanying data?

ANGELA: Well, I'm no expert but I think it supports as well.

BRENNAN: So based on this one sample it's clear that the donor bone came from someone in their sixties.

BOOTH: But how do we know that it's the bone that gave Amy cancer?

BRENNAN: Because of this. Magnify. The graft is riddled with cancer.

ZACK: Cancer consistent with morphology origin in the pleura, most likely mesothelioma.

BRENNAN: Whoever this is had terminal cancer. And now so does Amy.   (SydTV, *Bones*)

This conversation works both to explain the scientific evidence and to elucidate its significance for the case. At the same time, it could be argued that 'working through' a crime by examining such evidence is a 'pivotal' action for crime dramas such as this and could therefore also be seen to enact a narrative event. The distinction between 'enactment of narrative events' and 'communication of narrative causality' is thus not entirely clear-cut.[1]

3.1.5 MANAGING SCENE STRUCTURE AND SCENE CHANGES

As noted in Chapter 1, the structure of televisual narratives has been described in terms of acts and scenes. As they unfold over the course of the episode, elements of the plot(s) are developed or enacted in individual scenes. Dialogue can function to structure what happens within a particular scene as well as to manage scene changes.

For instance, several linguistic studies have identified greetings and leave-takings (e.g. *hi, hey, nice to meet you, bye, I'll be right back*) as frequent in television dialogue (cf. Chapter 2). In the sitcom *Friends*, for example, speakers arrive and leave frequently and scenes 'often start with the characters meeting one another' (Quaglio 2009: 35). It seems clear that greetings and leave-takings function to manage scene changes – marking the beginning or end of a scene – or to structure scenes internally. Thus, a conversation between two characters can be interrupted by a new character arriving, with a brief all-party conversation before the character departs again, as in example (12) from *Weeds*.

(12)

[conversation between the protagonist Nancy and her friend Celia; Doug arrives]

DOUG: Hey, Nancy. How's it going?

[eight turns between Celia, Doug, Nancy]

NANCY: You're welcome. Catch you later. I'll see you later, Doug.
DOUG: Oh. Okay. Yeah, later. [Doug leaves]
NANCY   [to Celia]: He's trying to find something nice for Dana. Her birthday is
          coming up.   (SydTV, *Weeds*)

It could also be argued that dialogue that orients viewers to simultaneous, past, and future events (see Section 3.1.1) additionally functions to manage scene changes, since it explicitly introduces and is followed by the next scene (e.g. *meanwhile ... ; ... we'll have to rewind to yesterday*).

3.2 Characters

The second major category of 'the communication of the narrative' concerns the construction of characters (characterisation) and includes anchorage of the characters, character biographies, social and individual character traits, relationships between characters, and narrative roles.

Kozloff (2000) uses the function of 'character revelation' to talk about how dialogue distinguishes characters from each other, for instance through accent or idiosyncratic linguistic practices. For Kozloff (2000: 43–6), this includes various aspects of character such as class, intelligence, personality, character psychology, emotional state, or motive. In another relevant non-linguistic study, Pearson (2007a: 43) proposes six elements of character identity: psychological traits/habitual behaviours, physical characteristics/appearance, speech patterns, interactions with other characters, environment, and biography. However, she is not interested in a detailed linguistic analysis of TV dialogue, but rather focuses on 'identifying the elements that constitute a character abstracted from the design of the text and existing in the story, that is, in the minds of producers and audiences' (Pearson 2007a: 43). With respect to language, I showed in Bednarek (2010a) that the main characters in the dramedy *Gilmore Girls* are distinguished by references to their relationships with others (e.g. mother–daughter) and their environment (e.g. workplace), as well as differences in levels of (in-)formality and evaluative/emotional preferences.

Building on these suggestions about elements of character, and also drawing on additional linguistic research on televisual characterisation (as reviewed in Bednarek 2017b), TV dialogue can function:

- to introduce and identify characters
- to inform viewers about characters' biographies
- to construct characters (social and individual character traits, expressive identity)
- to construct relationships between characters
- to inform viewers about the role of characters in the narrative.

This can happen either through self-revelation (characters' own dialogue) or when other characters comment upon a character (Kozloff 2000: 44–5) – what Culpeper (2001: 167) calls *self-presentation* and *other-presentation*.

3.2.1 ANCHORAGE OF THE CHARACTERS

As mentioned, the function 'anchorage of the characters' relates to the use of TV dialogue to identify and name characters. Here, dialogue in early episodes of a TV series is again important. Thus, in the first episode of *Community*, we find three instances of *My name's/is* and one instance of *her name is*, which work to introduce characters to each other and to the viewers (Figure 3.1).

he was angry, and he was angry because she's American. My name's Abed, by the way. <JEFF:> Abed, nice to know you, and then
I only talked to her once while she was borrowing a pencil, but her name's Britta, she's twenty-eight, birthday in October, she has two
at least 'til ten. <JEFF:> But who studies with strangers, right? My name is Jeff. <PIERCE:> Jeff, it's a pleasure, my name is Pierce
ngers, right? My name is Jeff. <PIERCE:> Jeff, it's a pleasure, my name is Pierce Hawthorne and yes, that is Hawthorne as in Hawthorne

Figure 3.1 Introducing characters in Community

The episode also features a humorous scene in which the (elderly) Pierce attempts to introduce Jeff to the other characters, getting everyone's name wrong but providing an elegant way of establishing who the characters are as well as revealing aspects of his character (old, racist, and sexist).

(13)

PIERCE: I'm also a Toastmaster so perhaps I should do the introduction.
JEFF: Definitely.
PIERCE: Right you already know Brittles.
BRITTA: Britta.
PIERCE: Abed, Abed the Arab, is that inappropriate?
ABED: Sure.
PIERCE: Roy, Roy, the wonder boy.
TROY: Troy.
PIERCE: Little princess Elizabeth.
ANNIE: Annie.
PIERCE: And finally this beautiful creature is named Shirley.
JEFF: Is that even close?   (SydTV, *Community*)

On the whole, this episode features several instances where names are used either to talk about or to address main characters: *Abed* (13 occurrences), *Jeff* (10 occurrences), *Britta* (7 occurrences), *Pierce* (6 occurrences), *Annie* (6 occurrences), *Shirley* (5 occurrences), *Troy* (4 occurrences). Such repeated use of character names in telecinematic discourse identifies characters and reminds audiences of who they are (Kozloff 2000: 36; Mittell 2015: 133).

3.2.2 CHARACTER BIOGRAPHIES

As already noted in relation to narrative causality, TV dialogue can communicate information on happenings that took place prior to the narrative. This includes information about a character's past experiences or background, as in example (14) from *The Big C*.

(14)

CATHY: We didn't have a lot of money growing up but we did have a pool in our backyard. My brother and I, we would spend all summer in it making up dives. My signature was the banana split and dive.
DOCTOR: Sounds fun.
CATHY: Except when Sean would hold me under the water and fart on my face.   (SydTV, *The Big C*)

In this conversation, the protagonist (Cathy) discloses information about her childhood, which provides a belated motivation for *why* she wants to install a pool in her backyard. It also indicates further biographical information (not being rich, family dynamics). In addition, this conversation features the first mention of Sean in the series, simultaneously identifying him to the viewers as her brother (= anchorage of the characters).

3.2.3 SOCIAL AND INDIVIDUAL CHARACTER TRAITS

Relevant linguistic research suggests that televisual characterisation includes the construction of social identities (more or less general, e.g. 'women', 'nerds', 'vegetarians', 'doctors', 'criminals'), personalities (individuals), and 'expressive character identity'. Using Queen's (2015: 154–81) terms, TV dialogue can establish social types and personae, the traits and stances of characters, and their personality. I use *social and individual character traits* as a cover term for all these aspects of character, covering both temporary and stable traits, including emotional reactions, desires, and other inner states. Where relevant, I will borrow Queen's (2015: 176) term *type characteristics* to refer to features associated with social variables like gender or age, and personae like nerds or jocks, while her term *trait characteristics* will be used to refer to features associated with personality and other individual characteristics (e.g. being quiet, energetic).

As noted in Chapter 1, a wide range of dialogue cues have been examined in relation to television characters. Most studies rely on a cognitive model where explicit or implicit dialogue cues give rise to the formation of impressions of characters in the minds of the audience (Culpeper 2001: 2, 163). From a sociocultural linguistic perspective, Queen (2015) draws on concepts such as indexicality to link language variation to characterisation, also showing that the *clustering* of linguistic features is important. This can be seen in the SydTV episode from the crime drama series *The Wire* (example 15).

(15)

BELL:	Him, on the ball, from Dunbar? He junior college now, but he goin' to bigger places if he can make them grades though. He our edge, right there.
BARKSDALE:	Where he goin'?
BELL:	I don't know. Uh, Terps, Hoyas, Missouri, Kansas, they all want this cat.
BARKSDALE:	Okay, so we in the mix, too, now. You know what I'm talkin' about?
BELL:	Blow Proposition Joe's mind. He ain't got nobody ballin' like this.
BARKSDALE:	He better not have one motherfucker ballin' like this. I'm sick and tired of losin' to these Eastside bitches every year. It's been three years runnin' now, man. Fuckin' with my morale, for real.

(SydTV, *The Wire*)

This conversation features an exchange between two African American characters whose ethnicity is partially established by their use of what many viewers would consider as features of AAVE. This includes lexical and pragmatic items (*this cat, ballin', these Eastside bitches, for real, you know what I'm talkin' about*, etc.), grammatical features such as zero copula (e.g. *He junior college now*) and multiple negation (e.g. *ain't got nobody*). At the phonological level, both characters produce the alveolar form [In] instead of [Ing] (e.g. *goin '*). While these features are not all exclusive to AAVE – for instance, multiple negation occurs in other varieties – this *cluster* of recognisable linguistic features constructs Bell and Barksdale as African American for the audience. As mentioned in Chapter 2, the construction of such and other social identities can be examined in relation to stereotyping and standard language ideologies. TV characters who belong to the same ethnic group can be distinguished from each other in the frequency with which they use linguistic variables (Gibson & Bell 2010; Queen 2015).

Past research has also shown that TV characters may share certain linguistic preferences (to construct similarities, for instance in terms of age) but are also constructed as unique. Thus, in *Gilmore Girls* the parents (Richard and Emily) are contrasted with daughter and granddaughter (Lorelai and Rory) in terms of shared attitudes and expressive resources, but individual characters also exhibit unique expressive identities (Bednarek 2010a). I made a similar point with respect to the sitcom *The Big Bang Theory*, arguing that the characters are all constructed as nerds but also as having unique personalities (Bednarek 2012b: 223). Thus, Sheldon is constructed as a stereotypical nerd but is differentiated from the others by his obsessive-compulsive and Asperger-like behaviour, his arrogance, and his lack of social skills. In example (16), the dialogue between Sheldon and other characters contributes to establishing the character's identity and illustrates my point that dialogue repeatedly presents other characters explaining social norms to Sheldon (Bednarek 2012b: 211).

(16)

PENNY:	Uh, Sheldon, I didn't see your present.
SHELDON:	That's because I didn't bring one.
PENNY:	Well why not?
HOWARD:	Don't ask.
SHELDON:	The entire institution of gift giving makes no sense.
HOWARD:	Too late.
SHELDON:	Let's say that I go out and I spend fifty dollars on you. It's a laborious activity, because I have to imagine what you need,

whereas you know what you need. Now I could simplify things, just give you the fifty dollars directly and then, you could give me fifty dollars on my birthday, and so on until one of us dies leaving the other one old and fifty dollars richer. And I ask you, is it worth it?

HOWARD: Told you not to ask.

PENNY: Well, Sheldon, you're his friend. Friends give each other presents.

SHELDON: I accept your premise, I reject your conclusion.

HOWARD: Try telling him it's a non-optional social convention.

PENNY: What?

HOWARD: Just do it.

PENNY: It's a non-optional social convention.

SHELDON: Oh. Fair enough.

HOWARD: He came with a manual.   (SydTV, *The Big Bang Theory*)

Without going into all the details here, the dialogue clearly shows Sheldon's predilection for formal (including academic) language (e.g. *I accept your premise, I reject your conclusion*) and his lack of understanding of social norms but willingness to learn about them (*PENNY: It's a non-optional social convention. SHELDON: Oh, Fair enough*). Sheldon clearly has a distinct personality that is constructed through dialogue, but at other times the dialogue establishes that he shares (stereotypical) traits with the other nerds, such as an interest in sci-fi and comic books. The character of Sheldon is thus a good example of the construction of social identities (nerds) and of the construction of personality. In Queen's words, these two facets of characterisation explain why 'a given character might be simultaneously stereotypical and uniquely individual' (2015: 155).

3.2.4 RELATIONSHIPS BETWEEN CHARACTERS

Characters are not just constructed in isolation: 'TV characters don't define themselves in a vacuum. They define themselves by how they relate to the other characters on the show' (Epstein 2006: 23). Hence, one important function of dialogue is to reflect and construe relationships between characters (Kozloff 2000: 46). These relationships can be constructed indirectly through linguistic cues such as innovative marked -*y* suffix adjectives (e.g. *Heart-of-Darkness-y*) in the fantasy action drama *Buffy the Vampire Slayer* (Mandala 2007) or the use of alignment patterns, terms of address, and question–response sequences in the dramedy *Sex and the City* (Bubel 2006, 2011). However, relationships may also be described directly, as in example (17) from the crime series *The Shield*:

(17)

VIC: Why'd you shoot up The Chez Club last night?
RONDELL: Hey, man. T-Bonz and Kern got this war goin' on, man. I'm just
            backin' up my boy.
VIC: Who's that? Kern? [. . .]
RONDELL: Yeah, man, look. Look, me and Kern, we've been hangin' since we
            was kids. We're still tight.   (SydTV, *The Shield*)

When being questioned about his involvement in a shooting, drug dealer Rondell explains to the police officer (Vic) that he was simply supporting his friend. When he clarifies who 'my boy' refers to and describes their relationship, he explicitly reveals the characters' inter-personal connection for the benefit of viewers.

3.2.5 NARRATIVE ROLES

From a narratological perspective, dialogue also establishes narrative roles such as 'hero' and 'villain' (e.g. Chatman 1978: 111–12, 125–31; Rimmon-Kenan 2002: 34, 37–8). There is a difference between what the character is like (character traits) compared with what he or she '*does*, in the plot' (Toolan 2001: 86, emphasis in original). Wodak (2009) analyses a *West Wing* episode in these terms. I will briefly consider an example from the political drama *House of Cards* here, which has been transcribed in more detail for this purpose and therefore includes information on pauses ([..] = medium pause), delivery speed (preceding speech, applies until another set of square brackets), and voice quality (following speech, applies up to preceding punctuation or pause). Italics indicate softness.

(18)

[Frank and Cathy alone in the Oval Office]

FRANK: You know, when I was waitin' for my transplant, I had the most vivid
          hallucinations. You wouldn't believe 'em. Do you know who I saw? [..]
          Peter Russo and Zoe Barnes, right here in this room. Zoe was tryin' to
          seduce me, right here on this couch, and Peter, he shoved my face,
          up against this glass. Cigarettes and razor blades and sex. It was
          terrifyin'. All I wanted to do was get out of this room that I worked so
          hard to get in. But of course it makes sense that they would've
          haunted me because, it's all true.
CATHY: What is?
FRANK: Everything Lucas Goodwin claimed. I killed them both, just like he said
          I did. [..] But of course, nobody believes it, and nobody ever will.

Because that's how good we are [..] [slower:] at making things [..] disappear [low and hoarse voice].
[Frank draws a letter opener and edges towards Cathy, then laughs, moves away from Cathy]
[Normal speed:] No, we didn't kill anybody. [laughs] But we would have [..] if it was necessary. So you're right. The time for negotiations is over. You will hand over your delegates, and you will serve on in my cabinet. And we will forget that any of this ever happened. [..] Because if you don't [..] [slower:] I swear to God [low and hoarse voice] [..] [even slower:] *I will never, ever, forget.* [~2 second pause] Do you *understand now?* [~ 4 second pause]

CATHY: *Yes.*   (*House of Cards*, season 4, episode 10/chapter 49)

This conversation between one of the protagonists, fictional US president Frank Underwood, and his Secretary of State Cathy Durant features Frank disclosing his evil deeds and threatening Cathy. Much of the menace is expressed through tone of voice, facial expression, etc. and would become fully apparent only through a multimodal analysis. As seen, the threat is spoken very slowly and menacingly. Even though Frank dismisses his disclosure through laughter as fake, the audience knows it is not (an instance of dramatic irony; cf. Chapter 4, Section 2.2) and Cathy may also be left with doubts. Dramatic irony is frequently used in this series to show characters' villainy, since viewers know they are lying outright, for instance when different people are promised the same job by Frank or his wife Claire.[2]

4 Concluding Remarks

This chapter has introduced a new model for analysing television dialogue (FATS) and has discussed functions relating to the communication of the narrative. I have introduced ten subcategories associated with establishing aspects such as setting, plot, and characters. Such functions are crucial for television series that construct a story for their viewers. The dialogue must provide adequate characterisation as well as communicate the who, where, what, how, and why of the narrative to the audience. But despite the importance of these functions, they do not represent the whole picture. Television dialogue also fulfils important additional functions such as those relating to aesthetic and interpersonal effect and commercial appeal. The next chapter will discuss these remaining functions and will also introduce some caveats about FATS, working as a conclusion to Part II as a whole.

4 *Other Functions of TV Dialogue*

1 Introduction

This chapter continues introducing the new functional approach to television series (FATS), now going beyond functions relating to the communication of the narrative. As in the previous chapter, I discuss each major category and its subcategories with multiple examples, mainly from SydTV. The final section then makes some important points about FATS as a whole, and concludes Part II (Chapter 3 and this chapter).

2 Functions Relating to Aesthetic and Interpersonal Effect and Commercial Appeal

I start by discussing functions associated with aesthetic and interpersonal effect and commercial appeal: control of viewer evaluation and emotions, exploitation of the resources of language, and opportunities for star turns.

2.1 *Control of Viewer Evaluation and Emotions*

Dialogue clearly functions to guide viewers' responses, for instance by controlling pacing, creating tension or suspense, setting up viewers for a surprise, drawing their attention to a plot element, guiding their interpretation, or eliciting their emotional responses (Kozloff 2000: 49–51). In example (9) in the previous chapter, the voice-over narrator introduces viewers to the backstory relevant to *Birds of Prey* but also guides viewer expectations regarding genre and narrative. With its mentions of New Gotham, Batman, Joker, and Catwoman, viewers are likely to expect a fantasy story, an expectation that will influence their reactions to the narrative.

Viewers' emotional responses can be elicited through the expression of character emotion, conflict, drama, tension, and so on. For instance, in the final episode of season three of the political drama *Homeland* (spoiler alert), one of the main characters (Brody) is publicly hanged, his death watched by another main character (Carrie), who is in love with him. In a highly emotional scene, viewers are exposed to both Brody's dying and Carrie's reaction, including her repeated shouting of his name. While Claire Danes's performance of Carrie's grief is multimodal and the graphic footage of Brody's death is also crucial, her shouts clearly contribute to eliciting viewers' emotional response to this scene. The scene can be viewed at www.youtube.com/watch?v= UlIzL8afSz8 (last accessed 3 December 2017), as a transcription would not do full justice to its powerful emotionality.

Additionally, certain dialogue lines create and foil viewer expectations, generate suspense, or arouse curiosity. As discussed in Mittell (2015: 83) in the final minutes of the pilot episode of *Veronica Mars*, the main character asks herself a range of questions: 'The Lilly Kane murder file – what's Dad been up to? . . . My surveillance photo from the Camelot – why is it in the Lilly Kane file? What was Mom doing there, and what business did she have with Jake Kane? And the million-dollar question: why did Dad lie to me?' Mittell discusses these questions as setting up story arcs, but they simultaneously create suspense.

Kozloff (2000: 50–1) also provides examples where dialogue helps viewers to interpret the visuals, for instance in relation to smell and beauty. In example (1), from the medical comedy-drama series *Nurse Jackie*, the eponymous Jackie converses with two elderly Jewish patients about their chicken soup (itself a stereotype). Since the audience cannot smell the soup, it is the dialogue that makes them vicariously experience it.

(1)

MRS ZIMBERG:	Chicken soup.
JACKIE:	Chicken soup. Is that what was in that bag?
MR ZIMBERG:	Yeah.
MRS ZIMBERG:	Smell.
JACKIE:	Oh, that smells good.
MR ZIMBERG:	Yeah, it is. [. . .] (SydTV, *Nurse Jackie*)

2.2 Exploitation of the Resources of Language

Kozloff (2000) explicitly associates the function 'exploitation of the resources of language' with Jakobson's poetic function. On a general level, exchanges between characters can be said to constitute a particular 'rhythm' (Kozloff 2000: 87). On a more specific level, the function is divided into four categories by Kozloff: poetic use of language, jokes/humour, dramatic irony, and on-screen verbal storytelling (where characters tell a story).

The poetic use of language includes characters' reciting of poetry as well as their use, in dialogue, of literary devices such as rhyming, alliteration, metaphor, repetition, contrast, and incongruity (Kozloff 2000: 52–3, passim). Both kinds of poetic language use occur in TV series. The *Nurse Jackie* pilot begins with the protagonist, a nurse, reciting in voice-over a fragment from a poem by T. S. Eliot (*Let us go then, you and I, when the evening is spread out against the sky like a patient etherized upon a table*) – which is also an instance of intertextuality (discussed below). In contrast, example (2) from SydTV (*Weeds*) shows how characters can jointly create poetic effects. Josh (a teenage drug dealer) and Nancy (a suburban mother and drug dealer) have a conversation about dealing to children, which ends with a poetic exchange. Josh's first turn is a poem in itself, but his second turn creates a rhyming effect as a response to Nancy's (*You're a poet*):

(2)

NANCY: Okay, listen, you stay away from my customer base, you don't deal to kids, are we clear?
JOSH: If they're too young to bleed, they're too young for weed. No grass on the field? No grass will they yield.
NANCY: You're a poet.
JOSH: You know it.   (SydTV, *Weeds*)

Another example of the poetic use of language comes from the British crime drama *River* (spoiler alert). In example (3), one of the protagonists of *River* (murdered detective Stevie, who appears and interacts with detective River) uses several literary devices (including rhyme and parallelism) as well as producing, in alphabetic order, the many synonyms British English offers to describe someone as mentally ill:

(3)

STEVIE: A question that sometimes drives me hazy: am I, or are the others, crazy?[1] Let me tell ya, from someone who knows ya – knew you – you're bananas. Barking, barking mad, batty, bonkers, crackers, crackpot, crazy, crazed, delirious, demented, deranged, distracted, doolally, frantic, gonzo, cuckoo. You've lost your marbles. Non compos mentis. Not right in the head. Not the full shilling. Nutty, nut,

nut. You – off your trolley, your rocker. Unsound of mind, out of your tree, unhinged, unstable, rabid, raving, wacko, raving loony tune. Find your way through your insanity. Find the order in your chaos. Otherwise, how will you ever find me?   (*River*, season 1, episode 4)

Kozloff's second subcategory of this function (jokes/humour) includes witty lines or jokes by characters, as in the final turn in example (4), from the dramedy *Gilmore Girls*:

(4)

EMILY: The entire school is talking about it [Lorelai kissing her daughter's teacher at parents' day]. And what do I say, how do I defend this?
LORELAI: Uh it was a mistake.
EMILY: A mistake? A mistake? Is that what you call it, a mistake?
LORELAI: Well I tried to call it Al but it would only answer to mistake.

(SydTV, *Gilmore Girls*)

Incidentally, Lorelai's punning here is also an allusion (intertextual reference) to a song by Paul Simon ('You Can Call Me Al'). I discuss such intertextuality in more detail below.

In addition, humour includes cases where we laugh at characters or their situation (Kozloff 2000: 54). The dialogue in example (5), from the medical drama *Grey's Anatomy*, is a good example, featuring an exchange between the hospital interns George, Alex, Meredith, Izzie, and Cristina. In this plotline, George has found out that he has syphilis and asks Alex to treat him, intending this treatment to be as private as possible. Instead, in a very funny scene, the female interns start coming in one by one, while George is face-down with his buttocks exposed:

(5)

[George and Alex in a treatment room by themselves]

GEORGE: Are you sure you know what you're doing?
ALEX: It's a shot of penicillin, George. Be grateful I'm even doing this. I've already seen more of you than I ever wanted to. I'll be fighting nightmares for a week.
GEORGE: Okay, you know what? Forget this.
ALEX: Do you wanna get rid of the syph or not? Just shut up and drop 'em.

[George pulls down his trousers and lies face-down on a treatment bed]

GEORGE: I cannot believe this. [Meredith pulls open the curtain] Meredith, go away!

MEREDITH [as she is coming in]: Oh, George. Thought you could use some moral support.

GEORGE: No! No, moral support. I'm indisposed here.

MEREDITH: George, it's not a big deal. And you have a cute butt.

ALEX: I have a cute butt too. You wanna see?

MEREDITH: Oh, get out. You're doing it wrong.

ALEX: Be my guest. [Meredith is taking over from Alex, Alex is leaving]

GEORGE: What? Alex. Alex! What? [George pulls the curtain to, which is immediately opened again by Izzie] Hey!

IZZIE: Ah. What are we doing here?

GEORGE: Breaking George's spirit. [pulls curtain to again]

MEREDITH: Curing George's syph.

GEORGE: I don't like needles.

MEREDITH: Good thing you became a doctor. Other side.

CRISTINA [from the outside]: Izzie?

IZZIE: Yeah?

CRISTINA: Uh, Mr Franklin's procedure's been scheduled [opens the curtain] for after lunch. Oh, what are we doing? [George pulls curtain to]

IZZIE: We are saving George from a future of festering sores and insanity.

CRISTINA: Oh, cute butt.

MEREDITH: Told you.

IZZIE: It is cute, like a baby's.

GEORGE [as he is getting up and pulling his trousers up]: You know, I have spent hours, days, years, imagining myself half-naked in a room with three women. The reality is so much better.

CRISTINA: I think he's gonna cry.   (SydTV, *Grey's Anatomy*)

Humour abounds in sitcoms, but also in other television genres, and can be the result of incongruity at all levels (Brock 2011), for instance breaches of conversational organisation (Stokoe 2008); incongruous or unexpected swearing, e.g. by members of the clergy (Walshe 2011);

or dialect dissonance, i.e. divergence from conventionalised norms and expectations regarding dialect use (Coupland 2016).

Kozloff (2000) mentions irony as the third subcategory of this function, focusing on dramatic irony, where viewers know more than the characters. I have already mentioned *House of Cards* in this respect (see example (18) in Chapter 3). Similarly, in the pilot episode from *Community*, viewers (but not the characters) know early on that the study group that Jeff pretends to run is purely an attempt to spend time with another character, Britta.

Another example from SydTV occurs in the sitcom *2 Broke Girls*. In this episode, the two female protagonists Caroline and Max, who want to start a cupcake business, attend a party to ask TV celebrity Martha Stewart to taste their cupcake. They dress as caterers to get in and the exchange in example (6) occurs while Caroline changes into her dress in the bathroom stall, and Max is outside it:

(6)

CAROLINE [in bathroom stall]:	[. . .] Martha Stewart is perfect. Her feet don't even touch the ground. The woman probably doesn't even go to the bathroom. [Sound of toilet flushing; camera shows Martha Stewart exiting the bathroom stall next to Caroline. Since Max is facing Caroline's bathroom stall she cannot yet see her.]
MAX:	Martha Stewart's hardly perfect. [Max turns around and notices Martha Stewart]
MARTHA STEWART:	And how are you this evening?
CAROLINE [in bathroom stall]:	No, you're right, Martha Stewart isn't perfect.
MAX:	Oh, I never said that!
CAROLINE [in bathroom stall]:	In fact, I hear she's a real ballbuster.
MAX:	Oh, you did not hear that.
CAROLINE [in bathroom stall]:	Yep, a real ballbuster, you know?
MAX:	No, I do not know.
MARTHA STEWART [to Max]:	Would you mind handing me a towelette please? Oh, one's fine. Thank you so much.
CAROLINE [in bathroom stall]:	But the fact that Martha Stewart is so tough . . .
MAX:	Caroline, you need to get out here right now.
CAROLINE [in bathroom stall]:	The fact that she is a real ballbuster . . .
MAX:	Oh, dear God, help me.
CAROLINE [in bathroom stall]:	Is what I like and respect about her. I mean, the woman's a genius.

MARTHA STEWART:	Now it's getting interesting.
CAROLINE:	And besides, you can't really believe gossip. Look at all that hate mail I got with people calling me a bitch, [starts exiting the bathroom stall] and I'm not a bitch.
MARTHA STEWART:	Well, that's debatable.
CAROLINE:	Martha Stewart, hi.
MARTHA STEWART:	Hello. (SydTV, *2 Broke Girls*)

Here the dialogue is funny because Caroline does not know that Martha Stewart is in the bathroom and can hear everything she is saying, while Max, Martha Stewart, and the viewers are aware of this fact. As mentioned in Chapter 1, pragmatic research has shown how humorous effects in TV series often rely on participation-based strategies. The humorous exchange in example (6) is prototypical for *2 Broke Girls* and other sitcoms in that the characters are not intentionally funny on the level of the diegesis (as would be the case if they deliberately joked), but the interaction is clearly intended to be humorous for the audience (Messerli 2016: 84–5). Dramatic irony can thus have various effects, including the creation of humour and the revelation of narrative roles as in the *House of Cards* example.

Kozloff's final subcategory for this function is on-screen verbal storytelling, especially where the storytelling is not relevant to the plot but 'compelling *as a story*, because of the intrinsic gratifications of storytelling' (Kozloff 2000: 56, emphasis in original). Perhaps example (7) might be considered a relevant example from the crime dramedy *Castle* – here crime writer Castle spins detective Beckett a hypothetical story about 'whodunnit':

(7)

CASTLE:	[. . .] What about the guy in eight B?
BECKETT:	Who?
CASTLE:	Eight B. Quiet guy, see him every day and only, you never notice him. Well he noticed Sara. She's young, beautiful, the kind of girl a guy like him never had a chance with. We all know girls like that, don't we? Well, at first, it was just a game, figure out her schedule, when does she do her laundry, when is she alone. Until it becomes something more, something that he can't control. Well, he uses the stairs, obviously, to avoid the elevator's cameras, and then he just waits, concealed in the shadows. When she comes into that laundry room, he pounces, and he looked into her vacant, lifeless eyes, he wanted to tell her, he never meant to kill her. All he ever

wanted was to be noticed. That's when he felt the heat of that dryer on his skin. So, he picks up her limp body in his arms and gently places it inside. He almost smiled at his good fortune when he found the quarter in his pocket, slipping it into the slot, buying the time to do what he does best, disappear. Just saying, better story.

(SydTV, *Castle*)

In addition to Kozloff's four subcategories (poetic use of language, jokes/humour, irony, on-screen verbal storytelling), I propose three additional subcategories: linguistic innovation, intertextuality (allusions to other texts), and metafictionality.

Linguistic innovation has already been discussed in Chapter 2. As mentioned, some TV series are lauded for invention, creativity, and play, and series with young adults who are close friends will include a high degree of linguistic innovation. In addition, sci-fi and fantasy series such as *Star Trek* or *Firefly* may create new words (e.g. *warp speed*; *gorram*) as well as new sociolinguistic environments (e.g. code-switching between English and Mandarin Chinese in *Firefly*; see Mandala 2008) or whole languages (e.g. Klingon in *Star Trek* or Dothraki and Valyrian in *Game of Thrones*). Such invention could be seen as the ultimate 'exploitation of the resources of language'. Linguistic innovation in SydTV will be the subject of Chapter 9, so no more will be said about it here.

Moving on, intertextuality occurs frequently in US TV series such as *Lost*, *Community*, *The Big Bang Theory*, or *Gilmore Girls* and exploits the common culture that viewers and the characters share. Such intertextuality functions to reveal the characters and their world but also to create pleasure in viewers and to bond with them, creating a community (Bednarek 2010a: 31–3; Queen 2015: 252).[2] Language is exploited because of its cultural value here. In example (8) – from *The Wire* – we can see a contrast between the speaker ('stick up man' Omar) and his allusion to a well-known fairy tale (*The Three Little Pigs*), which also recasts him as the 'big bad wolf'.

(8)

OMAR: Hey yo! Hey yo! Hey yo! Y'all need to open this door, man, **before I huff and puff**. C'mon, now, **by the hairs of your chinny chin chin**.

(SydTV, *The Wire*)

Intertextuality may also contribute to characterisation, for instance when *Buffy* characters reference *Star Trek* (Mandala 2007: 54), the nerds in *The Big Bang Theory* refer to sci-fi (Bednarek 2012b), or when the older character Mike from the political comedy series *Veep* references the TV series *Doogie Howser* from the late 1980s/early 1990s:

(9)

JONAH: And Mike you need to be there too okay, so no goin' home to walk
              your dog.
MIKE: Uh, don't tell me what to do, **Doogie fuckin' Howser**.
JONAH: I I don't know what that means.   (SydTV, *Veep*)

In example (9), Mike's reference to the television character Doogie Howser is not understood by the much younger Jonah, which emphasises the difference between these characters in terms of the social variable of age (type characteristics), but those audience members who are old enough to remember this programme may also bond with Mike. In other cases, characters may be constructed as sophisticated because they reference a particular text. Further examples of intertextuality in TV series are provided in Pearson (2007b: 248–9), Bednarek (2010a: 31–3), Queen (2015: 249–51), and in Chapter 9.

Finally, metafictionality exploits the potential of language to comment on language use itself (metalinguistic comments) but also includes dialogue that foregrounds the conventions or production aspects of TV narratives – such reflexive playfulness is a feature of many contemporary TV series (see Chapter 1, note 10).[3] For example, in the second episode of season 4 of the musical comedy-drama *Glee* the character Brittany explicitly comments on the show's use of voice-overs by saying, *Oh. I thought I was doing a voice-over*. In the final episode of the second season of the drama/thriller *Mr. Robot*, an FBI agent tells one of the characters (Darlene) *you are not on some TV show*, which plays with viewers' knowledge that yes, she is indeed on a TV show.

Another instance of metafictionality comes from the sitcom *Arrested Development*. In example (10), one of the main characters, the oldest son and part-time magician George Oscar (Gob), questions why a doctor would use ambiguous language, making the family think that his father has died when in fact he has escaped out of the hospital window (the doctor's words earlier in the episode are *We lost him. He just uh, got away from us. I'm sorry*). George Oscar comments directly on the doctor's dialogue and indirectly on the implausibility of the plot, hence foregrounding the constructedness of the narrative.

(10)

GEORGE OSCAR:	Why would a doctor say he's gone when he means he's escaped?
	[. . .]
GEORGE OSCAR:	Wouldn't you say "He left out the window", or "the room's empty"? (SydTV, *Arrested Development*)

Particular series exploit metafictionality to a high degree, while meta-communication can work in the service of other functions such as characterisation or control of viewer evaluation – as in the case of *The West Wing* (Richardson 2006).

2.3 *Opportunities for Star Turns*

Kozloff (2000: 60) suggests that some film dialogue functions to showcase a star and 'to keep our attention focused upon that star, and to give the star a chance to "show off"'. She argues that such dialogue can be identified because it is longer, requires above-average variety of emotional expression, and provides a platform for vocal skill. She also says that this category is 'primarily pertinent to a certain category of films, those designed as showcases for stars with unique histrionic talents' (Kozloff 2000: 60).

There are at least two aspects to be questioned here – first, whether this function is limited to such films, and second, whether length is a necessary criterion. In relation to contemporary TV series, much dialogue seems to allow actors a chance to 'show off'. It is too difficult to choose one dialogue extract that would illustrate this perfectly, and it would be very hard to demonstrate this without a video of the actor's performance. However, actors from TV series such as *House of Cards*, *Breaking Bad*, or *Homeland* are regularly nominated for awards and become known for their performance as a particular character. A web search for videos from these series will find many examples of particularly successful acting performances. But perhaps these do indeed tend to occur in particular kinds of TV series that might be considered as vehicles for known stars such as Kevin Spacey, Bryan Cranston, or Claire Danes.

In relation to length, certain *types* of dialogue arguably provide a platform for a star turn regardless of length. For example, dialogue by *other* actors may elicit a star performance, as when characters are given a bleak medical diagnosis by a doctor and must react to this. Even a story premise may provide a platform for showcasing performing skills as in *The United States of Tara*, *The Americans*, or *Orphan*

Black, where the same actor plays multiple personalities or persons and makes use of linguistic and other cues to distinguish these people. This can also occur in particular 'doppelgänger' episodes, as in *Buffy*, where the actor Alyson Hannigan performs both the 'normal' and the 'Vampire' version of the character Willow, each clearly distinguished (e.g. season 3, episode 16).

3 Functions Relating to Thematic Messages and Ideology

The next major function is associated with thematic messages and ideology, including explicit or implicit thematic messages, promotion of real-life products, and ideological representations.

3.1 Explicit or Implicit Thematic Messages

Like film dialogue, dialogue in TV series sometimes conveys explicit messages to the audience: Kozloff (2000: 56–7) mentions 'preachy passages' and 'overt moralizing' as examples of dialogue expressing a film's moral. Some TV episodes also have a 'moral', especially when they come from religious or quasi-religious narratives (e.g. *Highway to Heaven* (1984–9), *7th Heaven* (1996–2007)). A more recent example comes from the BBC series *Call the Midwife*, which occurs at the very end of the episode:

(11)

MATURE JENNY (voice-over):	It was a Christmas as unique as any other. For every year, the mystery unfolds itself anew. And later in life, I came to see that faith – like hope – is a rope and anchor in a shifting world. Faith cannot be questioned, only lived. And if I could not grasp it then, I felt its heartbeat, which was love. (*Call the Midwife*, 2012 Christmas special)

It is also possible to identify passages of TV dialogue where characters explicitly comment on social reality. Thus, the characters in *Gilmore Girls* discuss political issues related to women and feminism (Bednarek 2010a: 35, 39–40). The British TV series *Happy Valley* also includes discussions by policewomen about misogyny and sexism (season 2, episode 5). In example (12), Leslie and Ben – two of the protagonists of the sitcom *Parks and Recreation* – use a speech to directly address the sexism that female politicians face in the United States:

(12)

LESLIE: [. . .] Third, I'm now gonna give you permanent answers to all the silly questions that you're gonna end up asking me, and every other woman in this election, over the next few months. "Why did I change my hairstyle?" I don't know. I just thought it would look better. Or my kids got gum in it. "Are you trying to have it all?" That question makes no sense. It's a stupid question. Stop asking it. Don't ask it. "Do you miss your kids while you're at work?" Yes, of course I do. Everybody does. And then, you know, sometimes I don't.

BEN: Yeah. And by the way, no one's ever asked me that question. No one asks me, "Where are your kids?" Or, "Who's taking care of them?" [. . .] [one turn by Leslie]

BEN: Right. So, maybe Leslie doesn't fit your personal idea of what a candidate's wife should be. So what? That's good, because there shouldn't be just one idea anyway.

LESLIE: That's right. If you wanna bake a pie, that's great. If you wanna have a career, that's great, too. Do both, or neither, it doesn't matter. Just don't judge what someone else has decided to do. We're all just trying to find the right path for us. As individuals. On this Earth.   (*Parks and Recreation*, season 7, episode 9)

Mad Men is also famous for intentionally communicating feminist messages, as explicitly stated by its creator (see Goggin 2014: 82). But discussion of social issues is not just limited to feminist concerns – example (13) shows a critical comment on the US healthcare system, which occurs in a storyline from the dramedy *Weeds* after the main character, Nancy, has been shot and is in hospital:

(13)

MRS
TAFT: Hello, Botwin family. I'm Mrs. Taft, hospital administration. So sorry for your situation and so sorry to be clobbering you with this now, but we are a private hospital and blah, blah. How will you be paying? I have forms. They need to be filled out. **We're not Canada. We're not France. We're not Taiwan, Costa Rica, Iraq, Oman, Sri Lanka, Argentina, New Zealand, Spain, Ireland, Israel, Portugal, Germany, Ukraine, China. You get the point. We're America. We take all credit cards.**   (*Weeds*, season 8, episode 1)

I understand the comparison in example (13) of the US healthcare system with so many other countries as an explicit and intentional criticism of sociopolitical reality. Mittell (2015: 343) discusses an example from the finale of *Homeland*'s first season, where a video testimonial of one of the protagonists, Sergeant Nick Brody, makes a critical political statement about American drone strikes, which, he argues, the viewers are initially 'invited to endorse or at least consider as valid'. The first season of the comedy *Master of None* is an example of a TV series that successfully integrates humour with critical messages about contemporary life (for instance, racism on television in the episode 'Indians on TV'). In the British police drama *Life on Mars*, different strategies are combined to encourage viewers to critically engage with aspects of society, ranging from the personalisation and juxtaposition of different views to identification with characters and characters' explicit social critique (Richardson 2010a: 161–6).

There are also examples of contemporary TV narratives that include storylines that portray the LGBTQI community in ways that seem to elicit viewer sympathy (e.g. *Glee*, *Last Tango in Halifax*, *Please Like Me*), portraying for instance homophobia or negative reactions to 'coming out'. In example (14), from *Call the Midwife*, which takes place in the late 1950s/early 1960s, couple Delia and Patsy confront the now-historical reality in the United Kingdom of not being able to get married. I have included more detailed information such as pauses ([..] = medium pause), speed (preceding speech, applies until the next speaker's turn), and voice quality (following speech, applies up to preceding exclamation mark).

(14)

[In the street, after dark. Patsy runs after Delia, grabs and turns her.]

PATSY: [rushed:] You don't really want to get married, do you?
DELIA: Yes. More than anything. [Patsy looks shocked] To you, you fool! [Delia
          starts to tear up] But I can't [trembling voice]. [..] So that's that.
          [Patsy exhales and lets go of Delia's hand, as the latter is
          walking away.]   (*Call the Midwife*, season 4, episode 7)

The moving nature of this emotionally powerful exchange (reinforced through phonological and multimodal cues) elicits viewer sympathy for the women's situation and may trigger sympathy for people who are still in this situation in countries without such rights.

However, in relation to explicit messages where characters comment on social issues or praise/criticise other characters' behaviour, it is often hard to say whether audiences are positioned to agree or disagree. Another question is whether the characters are meant to be read as spokespersons for the TV series (Richardson 2010a: 165–6).

It is therefore difficult to find many clear examples of *overt* thematic messages in TV dialogue that can unproblematically be identified as a 'moral' for the audience. More often, viewers are presented with different morals and asked to reflect on them but are not necessarily *directed* to take sides. In general, it is possible to argue that overtly moral TV series would presumably put off some viewers, and representations that can be interpreted in different ways, depending on the viewer, are more interesting and appealing to audiences (Richardson 2010a; Raymond 2013; Bednarek 2015b).[4]

In addition to overt thematic messages, Kozloff includes less overt use of allegory to convey a social, moral, or political message. Such allegorical dialogue has a subtext, a double-layering (Kozloff 2000: 59–60). Douglas (2011: 33) mentions *The West Wing* and *Battlestar Galactica* as examples of political allegory in US TV series. Implicit messages are also apparent in TV series such as *Our Friends in the North* or *The Wire*, which explore sociocultural and political issues by way of fictional narratives, offering implicit critiques. Thus, the British *Our Friends in the North* critically portrays life in North East England from the 1960s to the 1990s. *The Wire*, according to creator David Simon, addresses 'what the drug war has become in America and what it was costing us as a society' (White House 2015: n.p.). Simon has stated elsewhere, 'I am not particularly interested in making the most entertaining stories unless they are actually contending with an argument that matters' (Chotiner 2015: n.p.). The storylines in the Netflix prison drama *Orange Is the New Black* can also be interpreted as criticisms of the American prison system and the way contemporary society views and treats those whom it has incarcerated.

In sum, certain TV series do make an argument, do have a thematic message, and do comment on human realities, and may do so in implicit, sophisticated ways. Both explicit and implicit thematic messages can critique, reinforce, or negotiate dominant/hegemonic cultural ideologies, including language ideologies (see Lippi-Green 2012: 17 for an example of the latter).

3.2 Promotion of Real-Life Products

In rare cases, the 'message' that is conveyed through TV dialogue is an instance of what I term 'verbal' product placement. There can be agreements between companies and networks, meaning that series are 'required by the networks to include specific products in their content' (Sandler 2007: KL 529–30). A clear example of a *verbal* product placement occurs in the musical drama *Nashville*:

(15)

DEACON: You had your meeting with that charity yesterday?
RAYNA: Oh, yeah, FosterMore.
DEACON: How'd it go?
RAYNA: So great. They are doing amazing work for these at-risk kids. Here
           in Nashville, all over the place.   (*Nashville*, season 4, episode
                                                                                  15)

This conversation between the country musicians and protagonists
Rayna and Deacon is essentially a plug for the real-life charity FosterMore. Between the final scene of this episode and the closing
credits, an advert for the charity is inserted (Figure 4.1).

TO LEARN MORE ABOUT

FosterMore

BECAUSE NO CHILD MAKES IT ALONE

VISIT FOSTERMORE.ORG TODAY

Figure 4.1 Still from Nashville *showing an advert for FosterMore*

A less clear example of verbal product placement is evident in
example (16), where one of the two characters in the HBO dramedy
Girls, Shoshanna, positively evaluates the dating show *Baggage* while
watching it:

(16)

HANNAH: What are you watching?
SHOSHANNA: Baggage.
HANNAH: Baggage? What's baggage?
SHOSHANNA: It's like, my favorite show on the game show network. Oh no
               she didn't.

HANNAH:	Oh, Marnie and I don't have cable so we haven't seen that.
SHOSHANNA:	Shut up, get over here now. Okay, so, there are three contestants. Today they're girls, and this guy Danny is looking for love, and they each have three suitcases, a little one a medium one and a big one, and then they have like, their secret baggage, and they reveal it, and if it's super freaky he eliminates them. Okay like, this chick?
HANNAH:	The black one or the blonde one?
SHOSHANNA:	No the black one. Her littlest baggage is that she spends a thousand dollars a month on her weave, which host Jerry Springer thinks is unbeweavable. Her medium baggage is that she plans her wedding after the first date and her biggest baggage is that she pokes holes in condoms. (SydTV, *Girls*)

There is a fine line between mentioning real-life products (such as genuine TV programmes) to create realism and anchor characters in a world similar to the audience's (see Section 4.2) and promoting such products. Extended positive discussions are more likely to fulfil promotional functions.

3.3 Ideological Representations

As we have seen, TV dialogue can convey overt thematic messages or have an intended subtext with an implicit message. In these cases, the assumption is that the relevant messages are intentional. However, there are many cases where it is not clear if aspects of the dialogue have been designed to create an explicit/implicit message, but where the dialogue nevertheless challenges, reinforces, or negotiates hegemonic ideologies. The function 'ideological representations' captures such cases. (In this respect, this is an exception to not making any assumptions about scriptwriters' intentionality.)

To give an example, there are thirty-one instances across eleven episodes of the adjective *fat* in SydTV where *fat* refers to body size, nutrition, etc. While some references occur with respect to men (*my fat ugly face* (Hot in Cleveland), *some fat old emir* (Dollhouse)) or unspecified/mixed gender (*I did not mean to imply that everyone here is fat and ugly* (Hot in Cleveland)), the vast majority of instances related to body image or dieting are used to refer to women, including the trope/stereotype of the 'former fat girl', which occurs in two different episodes in SydTV. In this way it could be argued that these episodes both reflect and reinforce cultural ideologies about gender and the obsession of the US and other cultures with the aesthetics of the female body. An extended example is discussed in Bednarek (2010a: 180–227), in relation to how *Gilmore Girls* reproduces the US mainstream ideology of eating meat.

It may not always be easy to distinguish 'ideological representations' from 'explicit or implicit thematic messages', but perhaps the latter occur in more marked contexts – for instance, in speeches, in longer stretches of dialogue, or in a voice-over at the beginning or end of an episode.

4 Functions Relating to Realism

This penultimate section discusses functions relating to realism. For Kozloff (2000: 47), to say that dialogue is 'realistic' means 'saying that it adheres to a complex code of what a culture at a given time agrees to accept as plausible, everyday, authentic'. Similarly, Mittell (2015: 221) argues:

Televisual realism is not a marker of accurate representation of the real world but rather is an attempt to render a fictional world that creates the representational illusion of accuracy – a program is seen as realist when it feels authentic even though no media text comes close to a truly accurate representation of the complex world.[5]

Scriptwriting advice notes that such believability is crucial to viewers caring about what happens to characters (Bull 2007: KL 834–8).

According to Kozloff (2000: 47) every mainstream film contains dialogue exchanges, which 'primarily function to replicate everyday encounters'. Also included are attempts at representing a particular cultural milieu accurately (Kozloff 2000: 48). I have subdivided functions relating to realism into two: imitating 'real' spoken and written language, and references to the 'real' world.

4.1 Imitating 'Real' Spoken and Written Language

Kozloff (2000: 47–9) suggests that one way of creating realism is to represent normal conversational activities such as ordering food, greetings, or small talk, which are strictly speaking not necessary for advancing the plot but which provide authenticity. Examples also occur in TV dialogue, such as the introduction in example (17) and the conventional politeness in the conversation with a dinner guest in example (18):

(17)

CAROLINE: [...] Alicia, this is Jay Van Zandt ...
JAY: Hi.
CAROLINE: Max's manager. Alicia's my lawyer.   (SydTV, *The Good Wife*)

(18)

BREE: Umm, Reverend, why don't you uh have a seat and I will get some
               refreshments.
               [two turns between Reverend and Bree's son Andrew]
BREE: Would you like some water? I have flat or bubbly.
REVEREND: Oh bubbly please.   (SydTV, *Desperate Housewives*)

However, most of these exchanges would simultaneously fulfil add-itional functions such as characterisation or plot development, since TV dialogue has a low tolerance for scenes that do not move the story forward (Bull 2007: KL 1893–6).

More generally – as already summarised in Chapter 2 – TV dialogue has to be realistic or authentic enough not to alienate viewers, and hence selectively imitates the features that we associate with 'real' (unscripted) speech, including institutional and casual encounters. Realism/authenticity can also be produced by successful representa-tions of particular language varieties (e.g. associated with professional or ethnic groups). Lopez and Bucholtz (2017: 23) talk about an *authenticity effect*, i.e. 'the result of carefully engineered artistic artifice and its ratification by audience members'.

I also include genre imitations under this function, for instance the creation of fictional but realistic CNN newscasts in season 4 of *House of Cards*, which report on the shooting of the fictional president. Similar examples occur in other series such as *Homeland* (Figure 4.2 and examples (19) and (20)).

Figure 4.2 Still from Homeland *showing a fictional newscast*

(19)

[Shot of the Brody family house, shot of Brody's children watching the television in the living-room, while we hear the television in the background]:	The turnout is overwhelming here at Andrews Air Force Base where Sergeant Nicholas Brody is scheduled to land [shot of TV screen] in just under two hours. Now a White House spokesman confirms that the Vice President [shot of children] will be on hand [children start talking to each other, television continues in background, becoming more difficult to understand] (*Homeland,* season 1, episode 1)

(20)

MIRA [reading from a newspaper]:	"In a stunning development at the Geneva summit, Iranian diplomats have offered IAEA inspectors full and unfettered access to the regime's nuclear sites in exchange for the lifting of economic sanctions." (*Homeland,* season 3, episode 12)

Here the scriptwriters have created fictional newscasts and print news stories that characters encounter in the narrative, imitating the kinds of newscasts and news stories that audiences are familiar with and encounter in their everyday lives. Such news items can also function to communicate narrative causality, for instance when they provide necessary background information.

4.2 References to the 'Real' World

TV dialogue also uses references to existing 'real-life' entities to anchor the narrative in the world known to the viewer. As Fludernik (2009: 42) notes, references to real places may hide the fictionality of a narrative, and Bruti and Vignozzi (2016b) point out that references to the cultural and historical background lend credibility to TV period dramas.

There are many instances of references to the 'real' world in SydTV, including *Lex* (Lexington Avenue in New York); *Beyoncé* and *Janelle Monáe* (singers); *DeGeneres and de Rossi* (celebrity couple); *Hugh Jackman* (actor); *Louis Vuitton* (brand); *Tetris* (computer game); *Tic*

Tacs (candy), *Spanx* (clothing product); *Mad Libs* (word game); *the 'Bucks* (coffee chain *Starbucks*); *vo-tech* (type of school); *Terps* (University of Maryland athletic team *Maryland Terrapins*); and *America's Most Wanted, Baggage* (reality television programmes). The SydTV episode of *2 Broke Girls* in example (6) above takes this realism further by not only referencing but also featuring Martha Stewart, as herself.

In TV series like *The Americans, Homeland,* and *Narcos* archival footage of events is integrated, for instance featuring utterances by real politicians in relation to actual events that have occurred. Even without dialogue such archival footage creates realism; that is, the dialogue is not necessary but can contribute to this effect. References to real historical events also occur, for instance in the voice-over narration in Netflix's *Narcos* or when characters in the drama *Mad Men*, which takes place at an advertising agency in the 1960s, discuss Richard Nixon's election campaign:

(21)

BERT: So Roger mentioned this Nixon thing.
DON: Yeah, he mentioned it. I just assumed it went away.
ROGER: It didn't.
DON: Last I read, Nixon was running without an agency.
BERT: Make no mistake, we know better what Dick Nixon needs, better than Dick Nixon.
DON: What does Dick Nixon think he needs?
ROGER: What he already has: Ted Rogers, the brains behind that Checkers broadcast. (*Mad Men*, season 1, episode 2)

Above, I suggested that intertextual references (allusions to other texts) can be discussed in relation to the exploitation of language for its cultural value. Insofar as intertextuality refers to 'real-life' phenomena (existing cultural texts such as films, novels, TV series), it also creates realism, since it shows that characters are 'embedded in a similar social world to that of the viewers themselves' (Queen 2015: 251).

5 Functions Relating to the Serial Nature of TV Narratives

The final category that I propose relates to functions of TV dialogue that have to do with the serial nature of TV series: the creation of consistency and continuity.[6]

5.1 Creation of Consistency

It is crucial for dialogue in TV series to create consistency across episodes and seasons. As explained in Chapter 1, TV narratives rely on 'consistent and persistent storyworlds and characters' (Mittell 2015: 22). The production process with showrunners helps to create this consistency. The television producer and writer Peter Dunne puts it strongly: 'In television, audiences are built on consistency. It is the number one rule in series TV' (Dunne 2007: 100). This includes consistency of characters, plot, and the general style, tone, and 'brand' of a show. In sum, a successful TV series is one that is consistent (Epstein 2006: 4).

As a TV series progresses, its dialogue should therefore remain in line with what audiences have come to expect of the series (e.g. in terms of humour, wittiness, and literary and aesthetic qualities) and of the characters (the way each character speaks and how they interact). Thus, a corpus linguistic analysis of dialogue produced by one of the protagonists in *Gilmore Girls* across all its seasons suggests that her style does remain fairly consistent and that a stable character 'adds to serial stability' (Bednarek 2011a: 194).

An obvious way of creating consistency is through catchphrases (e.g. Homer Simpson's *d'oh*) or salient 'signature interjections' (Bednarek 2010a: 137). But consistency does not mean that change is not possible, even in relation to catchphrases. For instance, *bazinga* is a catchphrase (and signature interjection) for the character Sheldon in *The Big Bang Theory* but is not used in all seasons. However, when characters diverge too much from the way they usually speak, this can become a source of meta-linguistic commentary and can be used stylistically for foregrounding (Bednarek 2010a: 110–11, 133).

Evidence for the importance of consistency also comes from what we know about the TV production process. Thus, show 'bibles' are sometimes given to new writers who join a scriptwriting team, which provide them with detailed information about the series, sometimes even information about characters' language choices (Douglas 2011: 34, 71).[7] Manuals on scriptwriting also advise novice writers to be consistent in their writing (e.g. Smith 2009: KL 751). They are told that in order to write 'in service to the show' (Douglas 2011: 263), they need to be familiar with its pace and style and to 'hear the characters' voices in [their] head' (Douglas 2011: 157). Showrunners also often talk about the voice of a series (e.g. Tracy Newman and Jonathan Stark in Prigge 2005: 110, 142; John Beck in Finer & Pearlman 2004: 205) or about writers learning the voices of the characters (e.g. Bill Lawrence in Priggé 2005: 182; Ron Hart in Finer & Pearlman 2004: 209), as further discussed in Chapter 10.

5.2 Creation of Continuity

The serial nature of TV series, which often feature plot lines that are continued across episodes (story arcs, cf. Chapter 1) means that TV dialogue must also function to create continuity. Serials in particular must do so, and often provide continuity for the viewer simply by including a recap sequence with dialogue from previous episodes at the beginning of a new episode, usually prefaced by *Previously on ...* (Richardson 2010a: 137). But the new episode itself can also include references to events that happened in previous episodes. For example, a conversation in the third episode of *Mad Men* between account executive Pete and secretary Peggy refers to a sexual encounter between them that happened in the first episode:

(22)

PETE: Peggy. When I came over that night, you know, before.
PEGGY: I was there.
PETE: You know, I'm married now.
PEGGY: I know.
PETE: So ...
PEGGY: Pete, I understand. It never happened.   (*Mad Men*, season 1,
                                                         episode 3)

Although he does not focus on linguistic analysis, Mittell (2015: 180–94) discusses many strategies for triggering and managing viewers' memories from recaps to embedded redundancies, diegetic retelling of happenings, voice-over, flashbacks, and so on. Particular series may develop their own strategies to update viewers, for instance to create continuity between different seasons (for an example, see Richardson 2010a: 137).

6 Conclusion

This chapter and the last have introduced a new functional approach to television series (FATS), offering a comprehensive framework that can be used to analyse the functions of television dialogue. I have deliberately included a large number of examples from different TV series, so that readers can better appreciate the complexity and multi-functionality of contemporary TV dialogue. Here, I will briefly highlight a few key points about FATS.

First, my main focus was on one mode (language), but television narratives are multimodal audiovisual texts (Bednarek 2010a, 2015a; Richardson 2010b; Toolan 2011, 2014). Hence, language interacts with other elements to fulfil these functions, and dialogue is 'not [...] the *only* means of accomplishing these ends' (Kozloff 2000: 62, emphasis in original). For example, viewers interpret television characters from speech, clothing, actions, etc. Realism can be created by the use of authentic music and sound effects, costumes, sets, camera techniques (such as the use of hand-held cameras), and so on. I have commented on this only in passing, where it has become clear that dialogue works in conjunction with camera shots to locate the narrative in space, in conjunction with shot sequencing to clarify the modality of happenings, and in conjunction with performance and shot content to elicit viewer's emotional responses, and that archival footage may also create realism without the inclusion of any dialogue. As Kozloff (2000: 17) puts it, 'the interaction between the visual and verbal tracks is always complicated and depends greatly upon the details of each instance'.

Second, I have predominantly discussed each dialogue extract with respect to one function only, for the sake of clarity. However, what Pfister (1988: 105) notes for drama dialogue and Kozloff (2000: 34) points out for film dialogue is also true for television dialogue: TV dialogue is polyfunctional, meaning that a piece of dialogue will most often fulfil more than one function at the same time (Bubel 2006: 255; Bednarek 2014a: 63). This was apparent in several examples, for instance in example (14) in the previous chapter, from *The Big C*, where Cathy talks about her childhood. These dialogue lines simultaneously establish the character's biography, identify Sean as her brother, and communicate narrative causality (reason for her desire for a pool). In this chapter, the line *Well I tried to call it Al but it would only answer to mistake* from example (4) is an intertextual reference that simultaneously functions to create humour. This multifunctionality is in line with scriptwriting advice, which states that scenes should fulfil several functions at the same time: no scene should merely explore character or be used only for exposition (Douglas 2011: 112, 114).

Third, there is no clear one-to-one relation between a particular type of dialogue cue and its function (Bednarek 2017b). For instance, while catchphrases and signature interjections create consistency, they are also important for characterisation and may create humour through repetition. Technical or specialised vocabulary establishes the professional identity of characters, creates realism, and indirectly conveys information about the setting. Non-standard language can construct characters' national or regional identity and identify the location but is also linked by Kozloff (2000: 82–3) to both realism and the poetic function of language. Intertextual references exploit the resources of language but also create realism and may contribute to characterisation. Names and nicknames identify characters (anchorage of the characters), but they also construct relationships such as friendship between these characters (relationships between characters). It has also been argued that the use of names and vocatives can foreground dialogue fragments and mark narrative salience (Zago 2015) – a usage that we can perhaps connect to the control of viewer evaluation and emotions. These are just a few examples; many more could be provided.

Fourth, it is an open question how many different functions should be posited and which subcategories should be distinguished. I have aimed for a compromise as far as generality and specificity are concerned, having a limited number of subcategories where they appear necessary and avoiding any double-classifications. The new model proposed here is not set in stone and can be adapted or developed further.

Finally, this chapter was concerned with describing and explaining the multiple functions that dialogue fulfils in televisual narratives, rather than providing details for *how* each function can be realised. In this respect, it has to be said that we know more about some functions than others – for instance, competing linguistic models exist for how characterisation works, and several linguists have investigated how humour is created in TV series. But other functions require more extensive analysis.

Notwithstanding these caveats, I hope that this new analytical framework will be useful for future research on television dialogue. I myself draw on it in this book, although not all functions will be equally relevant. For example, since SydTV contains only one episode per included TV series, it is not possible to analyse continuity. Further, corpus linguistic analysis of patterns *across* a range of texts does not lend itself well to analysis of narrative causality. For this, we would need to analyse linguistic patterns *within* an episode (intratextual analysis). The next chapter introduces the corpus linguistic approach in more detail.

Part III

Data and Approaches

5 *Corpora and Corpus Linguistic Methods*

1 Introduction

So far, I have provided relevant information on television dialogue and its linguistic analysis and have introduced a new functional approach to television series (FATS). But I have not yet explained the methods that are employed in this book. Before we get to the research results in Parts IV and V, it is necessary to outline the approaches used to arrive at these results. This chapter focuses on corpus linguistic methods, while the other approaches relevant to this book will be explained in Chapter 6.

In Chapter 1, I briefly introduced the Sydney Corpus of Television Dialogue (SydTV), and the previous chapters included many examples from this corpus. In this chapter I provide further information on the corpus contents (Sections 2.1 and 2.2) and also briefly assess the corpus (Section 2.3) and situate its use (Section 2.4). In addition, I describe the other corpora used for comparison (Section 3). I also introduce the corpus linguistic methods applied in this book (Section 4). The research results are reported in later chapters.

2 The Sydney Corpus of Television Dialogue (SydTV)

As outlined in Chapter 2, much linguistic research has focused on specific TV narratives, and much work has been undertaken on 'classic' or 'cult' shows: *Friends* (Tagliamonte & Roberts 2005; Stokoe 2008; Quaglio 2009; Heyd 2010; Dynel 2011), *Will & Grace* (Baker 2005), *The West Wing* (Richardson 2006; Wodak 2009), *Firefly* (Mandala 2008), *Star Trek* (Rey 2001; Mandala 2011), *Buffy the Vampire Slayer* (Mandala 2007), *Gilmore Girls* (Bednarek 2010a, b, 2011a, b), and *Sex and the City* (Bubel 2006, 2011; Paltridge et al. 2011; Urios-Aparisi & Wagner 2011). Existing corpora of US TV dialogue mostly contain dialogue from individual series, older series, or a small number of series, as reviewed in Bednarek (in press a). In my own research I have used corpora with dialogue ranging from one (Bednarek 2010a, b, 2011a, 2012b) to seven (Bednarek 2012a), ten (Bednarek 2011b), and twenty-seven (Bednarek 2014a) different series. It is clear that there is scope for linguistic research that examines a wider range of TV narratives, allowing a new focus on contemporary television dialogue as a language variety. The Sydney Corpus of Television Dialogue (SydTV) was designed to fill this gap, with the aim of enabling different types of linguistic analysis. The process of designing and building the corpus is described in detail in the corpus manual (Bednarek 2018), including justification of the criteria used in this process and following Sinclair's (2005: 8) advice to fully document such decisions. In Sections 2.1 and 2.2 I provide a summary of the key points.

2.1 Corpus Contents

SydTV is a small, specialised corpus representative of the language variety of US TV dialogue. TV dialogue is defined as the *actual* dialogue uttered by actors on screen as they are performing characters in fictional TV series (see Chapter 1). This on-screen dialogue differs from subtitles or dialogue present in shooting scripts and does not include screen directions and other elements present in such scripts (see Bednarek 2015a).

SydTV contains dialogue from one first-season episode of sixty-six different TV series whose country of origin is the United States and that were first broadcast between 2000 and 2012. This specific time frame was adopted because the first decade of the twenty-first century was characterised by the global rise of American TV series (Scripted Series Report 2010/11) and has been labelled the new 'golden age of television'. New seasons of some of the TV series included in SydTV are still being produced at the time of writing (e.g. *Veep*, *The Big Bang Theory*, *NCIS*), while most others are being shown as repeats or are available via services such as Netflix, Amazon, or iTunes. In total, the corpus contains about 275,000 words, although its size varies slightly depending on the token definition used (see Table A.2 in the Appendix).

The selection of episodes for the corpus was determined by the general goal to include a large number of different TV series and to achieve balance in terms of genre, textual time, and 'quality' versus 'mainstream': about half of the series can be classified as comedy genres and the other half as drama genres (using the labels provided by the Internet Movie Database, IMDb), with each category including

Table 5.1 SydTV: genre and quality (token definition: hyphens do not separate words; ' not allowed within word)

SydTV: Genre and quality (composition in number of episodes and words)				
	'Quality'		'Mainstream'	
Genre	*Drama*	*Comedy*	*Drama*	*Comedy*
Episodes/words	12/53,223	22/82,664	13/63,072	19/76,115
Total		34/135,887		32/139,187

genre combinations or hybrid genres such as crime/drama, action/drama, comedy/romance, or comedy/crime. In addition, about half the corpus consists of dialogue from 'quality' series, with the other half coming from other series (called 'mainstream' hereafter, for lack of a better label). Since *quality* can be defined in many different ways (see Thompson 2003; McCabe & Akass 2007; Richardson 2010a; Hassler-Forest 2014) and 'there is rarely any analytic clarity as to what precisely counts as quality television' (Mittell 2015: 211), a series was classified as 'quality' on the basis of Emmy or Golden Globe award nominations or wins for 'best/outstanding' TV series or 'outstanding writing'. Table 5.1 shows the composition of the corpus in number of episodes and words according to WordSmith ('tokens in text'), in terms of genre label and the subcategories 'quality' versus 'mainstream'.

To take into account the serial nature of TV series, the corpus includes episodes representing different moments of textual time within the season. As explained in Chapter 1, TV series are conceptualised and produced as seasons with a particular number of episodes, and even series that typically resolve storylines within an episode often have ongoing stories across episodes. The corpus hence contains a mix of pilot episodes, final episodes, and other episodes occurring towards the beginning, middle, and end of the respective season.[1] This consideration of textual time aims to ensure representation across the season to avoid a potential influence of particular kinds of episodes, especially pilot and final episodes, which are atypical and have very specific functions (Thompson 2003: 62; Douglas 2011: 53; Mittell 2015: 55–85). Table 5.2 shows the composition of the corpus in terms of textual time and the subcategories 'quality' versus 'mainstream', while Table A.3 in the Appendix includes all variables together.

One full episode per TV series was included, with the aim of building a 'full-text' rather than 'sample' corpus. This respects the 'integrity' of these artefacts (Sinclair 2005) and would be important for episode-based discourse and stylistic analysis. For each chosen

Table 5.2 SydTV: textual time (token definition: hyphens do not separate words; ' not allowed within word)

SydTV: Textual time (composition in number of episodes and words)

	'Quality'		'Mainstream'		Total	
	Episodes	No. of words	Episodes	No. of words	Episodes	No. of words
Pilot episodes	7	26,671	7	26,832	14	53,503
Final episodes	5	20,873	5	17,683	10	38,556
Episodes at the beginning	5	18,487	4	17,498	9	35,985
Episodes in the middle	9	35,586	8	37,426	17	73,012
Episodes at the end	8	34,270	8	39,748	16	74,018
Total	34	135,887	32	139,187	66	275,074

episode, dialogue was transcribed from scratch or on the basis of existing transcripts/scripts as explained in Section 2.2.

Although this was not used as a systematic variable during the design stage, SydTV contains a mix of broadcast/network television (forty-two episodes) and cable television (twenty-four episodes). It is important that a corpus contain series from such diverse distributors, since differences between these may impact on language use (cf. Chapter 1), and cable series such as *The Wire* and *Breaking Bad* are important cultural products in the contemporary television landscape. SydTV contains no Netflix, Hulu, or Amazon originals, since these were not as widespread during corpus design as they are now, and Netflix was not available in Australia until 2015. However, as mentioned above, many of the programmes included in SydTV are now distributed, if not created, via such platforms.

2.2 Transcription, Standardisation, Tagging

The vast majority of episodes (forty-eight episodes, about 70 per cent of the corpus) were transcribed from scratch by research assistants under my direction (mainly on the basis of iTunes, DVD, or streaming versions of episodes). In addition, two scripts and sixteen fan transcripts, freely available online on various sites, were used as starting points by the research assistants, who revised and corrected these texts by checking them against the audiovisual file of the respective episode. The transcription conventions are provided in the corpus manual (Bednarek 2018) and only summarised here.

Because of the expensive (time-consuming) nature of detailed transcription, transcription was mainly orthographic, although marked pronunciation variants such as *gonna* ('going to') and *c'mon* ('come on'), use of the alveolar form [In] in words ending in <ing> (e.g. *somethin'*), as well as contractions (e.g. *should've*), discourse markers (e.g. *oh*), hesitation markers (e.g. *uh*), listening cues (e.g. *mmm*), dis/agreement markers (e.g. *uh-uh*), and interjections (e.g. *ugh*) were transcribed. Several of these features are rarer in TV dialogue than in face-to-face conversation (cf. Chapter 2), and 'because they are rare, they can be more meaningful when they occur, so it can be important to capture them' (Queen 2015: 63).

Because of funding constraints, camera shots, scene information, background noise, character movements, actions, or gestures as well as delivery speed, voice quality, laughter, sighs, grunts, clearing one's throat, etc. could not be transcribed. Neither was punctuation consistently used to identify aspects such as pauses or intonation. In addition, dialogue in languages other than English was only sometimes transcribed, most often when mixed with English dialogue in the same turn (Figure 5.1).

In cases where English subtitles for such dialogue are provided to viewers, the subtitles were transcribed and dialogue was identified as subtitled (S), as seen in Figure 5.2.

Voice-over dialogue was also identified as such (V; VOICE), and audible dialogue emanating from media (e.g. radio, television) was transcribed (Figures 5.3–5.5).

Songs were transcribed only if they were sung by onscreen characters (Figure 5.6). Instances where characters read, recite, or clearly quote dialogue were marked "..." (Figure 5.7).

In terms of turn-taking structure, when characters speak in unison, utterances are repeated, although overlap is not explicitly identified;

```
<CLAUDETTE:> Manuel Ruiz! Ha visto este hombre? There.
<DUTCH:> Hey, hey hey you. You, amigo. Amigo.
```

Figure 5.1 Non-English dialogue mixed with English dialogue (The Shield)

```
<MR PAIK (S):> Why do you want to marry my daughter?
<JIN (S):> Mr Paik, I may be from a fishing village, but I have
ambitions.
```

Figure 5.2 Example of subtitled dialogue (Lost)

```
<JACKIE (V):> Ah morning. Such calm. I'm so quiet and so
peaceful. I can breathe it in. I can almost feel it inside.
Yeah, almost there. Almost. Yes!
```

Figure 5.3 Example of voice-over dialogue by a character (Nurse Jackie)

```
<VOICE:> Chuck continued to keep the secret ingredient of her
pies secret. Not even Olive Snook knew the baked goods she
delivered contained homeopathic mood-enhancers meant to pry
Chuck's aunts out of their funk.
```

Figure 5.4 Example of voice-over by a narrator (Pushing Daisies)

```
<TV:> ...seemed to indicate that voters approved of Senator
Palmer's honesty before a national television audience a little
more than a half-hour ago.
```

Figure 5.5 Example of dialogue from TV (24)

```
<NICK:> It's okay, hey, don't cry. I've, had, the time of my
life.
<COACH:> What is he doin'?
<NICK:> And I've never felt this way before, if it's true,
nananananana, and a somethin' somethin'.
```

Figure 5.6 Example of dialogue that is sung (New Girl)

```
<MAX:> "There's a certain slant of light, winter afternoons
that oppresses like the heft of cathedral tunes." That, my
friends is the first verse of a poem by Emily Dickinson. Now
read some of those tonight, and as you do, consider the fact
that Emily Dickinson writes convincingly about passion and
about the world in spite of the fact that she lived as a
virtual recluse. It'll help you appreciate her mind.
```

Figure 5.7 Example of dialogue that is recited (Gilmore Girls)

```
<RANDY:> Drink, drink, drink, drink, drink, drink.
<MAN 1:> Drink, drink, drink, drink, drink, drink.
<MAN 2:> Drink, drink, drink, drink, drink, drink.
```

Figure 5.8 Example of characters speaking in unison (My Name Is Earl)

```
<MAC:> I got it. Okay okay okay okay. Hold on a second. Ha! Ha ha! Ha!
<CHARLIE:> Give it to me! Okay you found it!
```

Figure 5.9 Example of characters speaking in overlap (It's Always Sunny in Philadelphia)

```
<HARVEY:> Stan it's nice to meet you. Has Mike...
<STAN:> Oh my God. Oh my God, is that them? Oh, Jeter. Hank
Aaron! No way, Merriths! That's not number sixty-one is it?
```

Figure 5.10 Example of interruption (Suits)

interruptions of another speaker are marked by dot points; repeats of full words are included (e.g. *I I I* or *I, I, I*). Figures 5.8–5.11 show example dialogue lines.

Much care was taken to ensure the accuracy of the transcription, but human error is still a possibility. Further, transcribers may disagree on particular dialogue lines, for example because of speaker overlap, mumbling, speedy delivery, etc. It is not possible to consult the script in such cases, since it 'will clarify which variant should have been used but not which was actually used, so it will account neither for production of the item in question nor for everyone's linguistic

```
<SELINA:> He's a tort guy, right, yes yes yes, of course.
<GARY:> No, this is the new cornstarch fork, see, I got the
cornstarch spoon.
<AMY:> Could we maybe table tableware for now Gary and focus on
filibuster reform?
<SELINA:> No no no no no, but Amy, look, look at this, this is
classic clean job stuff. I mean if I can get cornstarch
utensils in most federal buildings by the fall, well then, the
veep hath landed.
```

Figure 5.11 Example of repeats (Veep)

experience' (Adams 2013: 233). Needless to say, a transcript is only ever one version of on-screen dialogue. As many scholars have pointed out, transcription is not a neutral but rather a selective process of analysis, reflecting the researcher's interest and decisions and resulting in a single, partial, reductive, and fixed version (e.g. Toolan 2014: 460–1).

Technically, the corpus that I have just described is SydTV 3.0 and has previous incarnations, but I refer to it simply as SydTV throughout this book. SydTV 3.0 exists in two different versions: the original version (as transcribed) and a partially standardised version, as described in Table A.4 in the Appendix. The standardised version is useful for comparing word forms and n-grams across corpora (see Sections 4.1 and 4.2) and will be referred to as SydTV-Std. For example, standardising all instances of *fuckin'* to *fucking* allows the software to treat these as instances of the same word form. However, the original version is useful for analysis of non-standard language use.

All SydTV files are plain text files (.txt). In relation to tagging, the corpus is predominantly 'raw' text, although speakers were identified as such. For the version I used for this book, speaker names were simply marked by angle brackets, i.e. <JACKIE:> or <EARL (V):>. In the version now available to other researchers via an online interface, the tags are XML-compatible: <u who="JACKIE"> Hey. </u>. Information on access to SydTV is provided at www.syd-tv.com. When presenting examples from SydTV in this book, I have removed the angle brackets around speakers for the ease of the reader, except when concordances are displayed.

2.3 Corpus Assessment

Funding and time constraints impacted on both the amount of television dialogue that could be included in SydTV and the amount of detailed linguistic information present in the transcription, with both factors resulting in some limitations.

The most obvious limitation of the corpus is its small size, a result of the fact that most dialogue was transcribed from scratch. In this, SydTV is similar to many other corpora of spoken English.[2] To compile as much data as is contained in the spoken component of the British National Corpus (~10 million) requires considerable resources. The small size of SydTV equals less data, which in turn means lower frequencies of linguistic phenomena and the inability to investigate rarer features. For low-frequency items there is not enough evidence to examine patterns and phraseology.

I did briefly consider some alternatives in order to create a bigger corpus, namely using online scripts, subtitles, or uncorrected fan transcripts. However, these have several disadvantages, as discussed in Bednarek (2015a). The most important of these is that such documents do not represent on-screen dialogue accurately enough. As Jaeckle (2013: 5) emphasises, 'When scholars rely on screenplays and subtitles instead of on-screen dialogue, misquotations can and do occur.' Adams (2013) also points to variation among scripts, texts, and performances of a scripted work such as a TV series or film. Of the three options (subtitles, scripts, fan transcripts) fan transcripts are the closest to on-screen dialogue, as they can be 'fairly accurate and very detailed, including several features that scripts are not likely to present: hesitators, pauses, repeats, and contractions' (Quaglio 2008: 191–2). From my own experience with such transcripts, I would say that uncorrected fan transcripts are relatively accurate, but not completely accurate, and unsuitable for analysis of informality, colloquiality, discourse phenomena, performance features, etc. If transcripts are undertaken collectively, rather than by one dedicated fan transcriber, consistency is an issue that also affects other linguistic features. This does not render fan transcripts unusable, but they either need to be checked against videos or used only for analysis of lexical and grammatical features that are likely to remain fairly unaffected by these issues.

At the same time, the small size of SydTV has clear advantages: First, it means that I am highly familiar with the corpus – in fact, it made it possible for me to read every single text in the corpus so as not to approach my analyses 'from the position of *tabula rasa*' (Baker 2006: 25). External content such as episode recaps or information about characters and storylines was also consulted, to increase my knowledge about those narratives that I was not already familiar with. Second, the small size means that 'total accountability' (McEnery & Hardie 2012: 15) is easier to achieve (using the entire corpus and all relevant evidence emerging from it), and there is less need for downsampling – although high-frequency items or investigation of a large amount of different items still require researchers to randomly select a subset for analysis (see Chapter 7). Third, the small size of the corpus means that it is easier to compare instances against the relevant video of a given episode. These videos can easily be accessed by other scholars, via DVD or distributors such as iTunes, Netflix, or Amazon. The fact that the original data are publicly available is in line with the ethical duties of corpus creators (McEnery & Hardie 2012: 66). Importantly, examining the audiovisual context is both useful and necessary for the linguistic analysis of particular features such as interjections, discourse particles, intensifiers, etc. or for multimodal analysis.

Finally, while size is important, corpus design is arguably *as* important, if not more (Koester 2010: 68). In Mair's (2006: 356) words, 'small and tidy' corpora can be complementary to 'big and messy' corpora. In this respect, SydTV has been very carefully designed; it contains a highly accurate representation of actual on-screen speech, and it is an extremely balanced corpus that contains dialogue from sixty-six different TV series (comedy, drama; quality, mainstream; different moments of textual time). It is therefore more representative than bigger corpora that contain dialogue from only one genre or only one or a few series. Unlike other corpora, it does not rely on online scripts, subtitles, or uncorrected fan transcripts, which do not represent on-screen dialogue accurately enough for the purposes of this book.

Moving beyond size, the corpus could be enriched by more detailed transcription and annotation. Clearly, many aspects of spoken discourse are not captured in the transcription, thus 'drawing our eyes to some phenomena while leaving others in shadow' (Du Bois 1991: 71). While I may seek funding to be able to add annotation to SydTV (e.g. for character gender), I am not currently planning to have the data retranscribed. Rather, it is my hope that SydTV can be used as a starting point to identify interesting scenes for analysis, which can then be transcribed in more detail by researchers by accessing the original video. In this way, corpus linguistics could be combined with conversation analysis, interactional sociolinguistics, and other qualitative approaches to discourse that require and use more detailed transcription methods (see e.g. Du Bois et al. 1993; Clift 2016: 44–63).

Furthermore, SydTV is not suitable for comprehensive analysis of multilingualism. While the majority of characters use American English, the included series also feature characters that are English (e.g. O'Hara in *Nurse Jackie*), Indian (e.g. Raj in *The Big Bang Theory*; characters in *Outsourced*) or LX speakers from other countries (e.g. Gloria in *Modern Family*; Sophie in *2 Broke Girls*; Drazen in *24*).

Only lexicogrammatical aspects of these characters' speech are identifiable in SydTV, since accent is not captured in the transcription. Neither was all dialogue in languages other than English transcribed, as explained in Section 2.2.

Finally, SydTV was designed to be representative of TV dialogue as a language variety. This means that only one episode is included per series, in order to incorporate dialogue from many different programmes. This in turn makes the corpus unsuitable for a comprehensive analysis of *one* televisual narrative, which would require dialogue from a whole season or the complete series. This was an intentional decision, since there is already a large amount of linguistic research that focuses on dialogue from only one series, including some of my own past work. Given the fact that SydTV includes such varied data, it can act as a reference corpus for such research. Although it does not contain full seasons or series, it contains full episodes – which means that narrative or stylistic analysis of such episodes is still possible. Further detail on potential uses of SydTV for stylistic research are discussed in Bednarek (in press a). To enable other scholars to use SydTV as a reference corpus or to investigate TV dialogue more generally, I have made frequency lists publicly available and also offer free access to an online interface where analyses of SydTV can be undertaken. Information on both of these resources is provided at www.syd-tv.com.

2.4 Situating the Use of SydTV

In this book I exploit SydTV in two key ways:

(1) as a repository to identify functions of TV dialogue (for the previous two chapters) and to detect instances of non-codified language (Chapter 9)
(2) as a dataset for processing by corpus linguistic tools (Chapters 7 and 8, and to some extent Chapter 9).

To situate my use of SydTV more generally, I draw here on a new topology for the analysis of discourse, which I have developed in collaboration with Helen Caple to allow researchers to reflect upon and explicitly position their approach (Bednarek & Caple 2017a, b). We distinguish between four zones of analysis, depending on whether research focuses on one semiotic mode (e.g. language) or not, and whether research focuses on patterns within texts (e.g. discourse or genre structure) or patterns across texts. As the horizontal axis in Figure 5.12 shows, analysis can be limited to one mode (*intrasemiotic/monomodal*) or bring together analysis of several modes

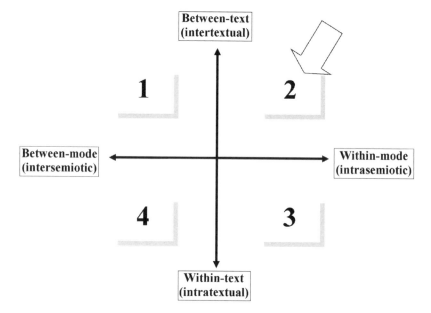

Figure 5.12 Situating this research project

(*intersemiotic/multimodal*). In addition, the vertical axis in Figure 5.12 shows that research can concentrate on uncovering patterns across a range of texts in a dataset (intertextual) or examine patterns that hold within texts (intratextual). These scalar parameters intersect and create zones of analysis, which are considered to be 'regions', rather than strict separate categories. That is, the term *topology* is used in analogy to Martin and Matthiessen (1991) to refer to scalar rather than categorical distinctions, which are typically represented in taxonomies.

The arrow in Figure 5.12 shows that I situate my analyses of SydTV mainly in zone 2: the focus is on language and the primary interest is in patterns across texts, rather than patterns within texts – except for limited examination of concordance plots, as explained in Section 4.4.

This focus on language is arguably typical of most corpus linguistic research but disregards the multimodal nature of TV narratives, in which aspects other than language can be highly meaningful and informative and combine with linguistic elements in important ways (see Chapter 4). In previous research on TV series I have therefore incorporated analysis of multimodal aspects (Bednarek 2010a, 2015a). However, 'corpus-assisted multimodal discourse analysis' (Bednarek & Caple 2014, 2017a) is a highly complex endeavour and not feasible in this book. As also noted above, the transcription of SydTV focuses on dialogue only, excluding gestures, actions, shot types, etc.

I did, however, exploit the affordances of a small corpus and watched episodes in SydTV so as to be familiar with the original audiovisual context. In addition, I often watched the respective scene when necessary for comprehending or interpreting corpus examples. In this book, I provide information on relevant non-linguistic aspects in some examples, even if these are not included in the transcription, but I do so only where this is crucial for understanding the particular dialogue lines or the point I make about them.

3 Other Corpora

In addition to SydTV, I make use of several other corpora, allowing a comparison of TV dialogue with different varieties of English. Table 5.3 on pp 94-95 provides a summary of these datasets.

While they are by no means perfect, these corpora are useful for different types of comparison. Because they represent a different national variety, the British corpora (BNC, BE06) are used only once when comparing similarities across different kinds of English-language corpora. The AmE06 is additionally used as a reference corpus for comparing both SydTV-Std and the LSAC against written American English (see Section 4.2). SOAP represents an interesting point of comparison for exploring how the language in SydTV is similar or different to other television corpora and is occasionally used for this purpose. Note that the SOAP corpus is restricted to one genre and it is somewhat difficult to identify the accuracy of the transcripts (see Bednarek 2015a).

The spoken corpora, C_CH and the LSAC, are used to compare TV dialogue (SydTV-Std) with unscripted spoken American English. The LSAC, in particular, is used for keyness analysis (Section 4.2), because it is bigger than C_CH and more representative of spontaneous conversation. However, since the LSAC contains spoken American English from an older time period than SydTV, the corpus is not useful as a point of reference when analysing non-codified language in Chapter 9. Instead, I primarily use COCA/S and GloWbE/US for this purpose (and very occasionally all of COCA), and will therefore say a few words about these two corpora here.

Davies (2009: 162) argues that the transcripts of unscripted TV and radio conversations that make up COCA/S are 'very accurate', 'almost completely spontaneous', and 'represent well non-media English'. Davies (n.d. a) states that COCA/S represents informal spoken English

Table 5.3 Summary of other corpora used in this book

Corpus name	Description
BNC	The British National Corpus (www.natcorp.ox.ac.uk/): 100 million words of spoken (10 per cent) and written (90 per cent) British English, the majority from 1985 to 1993; used as integrated in Sketch Engine (Kilgarriff et al. 2014)[a]
BE06	1 million words of published general written British English (five hundred 2,000-word samples from 15 genres), the majority of which were published between 2005 and 2007 (Baker n.d.)
AmE06	1 million words of published general written American English, the majority of which were published in 2006; same design as the BE06 (Baker n.d.)
SOAP	The Corpus of American Soap Operas (Davies 2012): 22,000 transcripts of ten American soap operas, 100,783,900 words, 2001–12 (ranging from about 2 million per year (2012) to about 11 million per year (2005)) (Davies n.d. b)
C_CH	Contiguous 10-minute segments from 24 American English telephone conversations (50,494 words; subset of CallHome), and 95 narratives, conversations, and interviews with and by North Carolina communities (198,295 words; from the Charlotte Narrative and Conversation Collection); taken from the second release of the American National Corpus (www.americannationalcorpus.org)
LSAC	The Longman Spoken American Corpus, a part of the Longman Spoken and Written English Corpus (Biber et al. 1999): about 5 million words representative of American English conversation produced by different speakers from different US states in the 1990s across a variety of settings (e.g. shop, park, home, classroom) and including different kinds of interactions such as casual conversations between family members or close friends, task-related interactions, service encounters, work-related exchanges, face-to-face and telephone conversations (Quaglio 2008, 2009; Al-Surmi 2012; Jack Du Bois, personal communication).
COCA	The Corpus of Contemporary American English (Davies 2008): 520 million words of spoken and written American English from 1990 to 2015, evenly divided between transcripts of TV and radio programs, various kinds of fiction (e.g. short stories, plays, books), different kinds of popular magazines, newspapers, and academic journals from different disciplines (Davies 2009)
COCA/S	Spoken part of COCA, consisting of American English media language: transcripts from 150+ different programmes from US radio and television (e.g. *All Things Considered, Today*

(continued)

Table 5.3 (cont.)

Corpus name	Description
	Show, Jerry Springer, Oprah), predominantly unscripted, 109,391,643 words, 1990–2015, about 4 million/year (Davies 2009)
GloWbE/US	US component of the corpus of Global Web–based English (Davies 2013): one of the two largest country components within GloWbE (Davies & Fuchs 2015: 22); 82,260 essentially randomly selected US websites (275,156 web pages), 386,809,355 words, 2012 (Davies 2015)

[a] The new version (BNC 2014) was released too late to be used for the analyses in this book.

well, although he does acknowledge that the media context means that speakers are likely to modify their speech, including 'relatively little profanity and perhaps avoiding highly stigmatized words and phrases like 'ain't got none'. It is crucial to keep this in mind – and COCA/S is best regarded as representative of unscripted spoken *media* language.

GloWbE/US was designed with the goal for the websites to represent informal language, with 60 per cent of the words coming from informal blogs (Davies 2015; Davies & Fuchs 2015: 3). Debates about GloWbE and its composition can be found in *English World Wide 36/1* – for instance in relation to 'the unknown heterogeneity of speaker types, language competencies, genres' (Mukherjee 2015: 35) or the question to what extent blogs can represent speech (Peters 2015: 42). Nevertheless, new media language exhibits a high degree of vernacularity (Squires & Iorio 2014: 331) and language change and innovation (Pitzl et al. 2008: 39; Lutzky & Kehoe 2016: 169). These are characteristics that make this corpus useful for analysis of non-codified language.

In analysing SydTV and the other corpora I use different corpus software and interfaces, namely WordSmith (Scott 2017a), GraphColl (Brezina et al. 2015), Sketch Engine (Kilgarriff et al. 2014), and Mark Davies's web interface to various corpora including COCA, GloWbE, and SOAP (http://corpus.byu.edu/).[3] These tools and interfaces are employed in this book for various corpus linguistic analyses, as explained in Section 4. In addition, WordSmith results were filtered and processed with the help of Excel (2016).

While I used the BNC, COCA, GloWbE/US, and SOAP as integrated in online interfaces, I had access to the files for the AmE06, BE06, C_CH, and the LSAC. To make these corpora more comparable to SydTV-Std, I produced partially standardised versions of these corpora, as described in Table A.5 in the Appendix, capturing some of the most important potential transcription differences. Since I use only one version of these corpora (the standardised version) I will simply refer to these corpora as AmE06, BE06, C_CH, and LSAC – rather than the more cumbersome AmE06-Std, BE06-Std, etc.

4 Corpus Linguistic Concepts and Techniques

In the remainder of this chapter I briefly introduce the main corpus techniques used in this book, without discussing debates surrounding them (see e.g. McEnery and Hardie 2012; Hunston 2013; Brezina et al. 2015). Importantly, information on the settings (thresholds, etc.) will be provided later in the relevant empirical chapters.

4.1 Frequency

Most corpus linguistic software programmes and interfaces permit analysis of the frequency of items (e.g. words), including their raw frequency (the actual number of instances) and their normalised frequency (their frequency per a given number of words, e.g. frequency per 100,000 words). The researcher can either look up the frequency of a *given* item or examine frequency lists, which provide information on the frequency of *all* items. Both types of frequency analysis are employed in this book. Frequency information can also be used to establish thresholds below which words are excluded from analysis (e.g. requiring a minimum frequency of two).

In addition to examining the frequency of words (word forms such as *walk, walks, walked, walking*), n-grams are also investigated, i.e. 'multi-word strings of two or more uninterrupted word-forms' (Stubbs & Barth 2003: 62). N-grams are recurring combinations of n-words, for example bigrams (two words, e.g. *of the, you know*), trigrams (three words, e.g. *at the end, you know that*), tetragrams (four words, e.g. *what are you doing*) or pentagrams (five words, e.g. *let me tell you something*). They are identified on a purely automatic basis, meaning that n-grams do not necessarily have grammatical, semantic, or pragmatic status (Stubbs & Barth 2003: 69) and can be either fragments or meaningful units (O'Keeffe et al. 2007: 61). Corpus linguistic analyses have revealed that n-grams are register/genre/text-type sensitive (e.g. Stubbs & Barth 2003; Culpeper & Kytö 2010), which means that they can provide useful insights into a language variety.

It is often interesting to compare the frequency of words across corpora. To do so, it is possible to use Sketch Engine's inbuilt

Comparing Corpora function, which allows the user to compare different corpora based on high-frequency words. The process is explained as follows on the website:

- for every two corpora
- top 5,000 words according to frequency (from every corpus separately)
- for every word from unification to count key word score
- next only top 500 words according to score
- arithmetic mean of their score is a similarity pair of corpora. (www .sketchengine.co.uk/user-guide/user-manual/corpora/compare-cor pora/, last accessed 6 March 2017)

In essence, the approach focuses on comparing high-frequency words – the lower the resulting value, the greater the similarity between the compared corpora. Thus, a value of 1.0 signifies identical corpora, while two corpora with a value of 2.48 are more similar to each other than two corpora with a value of 2.87. This functionality is used in Chapter 7 to explore similarities between SydTV-Std and various other corpora. However, the method that is used most often to compare corpora is keyness analysis.

4.2 Keyness

Keyness analysis enables the automatic comparison of frequencies across two corpora (e.g. Scott & Tribble 2006). In Culpeper's (2009: 34) words, '"keyness" is a matter of being statistically unusual relative to some norm'. How does this work in WordSmith? This software compares the frequencies of items in one corpus (variously called the node, target, focus, or study corpus) with their frequencies in a second corpus, which provides a baseline or norm (the reference corpus). The calculation takes into account the different sizes of the corpora and applies statistical tests – most often log likelihood (LL; G2). This test tells us if the difference between two corpora is statistically significant by providing a log likelihood value that corresponds to a particular p-value. A p-value of 0.05 (G2 = 3.84) means that we can be 95 per cent confident that the results are not due to chance (Baker 2006: 126; see further http://ucrel.lancs.ac.uk/llwizard.html, accessed 13 November 2015). Statistically significant key words do, however, vary in their raw frequency and distribution across corpus files (e.g. Culpeper 2009).

Another important factor is effect size – a key word may occur four times as frequently in the node corpus than in the reference corpus, eight times as frequently, fifty times as frequently, and so on. Differences in effect size can be considered by examining the log ratios for key words. As Hardie (2014) explains, 'The Log Ratio statistic is an "effect-size" statistic, not a significance statistic: it *does* represent how big the difference between two corpora are [*sic*] for a particular keyword' (emphasis in original).

In sum, a key words list is a list of items that are, statistically speaking, unusually frequent ('positive' key words) or unusually infrequent ('negative' key words) in the node corpus when compared with the reference corpus. The choice of reference corpus does influence the key words that are identified (Culpeper 2009: 34–5), even though it has been suggested that 'above a certain size, the procedure throws up a robust core of KWs [key words] whichever the reference corpus used' (Scott & Tribble 2006: 64). Researchers can compile a list of key words or key n-grams, both of which will be undertaken in this book.[4] I will use *key items* as a cover term for both. I focus on word forms and n-grams, rather than lemmas, to allow for better comparison with previous studies.[5] My specific interest is in those key items that are over-represented in the node corpus, i.e. 'positive' keyness, rather than those that are under-represented, i.e. 'negative' keyness.

While multidimensional analysis (MDA) is also used to analyse TV dialogue (see Chapter 2), keyness analysis was preferred, since it does not require predetermining linguistic categories or pre-processing of the data. Further, it appears that key words do capture important differences between language varieties and 'can be used to achieve an approximation to an MDA analysis' (Xiao & McEnery 2005: 76). Keyness analysis has been successfully applied in exploring other types of scripted language such as drama texts (e.g. Culpeper 2009; Culpeper's & Kytö 2010), and, crucially, the methodology has also been employed in the study of television dialogue (e.g. Baker 2005; Mittmann 2006; Bednarek 2012a).

In Chapter 7 I briefly investigate the key items that are shared by SydTV-Std and the LSAC, when both are compared with the AmE06. However, the bulk of the keyness analysis in this book consists of analysing key items in SydTV-Std when this is compared with the LSAC. Key items are often classified according to particular categories, a practice that I will also follow in this book.

4.3 Distribution

In addition to the frequency and keyness of words and n-grams, their distribution is important. In this book I pay attention to three different types of distribution:

- *Range* (Nation & Waring 1997): In how many files (i.e. texts) in a corpus does an item occur? This is important because some items with a relatively high frequency may occur in only a few documents in a corpus. I have analysed the distribution of key items across texts in a corpus for a while now, as a useful indicator of the core linguistic features of a register (e.g. Bednarek 2012a: 42). Analysis of range – sometimes called consistency analysis – is also useful for analysing similarity more generally (Taylor 2013). It makes sense to use range, since files in SydTV are meaningful units (one file is one episode) and not too dissimilar in size. In other cases, range may not be a useful measure (Stefan Gries, personal communication).

- *Dispersion*: How evenly is an item distributed within a corpus? Gries (2006: 198) has argued that dispersion analysis 'should belong to the standard procedure of interpreting corpus-linguistic data'. WordSmith provides users with a dispersion value for items in a word list, which indicates the extent of uniformity of the term's distribution. Generally, the WordList dispersion value lies between 0 and 1, and the closer the value is to 1, the more uniform the dispersion (Scott 2017b). According to Scott (2017b, email communication) the process works by dividing the corpus (based on size in bytes) into eight divisions and computing how each word is dispersed across the corpus (using one counter for each one-eighth of the corpus). The basis for the calculation is the whole corpus (all texts, rather than only the files in which items appear, which is the case for the dispersion value in Concord). The process takes into account the number of divisions, the mean of the frequencies over the divisions, and the standard deviation of the frequencies, using the most reliable of the three dispersion measures provided in Oakes (1998), i.e. Juilland's *D* (Juilland et al. 1970, cited in Oakes 1998: 190). Importantly, as is clear from the examples presented by Scott (2017b), a word with a high dispersion can have a low range. Note that the procedure assumes that there is no bias in the corpus itself and how it is structured and arranged (e.g. in terms of the order of files). It has recently been suggested that Juilland's *D* does not work well for large corpora divided into 100 or more parts but that the measure is 'relatively stable and reliable' (Biber et al. 2016: 440) when small corpora are divided into a small number of divisions, as is the case for SydTV. It has also come to my attention that there is now emerging corpus linguistic work on developing *text dispersion keyness*, a method that seems to produce higher-quality key words lists (Egbert 2018; Egbert & Biber in press).

- *Character diffusion*: By how many different characters is an item used? I have coined this term to refer to the way in which items may be assigned to particular characters. For example, is it only one character who uses a particular expression, or is it only characters from a particular region who employ a specific linguistic feature? Character diffusion can be important for stylistic and sociolinguistic analysis.

I use range as a threshold for examining keyness in SydTV-Std in Chapter 7, focussing on key items that occur across at least 20 per cent of the corpus. In that chapter I will also consider raw frequency and effect size, while Chapter 8 will pay special attention to key items below the range threshold as well as low-dispersion items. Chapter 8 will also examine the character diffusion of the stigmatised non-standard word form *ain't*.

4.4 Collocation and Concordancing

Another important corpus linguistic concept is that of collocation, which refers to the non-random association of words, i.e. the tendency of words to co-occur (e.g. Hunston 2002: 68). Collocation analysis usually proceeds by taking a word (the *node*) and identifying which other words typically co-occur in a given co-textual span. These co-occurring words are called *collocates*. For example, *oh*, *sake*, *knows*, *thank*, *my*, and *bless* are all collocates of *god* in British English. Typically, researchers examine a span of four or five words to the left and to the right of the node (Baker 2006; McEnery & Hardie 2012). These spans are referred to using the notation 4L:4R or 5L:5R.

Collocates are automatically identified using an in-built collocation measure, with different measures producing different results. Most association measures identify collocates by comparing how often they are expected to co-occur with the node with how often they actually occur (Brezina et al. 2015: 144). In my analysis of the collocates of *ain't* in Chapter 8, I use the MI3 measure (Daille 1995). MI3 is the cubed variant of the mutual information statistic, which reduces its low frequency bias – it gives more weight to observed frequencies and ranks frequently occurring (typical) collocations much higher than those that are uncommon (Brezina et al. 2015: 159–60). The top collocates produced with the MI3 score provide a mixture of high-frequency function and lower-frequency content words (Baker 2006: 102). To visualise the collocates of *ain't* I use GraphColl (Baker & McEnery 2015; Brezina et al. 2015), as seen in Figure 5.13. Each circle represents a word and the length of lines between words represents collocational strength (the shorter the stronger). Thus, Figure 5.13 shows that *ain't* collocates strongly with *nobody*, *nothin'*, *no*, and *nowhere* in SydTV, a finding that is explored in Chapter 8.

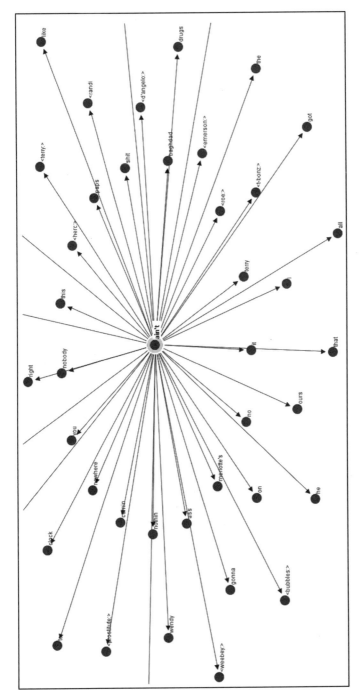

Figure 5.13 Extract from GraphColl visualisation for ain't

101

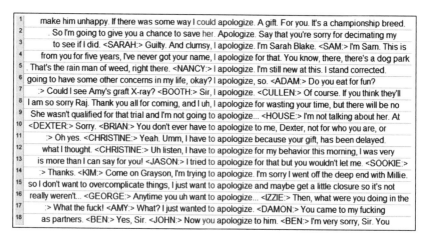

1	make him unhappy. If there was some way I could apologize. A gift. For you. It's a championship breed.
2	. So I'm going to give you a chance to save her. Apologize. Say that you're sorry for decimating my
3	to see if I did. <SARAH:> Guilty. And clumsy, I apologize. I'm Sarah Blake. <SAM:> I'm Sam. This is
4	from you for five years, I've never got your name, I apologize for that. You know, there's a dog park
5	. That's the rain man of weed, right there. <NANCY:> I apologize. I'm still new at this. I stand corrected.
6	going to have some other concerns in my life, okay? I apologize, so. <ADAM:> Do you eat for fun?
7	:> Could I see Amy's graft X-ray? <BOOTH:> Sir, I apologize. <CULLEN:> Of course. If you think they'll
8	I am so sorry Raj. Thank you all for coming, and I uh, I apologize for wasting your time, but there will be no
9	She wasn't qualified for that trial and I'm not going to apologize... <HOUSE:> I'm not talking about her. At
10	<DEXTER:> Sorry. You don't ever have to apologize to me, Dexter, not for who you are, or
11	:> Oh yes. <CHRISTINE:> Yeah. Umm, I have to apologize because your gift, has been delayed.
12	what I thought. <CHRISTINE:> Uh listen, I have to apologize for my behavior this morning, I was very
13	is more than I can say for you! <JASON:> I tried to apologize for that but you wouldn't let me. <SOOKIE:>
14	:> Thanks. <KIM:> Come on Grayson, I'm trying to apologize. I'm sorry I went off the deep end with Millie.
15	so I don't want to overcomplicate things, I just want to apologize and maybe get a little closure so it's not
16	really weren't... <GEORGE:> Anytime you uh want to apologize... <IZZIE:> Then, what were you doing in the
17	:> What the fuck! <AMY:> What? I just wanted to apologize. <DAMON:> You came to my fucking
18	as partners. <BEN:> Yes, Sir. <JOHN:> Now you apologize to him. <BEN:> I'm very sorry, Sir. You

Figure 5.14 Sorted concordance lines for apologize *in SydTV-Std (including speaker names)*

One of the most important corpus techniques that I make use of in this book is concordancing – producing all occurrences for a particular search term (the node), together with its surrounding text (co-text). Concordancing is particularly useful for qualitative analysis, as the co-text can be expanded, and because concordances can automatically be sorted in different ways. For instance, Figure 5.14 shows all instances of the word form *apologize* in SydTV-Std sorted alphabetically according to the left, with WordSmith's main (advanced) settings changed to show the speaker names (in angle brackets).

Concordances can be produced for single word forms (e.g. *hi*) or combinations of word forms (e.g. *a minute*) and the asterisk can be used as a wild card to stand for one or more characters (e.g. a search for *apolog** in SydTV retrieves instances for *apology, apologies, apologize, apologizing*). WordSmith also provides advanced search options such as the introduction of 'context words'. Using this function the user can produce a concordance for *no* occurring in the co-text of **n't* within five words to the right, aiding in the identification of negative concord (e.g. *this ain't no police station; I can't take no chances*). Another useful inbuilt function is the 'reduce to n' option, which provides the user with a random selection of *n* concordance lines for analysis (e.g. fifty lines). This enables random downsampling in cases where this is necessary.

I use concordancing for various purposes in this book, but most importantly, to investigate the meanings and uses of key items. In the displayed concordance lines the speaker names are always included in order to make it easier for the reader to understand the dialogue.

However, unless otherwise noted, in the corpus linguistic analyses the software was instructed to ignore speaker names. To be totally clear, even when concordance lines for particular key items include speaker names, this does *not* mean that the keyness analysis likewise included them. It is simply much more difficult to read a dialogue exchange between two speakers when the speaker names are elided.

Finally, the concordance plot shows the position of a word in the text: the left-hand side stands for the beginning and the right-hand side for the end of a text file, with black vertical lines showing occurrences of the search term and grey vertical lines showing the partition of the text into eight parts. In Figure 5.15, the word *mistake* seems to cluster in a particular scene of the relevant SydTV episode (as discussed in Chapter 8). This function permits the integration of intratextual analysis in corpus linguistic research (cf. Section 2.4).

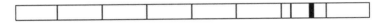

Figure 5.15 Concordance plot for the word mistake *in the* Gilmore Girls *episode*

5 Concluding Remarks

The corpus techniques introduced in this chapter will be drawn upon in the analyses of SydTV in Chapters 7 and 8. This corpus linguistic research permits examination of TV dialogue as a 'product' and can offer new insights into its salient features, functions, and uses. This can be usefully complemented by ethnographic research that connects such analysis to aspects of production and consumption. As mentioned, this book therefore reports on findings from a survey of pedagogic material, interviews with Hollywood scriptwriters, and a questionnaire with German university students. This triangulation of approaches allows the exploration of TV dialogue from different perspectives, which may support or contradict each other. It expands the scope of the research project beyond corpus linguistic analysis and provides added benefits, as we will see in Chapters 10 and 11. These ethnographic approaches are introduced in the next chapter, which also describes how SydTV was used as a repository to identify instances of non-codified language (see Section 2.4).

6 *Other Approaches*

1 Introduction

Before I present the findings from this comprehensive research project on TV series in Parts IV and V, it is necessary to explain further approaches employed in this book. In addition to corpus linguistic methods (outlined in the previous chapter), other approaches are also relevant to this book. These are introduced in this chapter.

As noted, SydTV is not only used as input for corpus linguistic processing and analysis, it is also used as a repository to identify instances of non-codified language. In this chapter I explain this approach (Section 2). In addition, this chapter presents information on the analyses that go beyond considering dialogue as a 'product': Section 3 describes the analysis of pedagogic material and interviews, while Section 4 discusses the investigation of aspects of consumption. The relevant project findings will be presented later in the book (Chapters 9–11).

2 Analysing Non-Codified Language in SydTV

2.1 An Introduction to Non-Codified Language

Before discussing how non-codified language was identified in SydTV, it is necessary to briefly introduce some relevant theoretical background. According to Trudgill (1999: 117) codification is a process in which a language variety gains a fixed, publicly recognised form, with the results of codification preserved in grammar books and dictionaries. I thus operationalise *non-codified language* as language use that has not (yet) been codified in dictionaries or other reference works such as grammar books. However, my main focus in this book is on non-codified word forms, rather than grammar rules, and my particular interest is in those non-codified word forms that may be considered as (1) linguistic innovation or (2) non-standard language.

Put simply, linguistic innovation refers to linguistic phenomena that can be identified as novel, recent, and innovative, for example new word formations and linguistic play as well as semantic or syntactic change. However, what is 'new' is not always easy to say:

> [T]he boundaries between already existent and new, between special vocabulary and so-called 'normal' words are not simple and clear-cut and may vary between different contexts and speaker constellations. [...] It is, however, particularly these 'grey' areas between normal and special, between existent and new that bear testimony to the vibrant nature of language in use and the ongoing linguistic change.   (Pitzl et al. 2008: 39)

I use *linguistic innovation* in a broad sense to refer to both recent and novel forms, as well as to creative uses of language. The label hence covers linguistic features that are already in circulation (albeit for a relatively short time, and perhaps only in specific communities of speakers, i.e. more likely to be infrequent) and those linguistic features that have been newly created (i.e. unattested). Linguistic innovations have the potential to spread more widely through a language community but can also remain ephemeral, one-off creations.

Non-standard language is arguably an even more problematic concept than linguistic innovation. It contrasts with standard language, which is usually defined as a social dialect that is codified, associated with educated speakers, and used predominantly in writing and education (e.g. Trudgill 1999: 120–4; Gramley 2012: 445; Hickey 2012: 2). Standard language is often conceptualised as supraregional, non-vernacular, and non-stigmatised. By implication, regional, vernacular, and stigmatised varieties are non-standard.[1] Further, (non-) standardness is associated in complex ways with power, ideology, social evaluation, and discrimination (Trudgill 1999: 127; Hickey 2012: 23–4; Lippi-Green 2012; Mair 2013: 258; Squires & Iorio 2014: 356).

Although standard language might have perceptual reality for language users, it has no ontological stability, i.e. is neither an unchanging nor objective quality and has a gradient nature (e.g. Mair 2013: 258; Coupland et al. 2016: 12). The analysis of telecinematic discourse over time can in fact provide insights into changes in the perceived standard, for example shifts from a non-rhotic to a rhotic prestige (Elliott 2000).

There are considerable debates around which language features are to be considered as non-standard, for example in relation to swear/taboo words, colloquial/vernacular features, and slang (for contrasting views, see e.g. Trudgill 1999: 120–1; Murray & Simon 2008; Gramley 2012: 446). In this book I use *non-standard* as cover term for dialectal, colloquial, slang, and swear/taboo words but not for technical/specialised vocabulary or non-English words.[2] In other words, the term is used in a broad sense, covering aspects of language that are marked for divergence from (written) standards that have influenced traditional broadcast speech. I acknowledge that a simple distinction between standard and non-standard hides the complex nature of linguistic variation, and underline that I do not consider non-standard varieties as deficient or inferior. Because there are clear differences between the various features labelled as non-standard here, I will also refer to them more specifically – for example as *colloquial language* or as *swear/taboo words*.

In sum, non-codified language is operationalised in this book as language use that is not (yet) featured in a given dictionary. This concept of non-codified language is a *relational* one: what is identified as non-codified will at least partially depend on the dictionary or reference work that is consulted (Osimk-Teasdale 2013: 4). Specialised dictionaries exist that list technical vocabulary or non-standard words, while such words may be absent from *general* dictionaries (i.e. they are non-codified only in relation to the latter). My use of different dictionaries is explained below.

2.2 Identifying Non-Codified Language in a Corpus

Different approaches have been applied to identifying non-codified language in a corpus, both top-down and bottom-up. For instance, researchers have annotated relevant language features at the stage of corpus building (e.g. Pitzl et al. 2008; Osimk-Teasdale 2013). To explore innovation and change, researchers have more often compared different corpora with respect to the frequency and use of particular lexical items or linguistic categories (e.g. Hundt & Mair 1999; Davies 2010). Or they have compared corpora from different time spans to identify newly emerging linguistic phenomena, without pre-selecting these features (e.g. Renouf 2007; Davies 2010). Further examples can be found in Grieve et al.'s (2017) useful overview and in the contributions to Deshors et al. (2016a). In addition to linguistic innovation, non-standard and specialised/technical words have also been identified by comparing words from a corpus with words in word lists, which are in turn derived from corpora or dictionaries (e.g. Csomay & Petrović 2012; Squires & Iorio 2014).

My own approach borrows some aspects of these, while exploiting the affordances of a small, specialised corpus like SydTV. First, I allow non-codified language features to emerge from the data, rather than deciding a priori which features to investigate. Second, I make use of a range of corpora and dictionaries. More specifically, my own approach trials the use of a spell-checker to provide insights into non-codified language in SydTV. It is precisely one of the advantages of a small corpus that it allows the kind of experimentation that necessitates a considerable amount of manual analysis, as is the case with this method. This approach can be called corpus-assisted since it starts with a computer-assisted manual analysis of the corpus, rather than employing more automatic, quantitative measures for identifying non-codified language. This initial stage is then complemented by follow-up analyses of the corpus, both quantitative and qualitative in nature.

First, each of the sixty-six text files that make up SydTV was opened separately in Microsoft Word 2007 and manually reviewed using the in-built spell-checker, which employs a red squiggly line to flag misspelled words or words that are not in the tool's dictionary (Curzan 2014: 67). I chose the 2007 version, since series in SydTV were broadcast between 2000 and 2012 and this represents an adequate midpoint. Words that were identified with a red squiggly line were categorised and submitted to further investigation as described below.[3]

In addition, I consulted two other dictionaries: the *Merriam-Webster Unabridged* online dictionary (http://unabridged.merriam-webster.com, henceforth MW) and the Urban Dictionary (www.urban dictionary.com/, henceforth UD). According to its website, the MW is based on *Webster's Third New International Dictionary, Unabridged* and represents the 'the largest, most comprehensive American dictionary currently available in print or online' (http://unabridged.merriam-webster.com/info/about-the-unabridged.html, accessed 23 March 2016). New content is continuously added to the site, with about 1,700 new words and 700 new word senses released in May 2015. Such a general dictionary will not include linguistic innovations that have not yet been established, neither will it list all non-standard words or highly technical words.[4] Dictionaries also select words according to particular criteria and editorial decisions.[5]

In contrast to the MW, the UD is not an official/prestigious dictionary created by professional editors, but rather an online slang dictionary, which allows users to submit and vote for entries and definitions. Cotter and Damaso (2007: 1) explain the UD as 'a collaborative project of over 1 million definitions for over 400,000 unique headwords', adding that it 'captures what most traditional dictionaries fall short of: recording ephemeral quotidian spoken language'. Grieve et al. (2017) use the UD to test the recency of emerging words on Twitter. The UD both stores and codifies meaning

(Cotter & Damaso 2007: 2, 8), with users of the UD regarding it as 'credible and even authoritative' (Cotter & Damaso 2007: 2). I thus consider word forms in the UD to be known to subsets of the general populace and 'codified' in a collaborative, 'citizen' dictionary. While the MW provides information on codified language from an 'official' perspective (as does Word's spell-checker dictionary), the UD is useful for offering a 'community-based' reference point, provided by ordinary users of the site rather than lexicographers. Both the MW and the UD were mostly consulted between September 2015 and June 2016.

In addition, certain word forms from SydTV were looked up in three corpora of American English – COCA/S (Davies 2008), GloWbE/US (Davies 2013), and SOAP (Davies 2012) – introduced in the previous chapter. Like dictionaries, corpora can be used as stable reference points for typical and established usage to allow identification of what is different and new (Pitzl et al. 2008: 25). Davies argues that COCA works well for capturing 'new forms that are just barely entering into the language' (Davies 2009: 182) and allows researchers to study 'linguistic change right up to the present time' (Davies 2010: 463).

The highly vernacular GloWbE/US (blogs) is also useful as a reference point, since new media language 'is constantly in flux [and] changes by the second' (Pitzl et al. 2008: 39). This makes it likely that new words are present in GloWbE/US. Davies (2015) and Davies and Fuchs (2015) emphasise the usefulness of GloWbE for low-frequency linguistic phenomena, noting that it will yield many more tokens for the same phenomenon than smaller corpora. Deshors et al. (2016b: 136) call GloWbE 'a goldmine for research into innovations'. My assumption is that if a word form occurs in SydTV (a small corpus of about 275,000 words) but is absent or rare in these large corpora (ranging from about 101 million words to about 387 million words; see Chapter 5), this is likely indicative of linguistic innovation unless other factors play a role (such as censorship in relation to swear/taboo words). To properly study linguistic innovation even larger corpora are required, but suitable data only exist for internet or social media varieties (e.g. Twitter), which are not representative of other registers (Grieve et al. 2017: 103). It must also be kept in mind that the comparative corpora (COCA/S, SOAP, GloWbE/US) do not represent unscripted, spontaneous spoken language in *non-media* contexts.

In sum, three steps were followed in the analysis of non-codified language in SydTV:

1. Use of a spell-checker to identify non-codified language in each text
2. Examination and categorisation of the word forms detected by the spell-checker

3. Follow-up investigations of particular categories/word forms, including comparison with other dictionaries (MW, UD) and corpora (COCA/S, GloWbE/US, SOAP).

This approach clearly has its limitations. First, the relational nature of codified language means that its identification is dependent on the codifying standard that is used. Thus, some of the word forms identified by the Microsoft Word 2007 spell-checker are *not* identified by the Microsoft Word 2010 spell-checker, because its inbuilt dictionary has been updated. It is partially for this reason that I also use the MW. In general, dictionaries such as the MW and the dictionaries used by the spell-checker lag behind actual linguistic usage. I have attempted to minimise this limitation by also consulting a community-based online dictionary (the UD).

Second, this approach will not detect non-codified grammatical usage, nor will it identify novel uses or meanings of existing words, i.e. semantic change. Third, the spell-checker will not identify *all* instances of linguistic innovation (in the broad sense in which I use the term). For example, creative nicknames and linguistic play are not detected when codified words are used (e.g. *Tiger Boobs, Harness Bitch, the Rain Man of weed; with them it is an every-day stand and I still know their names in the morning*). Innovative word formations are not identified when codified words are combined and spelled with a hyphen or as two separate word forms (for example, the nouns *jerk-off*, *meth heads*). An expression like *dollars to donuts* is therefore also not discovered. This is a seemingly innovative phrase that occurs in a SydTV episode from 2008 but that was not listed in the MW and was added to Macmillan's crowdsourced Open Dictionary only on 4 July 2017. Using a spell-checker is also time-consuming, which makes this approach suitable only for small corpora. Despite these caveats, Chapter 9 will show that this approach permits the identification of many interesting linguistic phenomena in SydTV and that it can provide useful insights into non-codified language use.

Together with Chapters 7 and 8, Chapter 9 forms a triplet of empirical studies that centre on the linguistic analysis of TV dialogue and provide new insights into language use in contemporary US TV series (Part IV). However, I also want to move 'beyond the product' and make connections between product, production, and consumption. To do so, I take the results from the analysis of TV dialogue – as presented in Part IV of this book – as a starting point. I then examine what scriptwriting manuals and scriptwriters have to say about TV dialogue (a 'production' perspective), and I explore the consumption practices, linguistic awareness, and attitudes of advanced learners of English (a 'consumption' perspective). It is important to note here that these studies in Part V are complementary to Part IV *as a whole* and do not focus on non-codified language per se. The following two sections explain the collection and analysis of pedagogic material and interviews, and of questionnaires with learners of English. The relevant project findings will be presented in Chapters 10 and 11.

3 Analysis of Scriptwriting Manuals and Interviews with Scriptwriters

To discover what pedagogic material might say about using non-codified language and about other areas of language use, it is necessary to analyse such material systematically. Handbooks or manuals on how to write for television have existed for a while, and new books are also being published. The genre is described by Batty (2016), who also argues that 'this type of discourse can and should be valued as an important type of research that benefits communities of practice outside of the academy as well as those within it' (Batty 2016: 63). Such manuals could be considered as 'regulatory texts' (van Leeuwen 2005: 83) that inform us about the 'semiotic rules' (van Leeuwen 2005: 47) that can help us understand how language is used in TV series. Following a search on the commercial platform amazon.com, I selected fourteen post-2000 publications (Table 6.1). This list consists of a variety of different titles, including manuals written by scriptwriters, books featuring interviews with scriptwriters (including showrunners), or a mix of the two. Venis (2013) brings together chapters written by ten working scriptwriters. I also examined an electronic booklet on writing for episodic television published online by the Writers Guild of America, West. For the sake of simplicity, I will refer to all of these as *scriptwriting manuals* or instances of *scriptwriting pedagogy*. Such manuals are read by industry professionals, students, emerging writers, and academics (Batty 2016: 64).

I did not include any manuals that focus on writing a pilot or those that concern products other than TV series, and included only manuals that focus on the American market. Notably, in the books with interviews, interviewees include industry professionals who have worked on some of the series contained in SydTV, for instance *According to Jim* (Tracy Newman and Jonathan Stark; John Beck and Ron Hart), *The Big Bang Theory* (David Goetsch, Bill Prady), *Bones* (Hart Hanson), *Castle* (Andrew Marlowe), *Dollhouse* (Joss Whedon, Steven S. DeKnight), *Fringe* (J. J. Abrams, J. H. Wyman, Jeff Pinkner), *Gilmore Girls* (Amy Sherman-Palladino), *The Good*

Table 6.1 List of the scriptwriting manuals surveyed in this book

Goldberg, L. & Rabkin, W. (2003). *Successful Television Writing*, Kindle edn. Hoboken, NJ: John Wiley.

Finer, A. & Pearlman, D. (2004). *Starting Your Television Writing Career: The Warner Bros Television Writers Workshop Guide*. Syracuse, NY: Syracuse University Press.

Wirth, J. & Melvoin, J. (eds.). (2004). *Writing for Episodic TV: From Freelance to Showrunner*. Los Angeles, CA: Writers Guild of America, West. Retrieved from www.writersguildtheater.org/content/default.aspx?id=156, 24 April 2017.

Priggé, S. (2005). *Created by . . . Inside the Minds of TV's Top Show Creators*. Los Angeles, CA: Silman-James Press.

Epstein, A. (2006). *Crafty TV Writing: Thinking Inside the Box*, Kindle edn. New York: Henry Holt.

Bull, S. (2007). *Elephant Bucks: An Inside Guide to Writing for TV Sitcoms*, Kindle edn. Studio City, CA: Michael Wiese Productions.

Sandler, E. (2007). *The TV Writer's Workbook: A Creative Approach to Television Scripts*, Kindle edn. New York: Bantam Dell.

Smith, E. S. (2009). *Writing Television Sitcoms*, 2nd edn. Kindle edn. New York: Perigee.

Douglas, P. (2011). *Writing the TV Drama Series: How to Succeed as a Professional Writer in TV*, 3rd edn. Studio City, CA: Michael Wiese Productions.

Vorhaus, J. (2012). *The Little Book of Sitcom*, Kindle edn. CreateSpace Independent Publishing Platform.

Venis, L. (ed.). (2013). *Inside the Room: Writing TV with the PROS at UCLA Extension Writers' Program*, Kindle edn. New York: Gotham.

Bennett, T. (2014). *The Official Companion to the Documentary* Showrunners: The Art of Running a TV Show, Kindle edn. London: Titan.

Landau, N. (2014). *The TV Showrunner's Roadmap: 21 Navigational Tips for Screenwriters to Create and Sustain a Hit TV Series*, Kindle edn. New York: Focal Press.

Cook, M. (2014). *Write to TV: Out of Your Head and onto the Screen*, 2nd edn. Kindle edn. New York: Focal Press.

Wife (Michelle King and Robert King), *Gossip Girl* (Josh Schwartz), *House* (David Shore), *Lost* (J. J. Abrams, Damon Lindelof), *Smallville* (Steven S. DeKnight), *The Shield* (Shawn Ryan, Kurt Sutter), *Southland* (John Wells), *True Blood* (Alan Ball), and *The Wire* (David Simon).

By systematically surveying each manual in turn, I was able to identify any extended discussion of aspects related to language. I omitted only chapters that were not about the writing process (e.g. 'A Battle Plan for Launching Your Career', 'What Makes a Good

Figure 6.1 Jane Espenson (left) and the author (right) after the interview (author's own photo)

Showrunner', 'The Pitch') or that were about writing other aspects such as outlines or scene descriptions rather than dialogue. I also examined tables of content and indexes where available.

In addition, I conducted semi-structured interviews with five Holly-wood television scriptwriters/showrunners: Jane Espenson, David Mandel, Doris Egan, Bob Berens, and one (female, European American) writer who preferred to remain unidentified. All of the interviewees have been involved in one or more of the series included in SydTV, and Jane Espenson has a background in linguistics (www .janeespenson.com/biography.php, accessed 1 May 2017). The inter-viewees were chosen opportunistically – the linguistic connection enabled initial contact with Jane Espenson (Figure 6.1), who then connected me with other writers, only some of whom consented to be interviewed. David Mandel (then showrunner of *Veep*) was involved in an event at the University of California, Santa Barbara, while I was a visiting scholar there, which prompted me to contact him.

The interviews lasted between thirty minutes and two hours depending on availability and were undertaken face-to-face in Los Angeles (at a hotel, in the writers' offices or homes) and via Skype (see Table 6.2). The difference in the length of interviews meant that not all scriptwriters answered all questions, but there was a core set of questions on the interview schedule that were answered by all inter-viewees. Leading questions with *yes/no* or *why* were avoided. A semi-structured interview was chosen in order to make the interview less artificial and more flexible, allowing the discussion of evolving topics and the posing of follow-up questions, as well as a more 'conversation-like' interaction. I recorded all interviews, and they were transcribed orthographically by a research assistant.

Table 6.2 Interviews with Hollywood scriptwriters

Interviewee	Location and mode	Date	Length
Jane Espenson	Circa 55 (restaurant), The Beverly Hilton, Los Angeles; face-to-face	12 March 2017	132 minutes
David Mandel	Goleta – Los Angeles; Skype	11 May 2017	35 minutes
Doris Egan	Writer's home, Los Angeles; face-to-face	1 April 2017	81 minutes
Bob Berens	Writer's office, Warner Brothers, Burbank, Los Angeles; face-to-face	31 March 2017	66 minutes
Unidentified female European American writer	Goleta – Los Angeles; Skype	10 May 2017	33 minutes

Interviews are a valuable research method in applied linguistics, as they are interactive and allow for in-depth discussion, flexibility, and responsiveness (Hyland 2010: 196). They can integrate an *emic* approach by focussing on participants' own experiences (Edley & Litosseliti 2010: 169). Interviewing has therefore been proposed as 'the most effective way of bringing the insider's perspective to the analysis, taking us nearer to a description of cultural practices in terms of its members' understandings' (Hyland 2000: 144). On the other hand, interviews have been criticised for various aspects, such as their artificiality and constraints, and cannot be regarded as neutral (Edley & Litosseliti 2010: 161). It is important to remain aware that relations between interviewer and interviewee may have an impact, that interviews can be used to negotiate identities, and that the interviewer plays a role in the construction of meaning (Starfield 2010: 58; Sunderland 2010: 24). To give a concrete example, the scriptwriters' answers are probably influenced by awareness of issues regarding race and racism in the United States, especially in relation to questions about the representation of dialectal features. They are likely to construct particular, non-racist identities for themselves in the interviews. In general, there is considerable debate about interviews as a research method in linguistics (see Edley & Litosseliti 2010). I acknowledge that interviews are interactional events, but nevertheless focus on interviewees' responses in this book, rather than analysing how their responses came about. The content from interviews therefore comes with the label 'treat with care'.

My research questions for the analysis of scriptwriting pedagogy and interviews are the following: To what extent are (budding) scriptwriters explicitly taught about linguistic features? And to what extent do scriptwriters (in the manuals they write or in interviews) refer to such features? My analyses of both the manuals and the interviews were guided by the insights revealed in the linguistic analyses of SydTV, to enable better connections to be made. For instance, I was specifically interested in what was said about non-standard language, including the representation of dialects and the use of swear/taboo words.

Both the discourses in scriptwriting manuals and those of industry professionals can be seen as 'normative discourses' (van Leeuwen 2011: 87) that surround TV narratives, influence the creation of TV dialogue, and provide important insights into semiotic rules. There are many other aspects of the development or production of TV series that could be analysed in future research – for instance, discussions in writers' rooms, comparing different versions of scripts, or analysis of production texts such as treatments (see further Bednarek 2015d: 224–5). Very occasionally I draw in this book on my consultation of official final scripts for relevant SydTV episodes that are archived in the Shavelson-Webb library (Writers Guild foundation, Los Angeles). But this material deserves further, more comprehensive analysis than I have undertaken so far.

4 Analysis of Questionnaires

My analysis of consumption focuses on LX viewers, in particular advanced learners of English in Germany. Germany was chosen for practical reasons, since I speak German as L1 and since a fellowship allowed me to administer questionnaires at universities there. US TV series are popular among German high school students (Dose 2013), and therefore most likely are also watched by many university students. Almost 600 undergraduate university students, mainly from the south of Germany, participated in a short questionnaire with a range of closed and open-ended items.

A written questionnaire was chosen as an efficient data collection instrument and to obtain answers from a large number of participants (Wagner 2010: 26). The questionnaire contained a set of eleven questions that investigated the subjects' reported consumption practices, linguistic awareness, and attitudes. German was used as the questionnaire language, which has the advantage that the respondents are less likely to experience comprehensibility problems (Wagner 2010: 34). I present my own translations of the questions in this chapter (in the order in which they were presented to the subjects), while the original German-language items are listed in Figure A.1 in the Appendix.

The first two of the eleven items elicited information about the students' degree, while other personal information was deliberately not collected:

1. What is your degree (example: BA/Linguistics)?
2. Which semester are you in? (example: 1 = first semester, 2 = second semester)

One multiple-choice item focussed on language choices regarding students' reported consumption of TV series:

3. When I watch fictional English-language TV series (for example, *Big Bang Theory*, *NCIS*, *The Mentalist*, *The Blacklist*, *CSI*, *Bones*, *Girls*, *Brooklyn 99*, *Game of Thrones*, *House of Cards* ...), I typically do so in the following way: [students select one of 6 options such as 'in English with German subtitles', including 'I don't tend to watch such series']

Six closed items provided students with options on a scale, from which they were to choose one:

4. I find such TV series useful for learning (better) English [5-point Likert scale[6]]
5. I would show examples from English-language TV series (for example *Big Bang Theory*, *NCIS*) when I teach English to others (in the future) or I have already done so (e.g. work experience in a school, tutoring ...) [5-point scale or the option to choose 'I don't intend to teach English and have never taught English']
6. English-language TV series are useful for showing pupils/students examples of spoken English. [5-point Likert scale]
7. When I watch English-language TV series I am aware that the language is scripted/artificial. [5-point scale]
8. My English teacher has used/shown examples from English-language TV series in the class-room. [5-point scale]
9. The language spoken by TV characters in English-language series is similar to the language spoken by 'real' speakers: [5-point Likert scale]

Two types of scale were used in these items, with the answers on the end points translatable as 'disagree'/'does not apply' (*trifft nicht zu*) and 'fully agree'/'fully applies' (*trifft voll zu*) as in Figure 6.2 or as 'not at all' (*gar nicht*) and 'very often' (*sehr oft*) as in Figure 6.3.

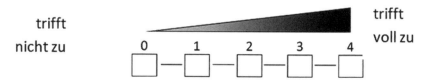

Figure 6.2 Five-point Likert scale

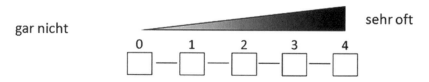

Figure 6.3 Five-point scale

The final two questions offered the students space for elaboration, with both items including a comment function. Item ten involved a multiple-choice task, while item eleven elicited purely qualitative information:

10. In my view there are linguistic differences between the language spoken by TV characters in such series and the language spoken by 'real' speakers
    ☐ No, there are no differences
    ☐ I don't know/am unsure
    ☐ Yes, the following differences exist: [space for comment]
11. I think that the following linguistic practices/phenomena are the most common in the language spoken by characters in English-language TV series (for example, particular words, expressions, ways of using language, speech acts …): [space for comment]

Respondents read each question or statement and either selected a choice among different options (closed items) or wrote their own response (open-ended items). Completion of all items was presented as optional. A total of 582 students from Mannheim (Universität Mannheim), Munich (Ludwig-Maximilians-Universität/LMU), Augsburg (Universität Augsburg), Freiburg (Albert-Ludwigs-Universität), Heidelberg (Universität Heidelberg), Aachen (Rheinisch-Westfälische Technische Universität/RWTH), and Erlangen/Nürnberg (Friedrich-Alexander-Universität Erlangen-Nürnberg) completed at least part of the questionnaire. These universities were chosen because of existing contacts to lecturers or closeness to my fellowship location (i.e. convenience sampling was used). Of the 582 participants, 231

(39.7 per cent) chose to provide a comment for question ten, while 315 participants responded to the qualitative question eleven (54.1 per cent). The textual data for items ten and eleven amounted to sixteen pages of single-spaced text. Thus, a sizable percentage of the survey population took the time to provide textual responses.

Questionnaires were distributed by the lecturer/tutor or by myself; participation was voluntary and anonymous. Most of the classes in which questionnaires were undertaken were undergraduate introductions to English linguistics, which students tend to take in their first or second semester. The exception was a class in Mannheim ('Introduction to English Linguistics'), which is typically taken by BA/teacher degree students in their second semester as well as students of business education(*Wirtschaftspädagogik*) in their sixth semester. The latter have chosen English as the second subject they would teach (in addition to business studies), an option available to them from the fifth semester. They would therefore not have had any linguistic training in previous semesters.

All completed questionnaires were processed by a research assistant who was instructed to put aside any forms where participants had indicated that they were not native speakers of German or that they were native speakers of English. As my interest is in German advanced learners of English, these responses were not considered. The research assistant provided the quantitative results and typed up a list of all comments provided in response to questions ten and eleven, separating them per student. These textual responses were then subjected to qualitative content analysis to extract meaningful categories – i.e., I classified answers into a limited number of broad categories. While no pre-defined categories were used and the categories arose from the data themselves, the categorisation was guided by the insights revealed in the linguistic analyses of SydTV, to enable better connections to be made between 'product' and 'consumption' (similar to the analysis of manuals/interviews). In this sense, the classification of responses could be said to be based on a mix of deductive and inductive analysis. Because of funding constraints, no other analyst/coder examined the qualitative data. Table 6.3 shows an example of the classification scheme, where colloquial/informal language and dialects/accents are used as broad subcategories, both falling under the more general category of non-standardness.

While some of the questionnaire results were tabulated and quantified in terms of frequency/percentages, I did not use any statistics to examine correlations between variables. Needless to say, findings are valid only for the surveyed cohort of students rather than all advanced learners of English in Germany, because non-probability convenience sampling was used (Wagner 2010: 25). The usual caveats concerning

Table 6.3 Example of the classification scheme used to analyse questionnaire responses

General category	Broad subcategory	Example response (German)	Example response (translation)
Standard and non-standard language	Colloquial/ informal language	*Weniger Umgangssprache*	Less 'everyday language'
	Dialects/ accents	*Meist weniger Akzente im Fernsehn*	Mostly fewer accents in television

the use of questionnaires in applied linguistics also apply, and it is important to acknowledge the limitations of such research. For example, the student respondents might have been unmotivated, impacting on the validity of the results, while some of their answers might have been prone to different forms of bias (Rasinger 2010: 63; Wagner 2010: 35). Most importantly, perhaps, asking students to reflect upon the linguistic characteristics of TV dialogue may actually raise their awareness. The fact that question 7 mentions the scripted (artificial, planned) nature of the language used in TV series might possibly have impacted on responses to questions 9 and 10.

5 Concluding Remarks

In this chapter and the previous I have described the various approaches used in this book. As mentioned in Chapter 2, the vast majority of linguistic research focuses only on TV dialogue, rather than analysing scriptwriting processes/pedagogy or aspects of consumption. In contrast, this book aims to move linguistic research beyond the product and to make connections between product, production, and consumption. As has become clear, this is a highly complex and time-consuming endeavour, requiring the collection and analysis of many different types of data. The next parts present the results of these analyses, first with a focus on TV dialogue (Part IV), then with a focus on pedagogic material and consumption (Part V). They show the rich insights that can be gained from a combination of different data and analyses, arguably making such a complex endeavour worthwhile.

Part IV
Analyses of SydTV

7 Salient Features of TV Dialogue

A Corpus Linguistic Approach

1 Introduction

This chapter is the first of three chapters dedicated to empirical analysis of SydTV. I adopt a corpus linguistic approach to explore some of the salient linguistic characteristics of US TV dialogue and investigate how it differs from unscripted language. This approach allows me to compare results with those by other researchers who similarly contrast corpora of TV dialogue with corpora of unscripted language (reviewed in Chapter 2). The corpus linguistic tools that assist me in this investigation are Sketch Engine (Kilgarriff et al. 2014) and Word-Smith (Scott 2017a), while the primary technique consists of keyness analysis (of word forms and n-grams, as explained in Chapter 5). All analyses make use of SydTV-Std. In Section 2, I briefly look at similarity between SydTV-Std and other corpora, while the bulk of this chapter (Section 3) deals with differences between SydTV-Std and a corpus of unscripted conversation, with a focus on over-represented words and n-grams.

2 TV Dialogue and Spoken and Written Corpora

The analysis of over-represented words and n-grams in SydTV-Std will show some of the ways in which US TV dialogue differs from unscripted spoken American English. However, this focus on difference is not to deny that there are also similarities. As pointed out in Chapter 2, TV dialogue selectively imitates unscripted language and includes language features associated with spontaneous conversation. I will briefly illustrate this point in this section: first, by comparing SydTV-Std with different spoken and written corpora; second, by examining the key n-grams that are shared by SydTV-Std and a corpus of spoken American English when they are both compared with a corpus of *written* American English.

2.1 Corpus Similarity

As a first step, I draw on corpus similarity information provided by Sketch Engine's *Comparing Corpora* function to test the following hypothesis:

If TV dialogue is a partial or selective imitation of unscripted spoken interaction, SydTV-Std should be more similar to corpora that contain such interactions (i.e. non-specialised spoken corpora) than to corpora that contain written language.

To test this hypothesis, I compared six corpora (as described in Chapter 5): SydTV-Std, C_CH, LSAC, BNC, AmE06, and BE06.[1] The comparison is based on word forms, with no differences between lower- and uppercase words. The results are presented in Table 7.1; lower values indicate a higher similarity between corpora. The lowest values in each row have been **bolded** to show which corpora are the most similar to each other.

The values in Table 7.1 show that SydTV-Std is most similar to the LSAC (unscripted American English conversations), followed by C_CH (narratives, interviews, face-to-face/telephone conversations), the BNC (mixed spoken/written British English), the AmE06 (written American English), and the BE06 (written American English). Thus, the hypothesis is supported by the results, since the TV dialogue corpus is more similar to the spoken corpora than any of the written or mixed corpora. It is nevertheless important to emphasise that there are vast differences between different types of spoken and written language. It is therefore plausible that SydTV-Std would be more similar to certain types of written corpora such as play texts or dialogue-heavy novels than to certain types of spoken corpora such as academic lectures.

Interestingly, SydTV-Std is marginally more similar to the BNC (British English) than to the AmE06 corpus (American English), although it is slightly more similar to the AmE06 than to the BE06. This is even more significant since the BNC was not standardised

Table 7.1 Results from corpus comparison (Sketch Engine)

	C_CH	LSAC	BNC	AmE06	BE06	SydTV-Std
SydTV-Std	2.13	**1.75**	2.77	2.79	2.81	(1.00)
BNC	2.94	2.74	(1.00)	1.55	**1.41**	2.77
BE06	2.95	2.92	**1.41**	1.51	(1.00)	2.81
AmE06	2.90	2.90	1.55	(1.00)	**1.51**	2.79
C_CH	(1.00)	**1.81**	2.94	2.90	2.95	2.13
LSAC	1.81	(1.00)	2.74	2.90	2.92	**1.75**

in the same way as the other corpora. It is likely a result of the BNC containing spoken as well as written English, in addition to including a significant amount of fictional texts that feature dialogue. This shows that the national variety of the comparison corpus is not as important as other variables such as mode (spoken, written, written as if spoken, etc.).

What is also noteworthy is that when the BNC (90 per cent written, 10 per cent spoken) and the written corpora (BE06, AmE06) are compared with the LSAC and SydTV-Std, both of the spoken corpora receive relatively similar scores (2.74/2.77; 2.92/2.81; 2.90/2.79). In all cases, SydTV-Std is slightly more similar to the three (primarily) written corpora than the LSAC is, reflecting TV dialogue's mode as written to be spoken. Interestingly, while C_CH is more similar to the LSAC (1.81) than to SydTV-Std (2.13), the LSAC is more similar to SydTV-Std (1.75) than to C_CH (1.81). This could be due to the fact that C_CH contains narratives and interviews as well as face-to-face/ telephone conversations.

This similarity between the LSAC and SydTV-Std is evidence of the fact that TV dialogue successfully imitates unscripted conversation. If we examine the word lists from the LSAC and SydTV-Std when they are both compared against the written American English corpus (AmE06) using Sketch Engine's Comparing Corpora function, 1,003 shared word forms are identified. It is not possible to examine and discuss all these here, but not surprisingly they include first- and second-person pronouns/determiners (e.g. *I, my, me, we, you*), contractions (e.g. *let's, ai [ain't], n't*), time/place references (*here, now*), discourse markers (e.g. *well*), politeness markers (e.g. *please, thanks*), response and dis/agreement markers (e.g. *mm-mmm, mm-hmmm, yeah, yep, yes*), interjections (e.g. *ah, gosh, oh, ugh, yay, yo*), hesitation markers (e.g. *uh*), informal lexis (e.g. *babe, fun, stuff, guys*), kinship and relationship terms (e.g. *mom, brother, dad, friend*), intensifiers (e.g. *really, totally, very*), emotion and cognition verbs (e.g. *love, likes, hated, believe, think, guess, want*), evaluative adjectives (e.g. *awesome, awful, funny, gorgeous, hilarious, horrible*), and swear/ taboo words (e.g. *ass, bitch, bullshit, damn, fucking*).

In the LSAC such items reflect the characteristics of spoken inter-actions (as non-monologic, spontaneous, on-line, expressive, informal, situation-bound talk), while in SydTV-Std they *construct* such charac-teristics for the audience. It is worth noting that hesitation markers and other dysfluency features may be introduced by actors in their delivery but are also partially scripted (Richardson 2010a: 65). The official final scripts for the SydTV episodes from *How I Met Your Mother, My Name Is Earl, Nurse Jackie, The Office, Royal Pains,* and

Supernatural – archived in the Shavelson-Webb library (Writers Guild foundation, Los Angeles) – contain at least one instance each of both *uh* and *um*, while the scripts for *30 Rock*, *Girls*, and *Vampire Diaries* contain at least one instance of *um*, and the scripts for *Breaking Bad*, *Dexter*, and *The Good Wife* contain at least one instance of *uh*. This differs from Richardson's (2010a: 65) findings for the script for a British TV series, but other scripts that I examined indeed include zero instances of either *uh* or *um*. Whether scriptwriters employ hesitation phenomena, discourse markers, and hedges depends on their relationship with actors, their attitude towards naturalism, and the particular stylistic functions at stake (Richardson 2010a: 83). Ultimately, the extent to which actors make changes to TV scripts in their performance varies and can be examined only by systematically comparing official final shooting scripts with on-screen dialogue. One should avoid drawing conclusions on the basis of analysing one TV series. In addition, elements introduced by actors in their performance can be deleted in the edit room.

This section has focused on shared word forms rather than longer syntagmatic structures. While it is not possible to use Sketch Engine's Comparing Corpora function to examine shared n-grams rather than word forms, a keyness analysis allows us to do this. For the purpose of triangulation, I will do so briefly in the next section, switching now to WordSmith.

2.2 Analysis of Shared Key n-Grams

As explained in Chapter 5, WordSmith can be used to produce key n-grams, i.e. n-grams that are statistically unusually frequent in the node corpus compared with the reference corpus. I am interested here in those positive key 2–5 grams that are shared between SydTV-Std and the LSAC when both are compared with the written American English corpus AmE06. In other words, I identify n-grams that are 'key' in SydTV-Std *as well as* the LSAC (i.e., shared key n-grams).

A quantitative summary of the results is presented in Table 7.2, while all key n-grams are available for download at www.syd-tv.com.[2] As predicted, there are many key n-grams in SydTV-Std that are also 'key' in the LSAC: in total, there are 1,024 shared bigrams, 379 shared trigrams, 75 shared tetragrams, and 7 shared 5-grams.[3] As Table 7.2 indicates, about 70 per cent of the n-grams that are key in SydTV-Std are also key in the LSAC. This is further evidence that TV dialogue is a partial imitation of unscripted spoken interaction and shares several characteristics with such language.

Table 7.2 Number of positive key n-grams in SydTV-Std and the LSAC (reference corpus: AmE06)

Key n-grams	No. of key n-grams in SydTV-Std	No. of shared key n-grams
Key 2-grams	1,367	1,024
Key 3-grams	576	379
Key 4-grams	136	75
Key 5-grams	26	7
Total	2,105	1,485 (70.5 per cent)

A comprehensive analysis of the shared n-grams (almost 1,500 in total) is beyond the scope of this section. However, the results appear to be in line with those presented in Section 2.1. Briefly, shared key n-grams include time/place references (e.g. *right now, in there, out here, out of here*), discourse markers (e.g. *I mean, well I/you, you know what I'm saying, you know what I mean*), routine formulae (e.g. *thanks for, see you later, thank you very much, nice to meet you, can I help you*), interjections (e.g. *oh god, oh man, oh my god*), informal language (e.g. *a ride, this guy, you guys, stuff like*), intensifiers/quantifiers (e.g. *a really, I'm very, a little bit, a lot of*), emotion and cognition verbs (e.g. *I like, I love, I guess, I think, I don't know*), and repeats (e.g. *I I, hey hey hey, no no no no, I know I know*). N-grams that incorporate first- and second-person pronouns (e.g. *you don't get, I don't even know, we're going to have to, let me tell you*), contractions (e.g. *that'd be, I've never, and I'll be, don't worry about, it's going to be a*), response and dis/agreement markers (e.g. *yeah and, no that's, yes sir, yeah I know, no this is*), hesitation markers (e.g. *and uh, and umm, uh I don't*), kinship and relationship terms (e.g. *my mom, my friend, your dad*), evaluative adjectives (e.g. *that's cool/funny/great, a really good*), and swear/taboo words (e.g. *the fucking, your ass, that shit, what the hell*) can also be found. In addition, there are n-grams that appear to point to the needs and desires of speaker or hearer (e.g. *I'd like to, you want to, I need, but I want to*), to the occurrence of questions (e.g. *can you, have you, what about, what do you, how did you, what are you going to*), and to the act of speaking itself (e.g. *to talk/tell, talk/ing about, talk to; are you talking about; tell her/him/me/them/you, told me/you, I told you; going to ask/call*). As mentioned above with respect to shared word forms, these n-grams help to construct TV dialogue as if it was unscripted talk. Heyd calls this 'staged orality' – 'the explicit staging of items that are perceived as typically oral, spontaneous, or intimate' (Heyd 2010: 34). This staging has multiple authors, as explained in Chapter 1.

It must be underlined that just because a particular word form or n-gram is 'key' in both SydTV-Std and the LSAC when compared with the AmE06 corpus, this does not mean that this item is used with the same frequency in the two corpora. Even if TV dialogue imitates unscripted conversation, there are also clear differences, as previous research has shown (see Chapter 2). The remainder of this chapter will tackle the question of difference rather than similarity through comparing the two corpora, using SydTV-Std as the node corpus and the LSAC as the reference corpus. The LSAC is chosen for two reasons: first, it is more similar to SydTV-Std than the other spoken corpus (C_CH), which is also smaller and less representative of spontaneous spoken language. Second, the LSAC or subsets thereof are also used by Mittmann (2006), Quaglio (2008, 2009) and Al-Surmi (2012), which makes my own analyses more comparable.

3 American English TV Dialogue and Unscripted Spoken Interaction

3.1 Categorising Key Items

A keyness analysis comparing SydTV-Std with the LSAC identifies items that are over-represented in TV dialogue with reference to this unscripted corpus of spoken American English. In total, 662 key word forms, 500 key bigrams, 188 key trigrams, 62 key tetragrams (4-grams), and 20 key pentagrams (5-grams) were identified by the software.[4] Thus, a very high number of key items are produced when no thresholds other than the p-value are applied. Not all of these items will occur across television episodes. To work with a manageable number of items and to exclude items that occur in only some of the episodes, I used Excel to set minimum *range* thresholds, focusing on key bigrams that occur across at least 33 texts (50 per cent of the corpus), key word forms and trigrams that occur across at least 20 texts (~30 per cent of the corpus), and key 4-grams and 5-grams that occur across at least 13 texts (~20 per cent of the corpus).[5] After testing various options, these specific range thresholds were chosen because they produce an adequate amount of items, and they ensure that all investigated items occur across at least 20 per cent of the corpus.

Once down-sampled in this way, the final list of key items includes 162 words, 74 bigrams, 28 trigrams, 15 tetragrams, and 4 penta-grams. The lowest-frequency key word in this list occurs with a raw frequency of 27, while the lowest-frequency bigram, trigram, 4-gram, and 5-gram occur 44 times, 23 times, 14 times, and 13 times, respectively. A raw frequency of 13 corresponds to a normalised frequency of about 4.7 per 100,000 words, or 47.3 per million words (token definition: hyphens do not separate words; ' not allowed within word; see Table A.2 in the Appendix). This is higher than the frequency thresholds used in other corpus studies of n-grams or lexical bundles, which typically range between 20 and 40 per million words (Chen & Baker 2010: 32). In the British National Corpus, the nouns *Christmas*, *forest*, and *journey* have comparable relative frequencies to the least frequent key item. Variation in frequency will be discussed below.

A large number of these key words and n-grams can be categorised into five broad pragmatic and stylistic categories:

1. *Routine formulae* (formulaic expressions that are routinely associated with particular speech acts): Greetings, introductions, and leave-takings; apologising; politeness; wishes; offers; suggestions; etc.[6]
2. *Interaction in the here-and-now* (features associated with interactivity and discourse immediacy): First- and second-person pronouns/determiners; terms of address; greetings, introductions, and leave-takings; spatial and temporal deixis; response, agreement, or discourse markers
3. *Formality*:
   a. *Colloquial/informal language*: Contractions; swear/taboo words; slang words, words referring to informal activities; informal terms of address, informal greetings, interjections, repeats
   b. *Formal language*: Titles
4. *Expressivity* (emotional, evaluative, emphatic language): Evaluative adjectives; emotion lexis; affective terms of address; interjections; swear/taboo words; verbs relating to speaker/hearer needs and desires, certain imperatives (alerts); other (e.g. words with negative connotations, intensifiers, repeats)
5. *Narrative concerns*: Lexical word forms or phrases associated with narrative content (used to refer to aspects of the plot, for example happenings, people/entities involved in the plot, or to provide backstory).

As we will see in the discussion of results in Section 3.2, many of the over-represented items in these five categories can be linked to the different functions of TV dialogue, as introduced in Chapters 3 and 4. The categories themselves arose from a combination of inductive and deductive research, i.e. examining the list of key items as well as looking at categories established by other relevant corpus linguistic studies (especially Quaglio's 2009 research on *Friends*). For example, studies by Mittmann (2006), Quaglio (2009), and Bednarek (2010a, 2012a) have all identified certain *routine formulae* as more frequent in US TV dialogue than in conversational corpora, and it is thus worth considering this as a distinct category.[7] The category labelled *interaction in the here-and-now* includes linguistic features that Quaglio (2009) associates with discourse immediacy: first- and second-person pronouns, terms of address, and greetings/leave-takings. These co-occur in context-dependent interactions where speakers focus on immediate concerns and happenings (Quaglio 2009: 132). In addition, I have classified temporal and spatial deixis (e.g. *here*, *tomorrow*) as well as response, agreement, or discourse markers (e.g. *alright, fine, of course*) as features associated with interactivity (turn-taking).[8]

The label *formality* is used as a cover term for both colloquial/informal language and formal language. Informal language is a category derived from Quaglio (2009), who mentions swear/taboo words, informal words (slang), informal greetings/leave-takings, terms of address, semi-modals, and repeats. In addition, I include contractions (e.g. *ain't, how'd*), words related to informal activities (e.g. *date, party*), and certain interjections (e.g. *whoa*). In contrast, titles are classified as formal language.

The category of *expressivity* refers to items that can be categorised as examples of emotional, evaluative, emphatic language. Quaglio's (2009) and Bednarek's (2012a) related category is called *emotional language*, although they include slightly different features. I classify the following as expressivity: evaluative adjectives, emotion lexis (denoting an emotional state/response), words with negative connotations, affective terms of address, interjections, swear/taboo words, intensification/emphasis, certain imperatives, repeats, and verbs relating to speaker/hearer needs and desires. On the other hand, I have *not* included words associated with danger and violence, such as *blood, dead, kill,* or the routine formulae *sorry, I'm sorry, thanks, thank you* or *please,* although these could be regarded as conventionalised expressions of emotion (Bednarek 2012a: 44). On some occasions, the use of such expressions will be infused with emotionality (*please,* for instance, may express intensity of desire or urgency), while on others they will be used purely as politeness formulae. Also not included are the copula verbs *look, feel, sound,* categorised by Quaglio (2009) as emotional language, since it is the co-text that (sometimes) carries expressivity (e.g. an evaluative adjective), rather than the verbs themselves.

Finally, the category of *narrative concerns* is a new category not to be confused with Quaglio's category of 'narrativeness' – associated with 'narrative discourse' (Quaglio 2009: 145), i.e. speakers telling stories about past happenings. Rather, this category relates to narrative content that characters talk about or reference in some way. That is, it covers references to (aspects) of the plot (e.g. happenings, people, or entities) or explanations of backstory.

Table 7.3 on pp 130–131 presents those key items that can be classified according to these five categories. For ease of reading, Table 7.3 includes only selected examples of key items with first- and second-person pronouns/determiners and contractions (because the table would be unwieldy if all instances were included). However, all original Excel lists are available at www.syd-tv.com.

The advantage of examining a range of different items, rather than say, just trigrams, is that different kinds of linguistic features can be identified – such as the term of address *honey* (key word form), the imperative *come on* (key bigram), the interjection *oh my god* (key trigram), the routine formula *nice to meet you* (key 4-gram), and the question *what are you doing here* (key 5-gram). The disadvantage is that it is beyond the scope of this chapter to analyse each of the almost 300 key items qualitatively. However, when we focus on formal properties and pragmatic and stylistic meaning potential, it is possible to classify, with a high degree of certainty, many items on the basis of such properties. For example, *ain't* and *isn't* can be classified as contractions, *crap* as a swear/taboo word, and *hi* and *hello* can be classified as greetings. It is also possible to draw on previous linguistic studies of the typical usage of particular items in TV dialogue – for example, the qualitative analysis of *out of here* in Bednarek (2012a) showed its association with expressivity.

Thus, some key items were categorised based on their properties or based on relevant prior research. But in the majority of cases, qualitative analysis was undertaken to check if a key item should be included in a particular category. WordSmith's 'reduce to n' function (Chapter 5) was used to examine fifty random instances for such items. If about half or more of these random occurrences (or of overall occurrences) could be placed in a particular category, the item was included; otherwise, it was not.[9] For example, of fifty randomly selected instances of the key word *baby*, only thirteen are used as affective term of address; the remainder have to do with plots about actual babies. Thus, this key word form – a potential candidate for either 'interaction in the here-and-now', 'expressivity', or 'narrative concerns' – was included only in the latter category. Cases where concordancing was undertaken are marked in Table 7.3 with a superscript dagger ([†]). The type of qualitative analysis varied. For example, with the word forms *lie* and *lying* I checked instances only to confirm that the majority are used to refer to not telling the truth (which has

Table 7.3 Key items in SydTV-Std (abbreviated table; [†] indicates that concordancing was undertaken)

Category		Subcategory	Key items
Routine formulae		Greetings, introductions, and leave-takings	hello, hi, this is my[†], to meet you[†], nice to meet you, let's go[†], see you[†], to see you[†], I got to[†], I got to go[†] [including I gotta go]
		Apologising, politeness, wishes, thanking, suggestions, etc.	excuse, excuse me, luck[†], sorry, I'm sorry, I'm so sorry, please, thank, thanks, thank you, let's[†]
Interaction in the here-and-now		First- and second-person pronouns/determiners	me, my, I am, I got, I'm a, I'm so, is my, of my, at me, to me, tell me[†], give me[†], I will, me to, me the
			you, your, you're, yourself, you to, you got, you think, for you, you and, you were, of you, to you, about you, to your, of your, with your, you in, for your, with you
			us, our, we're, let's . . .
		Terms of address	dude[†], man[†], honey[†], ladies[†], guys[†], mom[†], buddy[†], Mr[†], Mrs[†], Sir[†]
		Greetings, introductions, and leave-takings	hello, hi, this is my[†], to meet you[†], nice to meet you, let's go[†], see you[†], to see you[†], I got to[†], I got to go[†] [including I gotta go]
		Spatial and temporal deixis	here, tonight, right now, out of here
		Response, agreement or discourse marker	alright[†], fine[†], look I, of course[†]
Formality	Colloquial/ informal	Contractions	ain't, I'm, how'd, you're, would've, could've, should've . . .
	language	Swear/taboo words	ass[†], bitch[†], crap, hell, the hell

	Other (e.g. slang words, words referring to informal activities, informal terms of address, informal greetings, interjections, repeats)	kid†, kidding†, buddy†, shut†, date†, party†, dude†, guy, guys†, ladies†, honey†, man†, hey†, mom†, hi, uhoa, god, my god, oh my, oh my god, no no (no) (no), come on come on
Expressivity	Formal language	
	Titles (various uses)	doctor†, Mr†, Mrs†, Miss†, sir†
	Evaluative adjectives	best, crazy, fine†, beautiful, wrong, it's okay
	Emotion lexis	hurt†, love, loved, I love, I love you, trust, worry, happy, sad
	Affective terms of address	man†, buddy†, honey†
	Interjections	hey†, god, my god, oh my, oh my god, uhoa
	Swear/taboo words	bitch†, crap, hell, the hell
	Verbs relating to speaker/hearer needs and desires	need†, need you to†, I need, I need you, I need you to, I want you to
	Imperatives	listen†, shut†, stop†, wait†, come on, oh come on, come on come on
	Other (e.g. words with negative connotations, intensifiers, repeats)	broke†, lying†, kidding†, heart†, lose†, news†, seriously†, promise†, I'm so sorry, you're a†, you are†, no no (no) (no), come on come on, out of here
Narrative concerns	Lexical word forms or phrases used to refer to (aspects of) the plot (e.g. happenings, people/entities involved in the plot) or to provide backstory	baby†, bar†, brother†, boys†, date†, daughter†, die†, drink†, family†, found†, friend†, husband†, party†, sex†, blood†, body†, doctor†, police, dead†, death†, girl†, hurt†, kill, killed†, looking for†, men†, business†, safe†, alone†, met†, protect†, find†, help†, save†, shot†, son†, waiting†, wife†, woman†

negative connotations) rather than 'lying down'.[10] With other words or phrases, I also investigated how the word tends to be used in SydTV-Std (e.g. *ladies* as formal or as informal, as term of address, or as referring expression). Because of space constraints I am not able to provide details for *all* of the qualitative analyses in this chapter, but I will do so where possible.

Finally, it is worth pointing out that several key items have been classified in more than one category. For instance, certain uses of the informal word forms *hey* and *man* in TV dialogue convey emotional meanings such as excitement, alarm, or protest (Bednarek 2012a), and these key items can hence be classified as expressing *both* informality and expressivity. This approach to categorisation is in alignment with that taken by Quaglio (2009: 53), who notes that the same linguistic feature can represent different functions and defends this methodological decision as 'a reflection of the integrative nature of language in general and of conversation in particular' (Quaglio 2009: 53). Nevertheless, for the sake of clarity I attempted not to over-rely on double-classification.

3.2 Discussion of Results

To start with, several key items can be categorised as **routine formulae**. In line with Mittmann (2006), this category includes greetings such as *hello*, *hi*, or *nice to meet you* (used in introductions); leave-takings (e.g. *see you*, *let's go*, *I got to go*);[11] and apologising and politeness expressions (e.g. *excuse me*, *I'm [so] sorry*, *please*, *thanks*, *thank you*). Note that *good-bye*, another leave-taking expression, falls just below the range threshold, occurring in nineteen episodes.

To give some examples, concordancing showed that the key n-gram *(to) see you* is often used in greetings or leave-takings in phrases such as *good/great/happy/nice/pleased to see you* or *see you around/in a bit/ in the house/then/later/tomorrow*. As a routine formula (almost all instances), *to meet you* is preceded by *good*, *great*, *an honour*, *lovely*, *nice*, *pleased*, and *pleasure*. As Figure 7.1 demonstrates, the key tri-gram *this is my* is often used by characters in SydTV-Std to introduce someone (18 of 34 instances).

Interestingly, the study of SydTV-Std seems to confirm Bruti and Vignozzi's (2016b) statement (based on two series) that contemporary US TV series show a preference for colloquial greetings such as *hello* and *hi*, although a more extensive study comparing frequencies of all such formulae would need to be undertaken. Figure 7.2 on p. 134 illustrates the use of *hi* in greetings among friends, acquaintances, as well as strangers (as evident from the introductions in the co-text, e.g. lines 1, 4, 7, 11, 13, 15).

1	Thursday. <CHARLIE:> No, Sam, it's okay. Come on in. Everybody this is my daughter Sam. <SAM:> I'll just be a second, and I'll be out of
2	call them up and tell them not to come over. Tim! <TIM:> Oh hi Suse, this is my buddy Lamont. <LAMONT:> I brought peppermint schnapps.
3	:> Please put the gun away. My name is Rebecca Mynor, and this is my husband, Joel. We just bought this house. We did, right? You
4	Talbot? I'm a huge fan. <ANGIE:> You know her? <JANE:> Umm yeah. This is my best friend Stacy. When I told you about cocktails with
5	something to me if I knew who the fuck you were. <VINCENT:> Oh, this is my buddy Eric. <ERIC:> You can call me E. <BILLY:> E? Is that
6	is eighty more than the last time you played, I think. <RUFUS:> Lisa, this is my sarcastic son Dan and his friend Sarah. <LISA LOEB:> Hey.
7	night long. These are the freezing cold feet of my little brother, Dewey. This is my oldest brother Francis. He's the one I really like, so of course,
8	in Eagleton. <TOM:> Hi George Guernway, I'm Tom Haverford, this is my wife Wendy. She's my age. <GEORGE:> Hello. <WENDY:'>
9	is my oldest son. He's a very no-nonsense person like yourself. And, this is my youngest. He's about your age. <LESLIE:> Terrific. So umm,
10	tonight I'm the parks department's seventh wheel. <GEORGE:> This is my oldest son. He's a very no-nonsense person like yourself. And
11	made a judgment call. <WOMAN:> You made a mistake. <HANK (V):> This is my brother. <EVAN:> I'm Evan R Lawson CPA. <HANK (V):> He
12	police captain. Welcome. <ACEVEDA:> It's an honor to meet you, Sir. This is my wife, Aurora. <AURORA:> What a wonderful housing
13	:> Yes, can you send in Miss Smith, please? <SAMMY:'> Honey, this is my buddy Tom I was telling you about. He's going to take Richter.
14	:> How you doing? <MIA:> I'm doing great. <SALINGER:> Great. This is my daughter Kimmy. <MIA:> Oh hi, Kimmy. Nice to meet you.
15	:> Guilty. And clumsy, I apologize. I'm Sarah Blake. <SAM:> I'm Sam. This is my brother, Dean. <SARAH:> Dean? <DEAN:> Mmm?
16	champagne, please. <SAM:> He's not a waiter. I'm Sam Connors. This is my brother, Dean. We are art dealers with Connors Limited.
17	a surprise. <HARRISON:> Ah, you know me, I am full of them. <TRU:> This is my brother, Harrison. This is Jack. <JACK:> Hey. Jack Harper.
18	, hi. <MARTHA STEWART:> Hello. <CAROLINE:> I'm Caroline, and this is my business partner, Max, and we have a start-up cupcake

Figure 7.1 This is my used as a routine formula in introductions

#	
1	and over here we got Shannah. <ANDERS:> Hey. <JESS:> Hi. <ADAM:> So, where are you girls living at nowadays?
2	two lives today. Doctors are just people. Hi, Mrs O'hara, can I, hi, Doctor O'hara? My stethoscope, that you borrowed from me
3	Please come in. <MAX:> Oh yes. <JOY:> Hello. <VICTORIA:> Hi. <ELKA:> Is everybody ready? <MELANIE:> Yes.
4	. George Guernway, he's a city manager in Eagleton. <TOM:> Hi George Guernway, I'm Tom Haverford, this is my wife Wendy.
5	you still got to call Sarah, so. <SAM:> Sarah, hey. It's Sam. Hey, hi. Good, good, yeah, umm, what about you? Yeah, good, good,
6	. <MARNIE:> Okay. <HANNAH:> Oh you arrived, hi! <ELIJAH:> Hi. <HANNAH:> Hey, hey. <ELIJAH:> Hey. Hey. <HANNAH:>
7	Yes, can I help you! <CAROLINE:> Oh, my good, umm hi, hello I'm, are you, I'm, Caroline Miller from Malcolm's school. I
8	. For good, huh? <DARCY:> Okay, I'll hold you to that. <GAIL:> Hi honey, how'd it go this morning? <JOHNSTON:> Oh, the
9	association. <BOB:> Madam Vice-President. <SELINA:> Hi, how do you do. Please, come into my office. <BOB:> Thank
10	Mickelson from the office, and his wife, uh, Susan. <CLAIRE:> Hi. I do. Hey. <TOM:> Is your coat stuck? <CLAIRE:> It is. It
11	:> Hello? Hello? <JACK:> Can I help you? <MICHELLE:> Oh, hi, I I didn't see you there. Michelle Carey, Post Dispatch.
12	. What? Where? Alright, I'll be right there. I got to run. Nurse, hi. I'm looking, I got it. Okay, where's Megan? <CORRINE:>
13	:> Hi. <JIM:> I'm Jim by the way. <KATY:> I'm Katy. <JIM:> Hi Katy, nice to meet you. <KATY:> You sit out there don't you?
14	you! <LIZ:> How you doing. <GRAY:> Liz! <LIZ:> Hi. <GRAY:> Hi. Liz, this is Kiara, Francesca, that's Talbot and that's Armand.
15	<LOUIS:> He's probably still a virgin. <MIKE:> Mr Jacobson. Hi, Mike Ross, Harvey's associate. So sorry to keep you waiting
16	:> Quack! You are so obvious. <JANE:> Okay hold on. Hello? Hi Ms Talbot. Christie, I was just working on your case, and, yes,
17	a test! <RORY:> Where do you think you're going? <LORELAI:> Hi. <RORY:> It's one o'clock in the morning. <LORELAI:> I know
18	was hard. Hit the showers. <BECKY:> Thanks, Coach. <WILL:> Hi. Sue, you are unbelievable. <SUE:> And you are a terrible
19	. Okay, yeah, I love you too. Bye-bye. <MRS MCCLUSKY:> Hi there. I brought you some avocados. I have a tree in back but I
20	calling! <911:> Hello, nine one one emergency. <SERENA:> Hi, uh, we have an emergency, uh can you send someone right

Figure 7.2 Twenty instances where hi is used as a greeting, selected from twenty different TV series

134

According to Quaglio (2009: 47–8) and Bednarek (2012a: 44), greetings and leave-takings likely occur more frequently in TV dialogue than in unscripted conversation because of situational differences and principles of data collection.[12] At the same time, we can draw on what we know about the functions of TV dialogue to explain the keyness of these formulae. As discussed in Chapter 3, greetings and leave-takings can function to manage scene changes (marking the beginning or end of a scene) or to structure scenes internally. In addition, greetings and introductions present characters to the audience (anchorage of the characters), while conversational routines also establish interpersonal relationships between characters (e.g. familiarity, gratefulness). Routine formulae further create realism: they are representations of conventionalised conversational activities that viewers recognise from their own experience of everyday interactions. In drawing on such well-known conversational routines scriptwriters re-create recognisable and familiar linguistic exchanges. Thus, routine formulae fulfil functions relating to the communication of the narrative as well as functions relating to realism. This is in line with Richardson's (2010a: 51) assumption that routine dialogue is deployed by writers for 'ulterior, that is to say, narrative purposes'.

Moving on, several key items in SydTV-Std appear to be associated with **interaction in the here-and-now**. As explained above, included are first- and second-person pronouns/determiners (e.g. *me, I am, is my, your, yourself, you and, us, we're*), formal and informal terms of address (*dude, man, buddy, honey, mom, guys, ladies, Mr, Mrs, Sir*), greetings, introductions, leave-takings (e.g. *hello, hi, this is my, [to] see you, nice to meet you, let's go, I got to go*), response, agreement, or discourse markers (*alright, fine, look I, of course*), as well as temporal (*tonight, right now*) and spatial (*here, out of here*) deixis (illustrated in Figure 7.3).

The presence of many key items incorporating first- and second-person pronouns/determiners and of terms of address, greetings, introductions, and leave-takings reflects the focus of TV series on relations between people, the speaker–hearer relationship, and dialogic exchanges (Bednarek 2012a: 43). A small amount of interactional discourse management is also evident (*alright, fine, look I, of course*), perhaps indications of an overuse of particular discourse managing items in TV dialogue compared with unscripted conversation, while other features may be underused.[13] *Of course* and *alright* often occur at the beginning of turns in SydTV-Std, where they act as agreement or discourse markers – in contrast, only a few instances of *alright* are occurrences of BE *alright*.

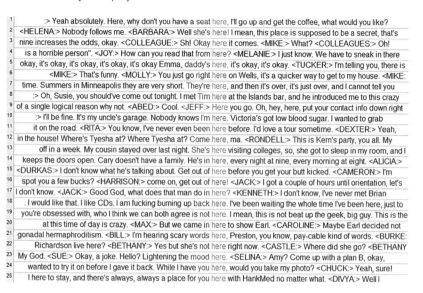

Figure 7.3 Twenty-five random instances of here, *selected from twenty-five different TV series*

This focus on characters' interaction in the here-and-now of the fictional world likely draws viewers into the televisual narrative by making them live these moments with the characters as they occur. There is perhaps an argument, then, for tying such features to the function 'control of viewer evaluation and emotions', but audience research would need to confirm this hypothesis. Some of the individual linguistic features in this category will fulfil specific functions, too, as explained in Part II: the functions of greetings/leave-takings have already been mentioned in the previous section. In addition, temporal/spatial deixis can be tied to the anchorage of time and space and the communication of narrative causality (e.g. anticipating events), while terms of address are associated with aspects of characterisation (anchorage of the characters and relationships between characters).

Interestingly, as the key items under **formality** show, there are indicators of both informal language and formal language. This result confirms a similar finding based on a corpus of dialogue from seven US TV series (Bednarek 2012a). In this study, I argued that the extent of formal language depends on generic aspects as well as aspects of character relationships, including power hierarchies. Many sitcoms feature relationships among friends and equals, while other genres such as medical or crime series feature professional hierarchies, with associated differences in linguistic levels of informality.

Classified as informal are swear/taboo words (*ass, bitch, crap*, [*the*] *hell*), informal words (e.g. *guy, kid, kidding, shut* [*shut* ... *up*]), informal greetings (*hi*), informal/intimate terms of address (e.g. *buddy, dude, honey, mom, ladies, guys*), words related to informal activities (e.g. *date* and *party*), the interjections (*oh*) (*my*) *god* and *whoa*, repeats (e.g. *no no no, come on come on*), and contractions (e.g. *ain't, I'm, how'd, would've*). *Ladies*, for example, is more often used informally than formally in SydTV-Std, with only seven instances of *ladies and gentlemen*. Some informal forms occur in more than one category because they are polyfunctional – for instance, *man* is used as informal reference, term of address, or interjection, while the informal *hey* is used in a greeting, as protest, etc.

For further illustration, Figure 7.4 on p. 138 shows some of the different ways in which the word form *kidding* is used in SydTV-Std, here most often as part of the idiomatic phrases *I'm (just) kidding* (lines 2–6), *are you ... kidding (me)* (lines 11–21), and *You're kidding (me)* (lines 22–25). Since many instances involve emotionality (e.g. intensification, disbelief, etc.), *kidding* has also been classified as expressivity.

As far as the functions of such informal language are concerned, Quaglio (2009: 120) argues that its overuse can be associated with humour, relationships between characters, and the attempt to make television language appear authentic. As I have put it elsewhere, the use of informal language 'may contribute to the "willing suspension of disbelief" on the part of audiences and allow them to engage with what they perceive as "realistic" characters, characters that are realistic because they use the same kind of colloquial language as viewers do' (Bednarek 2012a: 43). Informality can thus be tied to functions relating to realism (imitation of 'real' spoken language), functions relating to the communication of the narrative (relationships between characters), and functions relating to aesthetic and interpersonal effect and commercial appeal (humour).

As mentioned, there are also indicators of formal language among key items: titles such as *Mr, Mrs, Miss* (sometimes spelled *miss* in the corpus), *doctor, Sir*. Occurring as either title only or title and last name, they are most often used as terms of address (e.g. Figure 7.5 on p. 139, lines 3, 4, 8–9, 17, 21–25), as a reference (e.g. lines 2, 5–7, 16), or to introduce oneself (e.g. line 1).

Interestingly, these items occur across many different episodes, as summarised in Table 7.4 on p. 140. *Mr* is the word with the highest frequency and range, followed by *doctor* and *sir*. The female titles *Mrs* and *Miss* occur less frequently than *Mr/Sir* and have a slightly lower range across episodes, possibly reflecting a greater importance of male characters overall. Altogether, fifty-five episodes contain at least one

1	on. <SAMMY:> Have fun. <SALINGER:> You better be kidding me. No, no I don't think it's a good idea. <MIA:>
2	. Beautiful ladies. I want to bang you both! I'm kidding. I'm kidding, sweetheart. Uh. You know, in all seriousness, you
3	your little shop to the ground. Do you want to find out if I'm kidding? Yeah. Good-bye. <TED:> Hey, how's it going?
4	you miss me? <BRANDY:> Oh yeah. <DEAN:> I'm just kidding. Listen, I talked to my producer, and, uh, it is
5	. If I do have a threesome, you can't be part of it. I'm just kidding, yes you can. Can you bring a friend? <SHELDON
6	:> Oh my God. Raping? <KENNY:> Yeah, I'm just kidding. You mind if I pony up in here? <TERENCE:> Oh
7	, they clear brush. Fire prevention. <SAMMY:> No kidding? <TOM:> They clear brush faster than a crew.
8	. <KIM:> Law, not dessert. <GRAYSON:> I know. I was kidding. Five whole minutes before bringing up work, that's
9	, she told me you had an active imagination. She wasn't kidding. <KIM:> Who? <KRUGMAN:> Your friend. The one
10	. <NANCY:> Doug. <DOUG:> Jesus, Nance, you weren't kidding, this stuff is primo. want to climb in? <NANCY:>
11	owe you, Sir? <MAN:> Three dollars. <ANDY:> Are you kidding me? Three dollars? That's what he owes you?
12	. Will you sponsor me? <SAMMY:> Of course. Are you kidding? <JANILA:> And they said that I had to have a
13	<STAN:> I'm not signing some agreement, are you kidding me? I'm getting railroaded. <MIKE:> Should I go
14	. <JENNY:> Hmm, would you go? <MIKE:> What are you kidding me? No, I have a hard enough time pretending at
15	you letting me crash here, bud. <BEN:> Are you kidding? You're doing us a favor. No-Flush Tony just
16	recess. Honey, honey, what are you doing to me, are you kidding me? Baby! <ERIC:> Hello? <SHAUNA:> Eric, I
17	:> You didn't tell anyone, did you? <BUSTER:> Are you kidding? I don't need to brag, but some people haven't
18	Caroline could live with half the estate? <CARY:> Are you kidding? This is a gold-digger who wants to steal from our
19	and just be supportive of your sister. <MOLLY:> Are you kidding? That's all I ever do around here is support my
20	the emotional problems are there. <CHARLIE:> Are you kidding me? <SAM:> Ready to go dad. <CHARLIE:> I'll
21	, don't worry about me. <JACKIE:> Fucking pyxis, are you kidding me? They're going to replace you with a fucking
22	was done in here, they'd need a drain. <BOOTH:> You're kidding me. It's a drain? <MARTIN:> This is our sales
23	I dropped it in the warehouse last night. <SAM:> You're kidding, right? <DEAN:> Yeah, it's got my prints, my ID.
24	a while. <SARAH:> Welcome to the club. <SAM:> You're kidding me. <WAITER:> Here we are. <SARAH:> Thanks.
25	Way coming. <LORELAI:> Oh finished. <RORY:> You're kidding! It took me forever to read that. I had to renew it ten

Figure 7.4 Twenty-five random instances of kidding

#		File name
1	colleague along to help out. <CHASE:> Hi, I'm Doctor Chase. <NAOMI:> Hi. <CHASE:> Well,	House
2	like one. I hereby move to revoke the tenure of Doctor Gregory House and terminate his	House
3	MEDIC:> Give me the bag. <KATE:> Doctor! He just had lunch with the president.	NCIS
4	that you borrowed from me this morning, can I, Doctor O'hara, it's come to my attention that	Nurse_Jackie
5	is. It's kept me alive two years longer than any doctor predicted. It's all I need. <MRS	Nurse_Jackie
6	<SCOTT:> No, not at all. I don't get it the doctor said she'd be fine, but the bite's not	Teen_Wolf
7	critical. <BAILEY:> Doctor Stevens and Doctor Yang may have saved your life. If you	Greys_Anatomy
8	just goes so against my Christian work ethic, Miss B. Come on, help me out. I'd do it for you.	Weeds
9	Mr Dominic, would you leave us? <DOMINIC:> Miss DeWitt, I... <ADELLE:> I'll be perfectly	Dollhouse
10	. <DOROTA:> I know it's not my place, but, Miss Serena is, like the old days. <LILY:> What	Gossip_Girl
11	, our new member's here. <MIKE:> Excuse me miss, you just drove over my lawn. I'm going to	Anger_Management
12	down for anything. Hey, baby. How are the new Mr and Mrs Shepherd? <SERENA:> I didn't	Gossip_Girl
13	repulsive. <BOYD:> This is Boyd Langton for Mr Dominic. Yes, you need to take Victor off	Dollhouse
14	:> Do you know why I put up with this pitiful job, Mr Donaghy? Why I fetch these folks' lunches	Thirty_Rock
15	owe him after that? <DOCTOR:> Mr Morgan? Mr Morgan? <DEXTER:> That's me.	Dexter
16	, you will hold open auditions to fill her slot, and Mr Schuester will monitor them to make sure	Glee
17	Wilder meet Alicia Florrick. <CAROLINE:> Mrs Florrick. It's really nice to meet you. I, think	Good_Wife
18	. <VICTORIA:> Uh, "Say greeting to Mrs Ladypant. For best good times, be on dry".	Hot_in_Cleveland
19	. What? Oh, you can pull it off. <LYNETTE:> Mrs McClusky, you're back from the hospital	Desperate_Housewives
20	off. <JOHN:> If you want, but you don't have to. Mrs Solis, to take care of you? That's my	Desperate_Housewives
21	exactly my point! <SOOKIE:> What'll you have Sir? Anything that comes with the stuffed fried	Gilmore_Girls
22	the president would... <DRIVER:> Not mine, Sir. <FORNELL:> Not mine, either. <TONY:>	NCIS
23	we do something about this. So, please, Sir, I will ask you one more time. What is	24
24	For your little lady. <WAITER:> Thank you, Sir. <LINDSAY:> Oh, no, you ought to thank	Tru_Calling
25	that was a job well done. <BAER:> Thank you, Sir. <PRESIDENT:> What do you say we head	NCIS

Figure 7.5 Twenty-five random instances of doctor, Miss, Mr, Mrs, Sir, with file names

Table 7.4 Raw frequency and range for five key items

Key word form	Raw frequency	Range
Mr	154	35
Doctor	121	29
Sir	118	27
Mrs	71	21
Miss (excluding *miss* as verb)	56	24
All	520	55

instance of at least one of these five word forms, while no instances occur in the episodes from *According to Jim*, *Community*, *In Treatment*, *Jericho*, *Malcolm in the Middle*, *Mike & Molly*, *My Name Is Earl*, *New Girl*, *Supernatural*, *The Office*, and *Two and a Half Men*. Notably, eight of these eleven TV series are sitcoms, a genre that is associated with informality (see Chapter 2).

However, as Figure 7.6 demonstrates, these word forms do not express formality in *all* instances, even if they do so in a majority of cases. For example, *Miss* can be used in the titles of pageants (lines 2 and 38: *Miss America Pageant*, *Miss Mystic Falls*) and as part of informal nicknames (e.g. lines 15, 24, 29: *Miss Buzzkill*, *Miss Fluff-and-Fold*, *Little Miss Holdout*) or it can occur with an informal abbreviation as a nickname (as in the use of *Miss B* in lines 4–7). In most other cases, however, *Miss* occurs as term of address (e.g. lines 8, 16), as a reference (e.g. lines 10, 19), or to identify oneself (e.g. lines 26, 27), and in these instances it does seem to involve formality. Figure 7.6 also shows that titles have multiple functions in TV dialogue. For example, they identify characters and construct relationships between them. When used in innovative nicknames they exploit the resources of language, and they can also refer to real-life events (*Miss America Pageant*), constructing realism. Unequal uses of gendered titles in TV dialogue may also reflect and reinforce gender ideologies. Not to forget that a title like *doctor* reminds audiences of the character's profession. Thus, titles can fulfil functions relating to the communication of the narrative (characters), to aesthetic and interpersonal effect and commercial appeal (linguistic innovation), to realism (references to the 'real' world), and to thematic messages and ideology. Of these various functions, communication of the narrative (characters) does seem to be especially important.

Moving on, many key items can be classified under **expressivity**: evaluative adjectives (*best*, *crazy*, *fine*, *beautiful*, *wrong*, *it's okay*),

1	go. <BARBARA:> Helena, wait. <ALFRED:> Morning, miss. Alfred Pennyworth. How do you do? I've brought
2	. <CLAIRE:> Hmm. <PHIL:> So, what's your story? Miss America pageant in town? <CLAIRE:> Ah, you're
3	first baby! You're having a baby! <GUY:> Excuse me miss! <AMY:> Oh. Thank you so much! Thank you I
4	:> That just goes so against my Christian work ethic, Miss B. Come on, help me out. I'd do it for you.
5	drug. <NANCY:> Go away now, Josh. <JOSH:> Later Miss B. <COACH:> Let's go, team! Come on, hustle ou
6	all that. Whoa, you should take her easy on the lattes, Miss B. Don't kid yourself, caffeine is a serious drug.
7	:> Promise me you're not going to say anything, please, Miss B? <NANCY:> I'll think about it. <JOSH:> What
8	she's fabulous. <DISTRICT ATTORNEY:> Look, Miss Bingham, your client and the victim rented kayaks,
9	of clothes and a bathrobe? <DOROTA:> Miss Blair. <CHUCK:> So we have every hangover cure
10	is Blair's idea of a perverse double date. <DOROTA:> Miss Blair asks that you should wait there. She's on her
11	made of penises. You know I think he's a real sicko, Miss Brady. I got my major in art, not psychology, you
12	, correct? <DOCTOR:> Yes, But I just do the procedure, Miss Brennan. <BOOTH:> Doctor Brennan. <DOCTOR
13	everybody show's over, let's get back to work. <KID 4:> Miss Buchanan? <APRIL:> Yes? <JANITOR:> Where
14	yet, or not but uh. Of course you already know Miss Buchanan, and uh, then we got Mr Nesbit our
15	with another human being. <HOUSE:> Well, thank you, Miss Buzzkill. <CUDDY:> Well, you only cost us a
16	, we can't risk making any mistakes. <BRENNAN:> Miss Combs, tell me, what, what do you use these
17	> I did at one time, yes. <BRENNAN:> How do you feel, Miss Combs? Have you been coughing at all? Do you
18	grafts, I doubt you were wearing a mask. You're sick, Miss Combs, and I, I don't just mean in a mentally
19	. <BRENNAN:> Take a biopsy of this ulna graft from Miss DeMarco and compare it with the core sample
20	:> Well, I need to give it to you. That's all. <BOYD:> Miss DeWitt. <DOMINIC:> What do we do with Hearn?
21	:> Mr Dominic, would you leave us? <DOMINIC:> Miss DeWitt, I... <ADELLE:> I'll be perfectly safe.
22	:> I'll go first. I have to get two of these in one dress. Miss, do you have a shoehorn? <CAROLINE:> Come
23	just stay at the bar. <FREAMON:> Hmm. You know, Miss Ennis, it's a rare thing when we ask somebody to
24	up the dryer to take the other person's clothes out, finds Miss Fluff-and-Fold here instead. <ESPOSITO:> Now if
25	to keep me busy at the manor. I keep hoping that Miss Helena will change her mind and come live there.
26	the truth gets naked. <WOMAN:> Doctor Grey, this is Miss Henry from the nursing home. I'm calling about your
27	:> I think he's going to cry. <MISS HENRY:> Hi. It's Miss Henry again. Is this a better time? <MEREDITH:>
28	you couldn't be there for your mother. <MEREDITH:> Miss Henry, if my mother were lucid, she would
29	We've met. <MALCOLM:> Well, well! It looks like Little Miss Holdout has given up the goods. Brava! Did he
30	In fact, you two go wash your hands. <T BAG:> Evening Miss Holland. Don't you look lovely this evening?
31	. <TARA:> Yeah. That was a mile back. <LETTIE:> For Miss Jeanette, you got to go past where the devil's at.
32	demon of yours wouldn't let you. You must be Tara. I'm Miss Jeanette. You ready? Fully prepared, body and
33	to go to church. She need structure. <NATE:> Well Miss Johnson, this is uh this is kind of like church.
34	. <DIVYA:> Sorry about that. <ZOE:> No, please look Miss Katdare, we will have everything cleaned up in
35	:> You certainly are! Her name is Rose, named after Miss Kate Winslet in the movie Titanic. <KENNY:> you
36	:> And the Head is perfectly harmless and totally into Miss Liz Lemon. <LIZ:> Ha, ha. Not as much as he's into
37	doing, Doctor Brennan? <BRENNAN:> No, Sir. It's all Miss Montenegro. <MRS CULLEN:> Thank you Angela.
38	and their handsome escorts. This is Caroline Forbes, Miss Mystic Falls. Aren't they beautiful? <BONNIE:>
39	. Ladies and gentlemen, please welcome our stunning Miss Mystic Falls Court and their handsome escorts.
40	:> Oh! Are you kidding me? Hi! Luke's math teacher, Miss Passwater! <PHIL:> Passwater. <GLORIA:> Oh,
41	times today. <DOROTA:> I know it's not my place, but, Miss Serena is, like the old days. <LILY:> What are you
42	a very good time. <DOROTA:> Oh the wedding, I know. Miss Serena is here. <LILY:> Oh yes, I know. I've heard
43	reason we're here. <NINA:> Agent Dunham. <OLIVIA:> Miss Sharp. <NINA:> For what it's worth, it was not my
44	chance. Give it to her. <NIECY:> Yes, can you send in Miss Smith, please? <SAMMY:> Honey, this is my
45	. Will, I'm so inspired by your stunt that I'm insisting that Miss Sylvester do the same with the Cheerios. <SUE:> I
46	being extremely rude. <JAY:> We'd like you to release Miss Talbot immediately. <SECURITY:> The police are
47	And I promise this will never happen again. As soon as Miss Talbot's credit cards are unfrozen she will return for
48	guarantee it's going to. <POLICEMAN:> Just let it go, miss. <TRU:> What if she gets shot? What if she's
49	. <COOPER:> Someone you know? What's your name, Miss? <TRU:> I'd rather not say. <COOPER:> This uh,
50	we forget? <DAN:> Hey, uh, excuse me, Mr Bass, Miss Van der Woodsen. <LILY:> Not for long, thank you
51	. <DOROTA:> Miss Van der Woodsen, it is Dorota. Miss Waldorf's... <LILY:> I know who you are, Dorota,
52	at Blair's? You're supposed to be here. <DOROTA:> Miss Van der Woodsen, it is Dorota. Miss Waldorf's...
53	choice. <GREGGS:> Shardene Ennis. <FREAMON:> Miss, we need to talk. <SHARDENE:> About what?
54	orange T-shirt under a gray jacket. <COOPER:> Okay Miss, we'll send an officer to check it out. <TRU:> Thank
55	, our new member's here. <MIKE:> Excuse me miss, you just drove over my lawn. I'm going to have to
56	anywhere near him, but, uh... <REESE:> But? What? Miss, you saw something, didn't you? <MCNALLY:>

Figure 7.6 All instances for Miss *in SydTV-Std (excluding the verb)*

emotion lexis (*happy, sad, hurt, worry, trust, love, loved, I love [you]*), words with negative connotations (e.g. *fault, lie, lying, lose*), affective terms of address (e.g. *honey, man, buddy*),[14] interjections (e.g. *hey, [oh] [my] god, whoa*), swear/taboo words (e.g. *bitch, [the] hell*), intensification/emphasis (e.g. *I'm so sorry, seriously*), certain imperatives (*come on, listen, shut, stop, wait*), repeats (*no no [no] [no] [no], come on come on*), and references to speaker/hearer needs and desires (e.g. *I need, I want you to*). Indeed, qualitative analysis shows that the vast majority of *need* occurs with first- or second-person subjects. The category of expressivity also contains a few other items that are often used in an expressive co-text or with expressive meaning in SydTV-Std (e.g. *explain, broke, heart, kidding, news, promise, you're a, you are, out of here*). For example, *broke* tends to be associated with negative happenings (e.g. being broke, breaking limbs, breaking up, breaking rules), and *news* is often preceded by the evaluative adjectives *bad, big, biggest, excellent, glorious, good, great*, and *happy*, while *heart* is frequently used metaphorically to refer to feelings rather than with reference to physiology.[15] I have already mentioned the expressivity of *out of here* (cf. Bednarek 2012a).

With respect to swear/taboo words, one of the key items included under 'informal language' is missing here, namely the word form *ass*. This is because *ass* has many different usages, and especially with literal meaning ('buttocks') and as 'pronominal form' (Bednarek 2015b: 446), it appears foremost informal rather than expressing speaker emotion or attitude. Figure 7.7 shows twenty-five random instances for the word form *ass* in SydTV-Std (excluding hyphenated compounds such as *ass-kicking* or *short-ass*). Instances of literal meaning where *ass* refers to a taboo part of the body are apparent here (e.g. line 16), as is the pronominal form, where *ass* can be substituted by a pronoun with a specific referent (e.g. lines 6, 9, 23). In other occurrences the word form *ass* is indeed associated with expressivity (e.g. line 19: *You've been a real pain the ass*; line 21: *'Cause I will fuck your ass up*), but these make up less than 50 per cent of cases. In contrast, the key word *bitch* carries expressive meaning in almost all of its instances, as seen in Figure 7.8.

Another swear/taboo word, *damnit*, falls just below the range threshold, occurring across eighteen files.[16] In fact, *damn* itself is also overused in SydTV-Std (n = 57, range = 33) once spelling variation is taken into account (560 instances of *damn* in the LSAC, after exclusion of instances of *damn it, god damn* and *god damn it*, because these are spelled *damnit, goddamn* and *goddamnit* in SydTV-Std; LL = 17.99).

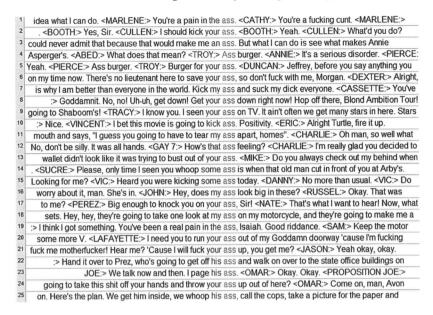

1 | idea what I can do. <MARLENE:> You're a pain in the ass. <CATHY:> You're a fucking cunt. <MARLENE:>
2 | . <BOOTH:> Yes, Sir. <CULLEN:> I should kick your ass. <BOOTH:> Yeah. <CULLEN:> What'd you do?
3 | could never admit that because that would make me an ass. But what I can do is see what makes Annie
4 | Asperger's. <ABED:> What does that mean? <TROY:> Ass burger. <ANNIE:> It's a serious disorder. <PIERCE:
5 | Yeah. <PIERCE:> Ass burger. <TROY:> Burger for your ass. <DUNCAN:> Jeffrey, before you say anything you
6 | on my time now. There's no lieutenant here to save your ass, so don't fuck with me, Morgan. <DEXTER:> Alright,
7 | is why I am better than everyone in the world. Kick my ass and suck my dick everyone. <CASSETTE:> You've
8 | :> Goddamnit. No, no! Uh-uh, get down! Get your ass down right now! Hop off there, Blond Ambition Tour!
9 | going to Shaboom's! <TRACY:> I know you. I seen your ass on TV. It ain't often we get many stars in here. Stars
10 | :> Nice. <VINCENT:> I bet this movie is going to kick ass. Positivity. <ERIC:> Alright Turtle, fire it up.
11 | mouth and says, "I guess you going to have to tear my ass apart, homes". <CHARLIE:> Oh man, so well what
12 | No, don't be silly. It was all hands. <GAY 7:> How's that ass feeling? <CHARLIE:> I'm really glad you decided to
13 | wallet didn't look like it was trying to bust out of your ass. <MIKE:> Do you always check out my behind when
14 | <SUCRE:> Please, only time I seen you whoop some ass is when that old man cut in front of you at Arby's.
15 | Looking for me? <VIC:> Heard you were kicking some ass today. <DANNY:> No more than usual. <VIC:> Do
16 | worry about it, man. She's in. <JOHN:> Hey, does my ass look big in these? <RUSSEL:> Okay. That was
17 | to me? <PEREZ:> Big enough to knock you on your ass, Sir! <NATE:> That's what I want to hear! Now, what
18 | sets. Hey, hey, they're going to take one look at my ass on my motorcycle, and they're going to make me a
19 | :> I think I got something. You've been a real pain in the ass, Isaiah. Good riddance. <SAM:> Keep the motor
20 | some more V. <LAFAYETTE:> I need you to run your ass out of my Goddamn doorway 'cause I'm fucking
21 | fuck me motherfucker! Hear me? 'Cause I will fuck your ass up, you get me? <JASON:> Yeah okay, okay.
22 | :> Hand it over to Prez, who's going to get off his ass and walk on over to the state office buildings on
23 | JOE:> We talk now and then. I page his ass. <OMAR:> Okay. Okay. <PROPOSITION JOE:>
24 | going to take this shit off your hands and throw your ass up out of here? <OMAR:> Come on, man, Avon
25 | on. Here's the plan. We get him inside, we whoop his ass, call the cops, take a picture for the paper and

Figure 7.7 Twenty-five random instances for ass

1 | prom. So you can either be fat and jolly, or a skinny bitch, it's up to you. Sit down. We're watching a
2 | follow my instructions! <JESSE:> Oh well heil Hitler, bitch! And let me tell you something else. We flipped
3 | Emily's not a bitch. <JOHNNY:> I was calling you a bitch for even thinking about calling her again.
4 | :> So what? <JOHNNY:> So you're a little glitch bitch! <TURTLE:> Blame the game makers, don't
5 | didn't call you back? Bitch. <ERIC:> Emily's not a bitch. <JOHNNY:> I was calling you a bitch for even
6 | actually, and I've been avoiding her ever since. The bitch is a psycho. <NATE:> What about her?
7 | know each other? <CHARLIE:> Yeah, it's the crazy bitch that punched me in my eye! <TERRELL:>
8 | :> Alright, let me in just one game. Domino bitch! <MAC:> This is bullshit, absolute bullshit. How
9 | , neither of which are cause to call a man a bitch. <CHUCK:> You're trying to kill Napoleon
10 | the killer. <OLIVE:> Oh, Lord. Don't make me cut a bitch. <OSCAR VIBENIUS:> Hey, I'm just here for
11 | . <DANNY:> You heard me. Go. <GUY 6:> Get lost, bitch. <THUG:> Who you calling a bitch?
12 | 6:> Get lost, bitch. <THUG:> Who you calling a bitch? <LEMONHEAD:> Get down! <DANNY:> Get
13 | , alright? <T-BONZ:> I'm going to get my money, bitch. <KERN:> Over my dead body, bitch.
14 | towards your mother. <KIMMY:> Mom's a bitch. <SALINGER:> Sh! You will never talk that way
15 | . <LYDIA:> Where's the mother? <SKYLAR:> That bitch broke up with me. <LYDIA:> Does she know
16 | > Purse? Let's do it. <ROYCE:> What kind of stupid bitch would go and do something like that?
17 | :> Now you think I got a motherfucking demon? Bitch, you as fucked up as your bus. <MISS
18 | the truck man. <LAFAYETTE:> Don't fucking creep bitch, you fucking creeping, what the fuck you doing
19 | <TARA:> Hey dog! <SAM:> Goddamn, son of a bitch and shit-ass fucking trailer. What are you, what
20 | at all that hate mail I got with people calling me a bitch, and I'm not a bitch. <MARTHA STEWART:>
21 | , hi. I'm melting, I'm melting. She is such a fucking bitch. <MIKE:> So uh, today at the three-thirty press
22 | time pack an espresso machine in your big fucking bitch bag. <GARY:> Oh my God. <SELINA:> Dan
23 | like Celia walked by? <DOUG:> She is such a bitch. Great tits, but, a raging bitch. Her husband's
24 | sitting up in there, right next to "dumb-ass white bitch". <HEYLIA:> Oh. Cornbread. <NANCY:> Oh,
25 | said about this one? <GREGGS:> That the stupid bitch didn't know how good the snort was at Little

Figure 7.8 Twenty-five random instances for bitch

In sum, since there are a large number of key items associated with expressivity, the SydTV-Std data provide persuasive evidence of the claim (based on data from seven series) that emotionality or expressivity is a defining feature of TV dialogue, regardless of series or genre (Bednarek 2012a). With respect to *Friends*, Quaglio (2009: 105) talks about a '"dramatic" effect'. More precisely, expressivity meets the demands of audiences for entertainment, makes them engage and care, and keeps them interested through the creation of emotional and dramatic tension (Bednarek 2012a: 57). In terms of FATS (as introduced in Part II), expressive language fulfils multiple functions in telecinematic discourse (Kozloff 2000; Bubel 2006; Quaglio 2009: 105; Bednarek 2010a, 2011c, 2012a: 56): functions relating to the communication of the narrative (social and individual character traits, revealing character's inner states; establishing intimate, friendly, or hostile relationships between characters) and functions relating to aesthetic and interpersonal effect and commercial appeal (control of viewer evaluation and emotions). It is possible that scenes with high expressivity also provide opportunities for star turns, as they call for the bodily enactment of emotion on the part of actors, but a systematic and multimodal analysis would need to confirm this hypothesis. Emotionality is also regarded as a key aspect of TV narratives in scriptwriting pedagogy (see Chapter 10).

The final category discussed in this section is **narrative concerns** (e.g. key words such as *baby, boys, business, looking for, met, waiting, woman*). Some of these words seem to concern socialising (*bar, drink, party, date, sex*), and several are relationship terms (*brother, daughter, family, friend, husband, son, wife*). Some of these occur in introductions, as seen in Figure 7.1 above. Key words like *baby, boys, brother, son, girl* are on occasion used as terms of address, but not in 50 per cent or more of occurrences. Rather, they refer to people that are usually in some way relevant to the narrative.

A word form such as *date* (as noun or verb, see Figure 7.9; found across twenty-nine corpus files) reflects a narrative concern with informal romantic relationships and simultaneously anchors the narrative in the world known to the US viewer. Only rarely does the word form *date* not refer to 'dating' in SydTV-Std (e.g. lines 4, 10–11 in Figure 7.9). 'Dating' arguably constitutes a specific North American cultural concept, with associated linguistic phrases such as *going [out] on a date, having a date, being on a date, asking someone on a date, a double date, bringing a date, being someone's date, the first/ second date*, etc. In languages like German *date* is now a colloquial loanword, possibly inspired by its occurrence in such mass media narratives.

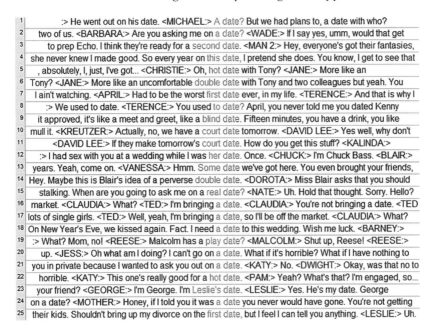

1	:> He went out on his date. <MICHAEL:> A date? But we had plans to, a date with who?
2	two of us. <BARBARA:> Are you asking me on a date? <WADE:> If I say yes, umm, would that get
3	to prep Echo. I think they're ready for a second date. <MAN 2:> Hey, everyone's got their fantasies,
4	she never knew I made good. So every year on this date, I pretend she does. You know, I get to see that
5	, absolutely, I, just, I've got... <CHRISTIE:> Oh, hot date with Tony? <JANE:> More like an
6	Tony? <JANE:> More like an uncomfortable double date with Tony and two colleagues but yeah. You
7	I ain't watching. <APRIL:> Had to be the worst first date ever, in my life. <TERENCE:> And that is why I
8	:> We used to date. <TERENCE:> You used to date? April, you never told me you dated Kenny
9	it approved, it's like a meet and greet, like a blind date. Fifteen minutes, you have a drink, you like
10	mull it. <KREUTZER:> Actually, no, we have a court date tomorrow. <DAVID LEE:> Yes well, why don't
11	<DAVID LEE:> If they make tomorrow's court date. How do you get this stuff? <KALINDA:>
12	:> I had sex with you at a wedding while I was her date. Once. <CHUCK:> I'm Chuck Bass. <BLAIR:>
13	years. Yeah, come on. <VANESSA:> Hmm. Some date we've got here. You even brought your friends,
14	Hey. Maybe this is Blair's idea of a perverse double date. <DOROTA:> Miss Blair asks that you should
15	stalking. When are you going to ask me on a real date? <NATE:> Uh. Hold that thought. Sorry. Hello?
16	market. <CLAUDIA:> What? <TED:> I'm bringing a date. <CLAUDIA:> You're not bringing a date. <TED
17	lots of single girls. <TED:> Well, yeah, I'm bringing a date, so I'll be off the market. <CLAUDIA:> What?
18	On New Year's Eve, we kissed again. Fact. I need a date to this wedding. Wish me luck. <BARNEY:>
19	:> What? Mom, no! <REESE:> Malcolm has a play date? <MALCOLM:> Shut up, Reese! <REESE:>
20	up. <JESS:> Oh what am I doing? I can't go on a date. What if it's horrible? What if I have nothing to
21	you in private because I wanted to ask you out on a date. <KATY:> No. <DWIGHT:> Okay, was that no to
22	horrible. <KATY:> This one's really good for a hot date. <PAM:> Yeah? What's that? I'm engaged, so...
23	your friend? <GEORGE:> I'm George. I'm Leslie's date. <LESLIE:> Yes. He's my date. George
24	on a date? <MOTHER:> Honey, if I told you it was a date you never would have gone. You're not getting
25	their kids. Shouldn't bring up my divorce on the first date, but I feel I can tell you anything. <LESLIE:> Uh.

Figure 7.9 Twenty-five random instances of date

Other words in the category 'narrative concerns' can be tied to emotional or physical harm, crime, illness, death, danger, or assistance (e.g. *safe*, *save*, *protect*, *hurt*, *body*, *doctor*, *police*, *dead*, *death*, *die*, *kill*, *killed*, *blood*, *help*), while *find* and *found* often (though not always) relate to the finding of evidence, the finding out of something or finding someone dead, lost, or missing. These word forms may be related to the enactment of narrative events or the creation of drama (control of viewer evaluation and emotions). They appear to be genre-related.

Take for example the key word form *blood*. This occurs sixty times across twenty-one files, predominantly series with 'supernatural' content (*Birds of Prey, Dollhouse, Fringe, Lost, Teen Wolf, The Vampire Diaries, True Blood*), crime (*Castle, Desperate Housewives, Dexter, Human Target, NCIS, The Shield, The Wire, Weeds*), or medical content (*Grey's Anatomy, House, The Big C*). Exceptions are the comedies/sitcoms *Entourage, Malcolm in the Middle*, and *Thirty Rock*, but occurrences in these episodes refer to financing a movie by *donating blood*, a comic book called *Young Blood*, and the idiomatic expression *it's in our blood*. Figure 7.10 presents twenty-five random occurrences of the remaining instances of *blood*, showing that many relate to generic aspects of the show (e.g. medical acts or findings,

#		
1	got to be other options. <ANDREA:> The blood sugar diet, the protein diet, the	Big_C
2	, he shot her. I saw her. She fell down and the blood went on the floor. <MOTHER:> Hush. It	Birds_of_Prey
3	list? No thank you Castle, little too rich for my blood. <CASTLE:> We could always make it	Castle
4	:> I was looking for a type match on the blood on Batista's collar. <LAGUERTA:> And	Dexter
5	sweet home. Is he taking me back before the blood? To a place where a boy was born?	Dexter
6	real brother. None of this foster bullshit. We're blood brothers, through birth and death.	Dexter
7	were there too. <BRIAN:> Two days, sitting in blood before they found us. You were young	Dexter
8	how we doing? <PETER:> Good, we got the blood work back. You were right, it is Marshall	Fringe
9	speaker. <WALTER:> So far so good, Olivia. Blood pressure one forty over ninety, not bad	Fringe
10	Patient presented with abdominal pain and blood in his urine. Once his workup came	Greys_Anatomy
11	right now. We'll see if you're right, check the blood. <FOREMAN:> Cameron quit?	House
12	:> It's hemorrhoids. <PATIENT:> But all that blood, that can't be right? <CUDDY:> Looks	House
13	inhibitors prevent the tumors from creating blood vessels. Without blood, the tumor	House
14	tumors from creating blood vessels. Without blood, the tumor starves. <SEAN:> That	House
15	by one of my charities. He offered to take my blood, not knowing it was strictly forbidden. My	Human_Target
16	arm in my hand and it feels like, I don't know, blood rushing to my head, making this	Human_Target
17	junk zaps the nervous system and it clots the blood. You convulse, and then you stroke.	NCIS
18	word. I mean, T-Bone's the one that spilled blood on my turf. I'm nothing if not a man of	Shield
19	boy! With no proof he spilled human blood. We go by the code.	Teen_Wolf
20	weak. <BILL:> Of course you do. I fed on your blood. You should take some vitamin B twelve	True_Blood
21	came here. <JASON:> I want some vampire blood. What time do you get off work? <PAM:	True_Blood
22	you get off work? <PAM:> You came for my blood? Yeah, you're right. You're nothing like	True_Blood
23	. <DEVON:> Ew. Shane just licked his own blood! <CHILDREN:> Ew! <CELIA:> Maybe	Weeds
24	for the fruit. Or are you just pretending it's blood, because we all know how much you	Weeds
25	we all know how much you love the taste of blood. Is that it, vampire? <SHANE:> Okay,	Weeds

Figure 7.10 Twenty-five random instances of blood, with file names

vampires feeding on blood, crime-related blood) but that some instances relate to other aspects of the narrative (e.g. line 6) or are metaphoric (e.g. line 3). Thus, the references in *Weeds* (lines 23–5) refer not to drug-related crime but to the teasing of a boy (Shane), while the instances in *Human Target* (lines 15–16) belong to dialogue about how two characters met and feel about each other, rather than dialogue about a committed crime. Nevertheless, it does appear that some of the key items in the 'narrative concerns' are indeed related to genres and the kinds of narrative happenings associated with these genres, for instance criminal acts.

As a whole, the key items in the 'narrative concerns' category show us the preoccupations of contemporary US television, both in terms of what the series (and genres) are about and in terms of what characters talk about or the activities they engage in. As the category name suggests, these items are primarily associated with the communication of the narrative.

3.3 Other Findings

There are a number of key items that cannot easily be classified into pragmatic or stylistic categories but share certain formal properties and can be categorised on that basis. More specifically, as Table 7.5

Table 7.5 Key items pointing to interrogatives and negation

Interrogatives	*Wh*-words	*what, what are, what about, what do, what happened, what are you, what are you talking, what are you talking about, what do you, what the hell, what the hell are, what the hell are you, what are you doing, what do you mean, what are you doing here, what's, what's going on, why, why are, why are you, why don't you*[†], *who*
	Interrogative fragments	*happened*[†], *am I, can I*[†], *don't you, do you mean, are you, you doing, are you doing, are you talking, you talking about, is going on*[†], *are you doing here, are you talking about, the hell are you*
Negation		*ain't, can't, don't you, why don't you*[†], *not, I'm not, I'm not a, not a, you're not*[†]
		no, you have no, you have no idea[†], *no no (no) (no) (no)*
		nothing, never

shows, a large number of key items contain *wh*-words or are interrogative fragments, while others express negation.

First, TV dialogue appears to be peppered with questions. If we assume that questions are most often addressed to others in dialogic exchanges, they again illustrate the interactive nature of TV dialogue. In two n-grams, discourse immediacy is shown by the presence of spatial deixis ([*what*] *are you doing here*). N-grams like *can I* and *why don't you* are associated with particular speech acts and could hence be classified as routine formulae. Some questions are also clearly related to expressivity, establishing conflict, hostility, or friendship or revealing characters' emotions (Bubel 2006; Bednarek 2010a, 2012a, 2014a) – as also evident from the presence of *hell* in several of these n-grams.

But questions are highly polyfunctional and are hence not simply classified as 'routine formulae', 'interaction in the here-and-now', or 'expressivity'. Research on *wh-* questions in US TV series has shown that these can fulfil the full gamut of functions, ranging from the communication of the narrative and the creation of realism to aesthetic and interpersonal effect and commercial appeal, as well as thematic messages and ideology (Bednarek 2013, 2014a). However, it is not usually questions on their own that fulfil these functions, but questions in their co-text – such as question–answer sequences.

The other category in Table 7.5 is negation. Certain n-grams with *not/no* in SydTV-Std are clearly related to expressivity, especially *you're not* and *you have no idea*, but this is not necessarily the case with all key items in this category. In general, negation can be associated with 'the contrast between the expected and the unexpected, between what is assumed to be the case and the unexpected deviation from this assumption' (Bublitz 1992: 567). Negation can thus be used to contrast, deny, or disclaim what is expected (e.g. Biber et al. 1999; Martin & White 2005). *No* can also occur as a response marker in interactive dialogue, e.g. as a reply to a question. In TV dialogue, negation can indicate 'an interpersonally loaded interaction between characters, for example, contradicting or questioning' (Bednarek 2010a: 73). Again, negation is polyfunctional.

To illustrate the complexity and multifunctionality of negation, Figure 7.11 shows twenty-five random occurrences of *no* in SydTV-Std, demonstrating that it can represent an answer to a *yes/no* question (e.g. lines 9, 16: *No, I don't like it*; *No, I just make them and sell them*), a correction (e.g. line 24: *No, I saw it* [car] *drive away* [rather than drop off the box]), a polite rejection of a gift (line 2: *Oh no! It, it looks so valuable*), surprise (line 6: *oh, no kidding*), a denial of a request (line 22: *Uh no* [in answer to a request to speak to someone]), an emotional exclamation (e.g. line 15: *She cannot know. No no no!*),

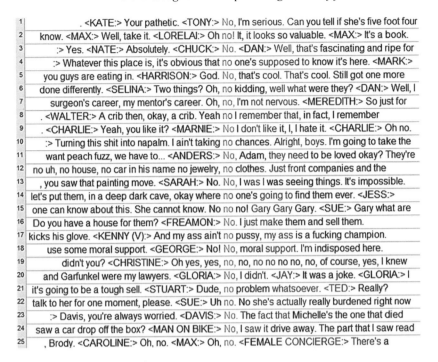

1	. <KATE:> Your pathetic. <TONY:> No, I'm serious. Can you tell if she's five foot four
2	know. <MAX:> Well, take it. <LORELAI:> Oh no! It, it looks so valuable. <MAX:> It's a book.
3	:> Yes. <NATE:> Absolutely. <CHUCK:> No. <DAN:> Well, that's fascinating and ripe for
4	:> Whatever this place is, it's obvious that no one's supposed to know it's here. <MARK:>
5	you guys are eating in. <HARRISON:> God. No, that's cool. That's cool. Still got one more
6	done differently. <SELINA:> Two things? Oh, no kidding, well what were they? <DAN:> Well, I
7	surgeon's career, my mentor's career. Oh, no, I'm not nervous. <MEREDITH:> So just for
8	. <WALTER:> A crib then, okay, a crib. Yeah no I remember that, in fact, I remember
9	. <CHARLIE:> Yeah, you like it? <MARNIE:> No I don't like it, I, I hate it. <CHARLIE:> Oh no.
10	:> Turning this shit into napalm. I ain't taking no chances. Alright, boys. I'm going to take the
11	want peach fuzz, we have to... <ANDERS:> No, Adam, they need to be loved okay? They're
12	no uh, no house, no car in his name no jewelry, no clothes. Just front companies and the
13	, you saw that painting move. <SARAH:> No. No, I was I was seeing things. It's impossible.
14	let's put them, in a deep dark cave, okay where no one's going to find them ever. <JESS:>
15	one can know about this. She cannot know. No no no! Gary Gary Gary. <SUE:> Gary what are
16	Do you have a house for them? <FREAMON:> No. I just make them and sell them.
17	kicks his glove. <KENNY (V):> And my ass ain't no pussy, my ass is a fucking champion.
18	use some moral support. <GEORGE:> No! No, moral support. I'm indisposed here.
19	didn't you? <CHRISTINE:> Oh yes, yes, no, no, no no no no, no, of course, yes, I knew
20	and Garfunkel were my lawyers. <GLORIA:> No, I didn't. <JAY:> It was a joke. <GLORIA:> I
21	it's going to be a tough sell. <STUART:> Dude, no problem whatsoever. <TED:> Really?
22	talk to her for one moment, please. <SUE:> Uh no. No she's actually really burdened right now
23	:> Davis, you're always worried. <DAVIS:> No. The fact that Michelle's the one that died
24	saw a car drop off the box? <MAN ON BIKE:> No, I saw it drive away. The part that I saw read
25	, Brody. <CAROLINE:> Oh, no. <MAX:> Oh, no. <FEMALE CONCIERGE:> There's a

Figure 7.11 Twenty-five random instances of no

conventional politeness (e.g. lines 21, 5: *no problem*; *no, that's cool*), and contrast (e.g. line 17: *And my ass ain't no pussy, my ass is a fucking champion*), to name but a few uses here. Figure 7.11 also shows that *no* may be part of multiple negation (e.g. lines 10, 17), an occurrence of the pronoun *no one* (e.g. lines 4, 14), or repeated several times within the same turn (e.g. lines 15,19).

In sum, further research is necessary to explore the typical functions of negation in TV dialogue in depth, which would also necessitate a close examination of the dialogic co-text (conversational structure, turn-taking). While such qualitative analysis is beyond the scope of this chapter, it is nevertheless a significant finding that both negation and interrogatives indeed seem to be overused linguistic structures in TV dialogue, confirming prior research based on more limited datasets.

In addition to interrogatives and negation, another result that goes beyond the pragmatic/stylistic categories in Table 7.3 has to do with lexis rather than grammar. Several key items include the word forms *talk/talking* or *tell* (Table 7.6). I have previously shown that these are important in the dramedy *Gilmore Girls* (Bednarek 2010a), but it

Table 7.6 Key items that include talk/talking *or* tell/told

talk/talking, tell	talk, talk to[†], to talk, to talk to, to talk to you, are you talking, you talking about, are you talking about, what are you talking, what are you talking about, tell, to tell, you tell, tell me, tell me what[†], to tell you, told you

appears that they are overused in TV series more generally. Space does not permit a fuller exploration here, but such key items seem to be connected to either narrative concerns (e.g. *talk to*) or expressivity (e.g. *tell me what*). Bednarek (2010a: 82ff.) includes qualitative analysis of how they are employed in *Gilmore Girls*, noting the association of *what are you talking about* with argumentative discourse or interpersonal conflict.

Finally, there are a few key items that remain unclassified because they are too polyfunctional or do not clearly fall into one of the above categories. These are provided in Table A.6 in the Appendix.

4 Variation of Key Words in Frequency and Effect Size

What I have ignored so far is that each individual key item in SydTV-Std varies in terms of raw **frequency** (how many times it occurs in SydTV-Std) and **effect size** (how much more frequently a key item occurs in SydTV-Std compared with the reference corpus). I will briefly explore this variation here with respect to key words (word forms, rather than n-grams). In addition to these variables, the key words also differ in terms of their statistical significance. However, since the p-value was set to 0.000001, all examined words are in fact highly significant and this type of variation will therefore not be investigated.

Starting with a brief look at raw frequency, the 162 key words range from 27 instances (*could've*) to 10,114 (*you*). Table 7.7 shows the twenty most and least frequent word forms in order of frequency. As expected, function words such as personal pronouns and determiners (*you, me, I'm, my, your, her, him*), *wh*-words (*what, why*), demonstratives (*this*), negation (*no, not*), prepositions (*about, for, with*), and forms of the primary verb BE (*I'm, you're*) are most frequent, but some lexical and pragmatic features are also highly frequent (e.g. *hey, god, please*). If we focus just on non-grammatical key words, we can see that frequent key words belong to all of the functional categories (expressivity, formality, etc.), although only a few are associated with narrative concerns (*help*, possibly *tell* and *talk*).

Table 7.7 Most and least frequent key words

20 most frequent key words	20 most frequent key words (excluding grammatical)[a]	20 least frequent key words
you, to, a, me, what, this, I'm, my, no, for, your, not, with, you're, about, here, her, him, hey, why	*hey, come, look, take, need, tell, man, sorry, alright, let, thank, god, guys, love, please, guy, let's, help, talk, wait*	*bar, die, save, ladies, promise, would've, lose, protect, broke, news, explain, lying, crap, lie, fault, luck, loved, sad, how'd, should've, buddy, could've*

[a] In addition to the usual function words (pronouns, articles, modal verbs, etc.), forms of the primary verb BE (*been, we're, what's, am*) and the adverb *never* are excluded here.

Table 7.8 Key words and log ratios

No. of key words with a log ratio < 1 (lowest value: 0.12: *to*)	56	Less than 2 times more common in SydTV-Std
No. of key words with a log ratio between 1.00 and 1.99	77	Between 2 and 4 times more common in SydTV-Std
No. of key words with a log ratio between 2.00 and 2.99	23	Between 4 and 8 times more common in SydTV-Std
No. of key words with a log ratio of at least 3.00 (highest value: 3.61 *protect*)	6	Between 8 and 16 times more common in SydTV-Std

The least frequent key words also belong to all of the functional categories, especially expressivity (e.g. *broke, lying, crap, fault, loved, sad*), informality (e.g. *buddy, ladies, could've, how'd*), and narrative concerns (*bar, die, save, protect*). As a whole, examination of frequency adds further information to the keyness analysis but does not seem to challenge the findings. What the results also show is that corpus linguistic analyses that focus on high-frequency items are less likely to discover key words associated with narrative concerns.

Another variation consists of the effect size (cf. Chapter 5), which can be investigated by looking at log ratios. Table 7.8 shows that the log ratios range from 0.12 (lowest value: *to*) to 3.61 (highest value: *protect*); hence there is considerable variation between key words in

Table 7.9 Highest and lowest log ratios

Log ratios	What it means	Key words
Key words with a log ratio <1	Less than two times more common in SydTV-Std than in the LSAC	*to, a, for, what, about, this, need, with, not, her, here, no, can't, you, an, take, who, been, what's, talk, night, never, we're, his, come, let's, our, let, keep, hi, Mom, why, find, away, knew, thanks, stay, guy, him, guys, us, own, look, I'm, my, hello, tonight, mind, tell, wrong, alright, head, drink, thank, you're, your*
Key words with a log ratio of 3 or more	At least eight times more common in SydTV-Std than in the LSAC	*whoa, could've, would've, Mrs, promise, protect*

terms of effect size. But in total, the majority of the key words (n=106) are at least twice as common in SydTV-Std than in the LSAC.

For comparison, Table 7.9 lists the fifty-six key words with a log ratio smaller than one as well as the six key words with a log ratio greater than three, sorted from smaller log ratios to higher ones (i.e. *Mrs, promise*, and *protect* feature the three highest log ratios).

In total, these ratios demonstrate that some key words, though statistically significant, occur only a little more often in SydTV-Std than in the LSAC, perhaps showing successful imitation of unscripted conversation with only slight overuse. On the other hand, those key words with a high log ratio demonstrate where TV dialogue diverges most from unscripted conversation, at least of the kind captured in corpora like the LSAC.

Just like range, frequency, or statistical significance, log ratios can be used for down-sampling, helping the analyst to choose which key words to focus on. Thus, while I focused on the key words with the highest range, I could also have sorted key words according to effect size, regardless of range. Instead, this section reported the variation in effect size for the respective key words (i.e. those with a particular range and p-value). Similar to the examination of raw frequency, the results do not seem to constitute radical challenges to the keyness findings, but do add useful information. Other aspects of variation (dispersion, range) are explored in Chapter 8.

5 Conclusion

This chapter used corpus linguistic techniques to examine language use in US television series. Given the fact that such series are consumed by millions of viewers worldwide, it is important to discover what this language looks like. What kind of language do L1 and LX viewers encounter by watching such series?

The chapter started out by using SydTV-Std to confirm prior assumptions that US TV dialogue artfully (but selectively) simulates naturalistic speech and features many examples of linguistic features associated with the latter. The analyses in Section 2 indeed showed linguistic similarities between US TV dialogue and unscripted spoken language, for example features that reflect the characteristics of spoken interactions (as non-monologic, spontaneous, on-line, expressive, informal, situation-bound talk). I do not intend to claim that TV dialogue is worthwhile to analyse *because* it is similar to unscripted language or that it can be used to study what goes on in spontaneous conversation. First, there are also *differences* (as seen in Section 3), and second, I entirely agree with Androutsopoulos (2012: 143) that tele-cinematic discourse is 'a legitimate area of [...] inquiry it its own right'. This makes this book a contribution to media linguistics – the study of TV dialogue *as* media language.

In Section 3, I therefore examined the words and n-grams that are key in SydTV-Std with respect to the new classification of functions of TV dialogue that was introduced in Part II (FATS). While some differences are due to principles of authentic data collection (cf. Chapter 2), many of the over-represented items can reasonably be linked to the different functions that dialogue lines fulfil for the viewers. In other words, they are ultimately associated with the participation framework of TV dialogue – its audience/overhearer/recipient design. This is supported by the fact that several of the listed key words and n-grams are also frequent in film dialogue (cf. Freddi 2009; Forchini 2012). I have also identified and examined the key words that are most and least frequent in SydTV-Std and proposed that a focus on high-frequency items may miss words related to narrative concerns. What is clear is that my approach in this chapter required breadth rather than depth of analysis and that many identified words and categories are worthy of further qualitative analysis.

Interestingly, the analyses confirmed many of the findings and assumptions from prior studies of TV dialogue where fewer series were examined. This indicates that TV dialogue exhibits a certain degree of conventionalisation. Bruti and Vignozzi (2016b) note that even British period dramas share some linguistic characteristics with contemporary US TV series. As evident from the analyses in this chapter, certain linguistic features are over-represented in many television episodes, characterising television dialogue as 'a distinctive register' (Bednarek 2011b: 62) with linguistic similarities. However, *similar* does not mean 'identical', and previous studies have indicated that there is variation between different TV series (see Chapter 2). The next chapter is dedicated to providing information on such variation. The implications of the results of this chapter for language learning and teaching will be discussed in Chapter 12, together with the results from the other chapters.

8 Key Words, Variation, and Further Insights into TV Dialogue

1 Introduction

This chapter is the second of three chapters dedicated to empirical analysis of SydTV. Again, I adopt a corpus linguistic approach with a focus on exploring variation within the corpus, on the basis of key words analysis. This chapter is therefore a companion piece to the previous chapter in that it adds further information and new analyses prompted by some of the findings. The software programmes I employ are WordSmith and GraphColl. I make use of two different versions of SydTV: the partially standardised version (SydTV-Std) and the original version (SydTV).

In the previous chapter, I focused only on key words that occur across a considerable number of files in SydTV-Std (at least twenty texts, about 30 per cent of the corpus) and did not discuss differences between key words in terms of their range and dispersion. This chapter offers such information.

2 Variation in Key Words

As Dose (2013) rightly cautions, one should not underestimate the variability between different TV series. According to her, such variation may result from differences in the linguistic awareness, skills, attitudes, and idiosyncrasies of scriptwriters and actors, as well as differences in the characters, turn-taking structure, or amount of voice-over speech. It may also result from generic differences (Al-Surmi 2012) or differences between individual narratives with their specific character relationships, settings, actions, events, and language (Bednarek 2011b). As I have put it elsewhere:

The language of a specific fictional television series will feature aspects related to the nature of fictional television series in general, but it will also include aspects particular to the genre it belongs to (e.g. we need to distinguish the language of sitcoms from the language of sci-fi [...]) as well as aspects unique to its character as a particular popular cultural artefact [...]. That is, each series will have its own linguistic profile, being a cultural artefact in its own right.   (Bednarek 2012a: 59–60).

Indeed, as summarised in Chapter 2, linguistic analysis has shown that TV series vary in a number of linguistic features such as filled pauses, discourse markers, and routine formulae. In addition, scriptwriting manuals also mention the uniqueness of particular series, with each series having 'a unique set of attributes that we should see, and that the audience expects to see, in each episode' (Smith 2009: KL 722–3). Other manuals mention the specific style of the dialogue of shows such as *The West Wing* (Venis 2013: 12), *Sports Night* (Vorhaus 2012: 89), *Buffy the Vampire Slayer*, *Dawson's Creek*, and *Gilmore Girls* (Epstein 2006: 103).

To a certain extent, the analyses of SydTV-Std so far have disguised the amount of linguistic variation in the data, because the focus was not on internal variation but rather on similarity and consistency. In the same way in which a focus on differences (which is generally more common in corpus linguistics) may 'create a "blind spot"' (Taylor 2013: 83) a focus on similarities may do so, too (Bednarek & Caple 2017a: 166). This section remedies this by investigating variation within SydTV-Std, looking specifically at word forms (rather than n-grams) that are 'key' when SydTV-Std is compared with the LSAC. As shorthand, I will hereafter simply use the term *key word* for these word forms. I have already explored variation in terms of raw frequency and effect size in Chapter 7; here I will focus on variation that is more insightful for exploring differences between the sixty-six files/episodes included in SydTV-Std, namely **range** (across how many corpus files/episodes a key word occurs) and **dispersion** (how evenly the key word is distributed). This section will briefly examine each kind of variation in turn.

2.1 Range

There is clear variation in terms of how widely distributed the SydTV-Std key words are, even after a range threshold is applied (at least twenty texts).

As Table 8.1 indicates, 23 key words occur in all 66 episodes included in the corpus (mostly function words), while 14 occur in about 30 per cent of the corpus (in 20–22 episodes). The remaining key words occur in 23–65 corpus files. The low-range key words include one marker of formality for female characters (*Mrs*), alongside key words associated with informality (e.g. *buddy*, *would've*) and

Table 8.1 Variation in range

Key words occurring in all 66 corpus files	*me, you, your, I'm, sorry, my, you're, tell, no, why, a, come, not, this, with, what, here, to, for, who, an, about, can't*
Key words occurring in 20–22 corpus files (~30 per cent)	*Mrs, protect, would've, bitch, blood, police, could've, should've, lie, husband, luck, brother, ain't, buddy*

narrative concerns (*police, blood, protect, husband, brother*), which is to be expected, since they relate to plot and genre aspects of only some episodes/TV series. The swear/taboo word form *bitch* (informality and expressivity) and the non-standard contraction *ain't* (informality) both occur in only twenty-one files. In the case of the swear/taboo word *bitch* this is likely caused by external factors like censorship: the Federal Communications Commission regulates the use of swear/ taboo words in network television but these rules do not apply to cable (Queen 2015: 210). This means that certain swear/taboo words are simply 'not allowed' in network TV, and therefore will not occur in episodes that come from such series (see www.syd-tv .com). However, it should be noted that such language-external factors do not entirely condition or determine linguistic usage – for instance, swear/taboo words that include the morpheme *fuck* do not occur in each cable TV series with the same frequency (Price 2015). What this means for linguistic research is that such external factors should be considered in the design and interpretation of television corpora, but that they do not fully explain the usage of swear/taboo words. The case of *ain't* requires further analysis, which I will undertake in Section 3.

As mentioned previously, only key words that occur in at least twenty texts or more were considered in Chapter 7 in order to exclude linguistic features that are characteristic of a particular episode or TV series rather than of TV dialogue as a language variety. Since this chapter explores variation, it is now appropriate to briefly consider those key words that occur in nineteen files or fewer. Table 8.2 shows that 359 key words occur across 1–5 episodes, 71 can be found in 6–10 episodes, and 70 are distributed across 11–19 episodes.[1]

Many of the key words with a low range consist of the names of characters (e.g. *Jess, Dewey, Harrison, Riley, Hank, Alice, Franklin*) or entities (*FBI*). Common 'Anglo' names such as *Charlie, Michael, Sue, Sam* occur across many episodes, reflecting an emphasis on Anglo-American culture. As a reminder, these names would be used

Table 8.2 Key words that occur across fewer than twenty files

Range (no. of corpus files)	No. of key words	Key words
19	7	mistake, good-bye, hospital, honestly, owe, sweetie, honest
18	7	damnit, surprise, calm, proud, private, alive, guy's
17	9	murder, cops, killing, hide, favour, respect, hurry, gift, offer
16	6	evidence, fucking, emergency, apologize, boyfriend, smell
15	8	fuck, yo, gun, cop, gay, ma'am, bullshit, kiss
14	7	cell, secret, must've, dating, club, drugs, freak
13	5	ID, gentlemen, wedding, bro, pretend
12	10	oh-oh, crime, lied, genius, might've, force, sweetheart, hiding, accident, dancing
11	11	agent, jail, arrest, asshole, why'd, bust, promised, punch, deserve, drug, guest
10	11	Charlie, detective, honor, prison, officer, apology, mm-mmm, lawyer, loser, breaking, bastard
9	11	Michael, Sue, killer, victim, patient, suspect, divorce, hero, charity, arrested, partners
8	11	cancer, bone, Sam, goddamn, goddamnit, bail, forgive, captain, corporate, basement, suicide
7	18	motherfucker, client, bones, princess, weapons, investigation, attempt, chase, trauma, weapon, trusted, inappropriate, pro, threat, dumped, roof, pm, boobs
6	20	Caroline, Max, Amy, Joy, mwa, Tony, anniversary, custody, Richard, dudes, firing, Booth, Derek, bear, stripper, pit, prom, uniform, memories, yay
5	17	Oscar, Lily, Todd, George, last-minute, uh-uh, wheelchair, HR, heroes, kidnapped, coach, revenge, couldn't've, murdered, fingerprints, secrets, promises
4	29	cupcake, FBI, Olivia, autopsy, Hank, Harris, president, Walter, Reese, therapist, cupcakes, Dean, hallucinating, backup, vampire, tumor, terrorist, elevator, emails, Nick, Davis, coma, Franklin, Walt, porn, assets, motive, agents, pussy

(continued)

Table 8.2 (cont.)

Range (no. of corpus files)	No. of key words	Key words
3	38	*Jake, Vince, senator, reverend, Jess, Riley, firm, Sophie, Dana, Marshall, vice-president, prisoner, Dewey, Victoria, Harrison, lieutenant, nanny, poisoned, anger, morgue, Martha, self-help, DVD, Ted, retard, biopsy, Blake, lung, Tim, Iraq, blowjob, bros, Sarah, Alice, Starbucks, robbery, Angela, double-check*
2	77	N/A [too many to list]
1	198	N/A [too many to list]

either as terms of address (to address these characters) or referentially (to talk about these characters), but not as speaker names (tagged and excluded by the software). There are also some potential terms of address (*honor, sweetheart, sweetie, ma'am*), and several identity labels (e.g. *killer, patient, vampire*), often professional roles (e.g. *cop[s], agent[s], detective, president, senator, reverend, vice-president, nanny, lieutenant, therapist, coach*). All of these key words fulfil functions relating to the communication of the narrative, including anchorage of the characters as well as establishment of social character traits and relationships between characters. Identity labels are also genre-related – for example, twenty of twenty-three instances of *vampire* come from the episodes from the fantasy/supernatural series *True Blood* and *Vampire Diaries*.

Further, several of the key words seem to be associated with crime or violence and realise generic aspects – in addition to *FBI, cop(s), agent(s), detective, killer*, this appears to be the case for many others, including *murder, murdered, evidence, killing, gun, terrorist, fingerprints, kidnapped, investigation, victim, suspect*. Others are related to medicine (e.g. *morgue, biopsy, lung, coma, hospital, cancer, tumor, bone*). The low range of these words reflects the generic diversity of SydTV in that not all episodes come from crime or medical dramas.

Some swear/taboo words also have a low distribution (e.g. *damnit, fucking, bullshit, fuck, asshole, motherfucker, goddamn, goddamnit*),[2] which is also the case for some informal variants (*yo, bro, bros*). This indicates that there is internal variation with respect to non-standard language, which is partially the result of language-external factors (especially US rules about swear/taboo words, as mentioned above).

But the presence of such words may also have to do with the kinds of characters that are part of the narrative world. For example, *yo* often (though not exclusively) gets used by non-European American characters (e.g. African American, Puerto Rican American) or young characters, and in one episode it actually stands for Spanish 'I'.

Words such as *mistake, surprise, apologize, kiss, freak, lied, genius, promised, deserve, apology, loser, forgive,* and *mwa* are likely associated with expressivity (at least in some usages), while other key words could be the result of different transcription conventions in the LSAC (e.g. *oh-oh*). The remainder of the low-range key words do not fall neatly in one category, and concordancing would be necessary to show how they are used in a variety of different ways across and within episodes. As there are too many key words to analyse all, I will briefly illustrate this point with four randomly selected words with different distributions across the corpus: *gay* (range = 15), *divorce* (r = 9), *penthouse* (r = 2), and *cup-pie* (r = 1).

Interestingly, the word *gay* occurs fifty-one times in fifteen different episodes. Many occurrences are tied to the communication of the narrative, as they relate to particular storylines. For example, in the *Desperate Housewives* episode, one storyline is related to reactions towards a son's coming out as gay in the previous episode – which also creates continuity. In *Entourage*, part of the episode revolves around one of the male protagonists (actor Vince) being asked by the director to perform oral sex on another male actor in a film scene. This is actually a 'test' to see if he has Vince's trust. In the *Girls* episode, one of the female characters (Hannah) finds out that her ex-boyfriend from college is now in a same-sex relationship, while the episode from *It's Always Sunny in Philadelphia* features a storyline where the main characters accidentally turn their pub into a gay bar. These storylines require further intratextual analysis with regards to the discourses and ideologies they represent, which is beyond the scope of this chapter. However, at least two of these episodes (*Entourage, It's Always Sunny in Philadelphia*) feature straight male characters' anxieties about (male) gay sexuality. The remaining instances of the word *gay* in the corpus are too varied to allow generalisation, except to note that they are all references to sexuality/queerness rather than used as a derogatory adjective (i.e. negatively evaluating an entity or behaviour as uncool, undesirable, nonnormative, or stupid, as in *that's so gay*; see Armstrong 1997; Woolley 2013). To be clear, this does not mean that being gay is seen as unproblematic by all characters in SydTV or that it is normalised in this corpus. Further, there are instances of derogatory *fag(s)*, *faggot*, and *dyke* in SydTV, representing characters' (not TV creators') homophobic attitudes in certain episodes.

One could argue that sexual identity and sexual behaviour is a topic well suited to the creation of drama and comedy, as 'this subject obviously carries a lot of useful tension with it' (Smith 2009: KL 669–70). But these references also show the anchoring of TV narratives in contemporary US life, where we can find different degrees of acceptance, insecurity, and rejection of gay sexuality and the LGBTQI community. By using the explicit identity label *gay*, this sexual identity becomes less invisible; however, in order to analyse the ideological nature of such representation one would need to examine in depth how the word is used in each episode. It has been pointed out that gayness is often stereotypically portrayed as white, middle-class, feminised, promiscuous (Lopez & Bucholtz 2017). In addition, Smith (2009: KL 666–70) argues that sitcoms more often include gay characters as supporting or visiting rather than main characters. There are TV series that do centre on LGBTQI protagonists, such as *The L Word* or *Will & Grace*, but they can still feature stereotypes such as the camp gay man (e.g. Baker 2005).

Moving on, the key word *divorce* occurs across nine episodes but is most frequent in *The Good Wife* – a legal drama where the majority of instances refer to a divorce case that the characters are involved in. In the crime dramedy *Castle* and in the action drama *Human Target* the occurrences refer to an intended future divorce, in *Human Target* explaining why a character has to fear for her life (communication of narrative causality). In the episodes from the other TV series, characters often reference their own (past) divorce, hence revealing something about the character's biography (*Enlightened, Parks and Recreation, Anger Management, The New Adventures of Old Christine*). In *The New Adventures of Old Christine*, the references also explain the nature of the relationship between two of the characters (example (1)). This is another instance where a pilot episode mentions happenings that occurred before the time represented on screen, for the benefit of viewers (cf. Chapter 3).

(1)

MATTHEW: You and Richard have a weird **divorce**.
CHRISTINE: It's not weird, it's great. My **divorce** is better than most people's marriages. We get along, we spend time together as a family. Nothing's really changed.   (SydTV-Std, *The New Adventures of Old Christine*)

Three instances involve younger characters. In *Gilmore Girls*, the behaviour of one of the teenage characters in the episode becomes

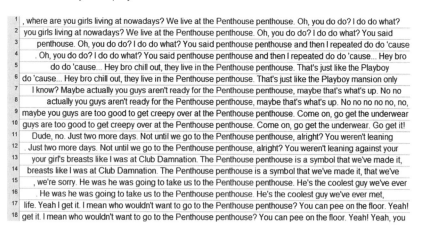

1	, where are you girls living at nowadays? We live at the Penthouse penthouse. Oh, you do do? I do do what?
2	you girls living at nowadays? We live at the Penthouse penthouse. Oh, you do do? I do do what? You said
3	penthouse. Oh, you do do? I do do what? You said penthouse penthouse and then I repeated do do 'cause
4	. Oh, you do do? I do do what? You said penthouse penthouse and then I repeated do do 'cause... Hey bro
5	do do 'cause... Hey bro chill out, they live in the Penthouse penthouse. That's just like the Playboy
6	do 'cause... Hey bro chill out, they live in the Penthouse penthouse. That's just like the Playboy mansion only
7	I know? Maybe actually you guys aren't ready for the Penthouse penthouse, maybe that's what's up. No no
8	actually you guys aren't ready for the Penthouse penthouse, maybe that's what's up. No no no no no, no,
9	maybe you guys are too good to get creepy over at the Penthouse penthouse. Come on, go get the underwear
10	guys are too good to get creepy over at the Penthouse penthouse. Come on, go get the underwear. Go get it!
11	Dude, no. Just two more days. Not until we go to the Penthouse penthouse, alright? You weren't leaning
12	. Just two more days. Not until we go to the Penthouse penthouse, alright? You weren't leaning against your
13	your girl's breasts like I was at Club Damnation. The Penthouse penthouse is a symbol that we've made it,
14	breasts like I was at Club Damnation. The Penthouse penthouse is a symbol that we've made it, that we've
15	, we're sorry. He was he was going to take us to the Penthouse penthouse. He's the coolest guy we've ever
16	. He was he was going to take us to the Penthouse penthouse. He's the coolest guy we've ever met,
17	life. Yeah I get it. I mean who wouldn't want to go to the Penthouse penthouse? You can pee on the floor. Yeah!
18	get it. I mean who wouldn't want to go to the Penthouse penthouse? You can pee on the floor. Yeah! Yeah, you

Figure 8.1 Penthouse penthouse *in* Workaholics

more understandable by references to her parents' divorce 'getting very ugly' and being discussed publicly in the news. In *The Big C*, the teenage son asks his parents if they are getting a divorce, because his father is staying elsewhere. Instances of *divorce*, then, fulfil various functions relating to the communication of the narrative, such as communication of narrative causality, character biographies, and relationships between characters. These occurrences also show the embedding of TV narratives in contemporary US culture where divorce is a fact of life.

Moving on, most of the occurrences of *penthouse* (19/20) occur in the episode from *Workaholics*, where the twenty-something male protagonists are introduced to three young women who 'live at the Penthouse penthouse' (as another character explains: 'just like the Playboy mansion only this time it's much more doper'). The name itself is an example of exploiting the resources of language for humorous effect. The location is then referenced several times throughout the episode – the promise of being taken along to the penthouse a major motivation for the characters' particular behaviour in that episode, which involves them befriending a potential paedophile (simultaneously establishing narrative causality and the young men's character traits). In total, eighteen occurrences of *penthouse* are instances of *Penthouse penthouse* (Figure 8.1). This key word is thus strongly associated with only one episode where it appears to be used to make fun of the male characters as well as the real-life Playboy Mansion and its surrounding culture (possibly even critiquing it). It fulfils functions relating to the communication of the narrative (narrative causality;

character traits), to aesthetic and interpersonal effect and commercial appeal (humour), and, possibly, to thematic messages and ideology (making fun of/critiquing the 'Playboy Mansion' culture).

Finally, the word *cup-pie* only occurs in one episode, namely *Pushing Daisies*, where it relates to a character's invention of a particular type of pie. In this series one of the characters (Ned) is a pie maker and owns a restaurant called *The Pie Hole*. The episode also features twenty-one instances of *pie*. The voice-over narrator refers to the character as *the pie maker* (four instances), while the characters themselves reference *the Pie Hole* (three instances), and other references to pie also occur throughout the episode. Perhaps there is an argument for saying that the choice of pie is another example of the cultural anchoring of TV series – pie being a popular and familiar type of food in the United States. The use of *cup-pie* is tied to this episode's plot, and, as a new word formation, is also an instance of exploitation of the resources of language (linguistic innovation – see Chapter 9).

Summing up Section 2.1, key words with a range below 30 per cent can be traced back to generic elements (e.g. crime, medicine, fantasy), anchor TV narratives in contemporary US life (creating a shared community with viewers), and are sometimes explicable by the socio-historical context of US television production (rules about swear/taboo words). Some of the key words fulfil functions relating to thematic messages and ideology (reflecting, reinforcing, or critiquing cultural ideologies), while others create humour. The majority of key words, however, appear to be associated with the communication of the narrative. This shows that lowering the range threshold for key words analysis may be fruitful when the research interest is in storylines and characters. In other words, researchers can use these key words to discover the 'aboutness' (Scott & Tribble 2006: 55) of particular narratives or genres.

2.2 Dispersion

While analysis of range tells us about the distribution of key words across corpus files, it does not tell us how evenly the key words are dispersed. Thus, the range analysis simply shows in how many texts in a corpus a key word occurs, but not whether the key word occurs evenly across the corpus or whether it clusters in particular sections. Such variation is automatically measured by WordSmith through the dispersion value in WordList. The closer the value is to 1, the more uniform the dispersion (Chapter 5 offers further explanation). To investigate this variation, I used Excel 2016 to automatically match the items in the key words list with the dispersion value of the same items in WordList

Table 8.3 Number of key words according to dispersion values

Key words (range ≥ 18 files; total number = 176)	
No. of key words with a value between 0.9 and 1	58
No. of key words with a value between 0.8 and 0.9	71
No. of key words with a value between 0.7 and 0.8	37
No. of key words with a value between 0.6 and 0.7	9
No. of key words with a value between 0.5 and 0.6	1

(using the VLOOKUP function). I chose to relax the range threshold slightly and included all key words that occur across at least eighteen files (27 per cent), since this added only fourteen items.

As Table 8.3 shows, the vast majority of the 176 key words have a high WordList dispersion value: 129 key words have a value higher than 0.8, with 58 of these having a value between 0.9 and 1. Further, there are only ten key words with a value between 0.5 and 0.7, and no key words with any values lower than 0.5.

A minimum value of at least 0.8 is a conservative cut-off applied to ensure a wide distribution of words (Biber et al. 2016: 441). Consequently, Table 8.4 lists the forty-seven key words that have a WordList dispersion value lower than 0.8. Note, for instance, that the non-standard contraction *ain't* has a fairly low value (between 0.6 and 0.7).

Table 8.4 Key words with a WordList dispersion value lower than 0.8

Key words with a dispersion value lower than 0.8	0.7–0.8	*Mr, Sir, killed, sex, dude, ass, alone, bitch, body, blood, case, honey, should've, shut, shot, luck, brother, crap, kid, party, die, eyes, knows, lose, men, explain, damnit, surprise, calm, proud, good-bye, hospital, owe, private, alive, sweetie, honest*
	0.6–0.7	*Mrs, doctor, police, boys, husband, ain't, bar, drink, mistake*
	0.5–0.6	*Ladies*

Only twelve of the forty-seven key words listed in Table 8.4 have a **Concord** dispersion value lower than 0.8: *alive, calm, crap, drink, good-bye, hospital, luck, mistake, private, proud, should've,* and *surprise*. This suggests that the remainder are relatively evenly dispersed *in the files in which they appear* (see Chapter 5 on the difference

Table 8.5 Information on three low-dispersion key words

Key word	Raw frequency	Files with most instances	Occurrences in the remaining files
mistake	41	*Gilmore Girls* (10, ~ 24%), *Dollhouse* (5 ~12%), *Enlightened* (4 ~ 10%)	between 1 and 3 instances per file
drink	73	*My Name Is Earl* (19, ~ 26%), *How I Met Your Mother* (5, ~ 7%)	between 1 and 3 instances per file
surprise	36	*The Big Bang Theory* (6 ~ 17%) and *Pushing Daisies* (5, ~ 14%)	between 1 and 3 instances per file

between the WordList and the Concord dispersion value). Of these twelve word forms, three were randomly selected for further analysis: *mistake* (raw f = 41; r = 19; WordList dispersion = 0.680; Concord dispersion = 0.657), *drink* (raw f = 73; r = 31; WordList dispersion = 0.654; Concord dispersion = 0.711), and *surprise* (raw f = 36; r = 18; WordList dispersion = 0.755; Concord dispersion = 0.745).

Table 8.5 provides more detailed information for these three low-dispersion key words, showing that 24 per cent of all occurrences of *mistake* occur in the episode from *Gilmore Girls*, 26 per cent of all instances of *drink* occur in the episode from *My Name Is Earl*, and 17 per cent of all occurrences of *surprise* can be found in the episode from *The Big Bang Theory*.

Table 8.6 shows the concordance plots for these three words in these episodes, indicating that the respective word form is clustered in particular scenes in *Gilmore Girls* and *My Name Is Earl*, while it is more dispersed across the narrative in *The Big Bang Theory*.

Table 8.6 Concordance plots of the three key words in the episodes with the most occurrences

Concordancing provides further insight into how these words are used in each episode. If we examine first the use of *mistake* in the *Gilmore Girls* episode, nine of the ten instances occur in one conversation, between one of the main characters, Lorelai, and her mother Emily. The exchange in example (2) is about Lorelai kissing her daughter Rory's teacher at Parents' Day and being observed doing so:

(2)

EMILY: The entire school is talking about it. And what do I say, how do I defend this?

LORELAI: Uh it was a **mistake**.

EMILY: A **mistake**? A **mistake**? Is that what you call it, a **mistake**?

LORELAI: Well I tried to call it Al but it would only answer to **mistake**.

EMILY: A **mistake** is when you throw out your credit card bill. A **mistake** is when you forget to RSVP to a dinner party. A **mistake** is when the gardeners miss trash day and the barrels are full for a week. This my girl, was not a **mistake**! Do you even know this man?   (SydTV-Std, *Gilmore Girls*)

This key word is thus crucially associated with a storyline of that particular episode, while also being associated with an *ongoing* story arc in other episodes of season 1, namely the relationship between Lorelai and Rory's teacher Max. It is not dispersed within the particular episode, as it primarily occurs in one scene. Its use also contributes to characterisation, contrasting Lorelai's attempt at a joke with her mother's wholesale rejection of the label *mistake* for what she sees as Lorelai's indefensible behaviour. The conversation occurs at the beginning of a more extended, emotional argument, and the conflict also constructs drama. In its co-text, the key word *mistake* hence contributes to each individual character's personality, while also construing their difficult relationship. The latter is related to a major continuing storyline of the series as a whole: *Gilmore Girls* is a series that 'gains its narrative momentum from intergenerational bonding and conflict' (Woods 2008: 127). In addition, Lorelai's joke *I tried to call it Al but it would only answer to mistake* exploits the resources of language (as already discussed in Chapter 4).

We can compare this with the use of *surprise* in *The Big Bang Theory*. As in *Gilmore Girls*, the word relates to a storyline of the particular episode, namely the throwing of a surprise birthday party for one of the main characters, Leonard. In the case of *The Big Bang Theory*, the word occurs in various parts of the episode (as indicated in the concordance plot), rather than in only one scene. Each instance is listed here as a bullet point:

- LEONARD: [...] I mean, when I was little I'd think maybe my parents would change their mind, and **surprise** me with a party [...]
- PENNY: Okay, here's the deal, we are going to throw Leonard a kick-ass **surprise** party for his birthday on Saturday.
- HOWARD: No, listen, see we're throwing my friend a **surprise** party and I'm supposed to keep him out of his apartment for two hours.
- PENNY: You have to, we all have to be there at the same time to yell **surprise**!
- LEONARD: You know, before you got all swollen up, I actually thought you were trying to keep me out of the apartment so you could throw me a **surprise** party.
- RAJ: [...] Dude! Everybody left an hour ago! **Surprise**! [...]

Overall, the word is primarily related to different aspects of this storyline, although in the wider co-text of the first instance viewers acquire personal background information about Leonard, which motivates Penny to organise the surprise party:

(3)

LEONARD: I don't celebrate my birthday.
PENNY: Shut up, yeah you do.
LEONARD: No, it's no big deal, it's just the way I was raised. My parents focused on celebrating achievements, and being expelled from a birth canal was not considered one of them.
          [Several turns]
PENNY: So you've really never had a birthday party?
LEONARD: No. But it was okay. I mean, when I was little I'd think maybe my parents would change their mind, and **surprise** me with a party.   (SydTV-Std, *The Big Bang Theory*)

The difficult relationship between Leonard and his parents (his mother) is also a recurring storyline of the sitcom as a whole, but it is not as major as in the case of *Gilmore Girls*, and Leonard's mother does not appear as a character in this particular episode.

Finally, an examination of all occurrences of *drink* in *My Name Is Earl* shows that eighteen of nineteen instances occur in one scene, where the protagonist Earl tells the backstory of how he came to marry his ex-wife Joy. Example (4) shows how Joy's girlfriends proceeded to get Earl extremely drunk in a bar before introducing him to (a pregnant) Joy. I have added relevant non-linguistic information.

(4)

EARL (V):   There's only one way to get a guy like me ready to marry a pregnant woman.
[Flashback: The camera shows us two women, as we hear a crowd chanting 'Drink, drink, drink, drink, drink, drink . . .', followed by a shot of Earl lying on his back, the contents from two different bottles being poured in his mouth by the two women. The chanting continues in the background, as the camera now shows us Earl's brother Randy chanting in the foreground, with two other men in the frame also visibly chanting, while the mouths of two women in the frame cannot be seen. The chanting of the three men, including Randy, has been transcribed as representative of the crowd chanting.][3]

RANDY: Drink, drink, drink, drink, drink, drink.
MAN 1:   Drink, drink, drink, drink, drink, drink.
MAN 2:   Drink, drink, drink, drink, drink, drink.
[Further shots of the women and Joy, with crowd chanting audible, indicating time passing, before the crowd chanting fades and the camera shows us Earl again.]

EARL: [very slurred] You girls are great. You're, girls are great. Wait what were we, what were we talking about?
FRIEND 1:   I think he's ready.
FRIEND 2:   Boo, if you think we're great, you're going to love our friend Joy.
EARL: Joy huh? She sounds great.   (SydTV-Std, *My Name Is Earl*)

In addition to providing background information on how Earl came to marry Joy, the scene also constructs ideological representations of masculinity/femininity and class, while simultaneously revealing personality traits/trait characteristics (e.g. past Earl liking to drink, being not very bright). The joint chorus-like repetition of *drink* can also be considered as an attempt to represent a conversational routine, expected of rowdy crowds in certain situational contexts. In the case of *My Name Is Earl* then, the scene with the key word *drink* communicates narrative causality. It is another example of a scene that provides viewers with information on events preceding the usual time period of the televisual narrative (see Chapter 3). At the same time, it contributes to characterisation, reinforces ideological expectations about a particular kind of masculinity, and adds to the creation of realism by using a conversational routine. Arguably, the scene is also humorous.

This brief examination showcases both similarities and differences in the 'overuse' of particular key words in one episode. In sum, it appears that those key words that have most occurrences in *one* episode do provide insights into the functions of TV dialogue, even if they are clearly related to the particularities of the respective episode. As a reminder, these three key words still do occur in many SydTV files, even if their overuse in a particular episode most likely contributed significantly to their identification as 'key'.

Summing up the discussion so far, Section 2.1 has focused on variation in terms of range, identifying the key words with most and least range. Section 2.2 moved on to analysing variation with respect to dispersion. It detected how many key words have a low dispersion and examined three low-dispersion key words in more detail. Together, these analyses made visible the 'blind spot' created by a focus on similarity and consistency in Chapter 7. In addition, they demonstrated that key words with a low range and low dispersion value are mainly associated with plot development and characterisation, i.e. communication of the relevant narrative.

Together, Sections 2.1 and 2.2 also revealed that the key word *ain't* is towards the lower end of the range threshold, occurring across twenty-one episodes, with a (WordList) dispersion value between 0.6 and 0.7. This word form is worth examining in further detail, since it is not only a clear instance of non-standard language use but also a socially stigmatised feature of American English. The next section is therefore dedicated to a brief case study of *ain't*.

3 A Case Study of the Non-Standard Contraction *Ain't*

Although *ain't* is one of the 'shibboleths of nonstandard usage' (Wolfram & Schilling-Estes 2006: 336), a social stereotype that is 'widely recognized as "bad grammar"' (Wolfram & Schilling-Estes 2006: 186), it is in fact used in a wide variety of American English vernacular dialects, including but not limited to African American Vernacular English (AAVE) (Wolfram & Schilling-Estes 2006: 17). Curzan (2014: 31) notes:

Criticism of *ain't* has been so pervasive and effective that despite the word's widespread use in many nonstandard varieties of American English, as well as in the colloquial speech of many standard American English speakers, many speakers of American English (nonstandard and standard) see the word as improper and the speakers who use it as violating fundamental principles or laws of English.

In my interviews with five Hollywood scriptwriters (see Chapters 6 and 10) I asked them what type of character would use *ain't*. Their responses (e.g. 'blue-collar', 'working class', 'less-educated', 'lower class', 'stupid/dumb') indicate that they associate the use of this non-standard contraction with aspects of education or class rather than ethnicity.

In another study (Bednarek in press a) I used SydTV to compare *ain't* with five other variants: [In], *gonna, wanna, gotta, 'cause*. The latter forms are colloquial variants of *going to, want to, got to*, and *because*, while [In] refers to the use of the alveolar form [n] at the end of words ending in <ing> (e.g. *goin', fuckin', somethin'*). This non-standard variant contrasts with the standard velar [ŋ] and is associated with AAVE as well as other varieties of English (Green 2002: 122). Although almost all speakers sometimes use this pronunciation (Queen 2015: 35) and this variant is predominant in some Southern American dialects (Finegan 2004: 26), it carries social stigma (Wolfram & Schilling-Estes 2006: 184).

Queen (2015: 39–40) summarises research that suggests that [In] signals social meanings such as 'masculine', 'informal', and 'friendly' as well as having an association with Western and Southern American English, whereas [Ing] signals 'articulate' and 'educated'. [In] is also used more in spoken language, in more informal, private, local, and unplanned situations, whereas [Ing] is more common in written language, in more formal, global, planned, and public contexts (Queen 2015: 88). In the US daytime television drama *Days of Our Lives*, the [In] variant does not have the same negative associations with education or social background as more stigmatised forms like *ain't* (Queen 2012). More recently, Queen has argued that [In] 'is especially prevalent in the narrative media among characters who are supposed to be southern or western, particularly characters who are also in Westerns (as a film/television genre)' (Queen 2015: 52–3). At the same time, Queen shows how the relative frequencies with which characters use the [Ing] or [In] variant map onto differences in personality, general orientation, and sexual orientation (Queen 2015: 166).

My comparison of these six variants in SydTV suggested that *gonna* is the most important: it is the most distributed (reaching almost 100 per cent) and most frequent; and it occurs almost nine times more frequently and has a wider range than its variant *going to*. *Wanna* is not as frequent, but has the second highest range, and occurs almost four times more frequently and has a wider range than its variant *want to*. The forms [In], *gotta*, and *'cause* are also fairly common (especially [In]) and occur in 85 per cent to 88 per cent of the corpus; however, they are less frequent and less widely distributed than their alternatives ([Ing], *want to, has/have to*).[4]

In contrast, *ain't* is the most stigmatised of the six forms: it has a lower frequency and a much lower range than the other variants, and its range and frequency are also lower than that of the spoken 'standard' variant *isn't*. It is similar in frequency to the written 'standard' variant *is not*, which reflects the fact that the dialogue imitates informal and spoken rather than formal and written American speech. The study also showed that *ain't* is over-represented in SydTV when compared with both COCA/S and SOAP, showing that TV series accept non-standard language more than more traditional types of media, where standard language ideology dominates and deviation from the standard is not accepted or is seen as a threat (e.g. Jaworski 2007: 272). Interestingly, *ain't* is most frequent in the fiction section of COCA (Szmrecsanyi & Anderwald 2018).

For this chapter, I undertook a new follow-up study of the use of *ain't* in SydTV (the original, non-standardised version). First of all, it is useful to examine not just the range of *ain't* across corpus files, but also its variation in frequency. Thus, *ain't* occurs once in the episodes from *Baby Daddy, Bones, Castle, Entourage, Jericho, Lost, My Name Is Earl, NCIS, Nurse Jackie, Southland,* and *Tru Calling*; twice in the episodes from *Breaking Bad, Dexter,* and *Prison Break*; three times in the episodes from *Human Target* and *Mike & Molly*; four times in the *Weeds* episode; and six times in the episodes from *Eastbound & Down, Pushing Daisies,* and *The Shield*. But the most instances occur in the episodes from *True Blood* (raw frequency = 16) and *The Wire* (raw frequency = 31), which are series that feature African American and white American characters from Louisiana (southern) and Baltimore (mid-Atlantic), respectively.

In order to find out more about its usage in those episodes and in SydTV more generally, I undertook collocation analysis. I used the MI3 statistic (Daille 1995) with the default cut-off of 9, a span of five words on each side of the node (5L:5R), and a minimum frequency threshold of 2. Figure 8.2 shows a GraphColl visualisation of the collocates of *ain't*. Tagged character names such as <chuck> are included as collocates (used to identify speakers).

While I will not comment on all collocates here, it is interesting that *ain't* appears to collocate with other non-standard variants (e.g. *til, y'all, gonna*), including word forms with [In] (*talkin', nothin', comin'*), and swear/taboo words (*ass, shit, motherfucker, fucked*). There are also indications of multiple negation (the collocates *no, nobody, nowhere, nothin'*) – 'one of the best-known features of "nonstandard" syntax, and certainly one of the most stigmatized ones' (Anderwald 2012: 301).[5] Both *ain't* and multiple negation are social stereotypes; that is, speakers are consciously aware of these features and they are associated with value judgments (Wolfram & Schilling Estes 2006: 187). Concordancing was necessary to confirm that there is indeed an association of *ain't* with multiple negation:

A WordSmith search for **n't* with the right-hand context words *no, nobody, nowhere, none* or *nothin(g)* (up to R5) produced thirty-nine

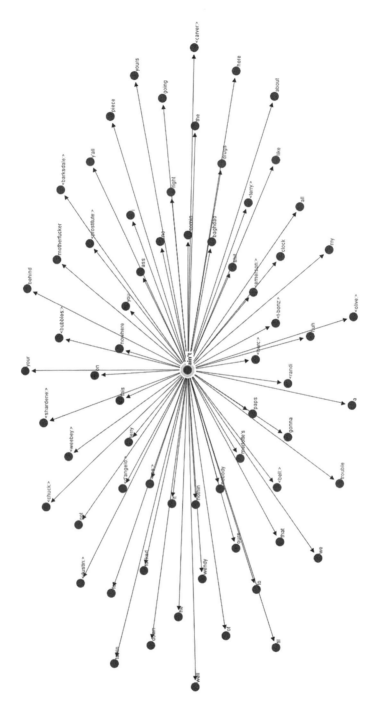

Figure 8.2 Collocates of ain't in SydTV (MI3, 5:5, min f = 2; stat >= 9 [default])

1	is a dick-wagging contest over a piece of ass? <T-BONZ:> This ain't about no piece of ass. This is about two millic
2	than the drugs, it's the money that matters. <D'ANGELO:> I ain't fucked nobody else if that's what you thinkin'..
3	. Let's get out of here before you get us both killed. <JASON:> I ain't goin' nowhere until I get what I came for. <AM
4	a prosthetic hand. John painted her nails different colors, but it ain't goin' nowhere. <LAGUERTA:> Except she w;
5	<BOOTH:> Well, this'll only take a minute. Uh, Mr Jessup, he, he ain't going nowhere. <MARTIN:> What's this abou!
6	:> Look I don't want any trouble, okay? <PROPOSITION JOE:> Ain't gonna be no trouble over no ball. <BARKSD/
7	gonna have to do something about your daughter. <TARA:> You ain't gonna do nothin' for me. <MISS JEANETTE:>
8	Billy first, but he turned it down. <VINCENT:> Yeah? <MAN:> He ain't gonna soft-soap nobody. Billy's a genius brot!
9	a buck forty I didn't even know was there. <WEEBEY:> Y'all ain't got no charge, right? <HERC:> No fucker we
10	, I'm thinkin' about gettin' clean, again. I was thinkin', you know, I ain't got no other place to go, maybe, that's wrong,
11	three months old. <WOMAN:> Mm-mmm, put this back. She ain't got no teeth, put it back. <RILEY:> So the first
12	I'm talkin' about? <BELL:> Blow Proposition Joe's mind. He ain't got nobody ballin' like this. <BARKSDALE:> I
13	:> Yo I said I don't wanna play. <D'ANGELO:> And you ain't gotta do nothin'. I heard you. Take it. Hurry up.
14	We can use the Lieutenant's office. <RAE:> No. <BUBBLES:> I ain't, I didn't asked for nothin'. Oh! What's up, Tash
15	know, he's, he's Linc. <LINCOLN:> I don't care who the guy is. I ain't killin' no one. <MAN 2:> I must've missed the
16	. You have the right to have an attorney present. <T-BONZ:> This ain't no police station, man. What's going on, Mac!
17	career, and Powers kicks his ass here. <KENNY (V):> And my ass ain't no pussy, my ass is a fuckin' champion. <TE/
18	they see this cocksuckin' faggot out in the sunshine? Like it ain't no thing to take my shit? <STOLTZ:> Kid's ev
19	<EARL:> That might upset the people behind us. <JOY:> There ain't nobody behind us. <EARL (V):> If tellin' Jessi
20	to go! <CHUCK:> Hello? <EMERSON:> He ain't down here! Ain't nobody down here! We been walking around
21	up before noon. Reveille! <LEMONHEAD:> T-Bonz! <KERN:> Ain't nobody else comin' out of there. Told you he \
22	your Paps. Paps has a lady connotation. And second of all, this ain't none of your business. <OLIVE:> Oh, yuck! S
23	that side of you and she will open up like a flower 'cause there ain't nothin' sexier in the world than a secure man I
24	. <ARLENE:> This ain't Baghdad, Terry. It's Merlotte's, okay? Ain't nothing anybody coulda done. <TERRY:> I'm
25	What are you doing? <ROYCE:> Turning this shit into napalm. I ain't takin' no chances. Alright, boys. I'm gonna tak
26	for this thing to go to trial I'll make it go away. <RONDELL:> I can't take no chances, Vic! <VIC:> The biggest ch
27	use the Lieutenant's office. <RAE:> No. <BUBBLES:> I ain't, I didn't asked for nothin'. Oh! What's up, Tasha? Yo
28	the world of light! <TERRY:> I froze up. I let everybody down. I didn't do nothin'. <ARLENE:> This ain't Baghdad,
29	computer skills, new technologies. <FRANKLIN:> Uncle Sam didn't teach me nothin' but cadence and kill. <MA!
30	mind. <WOMAN 2:> So bein' a Doll, you do whatever, and you don't gotta remember nothing, or study, or pay ren!
31	be okay. Your sister's gonna be alright. <LEMONHEAD:> I don't hear nothin'. <VIC:> Assholes like these don'
32	:> Only temporarily. Still working on that. <EMERSON:> This don't look like no pop-up book I had as a child. <C
33	the head than a hog is in the butt. <WAYNE:> Fuckin' a vampire don't make you no expert. <ROYCE:> You're cont;
34	tips? <SHARDENE:> Tips, drinks. You know, I'm just a B girl. I don't mess with nothin' beyond that. Some of the g
35	, Rondell, and that's who's giving you protection. <RONDELL:> I don't need no protection. <ACEVEDA:> Even if w
36	you, or me do. <WALLACE:> I just don't wanna play. I just don't wanna play no more. Alright? I was thinkin' a!
37	:> And if we're right, that means you got stabbed for a reason, it wasn't no carjacking. <BATISTA:> How did he knc
38	in my bar. <ROYCE:> Weren't for little Stackhouse bitch, there wouldn't be no vampires coming around here at all

Figure 8.3 Multiple negation in SydTV

occurrences of multiple negation across thirteen corpus files. Figure 8.3 shows that the vast majority of these include *ain't* (25), compared with *don't* (8), *didn't* (3), *can't*, *wasn't*, and *wouldn't* (1 each) – which is all the more significant considering that all of these word forms have higher raw frequencies in SydTV than *ain't*, which occurs only ninety-two times. This SydTV association of *ain't* with multiple negation seems to conform to usage in unscripted English (Queen 2015: 234). Negative inversion (Green 2002: 78–80) is also present, e.g. in line 20 (*ain't nobody down here*). Additionally, the concordance lines confirm the co-occurrence of *ain't* with other non-standard features such as slang (e.g. line 8: *soft-soap*; line 12: *ballin '*) and swear/taboo words (e.g. line 1: *piece of ass*; line 17: *pussy*; line 18: *shit*).

As explained in Chapter 2, conventionalised indexicalised meanings become attached to bundles of linguistic features, which can then be drawn upon in the narrative mass media to construct type and trait characteristics. While a corpus linguistic investigation will not detect pronunciation variants unless they have been transcribed, the analysis of *ain't* shows that collocation analysis may at least point to interesting packages that are used and thus could be a useful way of combining corpus linguistics with sociolinguistic and stylistic research into indexicality, stereotyping, and characterisation.

Returning briefly to the collocates shown in Figure 8.2, the collocates *drugs* and <*prostitute*> indicate that there might be an association with particular social groups, while the presence of character names such as <D'angelo> or <herc> suggests that *ain't* co-occurs with particular characters. That these characters may either be speakers or addressees is shown in example (5), where <herc> occurs at R2 of the first *ain't* (addressee) and at L2 of the second *ain't* (speaker):

(5)

<SAVINO:>   Like the man said, it **ain't** ours.
<HERC:>   It **ain't** yours, huh? So, you don't mind if we just take it off your hands?   (*The Wire*)

In order to explore further if *ain't* is produced by particular speakers or social groups, I examined its *character diffusion* (as introduced in Chapter 5). Overall, *ain't* is used by fifty-three different characters across SydTV, of which fewer than half (n = 24) are African American, and almost 80 per cent (n = 42) are men. This shows that *ain't* is not just used for stereotyping or 'Othering' African American speakers, although such Othering may indeed occur. The word form may have associations with masculinity, rather than femininity, but not always. It is also likely that less dialogue (in total) is produced by African American and female speakers in SydTV, which affects these numbers.

In some of the SydTV episodes, *ain't* is used by only one character, for example, Sawyer in *Lost*, Joy in *My Name Is Earl*, Emerson in *Pushing Daisies*, and Heylia in *Weeds*, including minor characters such as 'woman' (*Baby Daddy*), 'man' (*Entourage*), or 'elderly man' (*Castle*). This would indicate that it functions primarily for constructing character traits that are unique to one character, with potential for stereotyping – for example, in the *Weeds* and *Pushing Daisies* episodes the only characters to use *ain't* are African American, while Sawyer in

Lost is white and Southern American. The use of *ain't* by Southern American characters like Sawyer and Joy is in line with common representations of Southern American English in the narrative mass media (see Chapter 2).

In other SydTV episodes, two or more characters employ *ain't*, for example Kenny, Dustin, and Tracy in *Eastbound & Down*; Carl and Grandma in *Mike & Molly*; Rondell, T-bonz, Vic, and Kern in *The Shield*; and Lincoln and Franklin in *Prison Break*. This might indicate that these characters are constructed as sharing particular type characteristics; for instance, both Carl and Grandma in *Mike & Molly* are African American, while Kenny, Dustin, and Tracy in *Eastbound & Down* are Southern American (from North Carolina). In *The Shield*, most occurrences are produced by African American characters who are associated with rapping and/or drug dealing – only one instance is produced by a white character (detective Vic) and his is quite a specific use of *ain't* (*Knute Rockne he ain't.*) Again, there is potential for stereotyping here.

Most variation can be found in the two episodes from *True Blood* and *The Wire*, where *ain't* also occurs the most. In these episodes, the characters who produce the non-standard variant are fairly diverse and include both African Americans (eleven in *The Wire*, four in *True Blood*) and non–African Americans (four in *The Wire*, five in *True Blood*). In *The Wire*, one female character (Greggs) employs *ain't*, while in *True Blood*, five female and four male characters use it. Its use in *True Blood* again indexes the Southern setting and identity of the characters. Note that the characters who use *ain't* in the episode from *The Wire* include both those working in the drug trade (seven characters, plus two drug addicts) and those working in the police force (four characters, plus a drug counsellor). *Ain't* is thus not simply used to index education, gender, or ethnicity in this program, and may not be highly stigmatised by itself. At the same time, it could function in different ways: when used by male police officers it might be an index of their 'working-class speech style' (Lopez & Bucholtz 2017: 15), whereas it might signal other social dimensions when used by other characters.

In terms of usage, concordancing shows that the vast majority of usages of *ain't* are as variants of BE (*'m not, isn't, aren't*) or HAVE (*haven't, hasn't*), which are attested in most/all vernacular varieties in North America (Wolfram 2008: 524; Anderwald 2012: 313) – and are 'extremely common' in colloquial American English (Murray & Simon 2008: 405). Most of these occurrences are variants of BE rather than HAVE, and the majority of the BE variants correspond to *isn't*. There are only two possible instances of 'distinctive' urban AAVE use where *ain't* is a substitute for *didn't* (Wolfram 2008: 524). Both are uttered by African American characters:

(6)

BUBBLES: I ain't, I didn't ask[ed] for nothin'.   (SydTV, The Wire)

(7)

LETTIE: I ain't eat [ate] anything all day, like you said.   (SydTV, True Blood)

It must be noted that different viewers might disagree here on what they hear. When I played these two examples as audio files to an audience of American speakers (including some who are familiar with AAVE), there was no clear consensus about whether Bubbles in example (6) says *I ain't, I didn't* or *I didn't, I ain't* (both with reduced forms of *didn't*) or *I ain't, I ain't* or *I ain't even*. However, there did seem to be consensus that the character says *ask* rather than *asked* (heard by the transcriber), although the subtitles (which are not necessarily the 'correct' version) are *I ain't, I ain't even asked for nothin'*. With example (7), some audience members thought the speaker produces a reduced *didn't* rather than *ain't*, while others did hear the word form as *ain't*. Some heard the lexical verb as *ate* rather than *eat* (transcribed). These transcribed dialogue lines are therefore a prime example for the fact that viewers will not necessarily have the same linguistic experience of performed speech in TV series (Adams 2013).

If the example from *The Wire* is indeed a case of *ain't* corresponding to *didn't* rather than *haven't*, this would be another instance of *The Wire* featuring grammatical constructions of AAVE that are not usually encountered in TV dialogue (Lopez & Bucholtz 2017: 12). In any case, these two examples do not alter the general tendency for *ain't* uses to be dominated by usages that are largely familiar to audience members (i.e. corresponding to forms of BE or HAVE). This could be the result of audience design (comprehensibility) or unfamiliarity with AAVE, and mirrors findings that Bucholtz and Lopez (2011: 689) report for the use of *ain't* in Hollywood films.

In sum, non-standard *ain't* in SydTV is used for particular functions such as characterisation. There is a clear potential for such representations to reinforce linguistic stereotypes and language ideologies. The high number of occurrences in the episodes from *The Wire* and *True Blood* also shows the impact that particular series have on the linguistic landscape that is presented to viewers in contemporary television, including perhaps an increased diversity of represented speakers in some programmes. In order to investigate whether a particular TV series engages in stereotyping, it would be necessary to compile a larger corpus with episodes across seasons and engage more deeply with characterisation. The extent of linguistic stereotyping through characters' use of *ain't* (and other linguistic features) in *Lost*, *Weeds*, *The Shield*, *True Blood*, *The Wire*, and other TV series would hence need to be explored on a case-by-case basis. For instance, as Lopez and Bucholtz (2017) argue, language use in *The Wire* subverts certain hegemonic expectations while reasserting others.

4 Conclusion

This chapter used corpus linguistic techniques to examine language use in US television dialogue. Given the fact that there are so many TV series and that there are linguistic differences between them, it is crucial to consider variation.

In this chapter I examined variation with respect to the range and dispersion values of key words. As noted, these analyses had the goal of making visible the 'blind spot' created by the focus on similarity and consistency. The findings support previous claims made on the basis of different data that some linguistic features will not be found in all TV episodes, series, or genres, and showed that it is necessary to consider both language-internal and language-external factors that may influence linguistic variation. There is a need to tease apart the effects of storylines, characters, and genre, including narrative functions of dialogue such as characterisation and plot development. The latter in particular has been ignored in corpus linguistic research on television narratives and also takes a back seat in sociolinguistic studies. This is in line with a tendency in corpus linguistic research to focus on patterns *across* texts rather than *within* text (but see Flowerdew 2005, 2009; Toolan 2009; Barlow 2016). Genre also plays an important role, for example in relation to crime-related or medical vocabulary. The investigation of genre is challenging, however, since many TV series are hybrids (Dunn 2005: 138). There is also a non-negligible effect of language-external factors such as censorship associated with taboo/swear words.

The case study of the key word *ain't*, a stigmatised feature of American English, showed that it is often part of a bundle of non-standard features and may contribute to social stereotyping, although this is arguably less so the case in series like *The Wire*. The motivation behind the use of iconic or (stereo-)typical cues may lie in audience design, as this makes characters comprehensible as well as easily recognisable and interpretable (see Chapter 2). The lack of diversity in scriptwriting teams may also play a role, as it could limit writers' linguistic awareness of non-standard features.

In addition to *ain't*, several other results also involve non-standard language, including swear/taboo words. This suggests that it may be useful to examine types of non-standard language use in TV dialogue in more detail. This will be part of the next chapter, which analyses non-codified language, including but not limited to non-standard language. Chapter 12 will discuss the implications of the results of this chapter for language learning and teaching, together with the results from the other chapters.

9   *Non-Codified Language in SydTV*

1 Introduction

This chapter is the final chapter dedicated to empirical analysis of SydTV. I present a corpus-assisted study of non-codified language features – i.e. word forms that are not present in a given dictionary. In Chapter 6, I explained my approach to identifying such language in SydTV, which starts by using Microsoft Word's 2007 spell-checker. I then categorise the word forms that were identified by the spell-checker and undertake follow-up investigations prompted by some of the results. I interpret results in terms of the functional approach to television series (FATS) introduced in Part II. Also included are comparisons with dictionaries (Merriam-Webster Unabridged (MW), Urban Dictionary (UD)) and corpora (COCA/S, GloWbE/US, SOAP).[1] The non-standardised version of SydTV is used for all analyses. As a reminder, the year of first broadcast of the TV series in this corpus ranges from 2000 to 2012. I will list the respective year where relevant to allow for better interpretation of results.

2 Categorising Word Forms Identified by the Spell-Checker

The word forms identified by the spell-checker can be classified into seven broad categories, which are discussed in turn. In some cases, follow-up analyses are also undertaken.

2.1 Pronunciation Variants, Non-Lexical Forms, Colloquial Forms, Interactive Features

As expected, the spell-checker underlines some of the contractions, lexicalised reduced forms, non-standard pronunciation variants, and colloquial forms that were taken into account during the transcription process (see Bednarek 2018). This includes word forms such as *youse*, *oughta, woulda, kinda, gonna, gotta, wanna, lotta, outta, sorta, lemme, cuz* ('cousin'), *whatcha* ('what [do/did] you'), as well as words with the [In] variant (for instance, *nothin', goin'*), to name but a few. Also identified are many of the transcribed discourse markers, listening cues, hesitation markers, (dis)agreement markers, interjections, sounds, etc. For instance, the spell-checker identified the fairly recent interjection *booyah* (MW: first known use in 1990) as well as the innovative interjection *jeesh* (likely a blend of *sheesh* and *jeez*; not listed in the MW) and the attention-getter *yo* (indexically associated with African American Vernacular English (AAVE); listed in the MW). Most of the forms in this category are markers of orality and many are non-lexical or semi-lexical forms that we would not expect to be listed in a dictionary. Their presence again illustrates that TV dialogue artfully and selectively simulates naturalistic speech, creating realism.

This is the first case where I use the spell-checker results as a stimulus for subsequent corpus linguistic analysis, focusing here on variants for second-person plural *you* (like the non-standard *youse* identified by the spell-checker). Second-person plural pronouns are grammatical forms that distinguish standard English from many non-standard dialects (Trudgill 1999: 126) and can be found in almost all English vernaculars (Wagner 2012: 381). In American English the major forms of a plural second person are *y'all, youse*, and *you guys* (Queen 2015: 46).

Wolfram (2008: 525, 530) states that *y'all* occurs in AAVE (Southern and Northern) and in European American Vernacular English (Southern). Newman (2014: 92) notes that it is 'stereotypically southern' but that it is rapidly spreading outside that region. It is three times more common in American English than in British English conversation (Finegan 2004: 31). In contrast, *youse* occurs in Northeastern dialects in the United States (Wolfram & Schilling Estes 2006: 87); it is nationally 'quite rare, but [...] heavily concentrated in New York and vicinity' (Newman 2014: 91). Queen (2015: 46) notes that *youse* is also 'more commonly used by people in the working classes than in the upper classes'. *You guys* is a more generic colloquial expression that can be used to address males or females (Finegan 2004: 31; Murray & Simon 2008: 408). It is less restricted geographically and socially (Queen 2015: 46) and is an example of ongoing linguistic change, as its use has steadily increased over the past two decades (Heyd 2010: 36).

Table 9.1 shows the raw and normalised frequencies and range of all three forms (search terms: *you guys, y'all, youse*), showing that *you guys* is the most frequent, followed by *y'all* and *youse*. Interestingly, this order corresponds to survey results reported by Newman (2014:

Table 9.1 Raw and normalised frequency and range for variants for plural you

	Raw frequency	Normalised frequency	Range
you guys	135	49.1	40
y'all	25	9.1	9
youse	2	0.7	1

92) where more American English respondents said that they would use *you guys* (42.53 per cent) than *you all* (12.63 per cent) and *youse* (0.67 per cent). This again demonstrates that TV dialogue is capable of imitating unscripted spoken language (creating realism). The findings, which indicate that *you guys* is by far the most frequent and has the widest range, can also be compared with results by Heyd (2010) for *Friends*. In this sitcom, *you guys* is highly frequent (with a normalised frequency of 116.3 per 100,000 words), and Heyd (2010: 60) argues that it is 'strategically employed' for characterisation and to represent orality. As noted in Chapter 2, *Friends* is particularly informal, and Table 9.1 indeed shows that the frequency of *you guys* in television dialogue as a whole is much lower (with a normalised frequency of 49.1 per 100,000 words). Levels of informality in TV series vary depending on genre and character hierarchies (Bednarek 2012a: 48), and twenty-six episodes in SydTV have zero instances of the form. In general, the common and familiar *you guys* is nevertheless preferred to all the other variants.

Moving on to the second most frequent form, *y'all*,[2] the characters who produce this form in SydTV are both African American (e.g. Omar and Sterling in *The Wire*, Rondell in *The Shield*, Janila in *Southland*) and non–African American characters. The latter appear to be from the South as far as this can be determined (e.g. Sookie in *True Blood*, Kenny in *Eastbound & Down*) even when the series itself does not take part in the South (e.g. Kenneth in *30 Rock*). Similar to the use of *ain't* (cf. Chapter 8), this is in line with common representations of Southern American English in the narrative mass media, where *y'all* is used because it is recognisably or ideologically associated with this variety (Queen 2015: 165). It is therefore *type* characteristics that are indexed through *y'all*, and there is a clear potential here to reinforce linguistic stereotypes. Of the five Hollywood scriptwriters I interviewed for this book, all associated *y'all* with Southern American characters, with some being critical of its use. According to Jane Espenson, the use of *y'all* constitutes 'an easy way to say "this character is Southern" instead of genuinely thinking about how they would really talk'. David Mandel said he found it a bit insulting to include the form in a script and might leave it up to the relevant actor to add it in more naturally. On the other hand, the official final script for the SydTV episode from *30 Rock* in the Shavelson-Webb library (Writers Guild Foundation, Los Angeles) did contain an instance of *y'all*. The use of *y'all* in on-screen dialogue could thus derive from the scriptwriting team or be a contribution from actors (and/or dialect coaches).

Finally, there are only two occurrences of *youse*, both of which occur in an episode from *Human Target* and are produced by the Northern Irish character Connor. It is worth keeping in mind that although SydTV contains only episodes from US TV series, this does not mean that it includes only speakers of American English. Again, though, *youse* functions to index type characteristics and is recognisably associated with (Northern) Irish. In sum, contemporary TV series continue to exploit the well-known indexical meanings of non-standard language features such as *y'all* and *youse* to construct familiar social identities.

2.2 Repeated Word Forms

The spell-checker also identifies repeated words, but only if they are not separated by punctuation (e.g. it underlines *No no no no no*; *and and*). Such repeats may indicate character emotion or other cognitive states (Quaglio 2009: 119, Bednarek 2012a: 45–6), hence contributing to characterisation. More interestingly, repetition of word forms also includes non-codified means of intensification, as seen in examples (1)–(3), to which I have added some relevant non-linguistic information:

(1)

BARNEY: What I don't get is, why is Claudia marrying Stuart? She's way hotter than him. How way? [question asked by Barney himself; followed by a brief pause] **Way way**. [laugh track: laughter]   (SydTV, *How I Met Your Mother*, 2005)

(2)

ROBIN: [on the phone] Hello. Oh my God, tonight? You're kidding. [to Ted:] They want me to anchor the news tonight. [on the phone:] What? Really? Like, **anchor anchor**? What happened to Sandy? Okay, okay, sure, what time do you need me to, right now? Oh.   (SydTV, *How I Met Your Mother*, 2005)

(3)

DR HANSON: Mrs Wilder your husband is effectively brain dead. I'm sorry.
DAVID LEE: But not **dead dead**?   (SydTV, *The Good Wife*, 2009)

In these examples, we are dealing with a low-frequency phenomenon that Huang (2015: 80) calls 'lexical cloning'. According to Huang (2015), this can have functions such as intensification or singling out a particular sense of a lexical expression. Hohenhaus (2004: 297–8) suggests that such reduplications are 'nonce formations', i.e. '*new* word-formations which are produced actively in actual performance as opposed to lexemes which are retrieved ready-made from the lexicon' (emphasis in original). Huang (2015) notes that this is a novel, recent, and innovative linguistic phenomenon.

Considering the examples from SydTV, in example (1), the intensifier *way* is repeated to maximise its degree, and the reduplicated form can be paraphrased as 'very much hotter'. Interestingly, the intensifying usage of *way* is itself labelled by the MW as non-standard ('dialectal'). However, Finegan (2004: 33) notes that this use of *way* is 'extremely popular' in American English, especially among younger speakers. Barney, who produces the form here, is supposed to be in his mid- to late twenties like the other protagonists in *How I Met Your Mother*, and its use may index his age (type characteristic), in addition to creating humour as indicated by the laugh track.

In examples (2) and (3) we are dealing with a different kind of intensification, where the grading or scaling that is applied is not according to intensity/extent, but rather according to prototypicality – that is, what appears to be emphasised is 'a prototype reading' of the relevant item (Hohenhaus 2004: 297). These phrases can be paraphrased as 'properly' *anchor* or 'fully' *dead*, and in example (2) the reduplication appears to show Robin's excitement or disbelief.

Hohenhaus (2004) argues that instances of identical constituent compounding in TV or movie scripts are representations of informal, conversational language. Thus, they function to create realism. Supporting evidence comes from the fact that such usages can be found in contemporary American English – including occurrences of *way way* in COCA/S and *dead dead* in GloWbE/US. In addition, as the examples above show, they can create humour and express character emotion.

2.3 Non-English Words

Unsurprisingly, the spell-checker also identifies the use of languages other than English (e.g. *Well howdy there **muchachos***; *Spare me the **yo** *no se's*), including borrowed words, as illustrated in example (4) from *Nurse Jackie*. The conversation takes place in a hospital in New York and features a conversation between Jackie (the eponymous nurse) and an elderly Jewish patient, Mr Zimberg:

(4)

JACKIE:	Okay, so Mr Zimberg, umm, as soon as we speak to the cardiologist, I think we'll have a better idea ...
MR ZIMBERG:	No. No cardiologists. No more angioplasty. No more bypass. No more **bubkes**.
JACKIE:	I'm sorry?
MR ZIMBERG:	I'm sorry to be so irritable, but an old friend of mine used to say, "Well, that's life in the Balkans". I didn't know what the hell he was talking about. One thing I don't want, I don't want my wife to lose one minute of sleep over this. You got it? (SydTV, *Nurse Jackie*, 2009)

Newman (2014: 113) claims that *bubkes* ('nothing, the least amount') is a Yiddishism that has 'taken on an iconic role' and is understood by a general audience in New York. If we assume that Jackie's *I'm sorry* indeed relates to Mr Zimberg's *bubkes* in the previous turn and if we assume that the same conversational rules apply in the fictional New York as in the 'real' New York, then there should be no need for her query. Rather, the word should be known to her as a fellow New Yorker, although it might be clarified here for the benefit of the audience. Together with other linguistic elements in his speech and references to being Jewish elsewhere in the episode, the use of the Yiddishism *bubkes* in conjunction with Jackie's *I'm sorry* linguistically constructs Mr Zimberg as different, as an Other. Such Othering is connected to standard language ideology, i.e. to functions relating to thematic messages and ideology. In addition, the word establishes type characteristics (Mr Zimberg's Jewish identity), and hence contributes to the communication of the narrative, namely characterisation.

2.4 Technical/Specialised Vocabulary

Several occurrences of technical/specialised vocabulary, including initialisms and acronyms, are also detected by the spell-checker (e.g. *procoagulate*; *muskie* (a type of fish); *leos* (law enforcement officers)). Some of these words undergo innovative word formation processes such as conversion/zero derivation (e.g. *I only iso'd the epinephrine*; *while she was* **ALS-ing** *the uniform*) or shortening (e.g. *lipo, boty, tox screen/report, postnup*).[3] In certain cases, the meaning of word forms is unpacked through the TV dialogue itself (e.g. *a **Chud**, a Cannibalistic Humanoid*). Example (5) represents an extended case of such unpacking:

(5)

BARBARA: This machine will tell me if there's any biological evidence of the abilities you say you have. In other words, if you're **metahuman**.
DINAH: Meta-what?
BARBARA: In most people, less than five per cent of their neural cells are active. Your cerebral cortex activity is, over fifty per cent.
DINAH: So it's true. I'm officially a freak.
HELENA: Hey, watch it with the F word.
BARBARA: There are people in the world, Dinah, a lot of people with abilities beyond what we think of as human. Umm, no two metahumans have the same gifts. Don't ask me where their powers come from, no one knows. Natural mutations, biological experiments.   (SydTV, *Birds of Prey*, 2002)

This example shows the use of meta-discourse to clarify the meaning of specialised or technical vocabulary (to Dinah *and* the audience) and that such vocabulary partially depends on the genre of the TV series. In legal, medical, crime, mystery, fantasy, sci-fi, and related genres, such vocabulary functions to create particular worlds (e.g. supernatural) that are populated by particular characters (e.g. detectives, lawyers) undertaking specialised activities in particular settings (e.g. at court). Thus, TV series about medical staff in a hospital will include technical words relating to medical procedures, while legal dramas will comprise a considerable amount of 'legalese' (Csomay & Petrović 2012). Such word forms may also be used in the enactment of narrative events – for instance, when specialised/technical terms are used in key actions at court. This type of non-codified vocabulary hence appears to be primarily related to the communication of the narrative. Additionally, their use creates realism by representing language that is assumed to be used by particular professions. TV series sometimes have special consultants or tech advisers who help with this aspect of writing dialogue (cf. Cook 2014: 127; Landau 2014: 50, 65, 260). Some of these words would be codified in a specialised reference work such as a medical or legal dictionary (cf. Chapter 6).

2.5 Names and Cultural and Intertextual References

Also related to the communication of the narrative are character names (e.g. *Sookie, Toofer*) and nicknames (e.g. *Stinkum* or

Crabman), including terms of address for family members (*Mami, papi*) and shortening of names. The latter are very common in SydTV and include *Shue* (Schuester), *Shep* (Shepard), *Mr Linc* (Lincoln), *Lyd* (Lydia), *Jer* (Jeremy), *Tophe* (Topher), *Ders* (Anders), *Toof* (Toofer), and *Linds* (Lindsay), alongside many others.

More innovative and linguistically playful nicknames include *Autismo* (an insult), *Bretty boy*, *Rapey Reeves*, *Stevie "the Wheelie" Kenarban*, *Brosef*, *Annie McNoface*, *Nanny McDead*, and *Ri-gantor* (Riley). These are cases where scriptwriters exploit the resources of language via linguistic innovation. Nicknames are regular or one-off, self-selected, or chosen by others; they occur as terms of address or to refer to characters (example (6)).

(6)

MAX:	Oh my gosh! You are breathtaking, which at my age is dangerous.
ELKA:	Max, my eyes are up here.
MAX:	Just taking it all in. You are gonna be prom queen for sure.
ELKA:	Why, thank you. Not Agnes Bratford?
MAX:	You mean **Hagnes Fatford**?
ELKA:	Oh Max, that's terrible. (SydTV, *Hot in Cleveland*, 2010)

In example (6), Max is seen to play with a character's real name, turning *Agnes* into *Hagnes* and *Bratford* into *Fatford*, in turn implying that the character is both a 'hag' and 'fat'. This creates humour through linguistic creativity and expresses his solidarity with Elka (who called the same person *fat-ass hag-ford* earlier, though not in Max's presence).

But on the whole, the use of names in telecinematic discourse has a host of functions (see Part II), including anchorage of the characters and constructing relationships between characters. Mittell (2015: 181) claims that 'characters [...] call each other by name and reference their relationships more frequently than people do in everyday life, using dialogue as a way to keep crucial character information active in our minds'. In addition to characters, names may also refer to various other elements of the narrative such as settings or entities (e.g. *the* **Eastview** *Hotel, a box of Ozawa Industrial Brothers Mrs* **Ladypant** *Beneficial Dryness Force*). Further, the spell-checker identifies many names of real-life locations, people, products, which anchor the narrative in the world known to the viewer, creating realism (e.g. *vo-tech, Terps*; see Chapter 4).

In some cases, such references to the real world are associated with a particular storyline. Thus, the SydTV episode from *Workaholics* contains fourteen references associated with Canadian singer Justin

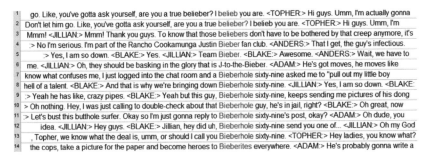

1	go. Like, you've gotta ask yourself, are you a true belieber? I belieb you are. <TOPHER:> Hi guys. Umm, I'm actually gonna
2	Don't let him go. Like, you've gotta ask yourself, are you a true belieber? I belieb you are. <TOPHER:> Hi guys. Umm, I'm
3	Mmm! <JILLIAN:> Mmm! Thank you guys. To know that those beliebers don't have to be bothered by that creep anymore, it's
4	:> No I'm serious. I'm part of the Rancho Cookamunga Justin Bieber fan club. <ANDERS:> That I get, the guy's infectious.
5	:> Yes, I am so down. <BLAKE:> Yes. <JILLIAN:> Team Bieber. <BLAKE:> Awesome. <ANDERS:> Wait, we have to
6	me. <JILLIAN:> Oh, they should be basking in the glory that is J-to-the-Bieber. <ADAM:> He's got moves, he moves like
7	know what confuses me, I just logged into the chat room and a Bieberhole sixty-nine asked me to "pull out my little boy
8	hell of a talent. <BLAKE:> And that is why we're bringing down Bieberhole sixty-nine. <JILLIAN:> Yes, I am so down. <BLAKE:
9	:> Yeah he has like, crazy pipes. <BLAKE:> Yeah but this guy, Bieberhole sixty-nine, keeps sending me pictures of his dong
10	> Oh nothing. Hey, I was just calling to double-check about that Bieberhole guy, he's in jail, right? <BLAKE:> Oh great, now
11	:> Let's bust this butthole surfer. Okay so I'm just gonna reply to Bieberhole sixty-nine's post, okay? <ADAM:> Oh dude, you
12	idea. <JILLIAN:> Hey guys. <BLAKE:> Jillian, hey did uh, Bieberhole sixty-nine send you one of... <JILLIAN:> Oh my God
13	, Topher, we know what the deal is, umm, or should I call you Bieberhole sixty-nine. <TOPHER:> Hey ladies, you know what?
14	the cops, take a picture for the paper and become heroes to Bieberites everywhere. <ADAM:> He's probably gonna write a

Figure 9.1 Concordance for bieber* *or* belieb* *in* Workaholics

Bieber, because of a storyline where one of the protagonists is a member of a Justin Bieber fan club and is sent sexually explicit pictures by *Bieberhole sixty-nine*, who the protagonists plan to identify, shame, and report to the police. These fourteen instances (Figure 9.1) include references to this character (lines 7–13 *Bieberhole sixty-nine, that Bieberhole guy*) as well as references to Justin Bieber fans (lines 2–3, 14: *belieber(s), bieberites*; line 4: *Justin Bieber fan club*), play with the words *belieber/belieb* (line 1),[4] their mission (line 5: *team Bieber*), and rap/hip-hop slang (line 6: *J-to-the-Bieber*). Some of these word forms are also in use in unscripted American English: COCA/S has two instances of *belieber*, while GloWbE/US has several instances of *belieber* (n = 25), *beliebers* (n = 40), and *belieb* (n = 2), with zero instances of *bieberites, bieberhole*, or *J-to-the-Bieber* in either corpus.

Intertextual references are also apparent in SydTV (e.g. *Superboy, Divine Secrets of the Ya-Ya Sisterhood, I'm basically **Darkwing Duck**, I like that **Wonderbug**, we're not a concierge **ghostbuster** service, I'm gonna leave my homework with **Slumdog Millionaire***). Characters can directly name a cultural product as in example (7), where the title of the US reality television programme *To Catch a Predator* additionally undergoes verbification.

(7)

BLAKE: Umm, alright, Topher, you know what, you cannot be here man because that girl is like the main reason we **To Catch a Predator'ed** you. (SydTV, *Workaholics*, 2011)

Characters can also more indirectly refer to a cultural product, as in example (8). This turn references a scene in the 1990 romantic comedy *Pretty Woman* where wealthy Edward (played by Richard Gere) pays for new clothes for Vivian, a prostitute with whom he has fallen in love (played by Julia Roberts).

(8)

[Sophie buying dresses for two other female characters]

SOPHIE: Yeah, this is fun day [*sic*]. I'm like Richard Gere and you're my two
                   hookers.   (SydTV, *2 Broke Girls*, 2011)

This intertextual reference to *Pretty Woman* relies on viewers' memory of the film, establishing communality with the knowledge and experience of the audience. As explained in Chapter 4, such references exploit the resources of language but also create realism and may contribute to characterisation. They show the engagement of TV series with contemporary US culture. In general, cultural-societal-historical items would be included in an encyclopaedia rather than a dictionary (Gramley 2012: 440), explaining why they are identified by the spell-checker.

By watching US TV series, then, viewers from other cultures do not just absorb aspects about the narrative world of the respective series, they are also exposed to many references to the 'real' world, including both globally known phenomena (such as the film *Pretty Woman*) and phenomena that are tied to US culture (such as *vo-tech*).

2.6 *Wordplay*

The spell-checker additionally detects various instances of wordplay, including play with word formation processes and play with similar sounding words (examples (9)–(11)). Linguistic play at this level is one of the ways in which humour is created in telecinematic discourse (Brock 2011).

(9)

SUE: But I just found you and now you're leaving? You gave me hope
                        but now everything just seems impossible.
REV TIM TOM: You know, **if you take the im off of impossible**, what do
                        you get?
SUE: Im?
REV TIM TOM: No, the other half.
SUE: Possible?
REV TIM TOM: That's right Sue Heck, possible.   (SydTV, *The Middle*,
                                                                                              2009)

(10)

AMY: So, Dan, are you enjoying working for Hallows?
DAN: Not really, she's the middle of the road, she's mediocre, really. **Of all the ocres, she's the mediest**. (SydTV, *Veep*, 2012)

(11)

SHOSHANNA: Her littlest baggage is that she spends a thousand dollars a month on her weave, which host Jerry Springer thinks is **unbeweavable**. (SydTV, *Girls*, 2012)

In both examples (9) and (10), characters play with word formation processes, correctly separating a prefix (*im-*) from the root (*possible*), and incorrectly analysing *mediocre* into two component parts, while in example (11) the play rests on sound similarity (*unbelievable/unbeweavable*). In all three examples, the wordplay seems to create humour and make audiences laugh, but it may also contribute to characterisation – for example, in relation to the incomprehensibility expressed by teenager Sue in example (9), which indicates that she is not exactly the brightest.

Another interesting example of linguistic play occurs in example (12), where I have added information about the laugh track to the transcription:

(12)

CHRISTINE: My marriage was like a game of hide-and-seek where both of us hid and nobody **seeked**. [laugh track: laughter] Sought. [laugh track: laughter] Slept together. [laugh track: laughter] Nothing's really changed. [laugh track: laughter] (SydTV, *The New Adventures of Old Christine*, 2006)

Here, the character attempts to play with unpacking the compound *hide-and-seek* into its two component verbs, resulting in the grammatically erroneous form *seeked*, which is self-corrected. Note that this is an exceptional case where the spell-checker detects non-standard *grammatical* usage – regularisation of an irregular verb by analogy. Again, this results in humour (as indicated by the laugh track), but the dialogue lines also introduce relevant background about the character to the audience. Additional examples for wordplay are presented at www.syd-tv.com.

2.7 Swear/Taboo Words

Perhaps unsurprisingly, the spell-checker also identifies some swear/taboo words, the final category in this section. As Chapters 7 and 8 have shown, such informal/expressive words are overused in SydTV compared with the LSAC, although certain words have a low range because of relevant US regulations. Some of the swear/taboo words identified by the spell-checker are in fact listed in the MW (e.g. *cocksucking*, *motherfucking*) but labelled as non-standard, for example as 'vulgar', 'offensive', or 'obscene'.

Further, the identified forms are often the product of word formation processes such as derivation, compounding or blending (e.g. *fuckable*, *butt-fuck*, *dickweed*, *dickwad/fuckwad*, *fucktard*, *ballbuster*). This is another case where I use the spell-checker results as a stimulus for subsequent corpus linguistic analysis, focusing on the use of swear/taboo words in word formation. A search for selected morphemes (*ass*, *shit*, *dick*, *fuck*) in SydTV shows that *ass* is especially productive in this corpus: *big-ass*, *ugly-ass*, *tight-ass*, *lame-ass*, *kick-ass*, *fiend-ass*, *fat-ass*, *stupid-ass*, *dumb-ass*, *creepy-ass*, *smooth-ass*, *smart-ass*, *short-ass*, *shit-ass*, *jackass*, *badass*, *ass burger*, *ass-clown*, *ass ache*, *ass-fucked*, *ass-kicking*, *bitch-ass*. This reflects the fact that *ass* is indeed a very productive affix, in AAVE as well as in general slang (Widawski 2015: 24–5), again providing evidence for TV dialogue's imitation of unscripted spoken language. But word formation also occurs with other taboo morphemes such as *shit*, *dick*, and *fuck*, including:

- *bullshit, dipshit, shit-ass, shitheads, shit-faced*
- *dickwad, dickweed, dickhead, limp-dick, dick-wagging*
- *fuck-up/fucked-up, fucktard, fuckwad, fuckable, butt-fuck/butt-fucking, ass-fucked, pencil-fucked, motherfucking, motherfucker.*[5]

Interestingly, most of these word forms cannot be found in COCA/S.[6] This could be because they have 'a rather ephemeral character' (Widawski 2015: 24) or because they are instances of wordplay (*ass burger* is a play on *Asperger*; see Bednarek 2014a). Even if a particular word form does occur in COCA/S, it is very infrequent in that corpus. Thus, *dumb-ass* occurs six times (a normalised frequency (n.f.) of 0.005 per 100,000 words), while *smart-ass* occurs eleven times (n.f. = 0.010). This is likely because COCA/S consists of mainstream media language, with 'relatively little profanity' (Davies n.d. a), making it unsuitable for the study of strong swear/taboo words.

If we briefly consider soap opera language, overall frequencies of *ass* are much higher in SOAP (2,335; n.f. = 2.317) than in COCA/S

(671; n.f. = 0.613), but much lower than in SydTV (81; n.f. = 29.4; excluding hyphenated words). These differences between SydTV and SOAP are due to language-external factors, since broadcast television is subject to different regulations than cable television and the time of broadcast also plays a role. This in turn may mean that certain swear/taboo words (e.g. *hell, damn*) might be overused in SOAP to compensate for the avoidance of others – just like particular swear/taboo words are overused in the sitcom *Friends* for similar reasons (Quaglio 2008: 205–6). Swear/taboo words are a prime example of the polyfunctionality of linguistic features in TV series (cf. Chapter 4). They can be used for characterisation (conveying type and trait characteristics as well as expressive character identity), but also for humour, as a plot device, as a catch-phrase, to create realism, or to control viewer evaluation/emotion (Bednarek in press b). Variation in the frequency of such words in SydTV is visualised at www.syd-tv.com.

3 A Closer Look at Word Formation

I now explore word formation in more detail, which cuts across the categories identified so far. To avoid repetition, I exclude from investigation word formation processes in the categories already discussed above. First, several word forms are detected by the spell-checker but are listed in the MW. What is noteworthy is that some of these MW entries are explicitly labelled as 'new', including the abbreviation *intel*, the adjective *metrosexual*, and the nouns *buzzkill* and *jegging*. Others are labelled as 'slang' (e.g. *skeevy, phat, hinky*; (*a*) *doozy*; (*to*) *case*), 'informal' (*creep out, perps*), or 'dialectal' (*ruinate, mush*). This provides further evidence that SydTV includes both new and non-standard word forms. Interestingly, characters sometimes comment on such word forms, unpacking them for viewers via meta-language, as seen in example (13).[7]

(13)

SOOKIE: A zucchini **toosh**?
JACKSON: Just *a temporary name.*
SOOKIE: You want me to serve my customers a genetically engineered vegetable *that's named after a butt?*   (SydTV, *Gilmore Girls*, 2000)

For the remainder of this section, I focus on word forms that are identified by the spell-checker but are *not* listed in the MW.[8] The spell-checker identifies examples for all common ways of forming new words, including:

- Derivation with prefixes and suffixes, e.g. ***supervillains***, ***unhear***, ***unspelled***, ***misjoked***, ***overthink***, ***untutorable***, ***unboyfriendable***, ***graftable***, *incentivizer*, *Social-Skills-**athon***, *Vape**tron***, *Trailer**ville***, *halves**ies***, *twins**ies***, *towel**ette***, *pod**ule***, *nib**let***
- Compounding, e.g. *amazeballs*, *low-carb*, *crimelords*, *freestylin'*, *motorboating*, *vaped out* (phrasal verb)
- Contraction/shortening, e.g. *sesh*, *nugs*, *special ed*, *home ec*, *low-carb*, *pic*, *vics*, *decomp*, *rezzy*, *'tron*
- Brand/trade/product names (eponymy), e.g. **Nascar** *moms, so you could* **Vespa** *to work*
- Conversion/zero derivation (e.g. changing of adjectives into nouns, nouns into verbs, also includes the use of trade names as adjectives or verbs as in the eponymy example above), e.g. *a lot of* ***vacants***, *You're not* ***webcamming*** *again, They're* ***vibing***
- Blends, e.g. *that* **handicapable** *bus* [*handicapped + capable*], *all* **pornalicious** [*pornography + delicious*], *some serious moral* **spankitude** [*spanking + attitude?*], **trestling** [*tetris + wrestling*]
- Reduplication: *schmancy* (copy/reduplicant without original *fancy*).

Given Mandala's (2007) research on linguistic innovation in *Buffy the Vampire Slayer* (see Chapter 2), it is worth noting that -*y* suffix adjectives occur in SydTV, including some 'marked' adjectives, where the suffix -*y* is used to 'create adjectives in unusual ways' (Mandala 2007: 55). In SydTV -*y* adjectives detected by the spell-checker include the following instances:

MAN 2: Hey, everyone's got their fantasies, right? A guy wants to know what it's like, you know, to be with another man. Just once, nothing **queeny**. (SydTV, *Dollhouse*, 2009)

KATHERINE: Hey you guys, looks like it's gonna rain outside, you guys are gonna wanna do some **insidey** things today okay? (SydTV, *Girls*, 2012)

MARIE: I like the support. My arches happen to be extremely **archy**. (SydTV, *Breaking Bad*, 2008)

JESS: I guess, it was something about the words you used, like sun-soaked and **beigey**.

SCHMIDT: What about these? These look **beigey** to you? (SydTV, *New Girl*, 2011)

JASON: Ooh, that looks **abortiony**. (SydTV, *United States of Tara*, 2009)

These do not all fulfil Mandala's criteria of markedness (for instance, she excludes adjectives formed from colour terms as 'too established to be called marked' [Mandala 2007: 57]), but they are certainly all non-codified. It is also questionable in how far these can be called 'established' if one considers their low frequency of occurrence: COCA/S includes no instances of *queeny*, *archy*, or *abortiony* and only one instance of *beigey* and *insidey* (with a different meaning). Similarly, GloWbE/US contains no instances of *abortiony*, *insidey*, or *archy* (except names/other unrelated usages) and only one equivalent usage of *beigey* and *queeny* ([derog. 'gay'], excluding instances as name).

As expected, the spell-checker does not identify all instances of innovative word formation, especially in relation to compounding when codified words are combined and spelled with a hyphen or as two separate words. It is, however, possible to undertake follow-up searches in SydTV by searching for *-*-* to identify instances where several word forms are conjoined (an example that we have already encountered above is *J-to-the-Bieber*).[9] In this way, we can identify innovative instances of conversion and derivation (*the risks of plus-one-ing me, You're cha-cha-cha-ing, the catwalk freeze-and-turn, It's like fifty rub-and-tugs for you, the first Spring Social-Skills-athon*) as well as linguistic play – for instance, the creation of humorous nicknames (*Miss Fluff-and-Fold, next to Lake No-one's-gonna-drive-that-far, you're Janelle I-have-no-Monae*).

Generally, the parts-of-speech that are conjoined in non-codified compounds (*-*-*) in SydTV vary (e.g. noun + conjunction + noun; preposition + noun), but many are used to modify nouns in an innovative and seemingly ad-hoc way, such as:

- *husband-and-wife stuff* (SydTV, *Lost*, 2004)
- *this whole you-and-my-mom thing* (SydTV, *Gilmore Girls*, 2000)
- *the spilling-the-fruit-punch type* (SydTV, *The Big C*, 2010)
- *the glow-in-the-dark ones* (SydTV, *Grey's Anatomy*, 2005)
- *your in-the-dark little brother* (SydTV, *The Vampire Diaries*, 2009)
- *an angry, out-of-control ball player* (SydTV, *Anger Management*, 2012)
- *it was roll-around-in money* (SydTV, *Dollhouse*, 2009)

Hohenhaus (2004) lists phrasal compounds like *shot-in-the-back face* as example for new word formations that are created during performance and are non-lexicalisable. If we assume that these word formations are created by the scriptwriting team rather than improvisations added in the performance, it is clear that these are pre-planned representations of such 'ad-hoc' creations – another example of staged or scripted orality, creating realism.

4 Comparison with Other Reference Points

Using the inbuilt Microsoft Word 2007 dictionary and the MW as reference points has clear limitations (cf. Chapter 6). I therefore undertake a brief comparison with three other reference points here: the UD, COCA/S, and GloWbE/US, using the spell-checker results as a starting point.

First, several word forms that are identified by the spell-checker and are not listed in the MW *are* listed in the UD. The most surprising occurrence perhaps is the compound *birthdate*:

- A fraudulent passport, Christie's picture, a new name, a new **birthdate** (SydTV, *Drop Dead Diva*, 2009)
- Write your name in the top right corner followed by the **birthdate** and social security number. (SydTV, *Eastbound & Down*, 2009)

These examples show that this word form is not particularly non-standard but rather used in relation to documents. The first instance is uttered in the formal context of a courtroom. It does appear to be a fairly recent word (the earliest instance in COCA/S dates from 1991), but it is unclear why there is no entry for *birthdate*, *birth date* or *birth-date* in the MW.

More often, word forms that can be found in the UD but not in the MW are colloquialisms and slang words (e.g. *bougie, sesh, unhear, overthink, home ec, pic, go in halvesies with, unboyfriendable, low-carb, webcamming, niblet, nugs, smush/smushed*),[10] including those relating to drugs, sex(uality), or subcultures (e.g. *jit, vaped out, queeny, motorboating* (a sexual act), *freestyling* (type of rap)). Unsurprisingly, many are examples of swear/taboo words (e.g. *fuckable, butt-fuck, poo-head, dickwad, fucktard, fuckwad*). In addition, the UD has entries for innovations such as *handicapable* and *spankitude*, and words associated with cultural products (*supervillain, trestling*). An entry in the UD does not mean that these word forms are in wider use; however, most of these forms occur at least once in either COCA/S or GloWbE/US, with the exception of *unboyfriendable, pornalicious, spankitude, jit, vaped out, trestling, rezzy*.[11]

To provide more detailed information on the frequency of word forms in SydTV compared with COCA/S and GloWbE/US, I examined thirty-three word forms that occur in SydTV and at least once in either of these two corpora.[12] Table 9.2 shows the raw and normalised

Table 9.2 Comparison of word forms across three corpora of American English

Word form	SydTV			COCA/S		GloWbE/US	
	Raw f.	N.f.	TV series (Year)	Raw f.	N.f.	Raw f.	N.f.
birthdate	2	0.7	Drop Dead Diva (2009), Eastbound & Down (2009)	58	0.053	295	0.076
handicapable	2	0.7	Glee (2009)	2	0.002	11	0.003
unhear	1	0.4	Outsourced (2010)	0	0	7	0.002
overthink	1	0.4	Parks and Recreation (2009)	6	0.005	133	0.034
freestyling ('spontaneous rap/spoken word performance')†	1	0.4	The Wire (2002)	0	0	20	0.005
webcamming	1	0.4	Castle (2009)	0	0	6	0.002
motorboating (a sexual act)†	1	0.4	New Girl (2011)	0	0	7	0.002
supervillains	1	0.4	Birds of Prey (2002)	2	0.002	111	0.029
crimelords	1	0.4	Birds of Prey (2002)	0	0	24	0.006
pic	1	0.4	Suits (2011)	41	0.037	2,548	0.659
vics ('victims')†	1	0.4	Birds of Prey (2002)	0	0	11	0.003
decomp ('decomposition')†	1	0.4	Bones (2005)	1	0.001	2	0.001
low-carb	1	0.4	Arrested Development (2003)	61	0.056	570	0.147
sesh	1	0.4	New Girl (2011)	0	0	22	0.006
beigey	2	0.7	New Girl (2011)	1	0.001	1	0.0003
nugs ('nuggets')† (drug refs included here)	1	0.4	Eastbound & Down (2009)	0	0	7	0.002
insidey	1	0.4	Girls (2012)	1	0.001	0	0

(continued)

Table 9.2 (cont.)

Word form	SydTV			COCA/S		GloWbE/US	
	Raw f.	N.f.	TV series (Year)	Raw f.	N.f.	Raw f.	N.f.
home ec	1	0.4	Glee (2009)	10	0.009	33	0.009
special ed	1	0.4	Malcolm in the Middle (2000)	55	0.050	227	0.059
bougie ('bourgeois or elitist or taking on attitudes/behaviour of whites')†	1	0.4	Glee (2009)	0	0	5	0.001
vacants ('vacant buildings')†	1	0.4	The Wire (2002)	0	0	3	0.001
halvesies	1	0.4	The Big C (2010)	1	0.001	0	0
niblet	1	0.4	United States of Tara (2009)	0	0	2	0.001
dickweed	1	0.4	Eastbound & Down (2009)	0	0	12	0.003
fuckable	1	0.4	Entourage (2004)	0	0	18	0.005
butt-fuck† (verb)	1	0.4	The Wire (2002)	0	0	4	0.001
poo-head	1	0.4	United States of Tara (2009)	0	0	5	0.001
dickwad	1	0.4	Veep (2012)	0	0	28	0.007
fucktard	2	0.7	Veep (2012), True Blood (2008)	0	0	58	0.015
fuckwad	3	1.1	Weeds (2005)	0	0	21	0.005
coochie† (excludes boochie coochie, coochie coo)	1	0.4	Breaking Bad (2008)	1	0.001	17	0.004
toosh† (and tush) (excludes use in names)	1	0.4	Gilmore Girls (2000)	22 (all tush)	0.020	52 (47 tush)	0.013
queeny (derog. 'gay')† (excludes instances as name)	1	0.4	Dollhouse (2009)	0	0	1	0.0003

frequencies of these forms. The words were chosen fairly randomly, except that word forms that are too difficult to disambiguate were not selected (e.g. *baller/balling/ballingest, vibing*). In cases where I did not expect extensive polysemy, the frequencies simply relate to occurrences of these forms (e.g. *birthdate, handicapable, unhear, overthink*). In other cases, concordances were consulted in order to check that the instance(s) in COCA/S or GloWbE/US are comparable with the way the word form is used in SydTV; for example, that *vics* is used as an abbreviation for *victims*, that *motorboating* is used to refer to a sexual act, that *butt-fuck* is used as a verb. These cases are marked with a superscript dagger ([†]). With items where several spellings are possible, the frequencies were added up – for instance, the frequency for *birthdate* combines frequencies for *birth-date, birthdate,* and *birth date* (other examples include *toosh* and *tush, nugs* and *nuggs, un-hear* and *unhear*). Frequencies are normalised per 100,000 words (n.f.), but no statistical tests were applied because of the low frequencies of occurrence, as evident from the raw frequencies (raw f.). Table 9.2 also provides information on the TV series in which a particular word form occurs.

Table 9.2 clearly shows that – with the exception of only one word form (*pic*) – all forms are more frequent in SydTV than in either COCA/S or GloWbE/US. Even *pic* is still more frequent in SydTV (0.4) than in COCA/S (0.037). Of the swear or taboo word forms, only two occur in COCA/S (*coochie, tush*),[13] while the word forms with the highest normalised frequencies in GloWbE/US are *fucktard* (58 occurrences; n.f. = 0.015) and *toosh/tush* (52 occurrences; n.f. = 0.013). In general, those word forms in Table 9.2 that occur with very low frequencies are unlikely to be present in the mental lexicons of many speakers and may be regarded as lexical innovations if a broad definition of the term is adopted (Baayen & Renouf 1996: 78). Table 9.2 also demonstrates that these word forms occur across a range of different television series and across a range of years. While these results apply only to the investigated word forms, they do seem to suggest a tendency for TV dialogue to feature *more* occurrences of particular non-codified language than other varieties of American English, including both unscripted media language and internet language. This is significant, since the latter exhibits a high degree of vernacularity and language change. As a reminder, 60 per cent of GloWbE/US comes from informal blogs that 'often contain language innovations which may already have appeared in speech but have not yet found their way into more conventional written texts' (Lutzky & Kehoe 2016: 169).

5 Summary of Spell-Check Results

The analyses prompted by the spell-check results identified many fascinating linguistic phenomena in SydTV. Most interesting for the purpose of this book are non-standard language use and linguistic innovation. Identified non-standard language features include dialectal features such as *youse* and *y'all*; colloquialisms such as *gonna, wanna*; slang such as *phat, skeevy*; and swear/taboo words such as *pencilfucked, cocksucking, fuckwad*. Many of these have multiple functions, most importantly:

- the creation of realism (selectively imitating unscripted spoken language)
- the construction of relationships between characters (e.g. solidarity, friendship)
- the indexing of character traits (e.g. character emotion, age, region, ethnicity).

The character traits and relationships that are constructed by these non-standard features may be temporary (such as emotional expression via swearing) or more stable (such as age, ethnicity, or regional identity indexed by specific non-standard features). As mentioned, the latter comes with a high likelihood of stereotyping.

Identified instances of linguistic innovation include different types of linguistic play (e.g. *Of all the ocres, she's the mediest*; *unbeweavable*), recent or new interjections (*booyah, jeesh*), and innovative word formation processes including lexical cloning (e.g. *way way*), innovative nicknames (e.g. *Annie McNoface, Rapey Reeves, Janelle I-have-no-Monae*), verbification (*To Catch a predator'ed*), word formation with swear/taboo words (e.g. *dickweed, fuckwad*), marked -y suffix adjectives (e.g. *abortiony*), and phrasal compounds (e.g. *this whole you-and-my-mom thing*). These are clear examples of TV dialogue exploiting the resources of language. They also seem to index speakers' trait characteristics (e.g. intelligence, wit) and type characteristics (e.g. age); they may express character emotion (e.g. swearing); and they construe TV dialogue as informal and spontaneous conversation, creating realism (e.g. via seemingly 'ad-hoc' word formations).

The spell-checker also identified additional linguistic phenomena, such as technical/specialised vocabulary (used for communication of the narrative, e.g. establishing the setting or a character's profession), non-English words (used to construct type characteristics, but possibly Othering), cultural-societal-historical items (references to the 'real' world; intertextuality), and character names (with multiple functions, e.g. anchorage of the characters). On the whole, the spell-check approach was useful in identifying a multitude of different phenomena in SydTV and in acting as a stimulus for follow-up analyses, but it does not detect *all* instances of linguistic innovation or non-standard language. It also identifies phenomena that are examples of neither (e.g. character names, cultural-societal-historical items). It is therefore useful to triangulate methods, which I will very briefly do in the final section in relation to linguistic innovation and change.

6 Beyond Spell-Checking

Rather than starting with word forms identified by the spell-checker, I now draw on Davies's (n.d. c) list of verbs that are more frequent in the Corpus of Contemporary American English in the 2000s than in the 1990s. Among the most significant fifty verbs we find many that relate to computer-mediated communication: *tweet, email/e-mail, blog, upload, voicemail, twitter, download, reboot,* and *google*. These are simply more frequent now because of external changes in the ways in which we interact with technology. A SydTV search for *tweet*, email*, twitter*, download*, voicemail*, blog*, upload*, reboot*,* or *googl** identifies twenty-eight instances across fourteen files (not all as verbs), represented in Figure 9.2.

These instances again demonstrate that TV dialogue anchors the narrative in the 'real' world of contemporary America and engages with the common culture that characters share with viewers. For comparison with other fictional narratives, Table 9.3 shows the raw and normalised frequencies of the three word forms *tweet, blog,* and *email* (regardless of part of speech) in SydTV and in COCA's fiction component (short stories, plays, books, movie scripts) in the years 2000–12 (about 31 million words). The results indicate that fictional television narratives engage with technological changes more than other types of fiction, and indeed have their finger on the pulse of time. (The obvious exception are TV narratives that are set in the past or future or in a fantasy world.)

Table 9.3 Comparison of the word forms tweet, blog, *and* email *(SydTV vs. COCA/F)*

Word form	SydTV (2000–12)		COCA/F (2000–12)	
	Raw f.	N.f.	Raw f.	N.f.
tweet	4	1.5	12	0.04
blog	3	1.1	89	0.28
email	6	2.2	203	0.65

1	is happening right now? <AMY:> Brett Kagan's blog picked up a tweet from us, quote seventy-six
2	right. This does hurt too much. <JACOB:> My blog has lit up with comments suggesting you
3	:> Alright, let's talk about, let's talk about this blog thing. <SELINA:> Guys? What's going on
4	:> Sorry. <SALINGER:> I think your wife's been blogging my wife. She's been getting all pissy
5	Hallows is on the ropes, she was reported by the blogs sayin' that the late Senator Reeves had a
6	any drugs except for my allergy medicine. I don't download music without paying for it. I never wear
7	. <ALICIA:> Is there any chance he could've downloaded a living will? <CARY:> From some
8	have to get one from America. And it can't be an email attachment. <DUNCAN:> Well, you've
9	television. Like I was checking my email at the same time. Like I wasn't really there.
10	through company emails? <EVAN:> There is no email on Sundays. <HANK:> I think you're
11	man. You gotta go. <SAMMY:> You didn't get the email, seriously? <KENNY:> No. <SAMMY:> Hey
12	for BioTech, but all we have to work on is this email address assigned to a fictitious name.
13	you waiting. <TORY:> That's okay. I got your email, with the list of other law firms. I respect
14	No no, this is from last night, the guys in security emailed it up to Louis this morning. <MIKE:> And
15	company I deal with, a virtual one. <BOOTH:> Emails, online financial transactions. <OGDEN:>
16	get into Max's house. Dig up anything you can, emails, songs, poems, anything that points to him
17	, you see this is why you never read company emails on Sundays, okay? <HANK:> I'm gonna
18	:> Isn't it your job to sort through company emails? <EVAN:> There is no email on Sundays.
19	wants to take over for me? I gotta go check my emails. Where can I do that? <ANDERS:> Right
20	now? <AMY:> Brett Kagan's blog picked up a tweet from us, quote seventy-six per cent of
21	river. Oh boy, it seems like with that cornstarch tweet we, we were hoist by our own retard. Uh.
22	History X. <CHARLIE:> Oh yeah, have fun, go tweet that. <MARNIE:> You look scary too.
23	his soul. <BARBARA:> Hey, did you fire your tweet monkey yet? Because that guy is a
24	people. <REPORTER:> Uh is your guy gonna be tweeting about this? <SELINA:> Okay well let me
25	:> Uh huh. And hello, gorgeous but deadly. Upload imprint to file drive. <BOYD:> Topher.
26	. I, I tried her cell phone, but it went straight to her voicemail. Then I tried here but, the machine
27	musical stylings of Ms Liza Minnelli. Straight to voicemail, okay. So I see you're ignoring my calls
28	talk to them. <CASTLE:> She was letting it go to voicemail. <MONTGOMERY:> Find this kid Brent

Figure 9.2 Word forms related to computer-mediated communication (SydTV)

In addition, some of the other most significant fifty verbs in the 2000s also occur in SydTV, namely *morph*, *overthink*, *repurpose*, *redact*, and *trump*, while others occur as a different part of speech (e.g. *manscape*, *incentivizer*):

- EVAN: [...] Okay, Hank get up here right now, because I don't think it's mold, I think it's ghosts, and, now the ghosts are **morphing** into bats! (SydTV, *Royal Pains*, 2009)
- LESLIE: Don't **overthink** it. (SydTV, *Parks and Recreation*, 2009)
- CAMERON: Actually, no, we **repurposed** it. (SydTV, *Modern Family*, 2009)
- VOICE: **Repurposed** and rejiggered, it [the decontamination system] no longer protected him from the outside world. (SydTV, *Pushing Daisies*, 2007)
- JONAH: Can I just, see that. Thank you. White House says we need to majorly **redact** this okay.
- MIKE: **Redact** your fuckin' face. (SydTV, *Veep*, 2012)

- PHIL: Did he **trump** me? (SydTV, *Modern Family*, 2009)
- VICTORIA: Oh well, I guess that **trumps** award-nominated actress. (SydTV, *Hot in Cleveland*, 2010)
- WILL: She can file all she wants. Wife **trumps** girlfriend. (SydTV, *The Good Wife*, 2009)
- WILL: My apologies, Your Honor. In legal terms wife **trumps** mistress. (SydTV, *The Good Wife*, 2009)
- JENNIFER: Sean's just too opinionated, plus his **manscape**'s really weird. (SydTV, *Anger Management*, 2012)
- MICHAEL: Coffee is the great **incentivizer** in the office. (SydTV, *The Office*, 2005)

This shows that TV dialogue reflects and possibly enhances ongoing change in unscripted American English. For instance, the normalised frequency of the verb form *trumps* in SydTV (1.1 per 100,000 words) is much higher than in any of the periods from the 2000s in COCA, which are as low as 0.12 (2000–4), 0.19 (2005–9), and 0.18 (2010–15). In Hundt and Mair's (1999: 236) terms, it appears that contemporary US television dialogue is a relatively 'agile' language variety that does not shy away from innovation.

7 Conclusion

The corpus-assisted analysis of non-codified language in SydTV identified non-standard features, linguistic innovation, and other linguistic phenomena. First, the use of a spell-checker identified examples of non-standard language use such as dialectal features, colloquialisms, slang, and swear/taboo words. There is the clear potential for such word forms to spread either nationally or globally, including to other varieties of English. American English slang and taboo items in particular may be unknown in national varieties such as British English (Gramley 2012: 459) and may be circulated through the mass media (Eble 2004: 382).

Analysis of features such as *y'all*, *youse*, and *bubkes* seems to confirm that easily recognisable cues are still used to index type characteristics such as ethnicity or regional identity. As explained in Chapter 2, the reason is likely linked to audience design, since such cues allow easy recognition and categorisation of characters. Those L1 and LX viewers who have not encountered such features elsewhere may thus form simplistic associations between non-standard features and particular identity categories. They might be socialised into dominant, potentially negative or stereotypical values about these identities. However, such constructs may be seen as less problematic if viewers have had enough exposure to non-standard varieties to recognise the stereotype or if they are media-literate enough to deconstruct the stereotype and understand its role and function in the TV narrative. Clearly, not all TV series feature equally stereotypical representations (see Chapter 8), and ultimately this question needs to be explored further (e.g. using Gibson & Bell's 2010 criteria introduced in Chapter 2). The question of stereotyping is one that is best addressed through case studies on one or a few individual TV series, as it requires systematic quantitative and qualitative investigation.

Second, the analysis of non-codified language also offered insights into linguistic innovation and creativity – permitting the identification of different types of linguistic play and innovative word formation processes. It was shown that SydTV includes both recent innovations (in use, e.g. words like *metrosexual, amazeballs, trump*; second-person plural *you guys*; marked -*y* adjectives; lexical cloning; words related to new technologies) and potentially novel words (e.g. *trestling, untutorable, unboyfriendable, trailerville, to plus-one* someone). Several innovations are more frequent in SydTV than in other corpora such as COCA/S and GloWbE/US. The higher frequencies in SydTV may suggest that TV dialogue accelerates language change and is *more* innovative than unscripted language. Hence it appears that the claim that researchers have made on the basis of intensifier usage in *Friends* may hold more generally, namely that TV dialogue 'provides a kind of preview of mainstream language. In fact, these media data appear to pave the way; language is more innovative in the media than in the general population' (Tagliamonte & Roberts 2005: 296). However, it is worth remembering the argument I made in Chapter 2: to make this claim more forcefully and reliably, we need a corpus of spontaneous spoken American English that includes similar types of interactions and participants from the same time period as SydTV. COCA/S, the main corpus used for comparison, is ultimately still a corpus of spoken *media* language. It can also be difficult to determine whether TV dialogue has picked up on an existing innovation or has created a new one.

Even though investigation of non-codified language has its difficulties, it showcases the creative nature of contemporary media language. As discussed in Chapter 2, some linguistic innovations in TV series will be ephemeral and quickly forgotten; others will be taken up by subsets of the community (e.g. *bazinga*) or larger numbers of speakers (e.g. *d'oh*), spreading through a language community. Not all will become conventionalised – this depends on a range of language-external and language-internal factors. Not all innovation results in change. The findings in this chapter can therefore provide a baseline for future research – will these word forms become more widely used? If so, what is their 'life cycle' (Renouf 2007: 87) and will they become codified in a dictionary?

In sum, contemporary US television series feature a wide variety of interesting linguistic phenomena, including but not limited to specialised/technical vocabulary, nicknames, cultural and intertextual references, wordplay, innovative word formations, swear/taboo words, slang, and colloquialisms. Some of the non-codified word forms are associated with particular narrative worlds (e.g. *metahuman*) or storylines (e.g. *bieberites*), but in general, functions are varied and wide-ranging (see Section 5). Ultimately, these functions can be tied to the participation framework of TV dialogue, since they allow viewers to be immersed in the narrative world, to be entertained, emotionally engaged, and aesthetically pleased. While non-codified language presents a challenge to comprehensibility (for instance, specialised vocabulary or slang), we have seen that meanings can be unpacked or elaborated through the dialogue to make it more accessible and that familiar expressions such as *you guys* are preferred to other forms. The implications of the results of this chapter for language learning and teaching will be discussed in Chapter 12, together with the results from the other chapters.

Part V

TV Dialogue in Pedagogy

10 'Take That Pencil and Just GO!'

TV Series and Scriptwriting Pedagogy

1 Introduction

While the previous chapters focused on television dialogue, this is the first of two chapters that move 'beyond the product'. It summarises the results from my survey of fourteen scriptwriting manuals and my interviews with five Hollywood scriptwriters (see Chapter 6 for explanation of this approach).[1] In so doing, I make connections to the linguistic analyses of TV dialogue presented in earlier chapters. I first discuss linguistic research on scriptwriting pedagogy in Section 2 before presenting my findings in Section 3.

2 Scriptwriting Pedagogy and Linguistics

Most of the research on scriptwriting pedagogy or dogma has taken place outside linguistics (e.g. Thompson 2003; Batty 2016; Macdonald 2016). Similarly, interviews with scriptwriters are typically undertaken by academics in other disciplines or, indeed, by journalists and other writers and not by linguists. Neither is Kozloff's influential study on film dialogue interested 'in the craft of screenwriting' (Kozloff 2000: 33).

In linguistics, studies that analyse TV dialogue only occasionally draw on either manuals or published interviews, and often do so in relation to a specific program such as *Buffy the Vampire Slayer* (Mandala 2007), *Gilmore Girls* (Bednarek 2010a), or *The Wire* (Lopez & Bucholtz 2017). In addition, linguists mainly rely on limited material, such as brief quotes from relevant scriptwriters, actors' memoirs, articles on how a series was produced, and scriptwriting pedagogy. For example, Dose (2013) cites one manual to argue that many scriptwriters have a negative attitude towards performance phenomena and discourse markers. Quaglio (2009) references five manuals in his work on the sitcom *Friends*.

In such analysis, there is some interest in linguistic attitudes and in the respective contributions of writers and actors to the production of non-standard language (Lopez & Bucholtz 2017 on AAVE). Thus, Lippi-Green (2012: 108) and Queen (2015: 238–9) discover a concern among TV creators/scriptwriters with avoiding or even countering linguistic stereotypes. Another important area of linguistic interest is scriptwriters' awareness of particular features – i.e., whether linguistic practices are 'a matter of conscious planning or intuition' (Mandala 2007: 66). There seems to be general agreement among scholars such as Mandala (2007), Quaglio (2009: 10–11), and Dose (2013) that linguistic information is neglected in scriptwriting pedagogy, that advice on dialogue writing relies on intuition, and that while conscious awareness 'clearly plays some part in writing dialogue that is both convincing and thematically effective, [...] the bulk of the process occurs below the level of conscious awareness' (Mandala 2007: 67).

In my own research (e.g. Bednarek 2010a), I have quoted from published interviews with creators and from scriptwriting manuals. I have also drawn on insights gained from auditing a university course on scriptwriting for television and on my interview with the lecturer of that course, an Australian scriptwriter. I have examined five script-writing manuals as well as online guidelines in relation to character-isation (Bednarek 2011c), and I have connected the presence of emotional language in TV dialogue to scriptwriting advice about heightening dramatic conflict and tension (Bednarek 2012a).

However, the most comprehensive outline in linguistics to date is by Richardson (2010a), who dedicates a whole chapter to scriptwriters' understanding of TV dialogue. To do so, she examines both manuals and online advice and relies on participation observation in a UK television writers' workshop. It must be noted that she does not discriminate between US and UK contexts, and therefore includes examples from both. She also cites a manual on writing dramatic dialogue in general (not limited to TV series). Her primary sources appear to be five manuals and three blogs, including one by Jane Espenson. While Richardson does not mention this, it is noteworthy that Jane Espenson undertook undergraduate and graduate studies in linguistics, and her insights into TV dialogue are likely informed by her linguistic background. In other words, it is difficult to extrapolate from Espenson to other US scriptwriters. She is indeed, as Richardson (2010a: 79) states, 'one of the most analytically minded writers about TV drama dialogue'.

Regardless of this caveat, Richardson's main conclusions are that scriptwriting advice focuses on aspects such as theme, plot, or story rather than dialogue and that the role of dialogue is to advance the plot, while '[c]haracterization through dialogue is allowed only to the extent that it respects this principle' (Richardson 2010a: 82). She argues that dialogue is seen as 'a potential *danger* to good storytelling' (Richardson 2010a: 74, emphasis in original) and that dialogue that is too expositional is evaluated negatively, while dialogue with subtext is evaluated positively. Citing one manual, Richardson (2010a: 74) appears to suggest that there is general agreement among scriptwriters on what constitutes good dialogue, namely that it is believable and reveals emotion and character, while also being witty and concise. Finally, Richardson shows that scriptwriters are consciously aware of certain linguistic features and their effects, including hesitation phenomena, discourse markers, and hedges. They are also aware that TV dialogue tends to exhibit only 'selective naturalism' (Richardson 2010a: 69–70).

This body of linguistic research has offered some important initial insights concerning linguistic awareness and processes of production. My own survey and interviews are meant to both test and complement this research. I also hope that this will encourage other 'TV linguists' to have a closer look at scriptwriting pedagogy and what scriptwriters themselves say about TV dialogue – incorporating analysis of the normative discourses that surround the creation of TV dialogue (cf. Chapter 6).

3 Insights from Scriptwriting Manuals and Interviews with Scriptwriters

In this section I summarise the major insights gained from my survey of scriptwriting manuals and interviews with scriptwriters.

Like Richardson (2010a: 65), I could not find any manuals devoted exclusively to television dialogue, but some of the surveyed manuals on TV series include chapter or section headings with *dialogue* (e.g. Finer & Pearlman 2004; Epstein 2006). However, only Smith (2009) and Cook (2014) include more in-depth discussion of linguistic features. Scriptwriters who happen to have read these particular two manuals might hence be more attuned to aspects of language than others. But on the whole, most of the fourteen surveyed manuals mention dialogue only in passing, have no index entry for dialogue, and do not use the word *dialogue* in any headings. This also confirms findings by Quaglio (2009: 10–11) that little to no linguistic information is provided in manuals on television writing, and is similar to observations about manuals on *film* screenwriting (Kozloff 2000: 6;

Jaeckle 2013). Scriptwriting advice does comment on storytelling aspects to do with dialogue such as voice-over narration, direct address, catchphrases, etc. Nevertheless, there is a clear emphasis on story or plot over dialogue, in line with what Richardson (2010a) found. Thus, writers advise that:

- 'Jokes and clever dialogue are certainly important, but story is what keeps eyes on the screen' (Smith 2009: KL 2128–9).
- 'the real basis of successful series television is the story structure' (Sandler 2007: KL 382)
- 'Structure is key'; 'you need that story-spine' (Bob Berens interview).

This emphasis on story and structure rather than dialogue reflects the fact that TV writers start with an approved outline (see Chapter 1). In fact, writers may import the outline – which already contains some dialogue – into their scriptwriting software and then reformat and rewrite it into a script (Jane Espenson interview). The focus on story also means that the key function of dialogue is to advance the plot. For instance, Bull (2007: KL 1893) writes, 'Every scene in your script must move the story forward.' But functions *other* than plot development are also mentioned, especially revealing character and creating humour, emotionality/conflict, and verisimilitude/authenticity. Further, Richardson's (2010a: 74) claim that dialogue is regarded as a potential danger to storytelling is perhaps too strong a statement, implying too much negative attitude on the part of scriptwriters. Writers talk about writing dialogue as 'fun' (Epstein 2006: 103) or 'enjoyable' (Smith 2009: KL 866). In the interviews, Bob Berens said how writing dialogue as a form of 'acting on the page' is 'the most enjoyable part of all of this'. Jane Espenson simply said: 'I love writing dialogue,' while another scriptwriter commented that dialogue is 'one of the most important parts of the storytelling process'.

In general, many scriptwriters express an evaluative point of view towards dialogue or scripts, using adjectives such as *sharp, subtle, sophisticated, literary, diverse, surreal, funny,* or simply *good* (all from the interviews in Priggé 2005). Short and concise dialogue as well as dialogue with subtext are evaluated positively (in line with Richardson 2010a: 78). In contrast, 'bad' dialogue is evaluated negatively (lines that are not funny; turns that are too long; dialogue that is too 'written', obvious, or overly expositional; clichéd phrases like *Houston, we have a problem*; *You have me at a disadvantage*). However, I did not identify a clear consensus among scriptwriters about what constitutes 'good' dialogue. Different manuals provide different definitions, such as the following:

- 'You want your characters to speak to each other in a way that sounds natural and real [not contrived or written]. That's what good writing is' (Bull 2007: KL 1936–7).
- 'The trick to great dialogue is making it clear to the audience what's going on while at the same time allowing the characters to reveal who they are by speaking unclearly to each other' (Epstein 2006: 102).

The interviewed scriptwriters said that great dialogue is difficult to explain, depends on the context, or is not precisely definable. For David Mandel, 'it's all about smoothness to the ear', while for another scriptwriter it is about dialogue that 'both captures the reality of the way people speak but then elevates it a little bit'. According to Jane Espenson, writers do not in fact agree on what makes good dialogue.

Moreover, the survey confirms the assumptions made in Bednarek (2010a, 2011c, 2012a) that emotionality is regarded as crucial. Emotional aspects of TV narratives are mentioned in many manuals.[2] However, in line with the general backgrounding of language, the manuals tend not to state how emotionality is linguistically expressed, except for advising against too obvious/direct or mushy lines such as *I'm really nervous* or *I love you. – No, I love you.* (Sandler 2007: KL 1688–91; Vorhaus 2012: 60). Smith (2009) is something of an exception, with a section that explicitly focuses on the 'emotional dynamics that affect speech' (KL 2547–8). In this section he associates arguing, fear, anxiety, happiness, and depressed state of mind with particular ways of speaking (e.g. swearing, yelling, stumbling over words). The scriptwriters that I interviewed explicitly about how emotion is expressed through dialogue mentioned relatively indirect ways of expressing emotional responses (for instance, bringing characters to the point of saying something and then cutting them off, using aborted sentences or backtracking, complaining/nit-picking to show that a character is depressed). They also mentioned more direct ways of expressing emotion (e.g. *I hate you*; *jerk*). Interestingly, both the manuals and interviewed writers seem to have a preference for characters not stating emotions directly, whereas the analyses in Chapter 7 have shown that certain words that directly label emotional states are in fact unusually frequent in TV dialogue (*hurt*, [*I*] *love* [*you*], *loved*, *trust*, *worry*, *happy*, *sad*).

The surveyed manuals also confirm my previous conclusions (e.g. in Bednarek 2010a) that characters are associated with individual, distinctive voices or ways of speaking (e.g. Epstein 2006: 102; Bull 2007: KL 438; Douglas 2011: 232; Cook 2014: 241) and that they are discussed in terms of attributes or traits as well as attitudes, goals, and desires (e.g. Smith 2009: KL 1912–14; Isaacs 2013: 178). In fact, the desires or goals of characters are seen as central to many storylines, and some writers even state that 'character is story' (Isaacs 2013: 177) or 'story *is* character' (Finer & Pearlman 2004, emphasis in original). Again, the connection between dialogue and character is somewhat neglected in most manuals, except for general comments: in line with Quaglio's (2009: 10) remarks, budding scriptwriters are instructed to write in a conversational or realistic style and in line with the characters' background. For instance, Finer and Pearlman (2004: 26) urge readers to 'make the characters sound real'. Others also state that characters should feel and speak like human beings in real life (e.g. Epstein 2006: 102; Bull 2007: KL 1932–7; Cook 2014: 157).

More specific advice, in the rare cases that it is provided (e.g. in Smith 2009; Chambers & Chambers 2013b; Cook 2014), lists aspects related to grammar/syntax (e.g. 'proper' grammar, double negatives, sentence structure) and vocabulary (e.g. difficult words, misuse of words, swear/taboo words) as well as signature lines or catchphrases. Smith (2009) also comments on aspects of pronunciation. When I asked the interviewed scriptwriters about how characters can be built through language, they also tended to mention aspects of syntax/ grammar and vocabulary as well as simply referencing characters' way of speaking or specific aspects about the language of a particular character. It is thus unlikely that writers actively draw on a complex analytical model of the kind linguists use to deconstruct how characterisation works. This does not make the linguistic models inappropriate; it just shows that the process of creating characters works differently and perhaps more subconsciously.

Quaglio (2009: 11) writes that some manuals advise using real speakers as a model and this is indeed the case (e.g. Finer & Pearlman 2004: 16; Sandler 2007: KL 1024; Cook 2014: 224, 230). Jane Espenson (interview) said that she pays attention to how real speakers use language, for example including divergences from standard grammar. However, manuals much more frequently list existing characters as models rather than real speakers. The advice is to study and capture the voices of these characters (e.g. Epstein 2006: 93; Douglas 2011: 201; Chambers & Chambers 2013a: 103, Cook 2014: 241). In other words, writers imitate TV characters more than real speakers, even though these characters might themselves be modelled on real speakers. The creator who comes up with the original characters in the pilot episode is thus an important influence on the subsequent creation of characters through dialogue. This is in line with the assumption that TV dialogue functions to create consistency (see Chapter 4).

Moving on to another important aspect of TV dialogue, it is clear that scriptwriters are aware that it is not fully naturalistic or, as one of the manuals puts it, is 'stylized' rather than realistic (Epstein 2006: 99). When I asked the interviewed scriptwriters about differences between how TV characters and 'real' speakers talk, they all mentioned aspects related to (dys)fluency and turn-taking structure (such as umming, straying from the main point, stopping and starting, broken or incomplete sentences, mistakes, overlapping speech, repetitions) and stated that these were mainly included in the script for particular effects (for example, to represent an emotion). David Mandel explained that a series like *Veep* strives to sound realistic, and the actors 'mess up' the script, for example by talking over each other or by ending conversations naturally rather than on the punchline. At the same time, pauses, repetitions, and hesitation phenomena are edited out unless they fulfil a specific narrative function. This, he said, makes TV dialogue an 'idealized version [...] of everyday speech'. Another scriptwriter said that writing dialogue is about 'giving characters the trappings of casual sounding-dialogue but [...] done better'.

When I asked them specifically about whether they would use discourse and agreement markers like *you know, I mean, like, well, yeah, right,* Bob Berens said he would not want to exclude them because 'That's how we speak', while Doris Egan would not use them a lot, only 'if it speaks to who they [characters] are', since too frequent use could be distracting. Another writer said that it depends on what a show wants to achieve (realism versus elevated speech) as well as on the characters (e.g. doctors versus twenty-somethings). David Mandel also suggested that they would be used only when they are necessary and that 'they serve their place'. Jane Espenson had conflicting views. On the one hand, she lamented the fact that these are often removed from scripts to shorten them, which makes the dialogue 'worse, less idiomatic'. On the other hand, she acknowledged that traditional television conventions mean that if you use these features too much, the result is that the dialogue does not sound like normal TV speech. Some of the interviewed writers explained that such devices may be left up to the actor to include, as this is easier and more natural – although such changes by actors are not permitted by all showrunners (see Chapters 1 and 7).

In addition, occasional reference is made to some of the linguistic characteristics of TV dialogue investigated in Part IV. This includes observations on the use of technical/specialised vocabulary such as 'legalese' (Landau 2014: 25) or 'cop/detective lingo' (Cook 2014: 244), which is linked to the creation of realism or authenticity. Intertextual or cultural references are also mentioned (e.g. Epstein

2006: 158–9; Sandler 2007: KL 523), with the caveat that these may become dated (Cook 2014: 103; Doris Egan interview). Scriptwriters, in particular those who write about humorous dialogue, also comment on different types of linguistic play such as puns and alliteration (e.g. Epstein 2006: 148; Chambers & Chambers 2013b: 137–8; Cook 2014: 104). Interviewed scriptwriters mentioned jokes or wittiness as an area where differences exist to language use in the 'real' world (Bob Berens, Jane Espenson, Doris Egan). David Mandel named similes, metaphor, and euphemism as common in TV dialogue. Further, manuals and scriptwriters are aware of the overuse of names in TV dialogue (Sandler 2007: KL 1723; Smith 2009: KL 2600; Cook 2014: 245; Jane Espenson interview), since these are 'notorious' (Doris Egan interview).

In relation to dialect and accent, at least some scriptwriters desire to avoid stereotyping. This is not widely discussed in manuals, although Smith (2009: KL 1146–53) comments on how foreign accents may be exploited for humour, while showing awareness that this is potentially problematic. He also advises to include only a few spellings in the script to identify mispronunciations, so as not to slow down the read (Smith 2009: KL 2531–3). In relation to ethnicity, Cook (2014: 243) instructs writers to remember that they are 'writing characters, not stereotypes' and to run dialogue by someone more familiar with the particular variety. Douglas notes that a second writer may be brought in for a 'cultural "wash"' when the original writer is not familiar with a character's background (Douglas 2011: 181). African American and Latinx writers may feel that they do not want to be seen to be just writing 'ethnic' characters or telling stories for specific audiences (Yvette Lee Bowser and Dennis Leoni, cited in Priggé 2005: 106, 196).

The European American scriptwriters that I asked about writing dialect stated that they would not want to offend anyone or make too many errors in cases where they did not know enough about the dialect (for example in relation to African American characters). They would therefore avoid being too specific in their writing, but might add some dialect flavour in the script to indicate a character's identity to casting. In general, they said they wanted to avoid stereotypes and would often leave it up to the actors to provide the necessary authenticity through dialect or accent. Doris Egan also noted that dialect has to be intelligible to the audience, which is in line with the assumptions made in Chapter 2. There is, then, grounds for hope in that at least some scriptwriters are aware of the dangers of stereotyping and also have a desire to avoid it. On the other hand, there are also grounds to think that these scriptwriters would have a desire to construct their identities in the interview as non-racist, which could affect their interview responses (see Chapter 6). In addition, scriptwriters are constrained by the collaborative process of writing and the commercial nature of TV series.

Finally, the use of swear/taboo words is arguably something that most scriptwriters know about, as it is conditioned by external regulations. Scriptwriters regularly comment on this when talking about premium cable versus broadcast television. Many find the restrictions of broadcast television artificial and unrealistic, as in the following three examples:

- '*NYPD Blue* was so good. However, there were some episodes where Sipowicz would throw some guy against a wall and say, "You dirt bag", when you knew he really wanted to say, "You shit head!"' (Shawn Ryan, cited in Priggé 2005: 93).
- 'And to be able to have a conversation where two people can talk the way two people would talk without artificial constraints was just amazingly liberating. It's as simple a thing as it is to have somebody be able to say "fuck", which I hear in my daily life 20, 30 times a day. Also, I'm from New Jersey, so I tend to use it a lot, and that kind of natural rhythm to dialogue in speech is invaluable' (Steven S. DeKnight, cited in Bennett 2014: KL 1927–30).
- 'You know the problem [. . .] is that you can't speak the way a career criminal would speak. It's these other words that you put in there, and so instead of saying "ass", you say "butt". "Oh, I'm gonna kick your butt." And they're just terrible; they're weak and they're vague. Instead of saying "scumbag", you have to say "dirtbag". And it makes you feel dirty that you're doing that, that you're not being true to the English language, not being true to humanity. It's a human, human life, you know, as it's really lived' (David Chase, cited in Lawson 2007: 214).

The two manuals that include some discussion on language have paragraphs on 'offensive language' (Smith 2009) and 'swear words' (Cook 2014). It is also easy to find examples online where scriptwriters discuss this issue, especially when it has created some controversy (for example, in relation to the historical drama/Western *Deadwood*).

In sum, my survey of scriptwriting advice and interviews with US scriptwriters suggest that the linguistic awareness of writers includes more than those aspects of language identified in previous research. At the same time, this awareness is primarily at play when writers are in what we might call an 'analytical' frame of mind – when they try to deconstruct television writing in manuals for the benefit of others or when they are asked to explicitly reflect upon dialogue in interviews.

In contrast, I suggest that this is *not* usually what happens during the process of writing TV dialogue. Often, the interviewed writers found it difficult to provide answers that dealt specifically with linguistic features. My interview with Bob Berens, for example, concluded with his explanation that he 'struggled sometimes talking about it 'cause [...] it's a frame that's so outside the process of it'. According to him, writers inhabit or act out the characters, as it were:

There's so many episodes of the show that you've seen so you've [...] internalised the voice to such an extent that it isn't necessarily a conscious or wilful act, it just kind of comes. And so it's [...] a little bit hearing it, but it's also [...] a little bit acting it whether I'm speaking out loud [...] or [...] speaking it in my head, like it's a [...] form of performance.

Jane Espenson also emphasised that she is not thinking analytically while writing:

so much of it is subconscious, like [...] I know why this is the right line [...] If I wrote it [a particular line of dialogue] I would write it and not think about why I was doing it [...] And so all writers are doing that, they're writing a line, [...] but they are not [...] consciously aware of it.

Alan Ball talks about writing as 'a kind of blind groping in the dark. I trust my own instincts' (in Priggé 2005: 108). Other writers emphasise a process of learning by doing (Brenda Hampton in Priggé 2005: 87) or say that they depend on inspiration – on 'feeling it' (Doris Egan interview). In addition, several writers talk about 'hearing' the characters' voices in their heads (Finer & Pearlman 2004: 228; Bull 2007: KL 444; Douglas 2011: 155). As Jane Espenson put it: 'You can just let the characters talk in your head and transcribe what they say.' Another interviewed scriptwriter said: 'When I am writing I hear it in my head almost like [...] composers hear music.'

Despite the institutional and commercial constraints in which the writing of TV dialogue is embedded, it is thus ultimately a creative process. The scriptwriters that make it into the writers' room have been selected among thousands of others vying for these positions and clearly have the craft and the skill to write entertaining and compelling dialogue. In so doing, they primarily seem to draw on their intuition, talent, and 'tacit understanding, *knowing how*' (Richardson 2010a: 64, emphasis in original) rather than on analytical thinking about language. This is why they are not necessarily able to name or explain all of the linguistic characteristics of TV dialogue that the analyses in this book have uncovered. In other words, only some of the linguistic features that define TV dialogue are the result of conscious planning (e.g. swear/taboo words), while others are more likely the outcome of intuitive, subconscious processes of creation. In addition, the recourse to linguistic stereotypes is not necessarily intentional.

4 Concluding Remarks

In this chapter I investigated TV dialogue from the perspective of production. This perspective complements the 'product' perspective adopted in the other chapters of this book that analysed TV dialogue as a particular type of language variety.

But what are the added benefits of examining production aspects? Exploring scriptwriting manuals and comments by scriptwriters is useful for various reasons. On the one hand, it provides insights into some of the normative discourses and semiotic rules that surround TV series (cf. Chapter 6). It can therefore help linguists explain some of the linguistic characteristics of TV dialogue. For instance, the unusual expressivity of TV dialogue (Chapter 7) seems to derive from the importance placed on emotional aspects of storytelling. More generally, observations about TV narratives in the manuals and by scriptwriters seem to provide some supporting evidence for using a framework that focuses on potential functions of TV dialogue. The functions mentioned by the industry professionals are clearly in line with the new FATS model proposed in Part II.

On the other hand, this investigation has provided insights into the process of writing TV dialogue, which is likely much more informed by intuition and tacit knowledge than by analytical thinking, at least at the level of language. It has also shown that linguistic analyses can make this tacit knowledge explicit – just like the scriptwriting manuals aim to do, but from a very different perspective. This chapter has offered sound empirical evidence that the linguistic analyses do not simply *reproduce* the knowledge of scriptwriters or the instructions and advice provided in scriptwriting manuals. Rather, linguistic analysis can contribute both new and complementary insights into our understanding of TV dialogue. This, in turn, could feed into the teaching of how to write for television, thereby making a contribution to both scriptwriting pedagogy and the television writing industry.

11 *Consuming Television Dialogue*

A Case Study of Advanced Learners in Germany

1 Introduction

In the previous chapter I have gone 'beyond the product' by focussing on scriptwriting advice, linguistic awareness, and the writing process. This chapter addresses another important aspect, namely that of consuming the 'product'. The context in which I do so is a transnational one, focusing on a cohort of German university students, as described in Chapter 6. Before I present the findings, I will provide a brief overview of relevant linguistic research on television audiences.[1]

2 TV Series, Language Learning, and the Audience

Like other mass media narratives, television series 'exist in a complex marketplace that depends on audiences for its continued existence' (Queen 2015: 222). Linguists have examined the ways in which audiences deal with media language and have identified different responses such as criticising, commenting, anticipating, transferring, appropriating, etc. (see overview in Bednarek 2017c). Such research shows the diversity of viewers' linguistic practices and simultaneously illustrates the *mediatisation* of contemporary societies (Androutsopoulos 2014). It contributes to our understanding of 'how active viewers negotiate responses to the staging of sociolinguistic difference' (Androutsopoulos 2012: 141).

In this chapter, I move away from the theme of functions of dialogue to focus more on sociolinguistic and other aspects of TV dialogue, including non-standard language. In this context, it is particularly interesting that some viewers clearly do notice and engage with representations of non-standard language in the narrative mass media: Bleichenbacher (2012) examines message board threads for reactions to multilingualism in Hollywood movies, showing that stereotypical or ideological representations are debated and that 'the audience does not just absorb, it talks back' (Bleichenbacher 2012: 171). Mitchell (2015) and Queen (2015) both provide examples where viewers comment explicitly on representations of regional accents or dialects, while Petrucci (2012) compares audience responses to translated (dubbed and subtitled) standard and non-standard styles. In relation to other aspects of non-standard language, an internet search will easily identify many examples where audience members either create supercuts (montages) of swear/taboo words (see http://justtheswearing.com/) or evaluate such language use explicitly.

It is also easy to find cases where viewers or reviewers comment on or recirculate instances of linguistic innovation in TV series. The following are just two examples selected because they refer to linguistic innovations in two episodes included in SydTV:

- *Hot in Cleveland*: 'Valerie Bertinelli (celebrity author Melanie Moretti) decides to throw a party to get to know her neighbors. To make a good impression, she serves **"Great Lakes Latkes, Drew Curry with LeBron Rice and to wash it all down, some cold, delicious Cuyahoga River Punch."** While there are no such dishes, there should be, particularly the LeBron Rice. It's done in seven minutes and sticks in the craw.' (www.cleveland.com/tv/index.ssf/2010/07/hot_in_cleveland_writers_nail.html, accessed 17 March 2016, boldface added)
- *Dollhouse*: 'But Joel punches back with maybe my favorite (and very Whedon-y) line of the night: "I'm sure I'm in serious need of some moral **spankitude,** but guess who's not qualified to be my rabbi?"' (www.avclub.com/tvclub/dollhouse-man-on-the-street-25543, accessed 17 March 2016, boldface added)

This suggests that there is linguistic awareness on the part of at least some audience members about both non-standard language use and linguistic innovation in US TV series, but a more systematic study of such awareness is lacking.

Crucially, the audience of contemporary US TV series includes international audiences outside the linguistic and cultural borders of the United States who engage with such series in various ways (Bednarek 2017a, c). As Androutsopoulos (2014: 21) puts it, 'media engagement clearly transcends the monolingual context'. Such audiences may encounter English-language TV series either in a translated or in the original version. Even if dubbed versions are broadcast on television in certain countries like Germany, platforms such as Netflix offer viewers easy access to the English-language version. As Mittmann (2006: 575) and Bleichenbacher (2008: 2) argue, films and TV series are a key medium through which learners encounter spoken English language and may therefore constitute an influential model for LX viewers.

As recently as 2015, Webb notes that 'television has been neglected to a large degree in the language-learning literature', partially because television may be seen as entertainment rather than an opportunity for education (Webb 2015: 160). Relevant linguistic research tends to focus on the usefulness of TV dialogue for language learning and investigates vocabulary coverage (e.g. Webb and Rodgers 2009; Csomay & Petrović 2012) or the extent to which TV dialogue is appropriate as a model of spoken English (e.g. Quaglio 2008; Al-Surmi 2012; Dose 2013). Many scholars argue that TV dialogue is similar enough to spoken language to be used as a 'surrogate', with differences seen as irrelevant or even advantageous. Such use can be both practical and appealing for those teaching English as a second language (ESL) (Quaglio 2008: 190). As Dose (2013) puts it:

> fictional television language might prove to be the perfect middle-ground between real-language material such as linguistic corpora of spontaneous spoken language (the latter displaying an abundance of performance phenomena unwelcome in the teaching context) and the often rather artificial, stiff and written-like representations of spoken language in traditional textbooks.

Grant (1996) also notes that TV soap conversations are more colloquial and more naturalistic than examples from teachers or textbooks and that such conversations meet the need to teach students about language use in informal conversations. Quaglio (2009: 149) suggests that television dialogue offers numerous adequate examples for ESL purposes and 'a vast potential for pedagogical purposes' as long as differences are acknowledged by teachers. In general, there appears to be agreement that television series are useful for vocabulary acquisition, cultural proficiency, listening comprehension, and fluency (e.g. Grant 1996: 64; Al-Surmi 2012: 671; Hanf 2015: 138; Webb 2015: 160–1).

Other research explores how TV series can best be used inside and outside the classroom, including best practices, benefits, and challenges (e.g. Hanf 2015; Lin & Siyanova-Chanturia 2015; Webb 2015). Some of the advantages of TV series discussed by these researchers include the following:

- their low cost and flexibility of access
- their multimodality
- that they engage learners, keep them motivated, and may reduce anxiety

- that TV series include representations of casual, everyday language
- that they enable extensive exposure to LX spoken input, including frequent encounters with topic-related words that are repeated across episodes of the same program.

Webb (2015: 160) even argues that television 'should represent the core material in an extensive viewing approach', since it 'offers advantages over movies, such as shorter running times and development of background knowledge through viewing different episodes of one program'. Specific strategies are also proposed to counter the challenges of TV dialogue (such as its difficulty and speed), in particular using classroom-based viewing and scaffolding activities in conjunction with out-of-class viewing, to make sure learners get the most out of watching TV series. Subtitles and repeat viewing can also be beneficial.

While providing a useful starting point for anyone interested in using TV series in a language-learning context, this body of research has not yet addressed the linguistic awareness of LX viewers or their responses to television dialogue. In the next section I report on findings from my questionnaire with a cohort of advanced learners in Germany (see Chapter 6 for explanation of this approach).

3 Questionnaire Results

3.1 Introductory Remarks

The focus of the questionnaire is on students' practices of consumption, views on pedagogical use, and linguistic awareness, with the aim of providing insights into the relationship of potential future teachers of English with English-language TV series. I provide a summary and discussion of key findings below. In so doing, I paraphrase the students' answers in English but will occasionally provide the original German, with translations either in the co-text or in an endnote. Note that questionnaire responses do not always add up to 582, since not all students completed all items, and some items include more than one response in cases where students did not follow the instructions.

3.2 Participant Information

The results from items one and two, which elicit background information (cf. Chapter 6), showed that of the 56 students from Mannheim, 37 were students of business education, 11 studied to become teachers, and 5 studied other degrees, in addition to three cases of unclear or no response. Correspondingly, most of the Mannheim students were in their sixth (n = 33) or second semester (n = 9).

Of the remaining students from the other universities, 226 indicated that they studied to become teachers, while another 25 said they were enrolled in a polyvalent BA (which includes an option to study to become a teacher). A total of 256 students listed other degrees (e.g. Bachelor), and there were 19 unclear/no answers. Note that those who listed *BA* or *Bachelor* might be enrolled in a polyvalent BA but might have chosen not to include 'polyvalent' in their response. The vast majority of these students were enrolled in their first (n = 440), second (n = 31), or third (n = 18) semester.

Together, these responses indicate that the surveyed students would have had only basic training in linguistics and that most would have completed 'high-school' in Germany the year before. Because of prior educational experience and entry requirements, participants are likely advanced learners of English with proficiency at levels B2 or C1 of the Common European Framework of Reference for Language. It is not possible to say with certainty exactly how many of them will end up teaching English as a foreign language, but it is likely to be a significant proportion. In response to item five, only 139 respondents indicated that they do not intend to teach English and had never taught English. In Section 3.3, the responses from all students (Mannheim included) will be reported together.

3.3 Other Questionnaire Responses

Regarding their consumption practices, it appears that the surveyed students do watch English-language TV series regularly, as the response *I don't tend to watch such series* was chosen only 26 times (of 614 responses to item three). Table 11.1 summarises the responses for language(s) of consumption. As can be seen, English is the preferred language (73 per cent of responses), and of the participants who watch TV series in the original version, most say they engage with the dialogue without subtitles. If subtitles are used, English subtitles are used more often than German subtitles. This suggests that many of these learners do regularly consume TV dialogue in English rather than in dubbed or subtitled German. In other words, the assumption that English-language dialogue has the potential to be an influential model for advanced learners of English is true for this cohort. The results also show the impact of new technologies that enable viewers to forgo the dubbed versions broadcast on television. On the other hand, it is possible that prestige bias (Wagner 2010: 35) played a role in these answers, as the choice of English would enhance respondents' standing.

Table 11.1 Reponses to the item: When I watch fictional English-language TV series (for example, *Big Bang Theory, NCIS, The Mentalist, The Blacklist, CSI, Bones, Girls, Brooklyn 99, Game of Thrones, House of Cards . . .*), I typically do so in the following way (on TV, Netflix, iTunes, Amazon, computer, internet, DVD . . .)

	German			English		
	German without subtitles	German with English subtitles	German with German subtitles	English without subtitles	English with German subtitles	English with English subtitles
	137	1	1	366	23	60
Total	139			449		

Nevertheless, these findings can be used as a baseline for a repeat study in the future to track changes in viewing habits as technologies develop.

Students also indicated that they found such TV series useful for learning (better) English, with 470 of the 582 participants (i.e., 80.8 per cent) selecting 3 or 4 on the Likert scale (where 0 stands for *trifft nicht zu* (~ 'disagree') and 4 stands for *trifft voll zu* (~ 'fully agree')), and only 33 students selecting 0 or 1. On the other hand, respondents were somewhat ambivalent about frequently using examples from English-language TV series in teaching, as shown by the responses summarised in Table 11.2. Nevertheless, a majority of students say that they would use them in teaching English or have already done so – excluding the above-mentioned 139 participants who state that they will not teach/have not taught English.

Table 11.2 Responses for the item I would show examples from English-language TV series (for example *Big Bang Theory, NCIS*) when I teach English to others (in the future) or I have already done so (e.g. work experience in a school, tutoring . . .)

0 (not at all)	1	2	3	4 (very often)
21	44	154	167	63

Indeed, the surveyed students agreed on the usefulness of TV series: when they were asked to rate how strongly they (dis)agreed with the statement that English-language TV series are useful for showing

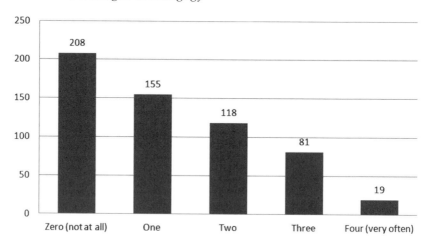

Figure 11.1 Responses for the statement My English teacher has used/shown examples from English-language TV series in the classroom

pupils examples of spoken English (questionnaire item four), zero respondents chose *trifft nicht zu/disagree*; 248 chose *trifft voll zu/fully agree*, i.e. option four; and 232 selected option three on the scale. This is surprising, given that they did not themselves experience TV series much in their own learning of English. As seen in Figure 11.1, 363 students selected 0 ('not at all': n = 208) or 1 (n = 155) for the statement *My English teacher has used/shown examples from English-language TV series in the classroom*. This means that TV series might still be underutilised in the English language teaching classroom. Together, these results suggest that the participants do find English-language TV series useful for learning and teaching English and that they are likely to use them when teaching English in the future. The contrast between how these students were taught and how they intend to teach indicates a potential generational shift in teaching methods, although these respondents would need to be observed in genuine classroom situations to confirm that they indeed act as they say.

As pointed out throughout this book, there are clear differences between TV dialogue and natural conversation, but students are not necessarily aware of these differences while they are watching TV series. This is suggested by their answers to item seven (*When I watch English-language TV series I am aware that the language is scripted/artificial*). The two highest options on the scale (three and four, 'very often') were selected only 147 times, while the two lowest options (zero, 'not at all', and one) were selected 206 times, and the

Table 11.3 Responses for the statement: The language spoken by TV characters in English-language series is similar to the language spoken by 'real' speakers

zero (trifft nicht zu)	one	two	three	four (trifft voll zu)
4	52	197	263	60

midpoint on the scale was selected the most (222 times), which might indicate that subjects are not sure of their experience.

The final two items on the questionnaire concern similarities and differences between TV dialogue and spontaneous conversation. First, responses for the statement in item ten, *The language spoken by TV characters in English-language series is similar to the language spoken by 'real' speakers*, are again mixed (Table 11.3), with a large proportion of answers for the midpoint (n = 197). However, zero (*trifft nicht zu*/strongly disagree) and one were chosen only 56 times, while a majority of respondents seem to agree with this statement (options three and four).

The uncertainty of participants also comes across in the responses to item eleven (*In my view there are linguistic differences between the language spoken by TV characters in such series and the language spoken by 'real' speakers*) where students could choose 'no', 'unsure', or 'yes'. Many respondents selected 'unsure' (n = 309), with 220 additional responses for 'yes' and 45 responses for 'no'. It is likely that this uncertainty reflects the fact that TV dialogue *selectively* imitates unscripted spoken English, as shown in Chapter 7. Another potential reason for these results might lie in students' awareness of the linguistic differences that exist between TV series. Indeed, this variation was mentioned by many students, and they often volunteered information about specific TV series in their responses, even though the questionnaire did not elicit such information. Representative answers from items ten and eleven include the following:

- *Kommt auf die Charaktere der Serie an* ('depends on the series' characters')
- *Hängt sehr stark von der Serie ab* ('strongly depends on the series')
- *Kommt auf das Genre an* ('depends on the genre')
- *je nach Serie unterschiedlich. Z.B. BBT und House Fachbegriffe, in anderen Serien oft Umgangssprache und Flüche* ('differs according to series. For example BBT [*Big Bang Theory*] and *House* technical terms, in other series often colloquial language and swearing')

- *kommt auf die Serie an, wo sie spielt* ('depends on the series, where it takes place')
- *Es kommt auf die Serie an. Z.B. in Comedy wird oft Sarkasmus verwendet.* ('depends on the series. For example, in comedy sarcasm is often used.')
- *Frage ist nur schwer zu beantworten, da Serien in vollkommen unterschiedlichen Milieus spielen. Natürlich sprechen Charaktere in Serien wie Game of Thrones nicht immer wie wir heute etc.* ('Question is difficult to answer, since series take place in completely different milieus. Of course, characters in series like *Game of Thrones* don't always speak like we do today etc.)
- *'posh', häufig weniger Umgangssprache, kommt jedoch stark auf die Serie an (Bsp. Misfits → authentisch)* ('posh, often less colloquial language, but depends strongly on the series [e.g. *Misfits* → authentic'])
- *wenig [...] Dialekt bei Serien wie 'FRIENDS', bei Serien wie 'HART OF DIXIE' Allerdings mit (Südstaaten-)Dialekt* ('little dialect in series like *Friends*, in series like *Hart of Dixie* on the other hand with dialect from the Southern states')
- *Ab und zu trifft dies zu (Downton Abbey), manchmal wiederum nicht (The Walking Dead)* ('sometimes this is the case (*Downton Abbey*), sometimes it isn't (*The Walking Dead*)')
- *Abhängig von der Serie, Sons of Anarchy beinhaltet sehr oft Slang, den man nur bei 'Gangs' hört, während Games of Thrones sehr auf 'hohe' Dialog bedacht ist* ('dependent on the series, *Sons of Anarchy* very often includes slang, which you hear only in gangs, whereas *Game of Thrones* values 'elevated' dialogue')
- *je besser die Serie (Breaking Bad, Sopranos, The Wire, ...) desto näher ist die Sprache an der Realität. Sowieso kann man nicht Comedy-Serien mit Kriminal-Serien und Serien wie BB, Sopranos, ... in einen Topf schmeißen.* ('the better the series (*Breaking Bad, Sopranos, The Wire,* ...) the closer the language is to realism. Anyway, you can't lump together comedy series with crime series and series like *BB, Sopranos* '.

Such comments suggest that many participants are aware of the linguistic variation that exists between TV narratives (as discussed in Chapter 8) and associate language features with a particular series or character, showing awareness of the uniqueness of narratives. It is interesting that respondents point to different levels of variation – at the level of the characters, series, and genre. This attention to variation is arguably a fairly sophisticated aspect of these students' linguistic awareness, but it also shows that their answers can be influenced by the particular series they consume. One could therefore make the argument that learners should be encouraged to watch a range of very different series.

Items ten and eleven also offered respondents space for elaboration. That is, if they selected 'yes' in response to item ten (i.e. 'yes, there are linguistic differences'), they could list these differences. A total of 231 participants chose to do so, although 21 of these had in fact selected 'unsure' rather than 'yes'.[2] Item eleven tried to ascertain to what extent subjects are aware of the most common linguistic features of TV dialogue. They were asked to elaborate on the following statement:

I think that the following linguistic practices/phenomena are the most common in the language spoken by characters in English-language TV series (for example, particular words, expressions, ways of using language, speech acts . . .)

In total, 315 students chose to provide comments in the provided space. I will summarise answers to items ten and eleven together here, with a particular focus on how they connect to the linguistic analyses of this book and mainly summarising general trends rather than responses offered by only one or two participants.[3]

A large number of relevant comments indicates that many students are aware of two aspects of TV dialogue discussed in Chapter 2: namely that TV dialogue tends to be intelligible and comprehensible, as well as more fluent and coherent than spontaneous conversation. Some 42 replies for item ten comment in some way on how TV dialogue is clear, intelligible/comprehensible, with a more controlled (slower, less relaxed) or extreme/exaggerated pronunciation/stress.[4] Some 12 responses to item eleven also mention this in some way. In addition, 49 comments on item ten refer to the 'fluency' of TV dialogue, for example that it has fewer fillers, pauses, less stuttering, less overlap/more monologue, fewer errors, fewer incomplete sentences, less topic shift, no repeats, and so on. Again, some replies to item eleven also point to these features.[5] It hence appears that the intelligibility/comprehensibility and fluency/coherence of TV dialogue are noticeable to at least some LX viewers who are advanced learners of English.

Moving on to aspects of TV dialogue investigated in Part IV, many participants spoke of standardness or non-standardness, in particular colloquial/informal language and dialects/accents. In response to item ten, many comments state that TV dialogue is more standard and features less slang and less colloquial language than unscripted conversation.[6] At the same time, it is acknowledged that colloquial/

informal language and slang are frequent in contemporary English-language TV dialogue: 53 responses to item eleven mention colloquial/informal/everyday language as frequent (*Umgangssprache, Alltags-sprache*, etc.), while 27 responses name slang as common (including two mentions of *Ghetto Slang/Ghetto-Sprache*). Only a few comments on item eleven mention standard English as frequent or colloquial language as infrequent.[7] These results suggest that students experience TV dialogue as full of colloquial language, even as they perceive it to be more standard than unscripted spoken English. Their awareness of colloquial language could be triggered by the fact that they are unfamiliar or less familiar with it from other contexts. As one participant comments:

Personally, I find this good [that colloquial language is frequent], since this allows you to learn expressions which you would not learn in this way in school/at university. (*Ich finde das persönlich jedoch gut, da man so Ausdrücke lernt die man in solcher Form in der Schule/im Studium nicht lernen würde.*)

As a reminder, Chapter 7 did indeed identify several colloquial/informal words and n-grams that are statistically speaking more frequent in TV dialogue than in unscripted spoken American English. Further, the dialogue used in some TV series is particularly informal/colloquial, although levels of in/formality vary depending on genre and series (see Chapters 2 and 9). In any case, results support the observation that these advanced learners are attuned to standardness and colloquiality.

As noted, dialects/accents were mentioned in many comments: 29 respondents state that these are common in TV dialogue (item eleven), with an additional three responses explicitly naming Southern American dialects/accents. However, replies to item ten indicate that students also think that they are *less* frequent than in unscripted spoken language; 27 participants mention that there are fewer dialects/accents or less dialect variation or that dialects/accents are less strong in TV series. Some students explicitly state that dialects/accents are exaggerated, stereotypical, unrealistic, or inaccurate (ten responses to item ten, four responses to item eleven).[8] On the whole, many respondents appear aware that there are differences between the ways in which language variation is represented in TV series and language variation in 'real' life. This is a promising finding, since there is indeed a clear potential for the use of non-standard language to reinforce linguistic stereotypes and language ideologies (cf. Chapters 2 and 8). As far as the teaching of televisual literacy is concerned, this finding suggests that it is possible to focus on such aspects with LX viewers.

In addition, particular aspects of (non)standardness such as swear/taboo words and terms of abuse are singled out in several comments.[9] In response to item eleven, fifteen students write that insulting/abusive language is frequent in TV dialogue (e.g. *Schimpfwörter, Beleidigungen*), while sixteen state that swear/taboo words are common.[10] Only three students comment that TV dialogue contains family-friendly language (*jugendfreundliche Sprache*) or few swear words. Replying to item ten, eight students volunteer that TV dialogue contains fewer instances of insulting/abusive language or swear/taboo words, while two students mention that it contains more swear/taboo words. Clearly, the mix of responses corresponds to the actual linguistic variation that can be found in TV series with respect to the use of such language (see Chapter 8). Nevertheless, the responses suggest that the surveyed students do consume TV narratives where this type of language is frequent. Students' awareness could also be triggered by the fact that swear/taboo words and insults are unlikely to be taught in the classroom or to occur in textbooks, while learners tend to be fascinated by them (Dewaele 2004: 205).

There are three other predominant themes in the responses: several participants assert that technical/specialised vocabulary (*Fach-sprache, -wörter, -ausdrücke, -begriffe, -vokabular, fachsprachliche Ausdrücke, wissenschaftl. Ausdrücke, wissenschaftliche Sprache*, etc.) is common in TV dialogue (22 responses to item eleven; 5 responses to item ten). In addition, 47 comments on item eleven and 19 comments on item ten name humour or wordplay as frequent (including jokes, puns, irony, sarcasm, witty replies (*schlagfertig*), wordplay, ambiguity, etc.), while an additional two responses refer to insider jokes between characters. Related to this area of linguistic creativity, a considerable number of students mention metaphors, unusual expressions, idioms, or literary/figurative/rhetorical devices as frequent (36 responses to item eleven; three responses to item ten). There is some overlap here with the areas of non-codified language identified in Chapter 9, including technical/specialised vocabulary and various types of linguistic play. In general, it seems that many students are attuned to 'exploitation of the resources of language' in TV dialogue. Potential reasons for their awareness include unfamiliarity, unusualness, and emotional effects (e.g. amusement, pleasure).

Together, the above categories make up the majority of responses and hence signal areas that *many* students who provided answers are aware of. In addition, a few (but not many) students do identify some of the other aspects of TV dialogue discussed in this book: repetitions/catchphrases (1x Q10; 8x Q11), invented expressions (3x Q10; 1x Q11), expressivity/emotionality (3x Q10; 3x Q11), references to the real-world/US culture (2x Q11), intertextuality/allusions (2x Q11), nicknames (1x Q11), and innovative word formation (1x Q11). Other areas that some students comment on include vocabulary and word choice, syntax/sentence structure, and pragmatic aspects (see Table A.7 in the Appendix). This shows that these areas of language use can be salient to individual LX viewers but are not as obvious to others.

Interestingly, several participants also nominate specific words or phrases as frequent in TV dialogue (just as the questionnaire intended to elicit through item eleven). The vast majority of these expressions are listed by only one individual, and only the following are named by two or more respondents:[11]

literally (2x), *basically* (3x), *kinda* (2x), *wanna* (3x), *(I'm) gonna* (5x), *are you kidding (me)* (3x), *(what the) hell* (2x), *fuck* (4x), *bitch* (2x), *dude* (5x), *bro* (3x); *oh my god/oh mein Gott* (2x), *I gotta go/gotta* (2x), *seriously/are you serious* (2x), *(oh) well* (2x), *awesome* (3x), *like* (including mentions of the quotative *X was like*: 8x)

Of these listed items, the following are 'key' in SydTV-Std when compared with the LSAC (regardless of range): *kidding*, *are you kidding*, and *are you kidding me*; *hell* and *what the hell*; *fuck*; *bitch*; *dude*; *bro*; *oh my god*; *I got to go*; *seriously*. Of the expressions that are not 'key' when SydTV-Std is compared with the LSAC, several are identified as 'key' when the reference corpus is the AmE06: *well* and *oh well*; *going to*, *I'm going*, and *I'm going to*; *got to*; *want to*; *kind of*; *awesome*; *like*. As a reminder, *kinda*, *gotta*, *wanna*, and *gonna* do not occur in the standardised version of SydTV used for the keyness analysis, which is why I report on findings for the standardised forms here. As reported in Chapter 8, the non-standardised version of SydTV contains more instances of *gonna* and *wanna* than of their variants *going to/want to*, while *gotta* is also fairly common in the corpus.

Together, these results indicate that some key words are not just statistically salient (i.e., overrepresented, 'key') but also cognitively salient (noticeable, memorable), at least to certain LX viewers. This also shows that the linguistic awareness of individual students is often in line with linguistic findings concerning frequency. In other words, the students may be aware of these words because they are overused in TV dialogue when compared with either unscripted spoken English or the kinds of published writing that students are exposed to in the classroom.

In general, it is interesting that almost all of the words/phrases listed by one or more students as common in TV dialogue can be classified (according to Chapter 7) as either or both colloquial/informal and expressive language. This includes:

- lexically reduced forms, colloquial expressions, swear/taboo words: *whatcha, nope, shrink, fuck, hoes, and sluts*
- evaluative lexis, imperatives, interjections, emotion lexis: *weird, terrific, pathetic, hang on, oh my gosh, bazinga, I don't like this.*

The forms *really, literally, basically, actually, seriously*, which are also mentioned by students, are highly multifunctional but can have interpersonal functions such as intensification or contrast. Respondents also list informal terms of address/reference such as *guys, dude, bro*, which can carry expressive meanings and also point to interaction in the here-and-now, as do some nominated forms that could function as response, agreement, or discourse markers (*alright, okay, whatever, you know, I think*). Finally, some of the listed utterances or utterance fragments can be classified as routine formulae (*What you doing? What's up, would you mind ..., let me think about that*).[12] A complete list of all the words, phrases, or utterances mentioned by students is included in Table A.8 in the Appendix.

4 Conclusion

In sum, the surveyed LX viewers, many of whom are potential future English teachers, appear to have a positive relationship with English-language TV series: they say that they watch such series regularly, and most often in the original version. The students state that they find them helpful for learning English and would at least sometimes use them in teaching English to others, as they deem them useful as sources for examples of spoken English. At the same time, questionnaire responses suggest that these learners did not experience such series themselves in their own classroom experience, indicating that English-language series may be underutilised in the English language teaching classroom in Germany. Although English language teaching research has long recognised the effectiveness of television and other popular media, and teachers may advise learners to watch English-language television outside the classroom (Lin & Siyanova-Chanturia 2015: 149), it is necessary to educate all stakeholders about the value of using television series for language learning (Webb 2015: 161, 166). This includes students, parents, and teachers. As the results from this questionnaire suggest, this may be less of a problem with the next generation of teachers.

For the other items, responses were more mixed (with many choosing the midpoint on the scale), namely in relation to awareness of the scripted/artificial nature of TV dialogue, whether the language spoken by TV characters is similar to that spoken by 'real' speakers, and whether there are linguistic differences between the two. On the whole, students either seem to lean towards similarity or are unsure. As the written comments indicate, this uncertainty might derive from students' awareness of the variability between series and genres, and from the fact that there are indeed both similarities and differences between TV dialogue and unscripted spoken English. Areas of difference that many students who provided comments identified are the following: intelligibility/comprehensibility, fluency/coherence, (non)standardness, technical/specialised vocabulary, humour/word-play, and literary/figurative/rhetorical devices. While more research is needed to identify if the latter are indeed more common in contemporary TV dialogue, the other categories clearly align with linguistic research, showing that these students' awareness is accurate. On the other hand, several of the linguistic features of TV dialogue that were identified in this book were mentioned by only a few students. The reasons why certain linguistic characteristics are more noticeable to a large number of students need further investigation, although unfamiliarity, rarity, and emotional effects could play a role.

In general, the results are arguably promising: it seems that there is a lot of experience and linguistic awareness that the teaching of televisual literacy could build on. Incorporating one or two sessions on TV dialogue into the university curriculum could suffice to equip advanced learners of English with the necessary critical awareness to use TV series judiciously in teaching English as a foreign language. For those students who will not go on to teach English, increased televisual literacy would be useful in helping them to recognise and question stereotypical representations, and would also be beneficial for language learning, as it would raise their linguistic awareness of particular features.

In conclusion, there are clear benefits of going 'beyond the product' to examine TV dialogue from the perspective of consumption. Consideration of the LX audience can help linguists understand how viewers outside the national and cultural borders of the United States experience the kind of American English deployed in TV series. Investigating the consumption practices, attitudes, and linguistic awareness of LX viewers can be useful in various ways: it shows the extent to which such language plays a role as a model of spoken English for learners and the extent to which it has been used in the past and might be used in the future in the English language teaching classroom. It can also help inform recommendations to learners (for example, encouraging them to watch a range of different series) as well as the teaching of televisual literacy at the university level. The students captured in my questionnaire are experienced viewers of English-language TV series and a considerable proportion show high levels of linguistic awareness. University lecturers should consider harnessing their students' interest and experience and introduce lectures dedicated to both televisual literacy and to using TV series in English language teaching.

Part VI
Conclusion

12 Conclusion

1 Introduction

The success of premium cable television and other developments, such as the DVD box set, and the increased 'cultural legitimacy' of particular narratives have raised the aesthetic and cultural value of television series (Mittell 2015: 37). Despite this increase in value, relatively few linguistic studies have been undertaken on contemporary television narratives, although recent years have seen a growth in such studies. This book has contributed to this emerging field of research and the endeavour to describe, interpret, and explain television dialogue from a *linguistic* point of view. In this conclusion, I first revisit each chapter before discussing implications for the classroom. The chapter also offers a brief reflection on my journey into television series. While I mention some possibilities for future research in this chapter, additional ideas for such projects are listed on the companion website to SydTV, www.syd-tv.com.

2 Linguistic Insights into Television Series

This book has pursued the ambitious aim of moving corpus linguistic research on TV series 'beyond the product' by combining analyses of TV dialogue with analysis of aspects of production and consumption. I started in the first chapter with explaining what I mean by television series and television dialogue and providing an introduction to the key features of televisual stories and characters as well as the participation framework of TV dialogue. The chapter also explained the production process of television series in the United States, such as the role of the famous 'writers' room' and the collaborative process of television writing.

The information provided in Chapter 1 constitutes an important background against which the features and functions of television dialogue need to be understood. While much of this information will be transferrable to other contexts, it must be emphasised that the production process of TV series in the United States does not apply everywhere. Even though it is clearly an influential model (see Redvall 2013 on the establishment of writers' rooms in Denmark), scholars investigating television dialogue in other countries are advised to undertake their own research into how TV series are produced in their specific cultural context. It is also necessary to remember that not every series follows exactly the same process of production. For instance, there are differences in the extent to which collaborative writing is used and whether showrunners allow actors to change the dialogue in their performance. While it is well known that actors can and do make changes to TV scripts, generalisations based on the analysis of one product should be avoided. Rather, future research should systematically compare final shooting scripts with on-screen dialogue, for a range of different television series. Access to the edit room would be necessary for an even fuller picture of this process, as features introduced by actors can be deleted at this later stage.

In Chapter 2, I provided a brief overview of relevant linguistic research on the extent to which language use in the narrative mass media is similar to unscripted spoken language. Also covered in this chapter were studies on non-standard language, linguistic innovation, and language change. It can be argued that for a medium where 'writers rule' (Lavery & Burkhead 2011: vii), a discipline that focuses on language is uniquely situated to provide novel insights. It is clear that linguistics has indeed made interesting discoveries about media discourse. For instance, stylistic research emphasises that 'dramatic dialogue can never be a mirror of naturally occurring conversation, since the impetus behind dramatization requires that every character-istic of natural speech be available for use as a stylistic device, whether this be in the service of character or plot' (McIntyre 2016: 434). At the same time, much of the research on television series has been limited in the amount and type of data analysed. This book has addressed this gap by drawing on a new corpus with dialogue from sixty-six different TV series (SydTV) and by combining corpus linguistics with media linguistics and other approaches.

Such a media linguistic approach implies that TV series are analysed *as* TV series. It examines the 'medium-specific' (Luginbühl 2015: 9) use of language in this context. Like other narrative audiovisual media, television series and television dialogue have unique properties:

Language in the narrative media differs from other forms of language in its paths of circulation and its relative polish once produced, and yet it shares with other forms of language an utter dependence on an audience and interaction. Narrative audiovisual media involve linguistic events that highlight the intention of the writers, actors, directors, and producers to entertain and engage the audience. Narrative audiovisual media also depend on predictable, recognizable forms of language that combine with the skills and styles of the people involved in the production, and the response of the audience, to form multilayered representations of social life.

(Queen 2015: 22)

This means that it is necessary not only to examine pretextual and contextual aspects of TV series such as their production and participation framework but also to develop specific frameworks that consider their nature as televisual narratives. Stylistic aspects are an important part of this nature, since such fictional narratives 'are shaped by an acute selectivity of presentation, conducive to the "telling" of a story and a sense of narrative arc' (Toolan 2014: 458). This storytelling function of TV dialogue has been regarded as essential, with other functions considered as 'value-added' (Richardson 2010a: 191).

The new functional approach to television series (FATS) developed and presented in Chapters 3 and 4 therefore includes functions relating to the communication of the narrative (settings, happenings, characters). In addition to other important functions (relating to realism; thematic messages and ideology; aesthetic and interpersonal effect and commercial appeal), this model also proposes the creation of consistency and continuity as functions relating specifically to the serial nature of TV narratives. Such a functional approach is not objective, but it 'can [...] strive for some degree of intersubjective plausibility in its demonstrations that particular functions [...] are performed by particular conversational exchanges' (Richardson 2010a: 156).

The new framework significantly adapts, refines, and extends Kozloff's (2000) pioneering research on film dialogue. It can be applied not just to TV series from the United States but also to other English-language series and could be adapted for TV series in languages other than English. My argument is that this new model has explanatory power and can be useful as an interpretive framework, moving beyond the pure description of linguistic patterns in TV dialogue. Significantly, a functional approach to television series extends linguistic analyses that neglect the constructed nature of televisual dialogue and that adopt a strategically 'naive reading position' (Richardson 2010a: 64–5). As demonstrated in this book, the analysis need not stop with the identification of these functions. Rather, researchers can tie such an analysis to larger sociolinguistic issues such as ideology and stereotyping or to production and consumption research. While the model does focus on *television* narratives, it could be modified for analyses of other fictional texts and could thus prove useful for stylistic, sociolinguistic, media linguistic, corpus linguistic, and other investigations of dramatic or narrative texts.

Chapters 5 and 6 introduced the data (SydTV and other corpora), approaches, and techniques used in this book. As a reminder, I have exploited SydTV both as a repository (Chapters 3, 4, 9) and as a dataset for processing by corpus linguistic tools (Chapters 7, 8, and to some degree Chapter 9). In so doing, I have drawn on frequency information, corpus comparison, keyness analysis, collocation, concordances, and distribution analysis (range, dispersion, character diffusion). Importantly, SydTV is now available to other researchers for their own analyses – for access information, see www.syd-tv.com. Scholars could thus use the corpus as a starting point to pinpoint linguistically interesting pieces of dialogue that could then be transcribed in more detail given the public availability of SydTV episodes via services such as iTunes, Netflix, Amazon, etc. This enables a combination of corpus linguistics with research that requires more detailed linguistic information such as the analysis of phonological variables, turn-taking structure, or discourse marking. To gain a fuller picture, it is also useful to examine multimodality in characters and in the product (Bednarek 2010a: 18–21).

In addition, the analyses of TV dialogue were combined in this book with analysis of aspects of production and consumption, thus contributing to 'the expansion of media linguistic investigations to cover the whole communicative process of production – product – reception' (Luginbühl 2015: 19). In outlining the data and methodologies for the various strands of analysis, Chapters 5 and 6 highlighted the highly complex nature of this endeavour, as further discussed in Section 4.

In Part IV (Chapters 7–9), I presented the corpus linguistic and corpus-assisted studies of SydTV. I will summarise the main findings of the three chapters together here[1] but will also refer to results in the next section. On the one hand, it is clear that television dialogue successfully imitates unscripted conversation. SydTV contains many language features that construct television dialogue as non-monologic, spontaneous, on-line, expressive, informal, situation-bound talk – for instance, first- and second-person pronouns, contractions, politeness markers, response and dis/agreement markers, interjections, hesitation markers, repeats, informal lexis, and evaluative adjectives. Several of the non-codified items identified in Chapter 9 also construe TV dialogue as informal and spontaneous conversation (e.g. colloquialisms, swear/taboo words, slang, seemingly 'ad-hoc' word formations). TV dialogue can thus be characterised as counterfeit conversation – what

Heyd (2010: 34) calls 'staged orality'. It simulates naturalistic speech, creating realism for the audience.

On the other hand, many words and n-grams are unusually frequent in SydTV when compared with a reference corpus of unscripted spoken American English. These over-represented items can be categorised as *routine formulae*, *interaction in the here-and-now*, *(in)formality*, *expressivity*, and *narrative concerns*. Surprisingly, interrogatives, negation, and items pointing to the act of speaking (e.g. *to talk to*, *tell me what*) are also unusually frequent. While some results derive from principles of authentic data collection and the nature of the compared corpora (cf. Chapter 2), many of the key items identified in Chapter 7 and many of the non-codified language features identified in Chapter 9 can be linked to the different functions that dialogue lines fulfil for the viewers. Ultimately, these linguistic characteristics of TV dialogue are thus associated with its audience/overhearer/recipient design.

Moreover, the corpus-assisted analyses in Chapter 9 show the inventiveness and creativity of those involved in the production of TV dialogue. The chapter illustrates that such dialogue is rich in linguistic expression and is innovative, creative, imaginative, expressive, novel, witty, and funny. These analyses also provide some evidence for the claim that TV dialogue is an agile language variety, reflecting and quite likely enhancing ongoing change in American English, while also generating lexical innovation. As seen, TV series fully engage with contemporary US society, and a corpus of television dialogue appears to capture cases of ongoing language change very well. There is the clear potential for linguistic innovations as well as other non-codified word forms to spread either nationally or globally. For instance, television series can popularise both existing and new words. However, it remains to be seen whether this will be the case for those language items identified in this book. Chapter 9 did not per se focus on the impact of these items, the extent of their conventionalisation, how they are spread, and if they have led to linguistic change. Such questions are a matter for future research.

Interestingly, the analyses in Part IV confirmed many of the results from prior studies of TV dialogue where fewer data or older series were analysed. This indicates that many lexicogrammatical aspects of TV dialogue are surprisingly conventionalised. Indeed, certain linguistic features are over-represented in many television episodes, characterising television dialogue as a register with linguistic similarities. However, Chapter 8 has shown that there is also variation between series, influenced by both language-internal and language-external factors (such as regulation concerning swear/taboo words). There is a clear need to tease apart the effects of storylines, characters, and genre, including narrative functions of dialogue such as characterisation and plot development.

Finally, the empirical studies have demonstrated that contemporary TV series continue to exploit the indexical meanings of non-standard language features such as *ain't*, *y'all*, and *youse* to construct familiar social identities. The motivation behind the use of such cues may lie in audience design, as this makes characters comprehensible as well as easily recognisable and interpretable. However, there is a clear potential for such representations to reinforce linguistic stereotypes and language ideologies – even if not in all series. Gieve and Norton (2007: 191) argue that representation of linguistic difference 'raises questions about how cultural groups are constituted, insider/outsider status, the nature of cultural difference, and how our relationships with cultural Others are ideologically constructed'. On the whole, today's US television landscape seems to be inhabited by an increased range of diverse characters, which is reflected in the use of non-standard language and other types of linguistic variation. Such representations may challenge views of a monolingual and monocultural United States, but we need to continue to be wary of stereotyping and linguistic ideologies.

Part V started to move 'beyond the product' to address the book's goal of combining linguistic analyses of TV dialogue with analysis of aspects of production and consumption. Chapter 10 summarised key insights gained from a survey of scriptwriting manuals and interviews with Hollywood scriptwriters. Manuals have a lot to say about TV writing in terms of aspects such as structure, plot, exposition, characterisation, and realism. These are dramatic/narrative questions. But only rarely do manuals contain any extended discussion of specific language features. An emphasis on story and structure was also evident in the interviews with scriptwriters, although there is awareness of certain linguistic characteristics of TV dialogue (e.g. the overuse of names, lack of dysfluency, presence of linguistic play). Importantly, this linguistic awareness includes more than those aspects identified in prior research. At the same time, my hypothesis is that this awareness is primarily at play when writers are in an 'analytical' frame of mind rather than during the process of writing, which is a matter of internalisation and tacit knowledge. With respect to the linguistic features of TV dialogue identified in Part IV, only some are the result of conscious planning (e.g. swear/taboo words), while others are more likely the outcome of intuitive, subconscious processes of creation. In sum, it is unlikely that writers actively draw on complex analytical models of the kind linguists use to deconstruct TV dialogue. This does not make the linguistic models inappropriate, but rather shows that linguistic analysis contributes different and complementary insights to those provided in the writings and statements of industry professionals.

Chapter 11 made a first step towards integrating audience analysis. The chapter reported on findings from a questionnaire with a cohort of advanced learners in Germany. The surveyed LX viewers, many of whom are potential future English teachers, seem to have a positive relationship with English-language TV series: they say that they watch such series regularly, and most often in the original version. An important finding is that such students have a wealth of experience and linguistic awareness that the teaching of televisual literacy could build on. This includes awareness of similarities and differences to unscripted spoken English, including dialects/accents, technicalised/specialised vocabulary, humour/wordplay, and linguistic variation between series. As far as particular words are concerned, the awareness of individual students is often in line with linguistic findings concerning unusual frequency (keyness). It is worth repeating here that more research is necessary across different regional and cultural contexts, as the results from this particular cohort of learners should not be extrapolated to foreign language learners or audiences in general. Further, linguists need to undertake additional studies on recirculation processes and audiences. As recent as 2015 it has been pointed out that 'very little of [research on film/TV audiences] has focused on questions of language' (Queen 2015: 233).

3 Implications for Education

Through analysis of TV dialogue, this book has provided new insights into the linguistic features viewers are potentially exposed to. Through questionnaires, we have seen how selected German viewers engage with English-language TV series. While it is unlikely that a particular viewer would have consumed exactly those episodes included in SydTV and no others, the corpus is representative of the type of language viewers encounter. The actual experience of particular viewers will vary, depending on the series they consume. This was apparent both in the questionnaire results and in the corpus linguistic identification of variation among TV series in terms of specific linguistic characteristics (e.g. in/formality, swear/taboo expressions, and non-standard language). It is important that teachers/lecturers remain aware of such variation and carefully choose dialogue from particular series for use in the classroom. In addition, learners should be encouraged to watch a range of very different series or genres outside the classroom. Three aspects to look out for include the type of television series (network, cable, subscription, etc.), its genre, and the constructed relationships between characters (equal or hierarchical), since all of these influence language use. Additional advice on the selection of television series for language learning purposes is given in Al-Surmi (2012: 691–2), Lin and Siyanova-Chanturia (2015: 154–5), and Webb (2015: 165).

Previous research has argued that TV dialogue can be used as a surrogate or model of spoken English in the English language teaching classroom, because it is similar enough to such unscripted language. While the studies in this book confirm the lexicogrammatical similarities between TV dialogue and unscripted spoken American English, differences have also been uncovered – such as the over-representation of particular language features as summarised above. Furthermore, such a corpus linguistic study does not address important aspects such as turn-taking structure and clarity of enunciation where there are differences between the two varieties (Quaglio 2008: 208).

Clearly, there are both similarities and differences between the language used in contemporary US television series and the language used by US speakers in the 'real' world. However, TV dialogue need not be identical to unscripted conversation to be useful for language learning and teaching. On the one hand, differences such as the lower amount of performance phenomena can be advantageous (Dose 2013). On the other hand, TV dialogue can and should be taught as an instance of dialogue emanating from a TV narrative. This means that the teaching of *media literacy* can be interwoven with the teaching of English language. The characteristics that differentiate TV dialogue from unscripted spoken varieties are not problematic if TV dialogue is taught *as* TV dialogue.

Some of the general advantages and challenges of using TV series inside and outside the classroom have been discussed in the previous chapter and will not be reviewed again here. Briefly, TV series are generally considered as helpful for being more colloquial/naturalistic than textbooks and useful for areas such as vocabulary acquisition, cultural proficiency, listening comprehension, and fluency. In this book corpus linguistic techniques were used to uncover the kind of language that LX viewers are likely to encounter by watching contemporary US TV series in the original version. The analyses confirm that much TV dialogue contains colloquial and informal language as well as other language features that also occur in spontaneous talk. The presence of recent and new expressions means that television narratives 'can offer the students a window onto current popular language use' (Dose 2013). In addition, viewers will encounter references to culture-specific phenomena and institutions. I have talked about the cultural anchoring of TV series. Television audiences thus become spectators of American culture (Richardson 2010a: 189). This could be useful when teaching cultural knowledge of the United States (*Landeskunde* in German). Similarly, variation in the use of swear/taboo words across TV series can be used to discuss social attitudes, norms, and censorship in the United States.

Together, the results indicate that TV dialogue can be useful for teaching pupils or students about many different aspects of language use, including expressions that might traditionally be neglected in textbooks or classroom teaching. This would need to be implemented in ways that are appropriate to both age and proficiency and would need to include information about appropriateness and contextual factors. This applies especially but not exclusively to the expression of emotionality and to swear/taboo words, which I will briefly comment on here.

In a comprehensive research program Dewaele (e.g. 2004, 2005, 2016a, b) has investigated emotion-laden words (including swear/taboo words) in the context of language acquisition and multilingualism. His studies suggest that the use of swear/taboo words can be challenging for language learners, that words in the L2 carry lower emotional force, that L2 speakers may differ from L1 speakers in their perceptions of offensiveness, and that 'many have lower levels of understanding of the rules that govern swearing in English because of less frequent practice and observation of swearing in various contexts' (Dewaele 2016b: 14). Dewaele (2004: 220) concludes that instructed learning should include material that is rich in swear/taboo words. TV series are useful in that respect because they feature many examples of use and variation in different kinds of words and phraseologies, which could constitute a starting point for teaching students about swear/taboo words, their emotional force, their functions, and contexts of appropriate and inappropriate use. As the questionnaire results in Chapter 11 suggest, the use of swear/taboo words in US TV series already constitutes an important source for some LX viewers. Every exposure to such words 'has the potential to push the user to consciously or unconsciously re-adjust, re-calibrate the meaning, reconsider the capacity to offend, and, at some future point, decide to mimic (or not) the use by L1 users' (Dewaele 2016a: 125). From an applied linguistic perspective it is therefore important to describe and analyse their use and distribution in media language. Before we integrate such material in the classroom it is vital to gain fuller understanding of their use in such media contexts.

More generally, when integrating TV series into the classroom – whatever the purpose of instruction – it is important for teachers and lecturers to either avoid the use of dialogue that includes derogatory, abusive, stereotypical, or 'Othering' language use or to utilise such dialogue to problematise and critique it in the context of media literacy. Again, this is a matter to be determined by the teacher/lecturer given their local contexts. As noted, there is a danger that LX viewers might be socialised into dominant, potentially negative or stereotypical values about particular identities, depending on the series they consume. It is possible to counter this danger by equipping viewers with the skills needed to deconstruct stereotypes and to understand their role and function in TV narratives.

In sum, the questionnaire results in Chapter 11 indicate that TV series might still be underutilised in the English language teaching classroom in Germany. This could be remedied with the help of thematic teacher handbooks, textbooks, or other targeted teaching and learning resources. While I agree with other scholars and practitioners on the usefulness of TV dialogue for language learning and teaching, I would add that it should be used to teach students not only English but also media literacy – especially in relation to linguistic stereotypes.

At the university level, too, the teaching of media or television literacy could be incorporated into the curriculum for future English teachers. It appears that TV dialogue does constitute an influential model for many students studying English at university in Germany. Rather than ignoring such practices of consumption it might be wise to harness this interest. As suggested in Chapter 11, university lectures should consider the introduction of material dedicated both to televisual literacy and to using TV series in English language teaching. This would go a long way towards equipping students with the necessary critical awareness to use TV series judiciously in the classroom at a later stage. As mentioned above, the teaching of television literacy could build on a considerable amount of experience and linguistic awareness on the part of students. For example, results suggest that it is possible to focus on non-standard language use, linguistic stereotypes, and language ideologies with advanced learners of English.

In addition, TV dialogue can be helpful in the linguistics classroom, including in the teaching of register variation (Quaglio 2009: 149), word formation, humour, linguistic play, and so on. The contributions to Beers Fägersten (2016) use television series to teach basic linguistic concepts such as morphology, word formation, syntax, pragmatics, language variation, and language acquisition. Squires and Queen (2011: 232) recommend the integration of mass media content across linguistics as 'an appropriate way to engage students in a lively class while broadening their applications of course concepts'. Media clips can be used in the classroom or out of class to illustrate linguistic phenomena or to evaluate student learning and performance, and have a positive impact on student engagement (Squires & Queen 2011: 221–7). In sociolinguistics, data from TV series or films can be helpful in teaching students about language variation, indexicality, and stereotypes (Queen 2013: 222). Indeed, Queen (2015) is a useful introduction to these and other sociolinguistic concepts with specific reference to the narrative mass media.

Finally, the results from the linguistic studies in this book could feed into the development of industry-appropriate guidelines for scriptwriters on how to build characters and narratives through words. As has become evident, very few manuals for aspiring or novice scriptwriters include any linguistic information on dialogue. By spelling out some of the major linguistic resources, writers' tacit knowledge can be made explicit. Such guidelines could usefully complement other pedagogic resources rather than substitute them, and could have an impact on professional education and practices.

4 Reflection

When I first started working on US TV series about a decade ago (Bednarek 2007) I began by analysing one series (*Gilmore Girls*). Since then, my interest has included both specific series (*Big Bang Theory*, *Flight of the Conchords*, *Nurse Jackie*, *Saving Grace*, *Weeds*) as well as TV series more generally. This book falls squarely in the latter category. In the endeavour to examine TV dialogue as a language variety I tried to bring together corpus linguistics with applied linguistics, media linguistics, and sociocultural linguistics.

The **corpus linguistic** approach centred on a small, specialised corpus (SydTV), which I assessed in Chapter 5. Using different approaches to explore the corpus, quantitative and qualitative analyses were combined in various ways and methods were triangulated. Since these analyses were primarily intrasemiotic and intertextual in terms of the topology introduced in Chapter 5, there is much room for future intersemiotic (multimodal) and intratextual analysis. With its focus on dialogue, the book can be classified as logocentrism (Toolan 2014:461), despite the multimodal nature of television narratives, which I have explored elsewhere (e.g. Bednarek 2010a, 2015a). This was primarily for practical reasons – it was simply beyond the scope of this book to undertake such analysis. In addition, a corpus linguistic approach lends itself to intertextual analysis much more than to intratextual analysis. To address this gap, corpus linguistic analysis needs to continue developing new corpus techniques and tools as well as making greater use of existing but underutilised tools such as the concordance plot (see Bednarek 2015c: 271–2) and cluster/n-gram analysis *across* sentence breaks (see Bednarek 2010a: 73; 2014d: 12–15). Alternatively, corpus linguistics can be combined with other approaches that focus on intratextual patterns (e.g. turn-taking structure or plot development).

The **applied linguistic** perspective meant examining TV dialogue in its professional context, and included analysis of scriptwriting manuals, interviews with industry professionals, and taking account of LX viewers. In Section 3 above I discussed implications of the results for education. The **media linguistic** perspective brought with it a focus on the specific characteristics of TV narratives and the recognisable functions of TV dialogue, as explained in Section 2 above. Since media linguistics has long focused on journalistic texts (Luginbühl 2015), such research continues the expansion of this subdiscipline. However, it has been necessary to exclude from consideration medium-specific processes such as subtitling and dubbing, which may provide different or added information to audiences.

With respect to **sociocultural linguistics**, the analyses paid particular attention to the relationship between language and society, for instance through the focus on non-standard language and linguistic innovation. Given the remit of the book and the constraints of the corpus, the analysis mostly ignored non-codified language at the level of phonology, syntax, and pragmatics/discourse as well as aspects such as crossing and stylisation (as discussed at www.syd-tv.com). One important insight is that collocation analysis can be a helpful way of combining corpus linguistics with sociolinguistic research into indexicality and stereotyping, pointing to interesting packages or bundles of linguistic features that are used for characterisation. In addition, corpus linguistic and corpus-assisted analysis of the use of non-standard language features can provide indirect insights into the language variation models of industry professionals, while interviews can illustrate their awareness and how this language variation is talked about. Questionnaire data and other types of audience research can be used to probe viewers' linguistic awareness and reactions to non-standard language and language variation.

As far as the analysis of linguistic innovation and change is concerned, it is clear that media language should not be dismissed entirely from its investigation. As Curzan (2014: 61) argues, changes in 'a few words here or there' may be rejected as 'not fundamental language change', but 'language change often happens word by word', and '[s]ingle words and individual innovations can make history'. However, we need better corpora of contemporary, spontaneous, casual spoken American English that have been carefully transcribed and that can act as suitable reference points for media language. The latter point also applies to other types of linguistic analysis (beyond linguistic innovation). For instance, features such as phonological reduction (e.g. *wanna*, *gonna*) can be meaningfully compared only across corpora that have been transcribed using the same procedures and with the same degree of reliability or accuracy.

Finally, the incorporation of methods such as interviews and questionnaires has allowed this book to make a contribution to the emerging combination of corpus linguistics with ethnography. I have already expanded on the relevance and usefulness of such an approach in the last two chapters. Ultimately, this helps to push linguistic research 'beyond the product', to provide complementary insights, and to make connections between product, production, and consumption. At the same time, it has to be said that such a project is highly ambitious, complex, and time consuming. Not only does it require the collection and analysis of many different types of data; it also requires expertise in different methodologies. This is not something that will always be possible in the linguistic analysis of the narrative mass media. Moreover, it can be difficult to meaningfully connect the different strands of analysis rather than treat them as separate research programs. My approach in this book was to use insights gained from the linguistic analyses of SydTV to guide the analysis of scriptwriting manuals, interviews, and questionnaires so as to make better connections and provide a more cohesive whole.

5 Concluding Remarks

Those involved in the production of television dialogue need to negotiate a number of constraints and norms. In addition to being constrained by particular business models and commercial imperatives, they need to consider the communicative norms and ideologies that hold in a particular society (e.g. politeness norms, language ideologies, conversational principles), the norms governing the particular format (e.g. narrative norms, genre norms, participation framework), legal or quasi-legal norms (e.g. censorship), and so on. They also need to strike a balance between adhering to generic conventions and linguistic innovation/creativity. The outcome or product of this negotiation is the TV dialogue that is consumed by millions of viewers worldwide. What I hope this book has demonstrated is that a linguistic analysis of this dialogue is not only worthwhile but can be meaningfully connected to aspects of production and consumption. Taken together, the results present significant and new insights into television dialogue that deepen our understanding of this important language variety and can impact on applications in the classroom and the profession.

Because SydTV is a static corpus, it captures a specific time frame of contemporary television and can provide a reference point for future research. New televisual stories and characters constantly arise and compete for the audience's attention, illustrating the continuing importance of such televisual storytelling in contemporary society. Whether *winter is coming* or you just need to *treat yoself*, there is no denying that TV series also offer us pleasure, even if the linguists among us may always have their analytical eye trained on the dialogue.

Appendix

Table A.1 *List of all episodes included in SydTV*

TV series[a]	Year	Episode Number	Episode name
According to Jim	2001	4	'Anniversary'
Anger Management	2012	1	'Charlie Goes Back to Therapy'
Arrested Development	2003	22	'Let 'em Eat Cake'
Baby Daddy	2012	1	Pilot
The Big Bang Theory	2007	16	'The Peanut Reaction'
The Big C	2010	1	Pilot
Birds of Prey	2002	1	Pilot
Bones	2005	20	'The Graft in the Girl'
Breaking Bad	2008	3	'And the Bag's in the River'
Castle	2009	2	'Nanny McDead'
Community	2009	1	Pilot
Desperate Housewives	2004	19	'Live Alone and Like It'
Dexter	2006	12	'Born Free'
Dollhouse	2009	6	'Man on the Street'
Drop Dead Diva	2009	12	'Dead Model Walking'
Eastbound & Down	2009	1	'Chapter 1'
Enlightened	2011	1	Pilot
Entourage	2004	7	'The Scene'
Fringe	2008	13	'The Transformation'
Gilmore Girls	2000	11	'Paris Is Burning'
Girls	2012	3	'All Adventurous Women Do'
Glee	2009	9	'Wheels'
The Good Wife	2009	21	'Unplugged'
Gossip Girl	2007	17	'Woman on the Verge'
Grey's Anatomy	2005	9	'Who's Zoomin' Who?'
Hot in Cleveland	2010	5	'Good Neighbors'
House	2004	18	'Babies and Birthwater'
How I Met Your Mother	2005	12	'The Wedding'
Human Target	2010	11	'Victoria'
In Treatment	2008	13	'Sophie: Week Three'
It's Always Sunny in Philadelphia	2005	1	'The Gang Gets Racist'

(continued)

Table A.1 (cont.)

TV series[a]	Year	Episode Number	Episode name
Jericho	2006	14	'Heart of Winter'
Legend of the Seeker	2008	14	'Hartland'
Lost	2004	17	'... in Translation'
Malcolm in the Middle	2000	1	Pilot
The Middle	2009	23	'Signals'
Mike & Molly	2010	3	'First Kiss'
Modern Family	2009	15	'My Funky Valentine'
My Name Is Earl	2005	21	'The Bounty Hunter'
NCIS	2003	1	'Yankee White'
The New Adventures of Old Christine	2006	1	Pilot
New Girl	2011	1	Pilot
Nurse Jackie	2009	3	'Chicken Soup'
The Office	2005	6	'Hot Girl'
Outsourced	2010	22	'Rajiv Ties the Baraat, Part 2'
Parks and Recreation	2009	6	'Rock Show'
Prison Break	2005	16	'Brother's Keeper'
Pushing Daisies	2007	7	'Smell of Success'
Royal Pains	2009	12	'Wonderland'
The Shield	2002	4	'Dawg Days'
Southland	2009	2	'Mozambique'
Suits	2011	10	'The Shelf Life'
Supernatural	2005	19	'Provenance'
Teen Wolf	2011	12	'Code Breaker'
Thirty Rock	2006	11	'The Head and the Hair'
Tru Calling	2003	15	'The Getaway'
True Blood	2008	7	'Burning House of Love'
24	2001	20	'7:00–8:00 pm'
2 Broke Girls	2011	24	'And Martha Stewart Have a Ball, part 2'
Two and a Half Men	2003	6	'Did You Check with the Captain of the Flying Monkeys?'
United States of Tara	2009	8	'Abundance'
The Vampire Diaries	2009	22	'Founder's Day'
Veep	2012	1	'Fundraiser'
Weeds	2005	1	'You Can't Miss the Bear'
The Wire	2002	9	'Game Day'
Workaholics	2011	8	'To Friend a Predator'

[a] Descriptions of each series can easily be found on the internet, and plot summaries of most episodes are available in relevant online episode guides.

Table A.2 Corpus size (in number of words) of SydTV and SydTV-Std depending on token definitions

Token definitions (WordSmith 'tokens in text')	SydTV	SydTV-Std
hyphens do not separate words; ' not allowed within word	275,074	276,899
hyphens separate words; ' not allowed within word	276,287	278,112
hyphens do not separate words; ' allowed within word	258,944	260,824
hyphens separate words; ' allowed within word	260,157	262,037

Table A.3 Composition of SydTV in number of episodes and words according to WordSmith ('tokens in text'), showing the variables of textual time, 'quality' vs. 'mainstream', and drama vs. comedy (token definition: hyphens do not separate words; ' not allowed within word)

	SydTV: Number of episodes and words			
	'Quality'		'Mainstream'	
Textual time	Drama	Comedy	Drama	Comedy
pilot episodes	0/0	7/26,671	2/10,053	5/16,779
final episodes	2/10,334	3/10,539	1/3,664	4/14,019
episodes at the beginning	2/8,675	3/9,812	1/4,958	3/12,540
episodes in the middle	5/20,314	4/15,272	5/24,065	3/13,361
episodes at the end	3/13,900	5/20,370	4/20,332	4/19,416
Total	12/53,223	22/82,664	13/63,072	19/76,115
	135,887		139,187	

Table A.4 Variants and their standardised forms

Variant	Standardised form[a]
percent; %	per cent
gonna	going to
wanna	want to
gotta	got to
oughta	ought to
coulda	could have
kinda	kind of
woulda	would have
shoulda	should have
lotta	lot of
sorta	sort of
	(continued)

Table A.4 (cont.)

Variant	Standardised form[a]
c'mon	*come on*
lemme	*let me*
gimme	*give me*
gotcha	*got you*
'em	*them*
y'all	*you all*
'til	*until*
'round	*around*
outta; outa	*out of*

[a] To produce a partially standardised version of SydTV 3.0 I used WordSmith's Text Converter function to standardise the lexicogrammatical items listed in in this table. I focused on items that I knew (from pilot studies) to have a significant influence on the calculation of keyness. Most of the variants were automatically standardised using a conversion file (settings: within file conversion, whole word, not case sensitive), with some changes made separately (using the 'just one change' setting). A test file was converted first and results checked, before SydTV was converted. In addition, I manually changed every instance where the alveolar form [In] was used in words ending in <ing> (e.g. *somethin'*, *goin'*, *fuckin'*) to *-ing* (e.g. *something, going, fucking*). I did not standardise any contractions since I am interested in their occurrence and since they are also present in the corpora to which I compare SydTV.

Table A.5 Information on standardisation

Variant	Standardised form[a]
OK	*okay*
all right	*alright*
awhile	*a while*
mum/mum's/mums	*mom/mom's/moms*
girl friend/girl friend's/girl friends; girl-friend/ girl-friend's/girl-friends	*girlfriend/girlfriend's/ girlfriends*
Mr., Mrs., Dr.	*Mr, Mrs, doctor*
um	*umm*
hm, hmmm, hum	*hmm*
uh-huh, uhhuh	*uh huh*
mm	*mmm*
mm-hmm, mhm, mmm-hmm, mmm-hmmm, mmm hmm, mmhmm, umm-hmm, umm-huh, umm huh, umm-hum, umm hum, umm-mmm	*mm-hmmm*

(continued)

Table A.5 (cont.)

Variant	Standardised form[a]
er	*uh*
shh, shhh	*sh*
till ['until']	first converted into *'til*, then into *until* (see Table A.4)
aah, aaaah, ahh	*ah*
oooh, ohhh, oohh	*oh*
ya	*you*
yup	*yep*
geez	*jeez*
good bye, goodbye	*good-bye*
bye bye	*bye-bye*
lets ['let us']	*let's*
*in'	**ing*
gawd	*god*

[a] The AmE06, BE06, C_CH, and LSAC were also partially standardised, for the purpose of comparing them with SydTV-Std in Sketch Engine (all corpora) and for keyness analysis (LSAC). The spoken corpora were used with speaker names either in angle brackets or deleted. In addition to standardising these corpora according to Table A.4, several forms were changed to their SydTV spelling (in Table A.5). The forms to be standardised were primarily identified based on a pilot study using Sketch Engine's Comparing corpora function as well as a pilot keyness analysis using WordSmith.

I also drew on some (limited) information about the transcription conventions for the two components of C_CH, namely the CallHome corpus and the Charlotte Narrative and Conversation Collection (Charlotte): the documentation available on CallHome via the Linguistic Data Consortium (https://catalog.ldc.upenn.edu/docs/LDC97T14/ch_eng.txt, last accessed 15 April 2017) and information about how the Charlotte corpus was transcribed (provided by oral historian Tina Wright). For example, CallHome makes use of *um, mm, hm* rather than *umm, mmm, hmm*, while Charlotte includes interviewer responses as *uh-huh* and *um-hum* (according to the instructions, although I also found other forms in the corpus). It must be noted that Charlotte may not contain all non-verbal utterances. The guidelines note that these are not included when used by speakers (e.g. *you know, um, it* ... is transcribed as *you know, it* ...). However, a search of the Charlotte data in fact discovered almost two thousand instances of *um*. In general, Charlotte was conducted as a student project, so transcription may not always adhere to the guidelines (Tina Wright, email communication). Both corpora include some information in square/round brackets – for example, audible actions/sounds like 'laughter', 'cough', 'buzz', inaudible/unintelligible speech and 'best guesses' as well as speech in another language and transcriber comments (e.g. [[previous word lengthened]]). Any content in brackets was removed. I also made some other changes to C_CH, deleting redundant spaces, manually removing any speaker initials (e.g. *BH:*), and converting dashes and hyphens to three dots when indicating ellipsis. Symbols were also removed (#, //, + **, %, &), which mark simultaneous speech, asides, mispronunciations, idiosyncratic words, hesitation words, and proper names/place names (in CallHome). Information such as *START OF TAPE 1, SIDE A* was also deleted (in Charlotte).

On the whole, the aim of the partial standardisation was to ensure that most of the items identified by the comparative analysis are not simply the result of differing transcription conventions (e.g. *okay* in SydTV vs. *OK* in parts of C_CH; different conventions for semi-lexical features, etc.). As with the standardisation of SydTV, most of the variants were automatically standardised using WordSmith's Text Converter function and a conversion file (settings: within file conversion, whole word, not case sensitive), with some changes made separately (using the 'just one change' setting). Some forms were corrected manually in each file where they occurred, e.g. *lets* to *let's* (when standing for *let us*) and **in'* to **ing*. In the case of the LSAC, which includes 406 instances of **in'*, I first identified the different types and then prepared a conversion file that included all of the 96 identified types before converting them (e.g. 'somethin' → 'something'; 'lovin' → 'loving').

Generally, a test file was converted first and results checked before all the corpora were converted. In cases with known ambiguities and wherever this was possible, I double-checked results to make sure that there were no incorrect conversions: for example, in the written BE06 and AmE06 corpora *mm* frequently stands for 'millimetre' and *er* may stand for 'emergency room', neither of which were converted. Similarly, *till* was converted into *until* only where appropriate. Such double-checking was not possible if instances ran into the thousands.

This standardisation is of necessity incomplete, and some differences remain (e.g. how acronyms and numbers are spelt, the inclusion of partial words and abbreviations, and the spelling/inclusion of additional semi-lexical features and non-lexemes). There are clear limits to retrospective standardisation. In other words, this process minimises the interference of transcription differences considerably, but does not eliminate it completely.

Das Ausfüllen dieses Fragebogens ist freiwillig. Die Erhebung der Daten wird absolut anonym durchgeführt. Sie sind durch Ihre Antworten nicht identifizierbar und alle Ergebnisse werden nur in Zusammenfassung publiziert. Bitte beantworten Sie die Fragen in der vorgegebenen Reihenfolge. Der Fragebogen hat zwei Seiten – **bitte beide Seiten ausfüllen (WICHTIG!)**

Dauer: ca. 10 Minuten. Herzlichen Dank für Ihre Mitwirkung – Sie helfen mir damit sehr bei meiner Forschung!

1. Studiengang/Abschluss (Beispiel: Englisch Staatsexamen Lehramt Gymnasium): _____

2. Semesterzahl (Beispiel: 1 = 1. Semester; 2 – 2. Semester): _____

Bei den folgenden Fragen bitte nur EINE Antwort ankreuzen: ⊠

3. Wenn ich mir englisch-sprachige TV Serien (z.B. *Big Bang Theory, NCIS, The Mentalist, The Blacklist, CSI, Bones*) anschaue (im Fernsehen, Netflix, ITunes, Amazon, Computer, Internet, DVD...), dann typischerweise:

☐ auf Deutsch ohne Untertitel

☐ auf Deutsch mit englischen Untertiteln

☐ auf Deutsch mit deutschen Untertiteln

☐ auf Englisch ohne Untertitel

☐ auf Englisch mit deutschen Untertiteln

☐ auf Englisch mit englischen Untertiteln

oder:

☐ Ich schaue mir solche Serien gar nicht oder nur sehr selten an

4. Ich finde solche TV Serien nützlich, um (besser) Englisch zu lernen

trifft nicht zu — trifft voll zu

$$0 - 1 - 2 - 3 - 4$$

5. Ich würde im Englischunterricht Beispiele aus englisch-sprachigen TV-serien (z.B. *Big Bang Theory, NCIS*) zeigen/verwenden oder habe das schon getan (z.B. im Praktikum, Nachhilfe)

gar nicht — sehr oft

$$0 - 1 - 2 - 3 - 4$$

oder:

☐ ich habe nicht vor, Englisch zu unterrichten und habe noch nie Englisch unterrichtet

6. Englisch-sprachige TV Serien sind nützlich, um SchülerInnen Beispiele von gesprochenem Englisch zu zeigen

trifft nicht zu — trifft voll zu

$$0 - 1 - 2 - 3 - 4$$

WICHTIG: Bitte umdrehen und zweite Seite ausfüllen

Figure A.1 Questionnaire in German

7. Wenn ich mir englisch-sprachige TV Serien anschaue, fällt es mir auf, dass die Sprache ‚gescripted' (d.h. künstlich, vorher ersonnen) ist:

gar nicht   sehr oft

0   1   2   3   4

8. Mein/e English Lehrer/in hat im Unterricht Beispiele aus englisch-sprachigen TV-serien gezeigt/verwendet.

gar nicht   sehr oft

0   1   2   3   4

9. Die gesprochene Sprache von TV Charakteren in englisch-sprachigen TV Serien ist der gesprochenen Sprache von 'realen' Sprechern ähnlich.

trifft   trifft
nicht zu   voll zu

0   1   2   3   4

Bei der folgenden Frage bitte nur EINE Antwort ankreuzen (und gegebenenfalls Ihre Antwort gut leserlich in das vorgesehene Textfeld eintragen):

10. Es gibt meiner Meinung nach sprachliche Unterschiede zwischen der gesprochenen Sprache von Charakteren in englisch-sprachigen TV Serien und der gesprochenen Sprache von 'realen' Sprechern:

☐ Nein, es gibt keine Unterschiede

☐ Ich weiß nicht/bin mir unsicher

☐ Ja, es gibt die folgenden sprachlichen Unterschiede:

_____
_____
_____
_____

Offene Frage: Bitte tragen Sie Ihre Antwort gut leserlich in das vorgesehene Textfeld ein.

11. Am häufigsten kommen meiner Meinung nach in der gesprochenen Sprache von Charakteren in englisch-sprachigen TV Serien folgende sprachliche Phänomene vor (z.B. spezielle Wörter, Ausdrücke, Sprachgebrauch, Sprechakte,…):

_____
_____
_____
_____
_____

Bei Fragen zu diesem Fragebogen bitte einfach eine Email an mich senden: Monika.Bednarek@sydney.edu.au

Figure A.1 (cont.)

Table A.6 Unclassified key items

Other key items	
unclassified, e.g. because of varied usage/multiple functionality, difficult to classify, requiring more in-depth analysis, or because not concordanced	*a, about, am, an, anyone, away, been, believe, case[†], chance, clear[†], come, eyes[†], everyone, for, happen[†], head[†], her, him, his, keep, knew, knows, let, life[†], look[†]* (varied usage, sometimes discourse marker, sometimes imperative, sometimes with evaluative adjective, and other usages), *meet, mind[†], night[†]* (varied usage, only a few instances of *good night*), *own[†], someone, stay[†], take[†]* (mostly not used as imperative/alert), *this, to, truth[†], understand[†], with, about this, going on, out of, to take, know what, with a*

Table A.7 Other responses to questionnaire items

Other responses to questionnaire items	
Vocabulary and word choice	well thought-out/clear/precise choice of words: 3x Q10, 1x Q11; limited vocabulary (dependent on topic/theme): 2x Q10; wider vocabulary range: 1x Q10; vocabulary dependant on theme and target audience: 1x Q11; some outdated expressions: 1x Q10; archaic/older language (examples *Game of Thrones, Downton Abbey*): 2x Q10; 4x Q11; some use of individual words that won't be understood everywhere (. . . *aber oft werden einzelne Wörter, die nicht überall verstanden werden, benutzt*): 1x Q11
Syntax/sentence structure	elaborated syntax/sentences: 3x Q10; 1x Q11; short sentences: 1x Q11
Pragmatics of communication	fewer trivial things/details are mentioned/discussed; less small talk: 3x Q10; successful communication (fewer misunderstandings unless planned): 1x Q10; misunderstandings/miscommunications: 2x Q11; illocution not working as planned [*Fehlschlagen der Illokution*]/indirect speech acts that are not understood: 2x Q11; replies are more direct without expressions such as *on the one hand, on the other hand* [*auf der einen Seite. . . auf der anderen Seite*]: 1x Q10; indirect language: 1x Q11; deviations from rules: 1x

(continued)

Table A.7 (cont.)

Other responses to questionnaire items	
	Q11; stereotyped (overused) conversations/ exaggerated conversational situations: 2x Q10; short conversations/speech acts: 1x Q11; less sensibility [*Sensibilität*] towards the addressee [*Gegenüber*]: 1x Q10; talking to oneself [*Selbstgespräche*]: 1x Q10; 'lectures' [*Belehrungen*]: 1x Q10; (white) lies [(*Not*)*lügen*]: 1x Q11; anecdotes: 1x Q11; questions; question/answer sequences: 2x Q11; in the language of real speakers there are more cultural 'tricks' that can be incomprehensible to other cultures: 1x Q10 [*Außerdem, kann es mehr kulturelle 'Tricks' geben, die nicht immer ganz verständlich für andere Kulturen sein können.*]
Other	fewer interjections: 1x Q11; idiomatic language: 1x Q11; higher pitch level towards the end of sentence: 1x Q11; repetitions: 1x Q11

Table A.8 Words/expressions listed by students in the questionnaire in response to item 11

Words/expressions	Number of mentions
really	1
literally	2
basically	3
actually	1
obviously (*Sherlock*)	1
seriously?; *are you serious?*	2
are you kidding (*me*)	3
we have to get out of here	1
I don't like this	1
ouh	1
ewaa	1
come on	1
hang on	1
oh nein, oh mein Gott	1
oh well; well	2
oh my gosh	1
oh my god	1

(*continued*)

Table A.8 (cont.)

Words/expressions	Number of mentions
bazinga (BBT)	1
bitch	2
damn	1
fuck	4
what the hell, hell	2
awesome (HIMYM)	3
brilliant (UK)	1
terrific (Family Guy)	1
pathetic	1
weird (Friends)	1
guys	1
dude	5
bro	3
mate (British; *Sherlock*)	3
hey man	1
nope	1
kinda	2
I gotta go; gotta	2
wanna	3
gonna; I'm gonna	5
ain't,	1
like; and she was like; I was like, and than he was like [sic]	8
blimey, innit	1
you know	1
whatever, I think, sure	1
what you doing?	1
what's up	1
whatcha	1
shrink	1
hoes & sluts	1
alright	1
okay	1
to put out a BOLO for so (Mentalist)	1
hit the bucket	1
I'd say	1
let me think about that	1
would you mind...	1
on fleek, basic, hashtags	1
newbie (Scrubs: Dr Cox)	1
to be supposed to	1

Endnotes

Chapter 1

1 Syndication means selling TV series to stations and foreign markets after they have had their run on a network (Douglas 2011: 287).

2 As explained in Chapter 6, *non-codified language* refers to language use that has not (yet) been codified in reference works such as dictionaries or grammar books.

3 I use *genre* to refer to categories of TV programmes such as comedy, drama, dramedy, crime, legal, medical, sci-fi, family, action, adventure, and so on. This use differs from the more technicalised term *genre* used in linguistic theory.

4 Lippi-Green (2012: 61) argues that it is problematic to continue to use terms such as *standard* and *non-standard*, since they are inaccurate and ideological. I nevertheless use them in this book to make connections to relevant sociolinguistic research, but the reader should imagine 'scare quotes' around the words.

5 Different definitions of *narrative* either exclude or include films (and by extension TV series) and drama (Fludernik 2009: 4–7; Abbott 2014: 15). For example, Pfister distinguishes narrative texts from dramatic texts and argues that film is 'a form which combines structural features of both narrative and dramatic texts' (1988: 25), since the camera (and editing) can be considered as mediating communication system. Fludernik states that drama and film can be considered as verbal-visual narratives (2009: 7) and further that 'film is widely recognized as a narrative medium, although its affinity with drama cannot be completely denied' (2009: 114). Kozloff (2000: 16–17) points to differences between film dialogue, stage dialogue, and dialogue in novels. Thompson (2003: 79) uses the term 'enacted narratives' for film and television. As indicated by the fact that I use the term *televisual narrative*, I do consider TV series as being concerned with the telling of stories. In addition, some TV series have narrating voice-overs (a character like in *Mr. Robot* or a narrator like in *Pushing Daisies*). However, this book does not situate itself within the field of narratology and is not overly concerned with describing the narrative elements or structure of TV series, although I briefly discuss this in Section 3. I sometimes use the term *TV narrative* as synonym for *TV series*.

6 In *series*, storylines tend to be completed in one episode even though there may also be a few that continue across episodes and/or seasons. *Serials* have more continuing storylines where the narrative is open-ended, i.e. extends across individual episodes within or across seasons. A more in-depth discussion of the difference between series and serial is provided in Bednarek (2010a: 12), and of the terms *narrative*, *fictional/imaginative*, and *scripted* in Queen (2015:

12–14). Soap operas are long-running, open-ended TV serials but excluded in this book, which focuses on series that have a limited number of seasons. For the same reason, close-ended miniseries are also not discussed.

7 Throughout this book, the abbreviation *KL* refers to Kindle locations for e-books that have no page numbers.

8 Possibilities of character changes and the atypical case of Walter White in *Breaking Bad* are discussed in Mittell (2015: 132–63). From a linguistic perspective, character change and stability in TV series are explored in case studies by Bednarek (2011a) and Mandala (2011).

9 The same holds for Lambrou's (2014) and Short's (2014) analyses of characters and character relations in novels, plays, and films through turn-taking patterns, speech-acts, conversational maxims, and politeness patterns. Kozloff (2000) discusses many examples where film dialogue functions to establish characters and their relationships, from the amount, speed, and volume of spoken dialogue to intonation, stuttering, and repetition; vocabulary and syntax; speech acts (e.g. commands, questions); turn-taking structure (e.g. overlaps, interruptions, punch lines); dialects; and so on. Elliott (2000) examines rhoticity in relation to the gender as well as the social and moral status of film characters. Much sociolinguistic research has explored the use of non-standard language in films with respect to the (stereotyped) construction of characters (see Chapter 2).

10 Mittell (2015) provides a much more sustained discussion than I am able to here, but very briefly, complex narratives may involve play with serial and episodic norms, foreground stories that are ongoing (rather than closure and resolution), interwoven storylines, temporally fractured or reordered narratives, complex characters (sometimes antiheroes), genre mixing, and self-conscious or reflexive aspects (including narrative spectacles/special effects that foreground the construction of the narrative; devices like split screens, freeze frames). They often include storytelling devices such as flashbacks, dream or fantasy sequences, voice-over narration, direct audience address, or telling stories from different perspectives.

Chapter 2

1 Metafictional comments are explicit comments in TV dialogue on the conventions or on production aspects of TV narratives.

2 However, the unscripted corpus used in Berber Sardinha and Veirano Pinto (2017) appears to come mostly from 1960–70s British English, while the American English television data come from 2009 to 2014.

3 No doubt, there are also similarities between TV dialogue and other constructed dialogue, whether in film (e.g. Zago 2016) or drama/novels (e.g. Fludernik 2009: 65). Richardson (2010a: 62) suggests that dialogue in film and TV drama is the most similar (compared with other types of representational talk), but that it is not identical. However, comparing different types of constructed dialogue is an endeavour for future research.

4 I am adopting Dewaele's (2017: 3) use and definition of *LX* in this book to refer to 'any foreign language acquired after the age at which the first language(s) was acquired, that is after the age of 3 years, to any level of proficiency'. The 'foreign language' in this case is English. I thus speak of LX varieties and LX users, which are contrasted with L1 varieties and users.

5 For reasons of scope, and because SydTV is not well suited to explore such issues (cf. Chapter 5), I do not discuss here how languages other than English are represented (see Bleichenbacher 2008 on multilingualism). In line with the remit of this book I also focus on research on telecinematic discourse, rather than fiction in general, although many findings appear similar (cf. Penfield and Ornstein-Galicia 1985; Wolfram & Schilling Estes 2006: 339–43; Lippi-Green 2012: 104). Non-linguistic research is also disregarded, as it does not tend to focus on issues to do with language (with some exceptions, e.g. Kozloff 2000; Buscombe 2013; Chung 2013).

6 Various labels are used to refer to this variety; see Green (2002: 5–8), Wolfram and Schilling-Estes (2006), or Widawski (2015: 2–7) on relevant debates. I use *African American Vernacular English* (AAVE) 'to refer to that variety spoken by and considered to be a key part of the ethnic heritage and cultural identity of many people of African descent in the US' (Wolfram & Schilling Estes 2006: 17–18). AAVE is characterised by a set of core features and is hence a supraregional language variety, although it does exhibit regional, social class, and stylistic variation (Wolfram & Schilling Estes 2006: 218). It is a 'linguistic system of communication governed by well defined rules' (Green 2004: 77). Many adolescents in the United States attempt to use it to index coolness (Eckert 2004: 369), although it is a stigmatised language variety in other contexts (Lippi-Green 2012: 196, 200). Widawski (2015) states that 'African American slang is more and more popular among Americans regardless of their ethnic origin and exerts an increasingly marked influence on general American English' (ix). Indeed, words of AAVE origin such as *cool*, *gig*, and *hip* are 'now a part of at least the recognition vocabulary of all generations and all segments of American society' (Eble 2004: 383). Grieve et al. (2017: 124) also found that many of the emerging words they identify in Twitter data come from the African American community.

Chapter 3

1 In narratology/poetics, narrative causality is discussed in relation to elements such as appointments, deadlines, dangling causes, narrative statements, and narrative enigmas (Thompson 2003; Mittell 2015). It would be an interesting endeavour for future research to investigate exactly how dialogue contributes to these elements. For example, questions can establish narrative enigmas (Mittell 2015: 79).

2 *House of Cards* is also a good example of an antihero as lead character, common in many complex serials (Mittell 2015: 13).

Chapter 4

1 The internet attributes this to Albert Einstein, but I have not been able to confirm this reliably. A similar quote has also been used in the TV series *Criminal Minds*.

2 Intertextual references are mentioned by Kozloff (2000, passim) but not distinguished as a subcategory in her chapter on the functions of film dialogue. She proposes that 'such lines function both as an inside joke for the film-makers, and to flatter viewers who are in the know, to make them feel like insiders' (Kozloff 2000: 178).

3 Kozloff (2000: 178) briefly mentions 'self-conscious' dialogue in a footnote, explaining it as 'dialogue that in some way lays bare the film's status as a film'.

4 Compare Chatman's (1978: 247) point about film: 'Modern films are generally chary of overt comment. A narrating voice-over of any sort is unfashionable, but especially one that moralizes, or interprets.' Kozloff (2000: 56–7) also comments on critical attitudes towards overt moralising in films.

5 The concept of realism in telecinematic discourse is a complex issue and worthy of further discussion. In linguistic studies of telecinematic discourse, realism is often defined as 'simulating contemporary conversational exchanges' (Zago 2016: 55), although Bleichenbacher (2008: 26) ties realism more broadly to 'the desire to represent a situation [...] in the story as faithfully as possible'. Dynel (2015) talks about *verisimilitude* and appears to conceptualise this as plausible, convincing, conceivable representation. McIntyre (2016) distinguishes realism/authenticity (dialogue 'reflecting naturalistic speech patterns' (434)) from credibility ('dialogue that is convincing as an imitation of naturally occurring speech or seems plausible as a historical variety' (431)) and argues that non-authentic dialogue can be credible in the context of a particular fictional world and realism/authenticity 'is secondary to credibility' (431). From a sociolinguistic perspective, Queen (2015: 160–3) discusses both realness and authenticity in the context of characterisation, noting that the concept of *authenticity* is more useful than the concept of realness or accuracy. However, Richardson (2010a: 4) notes that the line between inauthentic and authentic speech is difficult to draw. Lopez and Bucholtz (2017: 4) theorise authenticity as 'the result of authenticating practices that are enacted by users of language and other semiotic systems and ratified by those who observe these practices. Recognizing authenticity as a jointly produced semiotic effect shifts the focus of linguistic analysis from efforts to empirically verify the authenticity of some language sample to understanding how authenticity is accomplished for and with particular audiences.'

6 The creation of consistency is called 'continuity' in Bednarek (2017b).

7 Real examples are provided in Goldberg and Rabkin (2003), but in practice there is often no bible, and guidelines have to be inferred from the scripts or episodes (Epstein 2006: 38).

Chapter 5

1 An episode was classified as a 'beginning' episode if it occurred in about the first third or 30 per cent of a season. The first episode was labelled separately as *pilot*. Further, an episode was classified as a 'middle' episode if it occurred between 41 per cent (e.g. episode 9 of 22) and 75 per cent (e.g. episode 15 of 20). Finally, an episode was classified as an 'end' episode if it occurred between 78 per cent (e.g. episode 7 of 9) and 96 per cent (e.g. episode 23 of 24). The final episode (season finale) was identified as such.

2 For example, the Santa Barbara Corpus of Spoken American English, the London Lund corpus, the Michigan Corpus of Academic Spoken English, the Bergen Corpus of London Teenage Language, and the spoken components of ICE corpora range in size from 250,000 words to 600,000 words.

3 Prior to using files with Sketch Engine and GraphColl I used EncodeAnt (Anthony 2016) to convert all files to UTF8.

4 To produce key n-grams, one compiles an index before computing n-grams.

5 In addition, an initial pilot study of key lemmas showed that most of the results are covered by the investigation of key word forms and that a qualitative analysis of lemmas would have been too time-consuming. Where relevant elsewhere in this book, the difference between lemmas and word forms is marked by using all caps for lemmas (e.g. BE includes the word forms *be*, *is*, *are*, *was*, etc).

Chapter 6

1 It has been argued that Standard American English does not correspond to an actual variety spoken by any population of speakers but is rather a construct, a myth, or an ideology (Kretzschmar & Meyer 2012; Lippi-Green 2012). Further, linguists have pointed out that there are informal (vernacular) standards as well as regional standards (e.g. Wolfram & Schilling Estes 2006: 11–13; Gramley 2012: 444) and that variation exists at all levels within both standard and non-standard varieties, such as AAVE or Latinx/Hispanic English (Wolfram & Schilling Estes 2006: 18; Lippi-Green 2012: 260–1).

2 It is difficult to draw the line between concepts such as slang, colloquialism, and swear/taboo words. Slang – which 'is one of those terms that gives dialectologists fits' (Wolfram & Schilling Estes 2006: 70) could be seen to include swear/taboo words, for example, and can be characterised as highly colloquial and informal. Indeed, *colloquialism* and *vulgarism* may be used as synonyms for *slang* on occasion, while at the same time not all colloquial expressions are slang, and not all slang is vulgar (Widawski 2015: 8–9). For further discussion of these issues and criteria for defining slang, see Eble (2004), Wolfram and Schilling Estes (2006: 70–4), and Widawski (2015: 7–12). Another problem is that there are different definitions and conceptualisations of the term *swear/taboo word* (Bednarek in press b).

3 Other reviewing options such as grammar/style errors were not applied – compare Curzan (2014) on problems associated with the Microsoft Word

grammar and style checker, and for a more extensive discussion of grammar checkers and prescriptivism.

4 The presence of certain non-standard words in dictionaries is an indication of their longetivity and legitimacy, even as a label may question the latter (Curzan 2014: 93–4, 104).

5 This means that some instances of technical/specialised vocabulary, swear/taboo words, and colloquialisms are codified in the spell-checker dictionary (e.g. *arterial thrombosis, motherfucker, c'mon, could've, whoa*), while others are not (e.g. *procoagulate, fuckwad, yo, sh, booyah, shazam*).

6 A Likert scale is a rating scale used in closed questions, which require 'the respondent to indicate the extent to which they agree or disagree according to a numerical scale. For example, a five-point Likert scale ranges from 1 (strongly disagree) to 5 (strongly agree)' (Woodrow 2010: 304).

Chapter 7

1 I used the BNC as included in Sketch Engine; all other corpora were uploaded. Since the tool does not ignore tagged words, I uploaded a version of SydTV-Std and the LSAC where all tagged words (e.g. the names of speakers) were deleted (using WordSmith Text Converter: just one change: convert <*> to 'nothing'). To process the corpora I used the settings recommended by the software: English 3.1 for TreeTagger pipeline v2; English (TreeTagger - PennTB) for terms extraction 2.3; recommended structures and attributes. No changes were made to any of Sketch Engine's default settings.

2 Summary of settings:

The tagged versions of both corpora were used, but all mark-up <*> was ignored.

Language settings:

Hyphens do not separate words; ' allowed within words
Index settings:

Thorough concordancing; show if frequency at least 1; clusters (5–5 words; stop at sentence break); omit phrase frames, do not omit dispersion
Settings for computing n-grams from the index:

Cluster size 2–2; 3–3; 4–4; 5–5 (to compute 2-grams, 3-grams, 4-grams, and 5-grams, respectively); minimum frequency = 2; omit any containing #, omit phrase frames, do not omit dispersion, stop at sentence break.

Keyness settings:

p-value threshold = 0.000001
max. wanted: 4,000
min. frequency = 2

exclude negative KWs; no thresholds set for minimum percentage of text or minimum log ratio, as this is done at a later stage using Excel's filtering mechanisms.

My approach to settings is to set only one threshold in WordSmith, namely the p-value, then downloading the full list as an Excel file and applying additional thresholds at a later stage using Excel's filtering mechanisms. The p-value chosen as threshold is the default value, corresponding to one-in-one-million risk that results are due to chance. This setting is recommended for obtaining fewer key words since 'the notion of risk is less important than that of selectivity' in keyness analysis (Scott 2017b).

Because the reference corpus (AmE06) is fairly small (~1 million), the percentage of words found in the reference corpus (as indicated by a Word-Smith message) is low, especially when the larger LSAC is compared with the AmE06 (the message occurs for all n-grams) or when longer n-grams are concerned (the message occurs for 3–5 grams in SydTV-Std). According to Scott (2017b) it is not unusual to receive the message 'Only X% of words found in reference corpus' when the reference corpus is small (and much more likely with n-grams), and the message can be ignored if the researcher knows that there is nothing strange or wrong with the corpora or the analysis. However, using a small corpus like the AmE06 does make the comparison less reliable than a bigger reference corpus, which is another reason why I only briefly discuss the results here.

3 Shared n-grams were identified by merging the two lists and then using a pivot table in Excel to provide counts of any items occurring twice. The actual number of shared n-grams might be higher since some n-grams may not be identified as shared because they are spelled differently in the two corpora.

4 The software settings for producing key items are identical to those used above in the comparison with the AmE06. Because the LSAC is much bigger than SydTV-Std it is only in the case of 5-grams that WordSmith provided a message that only 39 per cent of the words in the word list were found in the reference corpus.

5 Importantly, the fact that a key item occurs across at least twenty texts does not mean that it is independently 'key' in each of these texts. Rather, it means that the item is 'key' in the corpus as a whole and occurs across at least twenty files. To identify words that are 'key' in most or many texts, one would need to calculate 'key key words', but this approach works best with 'a lot of text files (say 500 or more)' (Scott 2017b).

6 Usually important for phatic communication. They are also known as conversational routines, pragmatic routines, or socio-pragmatic formulae (Bruti & Vignozzi 2016b).

7 Quaglio (2009) does not include routine formulae as a separate category, but mentions *thank you so much* as a feature of emotional language and the greetings/leave-takings *hi, hey, bye, bye-bye* as informal language.

8 Quaglio (2009) includes *of course* as a stance marker and *fine* (as non-minimal response) under 'emotional language', while other non-minimal responses are included under 'narrativeness'.

9 This method is inspired by Culpeper's and Kytö's (2010) technique for categorising trigrams. However, my analysis was a single-researcher analysis and I used different categories than these researchers, also allowing

for double/multiple classification in cases where a key item seems to fulfil more than one important function. For example, if almost half of the analysed instances are examples for one function, and the remainder are examples for another function, the item is double-classified. The 50 per cent threshold was sometimes relaxed slightly when it seemed appropriate.

10 Which is the case, with only four exceptions: *lie awake, lie down, lie still; take that lying down.*

11 As a reminder, *got to* stands for both *got to* and *gotta* in the standardised version of SydTV.

12 More specifically, TV series are 'structured around frequent changes of different communicative situations' (Bednarek 2012a: 44), while 'conversations are usually recorded in particular places without much "movement" of speakers' (Quaglio 2009: 135). For example, the scenes in *Friends* 'change constantly and the characters frequently arrive in places (especially at the beginning of scenes). This situational circumstance results in several exchanges where the characters meet, producing a large number of greetings' (Quaglio 2009: 47–8). In addition, the phone conversations included in the LSAC mostly do not include the dialogue of all speakers (Quaglio 2008: 193); hence, there are fewer greetings, as only one side is represented. It would also not be ethical to start recording strangers before introductions are exchanged and permission is obtained, so formulae such as *nice to meet you* may be relatively infrequent in spoken corpora for this reason (Bednarek 2010a: 79–80).

13 For instance, Quaglio (2009) asserts that the discourse marker *you know* is under-represented in *Friends*, while Mittmann (2006) states that forms such as *you know, like, I mean, I think* are under-represented in her TV data (*Friends, Dawson's Creek, Golden Girls*).

14 Many instances of the key item *man* also appear to be tinged with emotionality and it is at times difficult to distinguish its use as term of address from its use as an interjection. *Sweetie* is also key but occurs in only nineteen files, just below the range threshold.

15 Some of these items (especially *broke, lie, lying, lose*) could perhaps be double-classified as 'narrative concerns'. For example, lying is mentioned by Chambers and Chambers (2013a: 108) as common action in comedic stories (see also Epstein 2006: 89; Sandler 2007: KL 1673–80).

16 Since *damnit* could be 'key' as a result of spelling variation, I double-checked the results by comparing instances of *damnit* in SydTV-Std (n = 22) with occurrences of *damn it* in the LSAC (n = 42; not counting *God damn it*, which is spelled *goddamnit* in SydTV-Std). The difference is indeed statistically significant (LL = 53.12; calculated using the log likelihood calculator at http://ucrel.lancs.ac.uk/llwizard.html, accessed 26 April 2017).

Chapter 8

1 The analysis of these key words is based on qualitative analysis only when this is explicitly stated.

2 To rule out that these are only 'key' because of different spelling conventions, I searched for the following forms in the LSAC: *god damn/goddamn/god damnit/god dammit/goddammit/goddamnit*; *bull shit/bullshit*; *ass hole/asshole*; *mother fucker/motherfucker* and used an online log likelihood calculator (http://ucrel.lancs.ac.uk/llwizard.html, accessed 13 May 2017) to compare the frequencies of these forms in the LSAC with their corresponding frequencies in SydTV-Std. In all cases, there is statistically significant overuse of the swear/taboo words in SydTV-Std compared with the LSAC:

- *Goddamnit* (and variants): Raw f LSAC: 36; raw f SydTV-Std: 10; LL = 15.18
- *Goddamn* (and variants): Raw f LSAC: 38; raw f SydTV-Std: 21; LL = 52.29
- *Bullshit* (and variants): Raw f LSAC: 119; raw f SydTV-Std: 24; LL = 26.04
- *Asshole* (and variants) Raw f LSAC: 54; raw f SydTV-Std: 22; LL = 45.28
- *Motherfucker* (and variants): Raw f LSAC: 45; raw f SydTV-Std: 24; LL = 58.56.

3 The 'keyness' of the word form is also the result of particular transcription conventions. In this case, in addition to crowd chanting, six instances of *drink* seem to be uttered by three men each – that this is counted as eighteen instances (three turns) relates to the transcription conventions for two or more speakers saying the same thing (see Chapter 5). Instead of making the three men representative of the crowd, this scene could also have been transcribed as *CROWD: Drink, drink, drink, drink, drink, drink* (and many more), but this would have resulted in even more occurrences if all audible occurrences had been transcribed.

4 These results rely on the accuracy and consistency of the transcription by the research assistants.

5 Multiple negation can be found in most non-standard dialects of English (Trudgill 1999: 125; Wolfram 2008: 523) but is 'generally evaluated as reflecting lack of education' (Eckert 2004: 370). Chambers (2012) calls it 'a vernacular universal' (265), which is 'outlawed in standard dialects' and 'does not occur in contemporary standard grammars in any national variety' (263); nor does it tend to occur in middle-class dialects (265). Multiple negation is more common in North America than in Australia or Britain (Anderwald 2012: 301) as is the case to an even larger extent for *ain't*.

Chapter 9

1 According to Mark Davies (email communication), the size of COCA, GloWbE/US, and SOAP is calculated using the following token definition: hyphens do not separate words (i.e., *force-feed* would count as one word); ' is not allowed within words (i.e., for contractions like *don't*, *don* counts as one word, and *t* counts as another). In this chapter I will be using the same token definition for SydTV when normalising frequencies (i.e. raw frequencies are

normalised with respect to a corpus size of 275,074 words; see Table A.2 in the Appendix).

2 The information in Table 9.1 relates to *y'all* rather than *you all*. Examination of *you all* showed that only some fall pronunciation-wise between one and two syllables. This includes one instance produced by an African American character in *The Wire* (drug dealer Bodie, played by New Jersey actor J. D. Williams) and one instance produced by McNulty in the same series (the character is a white, Irish-heritage Baltimore detective; the actor, Dominic West, is English). Lippi-Green (2012: 50) suggests that Yorkshire-born West does not convincingly portray 'a tough Baltimore homicide detective'.

3 The line between specialised and non-specialised vocabulary is not clear – I treated *postnup*, *prenup*, *lipo*, *boty*, *benzos* as specialised but not *decomp* or *low-carb*, as I considered the latter to be more widely known.

4 Upon reviewing this scene it was unclear to me if the word is *believe* or *belieb*, although it was transcribed as *belieb* by the research assistant. A Google search on 17 June 2016 for <Workaholics are you a true belieber "I **believe** you are"> resulted in only one quote from this episode, while a search for <Workaholics are you a true belieber "I **belieb** you are" and <Workaholics are you a true belieber "I **beliebe** you are"> turned up nine quotes from the TV series (in total). This suggests that the preferred auditory interpretation of this piece of dialogue involves wordplay.

5 Instances of infixing also occur (e.g. *Doogie fuckin' Howser*) – a phenomenon discussed in more detail in McMillan (1980).

6 To account for potential spelling variation in COCA/S I searched for three alternative spellings: with hyphen, as two separate word forms, or as one word (e.g. *smart-ass*, *smart ass*, *smartass*). No instances of the following word forms were found: *tight-ass*, *lame-ass*, *fiend-ass*, *smooth-ass*, *shit-ass*, *short-ass*, *ass burger*, *ass-clown*, *ass ache*, *ass-fucked*, *bitch-ass bitch*, *dipshit*, *shitheads*, *shit-faced*, *dickwad*, *dickweed*, *dickhead*, *limp-dick*, *dick-wagging*, *fuck-up*, *fucktard*, *fuckwad*, *fuckable*, *butt-fuck/butt-fucking*, *ass-fucked*, *pencil-fucked*, *motherfucking*, *motherfucker*.

7 *Toosh* is listed with a different spelling in the MW (*tush*).

8 I used the standard search function provided by the dictionary.

9 A search for combinations of two words (*-*) resulted in more than 1,000 instances, many of which were standard compounds – hence the search for the less frequent *-*-*. I exclude from discussion irrelevant instances such as *uh-uh-uh*, *la-di-da* as well as names of brands or businesses (real: *Filet-O-Fishes* and fictional: *Rent-a-Ruminant*, *Dip-a-Pet*) and codified compounds that are listed in the MW (e.g. *brother-in-law*, *chief-of-staff*, *great-great-grandparents*, *tete-a-tete*, *black-and-white television*, *before the black-and-whites show up* ['squad car'], *matter-of-fact*, *a rock-and-roll town*, *a stick-in-the-mud*, *know-it-all*, *what's-his-name*, *hide-and-seek*, *neck-and-neck*). Numbers are also excluded – most occurrences are age and year references, although more innovative compounding also occurs, for instance noun modification: *a* **ninety-thousand-dollar** *bullet, a* **forty-million-dollar** *motive, the* **forty-million-dollar** *estate, a* **forty-million-dollar** *divorce,* **multi-million-dollar** *deals, a*

one-in-a-million shot, a *two-hundred-dollar piece of*, a *twenty-four-hour ceasefire*, a *thirty-five-second hug*.

10 In relation to *nugs*, its use in SydTV does not refer to drugs, although the word tends to be defined (in the UD) and used (e.g. in GloWbE) more often in relation to marijuana.

11 Vice versa, only the following words occur at least once in either COCA/S or GloWbE/US but are *not* listed in the UD: *crimelords*, *insidey*, *vacants* (two entries for *vacant* with different meanings), *decomp* (for 'decomposition', but the UD has a related entry for *decomp* as 'decomposing body').

12 Several word forms in SydTV do not occur in COCA/S or GloWbE/US and are not listed in the UD (as this particular part of speech), including but not limited to: *vespa* (as verb, from *The Big C* (2010)), *trailerville* (from *Bones* (2005)), *plus-one-ing* (from *Outsourced* (2010)), *misjoked* (from *Veep* (2012)), *untutorable* (from *Community* (2009)).

13 The word *coochie* (*Breaking Bad*, 2008) is listed as African American slang meaning 'the vulva' in Widawski (2015: 162) but is used by a non-African American character in SydTV, a male white detective.

Chapter 10

1 The advice cited in the chapter title to 'Take that pencil and just GO!' comes from Amy Sherman-Palladino, cited in Priggé (2005: 86, emphasis in original).

2 Thus, manuals talk about the 'emotional heart' of an episode (Epstein 2006: 41) or characters' emotional base or journey (Smith 2009: KL 1913; Vorhaus 2012: 70) and advise writers 'to add real emotion' (Bull 2007: KL 1815), to identify characters' feelings (Sandler 2007: KL 930), to get the 'emotional juice' out of scenes (Witten 2013: 87), and to emotionally engage the audience (Priggé 2005: 149; Douglas 2011: 160; Chambers & Chambers 2013a: 113; Witten 2013: 87; Landau 2014: 56). It is pointed out that '[g]ood stories come from emotional issues' (Sandler 2007: KL 585), that '[d]ialogue must carry emotional baggage' (Sandler 2007: KL 1686), and that 'emotional change of state is the engine that drives story' (Vorhaus 2012: 64). Finer and Pearlman (2004: 30, 45) and Smith (2009: KL 2639) argue that it is important to reveal characters' emotions and goals through dialogue. Joss Whedon mentions 'the emotional truth of a moment and what's funny about it' as 'the real basis of all writing' (cited in Priggé 2005: 84). There is also recognition that TV characters are more emotional than 'real' people (e.g. Bull 2007: KL 2353).

Chapter 11

1 As it is not relevant to this chapter, I will ignore the large body of non-linguistic research on television audiences, which often has a focus on fandom (e.g. Jenkins 1992; Hills 2002; Petersen 2014; Mittell 2015).

2 A few students chose 'yes' but did not list any differences in the available space.

3 This summary disregards any highly general comments such as *nicht so spontan* ('less spontaneous'); *Die Sprache* [...] *ist* [...] *klarer strukturiert* ('the language is more clearly structured'); *Wahrscheinlich gibt es ein Script* ('probably there's a script'); *zudem ist es leichter Inhalte zu verstehen, wenn man den Kontext der Serie kennt* ('in addition, it's easier to understand content when you know the context of the series'); *Stereotype* ('stereotypes'), etc. Also disregarded are any vague comments (e.g. entries such as 'expressions' (*Ausdrücke*), 'dialogues' (*Dialoge*), 'dialects' (*Dialekte*), 'register/vocabulary' (*Register/Vokabular*), 'special speech acts' (*spezielle Sprechakte*), 'use of swear words' (*Benutzung von 'Swear words'*), etc.) that are not specific regarding the differences (for instance, whether TV dialogue makes *less* or *more* use of swear words). Comments on translations (dubbing or subtitles) are also ignored, as I am interested in students' experience of the original dialogue and the questionnaire did not specifically aim to elicit comments on audiovisual translation. There are also entries where it is unclear what students mean, which were ignored. For instance, does *spezielle Wörter* refer to 'particular words' or 'specialised/technical vocabulary'? What exactly is meant by *dramatische Sprache* ('dramatic language')? Several students mention abbreviations or short forms (*Wordabkürzungen* [*sic*], *Abkürzungen*, *Kurzformen*), but it is usually not clear what students mean by this as they tend not to give any examples – they could refer to acronyms (one student mentions *m, i, a* as example) or lexically reduced forms (e.g. *gonna*). Further, even though the questionnaire items were not oriented to this aspect of TV dialogue, a few students commented on its functions (see Part II), for instance pointing to the use of language to build character personalities, that the conversations have the goal of propelling the plot, that TV dialogue may convey moral messages, or that there is more explanation/exposition. Individual students also mention conventions such as the laughtrack (*Pausen für Lacher/*'pauses for laughs') and voice-over narration (*'lautes Denken'/*'thinking aloud'). Again, my summary here does not include such comments.

4 In addition, three responses to item ten mention that the intonation is artificial or unnatural.

5 For example: *Sprachliche Eloquenz* ('linguistic eloquence'); *keine authentischen Versprecher* ('no authentic slips of the tongue'); *insgesamt sind nur beabsichtigte Versprecher drin* ('on the whole there are only intentional slips of the tongue'); *kein realer Sprecher würde* [...] *so eloquente Sätze verwenden und ihm niemand zwischendurch ins Wort fallen* ('no real speaker would use such eloquent sentences and not be interrupted'); *insgesamt die Pausen in den Sprechakten zu gut getimt = manchmal sucht man nach einem Wort, verhaspelt sich oä* ('on the whole the pauses too well timed – sometimes you search for a word, splutter, or similar'); *Monologe* ('monologues'). There are very few dissenting students with respect to these two aspects, who state, for instance, that they find it easier to understand 'real' speakers (*Oft finde ich es leichter, 'reale' Sprecher zu verstehen*), that real speakers often speak more slowly and clearly than TV characters (*Reale Sprecher sprechen erstaunlicherweise oftmals langsamer und deutlicher als TV-Charaktere*), that TV dialogue is not

well enunciated by the actors (*die Schauspieler achten nicht auf die 'schöne' Artikulation*), or that words are swallowed by characters (*Ich finde* [. . .] *gerade im amerikanischen Tv, dass sie Wörter verschlucken*).

6 E.g. *Tendenz zu* [. . .] *Standard English; meistens sprechen alle Figuren Standard-Englisch; in der 'TV-Sprache' eher gefiltertes Englisch; 'posh'; gewählter; Slang wird ausgelassen; je nachdem sprechen Seriencharaktere GA oder RP.* Translations: 'tendency to standard English'; 'in most cases all characters speak Standard English'; 'in TV language rather filtered English'; 'more refined'; 'slang is left out'; 'characters speak either GA or RP'.

7 In response to item ten some students also note that TV dialogue contains simple, colloquial language (2x) or language that is 'too' colloquial/real (2x).

8 In addition, some students name only *Dialekte/Akzente* ('dialects/accents') or make similar vague entries (both excluded from the count here, cf. note 3).

9 Further, eight replies to item ten comment that TV dialogue uses 'better' or more correct grammar. Answers to item eleven include 'correct grammar' (1x: *grammatikalisch einwandfreie Sätze*), 'weird grammar' (1x: *seltsame grammatik*), and 'simple language/grammar' (5x: *vereinfachte Grammatikformen; einfache Sprache; 'einfache'-/umgangssprache; Sprache ist oftmals sehr einfach gehalten; nicht zu komplizierte Ausdrucksweisen*). Other aspects are mentioned by only one or two students: 'ellipses' (2x: *Ellipse*), *weak forms* ([*sic*], 1x), 'teen language' (1x: *Jugendwörter/sprache*), 'internet language' (2x: *'Internet Lingo'; Internetsprache*), geek or nerd terms ([*sic*], 1x).

10 E.g. *teils übermäßiger Gebrauch von Kraftausdrücken; sehr viele swear-words oder andere Formen von 'explicit language'; ich höre voll oft Kraftausdrücke wie 'Fuck!'* Translations: 'in part overuse of swear words'; 'partly frequent use of insults/vulgarity'; 'very many swear words or other forms of explicit language'; 'I hear swear words like "Fuck!" really often.'

11 Excluded here are words such as *mate, blimey, innit, brilliant* that students associate with British rather than US series.

12 Only the following word forms and expressions listed by students cannot easily be classified in such ways: *to put out a BOLO for so, hit the bucket, I'd say, newbie, to be supposed to, on fleek, basic, hashtags.*

Chapter 12

1 In this concluding chapter I use *SydTV* as a cover term for both the original and partially standardised version of the corpus.

References

Abbott, H. P. (2014). *The Cambridge Introduction to Narrative*, 2nd edn. New York: Cambridge University Press.

Adams, M. (2003). *Slayer Slang: A Buffy the Vampire Slayer Lexicon*. New York: Oxford University Press.

Adams, M. (2013). Vignette 13b. Working with scripted data: Variations among scripts, texts, and performances. In C. Mallison, B. Childs and G. van Herk, eds., *Data Collection in Sociolinguistics: Methods and Applications*. New York: Routledge, pp. 232–5.

Adams, T. (2017, 24 September). Secrets of the TV writers' room: Inside *Narcos*, *Transparent* and *Silicon Valley: The Guardian/The Observer*. Available at www.theguardian.com/tv-and-radio/2017/sep/23/secrets-of-the-tv-writers-rooms-tv-narcos-silicon-valley-transparent, 28 September 2017.

Al-Surmi, M. (2012). Authenticity and TV shows: A multidimensional analysis perspective. *TESOL Quarterly*, 46(4), 671–94.

Anderwald, L. (2012). Negation in varieties of English. In R. Hickey, ed., *Areal Features of the Anglophone World*. Berlin: Walter de Gruyter, pp. 299–328.

Androutsopoulos, J. (2012). Introduction: Language and society in cinematic discourse. *Multilingua*, 31(2–3), 139–54.

Androutsopoulos, J. (2014). Mediatization and sociolinguistic change: Key concepts, research traditions, open issues. In J. Androutsopoulos, ed., *Mediatization and Sociolinguistic Change*. Berlin: de Gruyter, pp. 3–48.

Anthony, L. (2016). EncodeAnt (Version 1.2.0). Computer software. Tokyo, Japan: Waseda University. Available at www.laurenceanthony.net/.

Armstrong, J. D. (1997). Homophobic slang as coercive discourse among college students. In A. Livia and K. Hall, eds., *Queerly Phrased: Language, Gender and Sexuality*. Oxford: Oxford University Press, pp. 326–34.

Baayen, R. H. & Renouf, A. (1996). Chronicling the Times: Productive lexical innovations in an English newspaper. *Language*, 72(1), 69–96.

Baker, P. (2005). *Public Discourses of Gay Men*. London: Routledge.

Baker, P. (2006). *Using Corpora in Discourse Analysis*. London: Continuum.

Baker, P. (n.d.). Professor Paul Baker. Available at www.lancaster.ac.uk/linguistics/about-us/people/paul-baker, 10 March 2017.

Baker, P. & McEnery, T. (2015). Introduction. In P. Baker and T. McEnery, eds., *Corpora and Discourse Studies. Integrating Discourse and Corpora*. Basingstoke: Palgrave Macmillan, pp. 1–19.

Bal, M. (1997). *Narratology: Introduction to the Theory of Narrative*, 2nd edn. Toronto: University of Toronto Press.

Baños, R. (2013). 'That is so cool': Investigating the translation of adverbial intensifiers in English-Spanish dubbing through a parallel corpus of sitcoms. *Perspectives: Studies in Translatology*, 21(4), 526–42.

Barlow, M. (2016). *WordSkew*. Linking corpus data and discourse structure. *International Journal of Corpus Linguistics*, 21(1), 105–15.

Bateman, J. A. & Schmidt, K. H. (2012). *Multimodal Film Analysis: How Films Mean*. Oxon: Routledge.

Batty, C. (2016). Screenwriting studies, screenwriting practice and the screenwriting manual. *New Writing*, 13(1), 59–70.

Bednarek, M. (2007, October). 'What the hell is wrong with you?' A corpus perspective on evaluation and emotion in contemporary American pop culture. Plenary presented at the 1st International Free Linguistics Conference, University of Sydney, Australia.

Bednarek, M. (2010a). *The Language of Fictional Television: Drama and Identity*. London: Continuum.

Bednarek, M. (2010b). Corpus linguistics and systemic functional linguistics: Interpersonal meaning, identity and bonding in popular culture. In M. Bednarek and J. R. Martin, eds., *New Discourse on Language: Functional Perspectives on Multimodality, Identity, and Affiliation*. London: Continuum, pp. 237–66.

Bednarek, M. (2011a). The stability of the televisual character: A corpus stylistic case study. In R. Piazza, M. Bednarek, and F. Rossi, eds., *Telecinematic Discourse: Approaches to the Language of Films and Television Series*. Amsterdam: John Benjamins, pp. 185–204.

Bednarek, M. (2011b). The language of fictional television: A case study of the 'dramedy' *Gilmore Girls*. *English Text Construction*, 4(1), 54–83.

Bednarek, M. (2011c). Expressivity and televisual characterisation. *Language and Literature* 20(1), 3–21.

Bednarek, M. (2012a). 'Get us the hell out of here': Key words and trigrams in fictional television series. *International Journal of Corpus Linguistics*, 17(1), 35–63.

Bednarek, M. (2012b). Construing 'nerdiness': Characterisation in *The Big Bang Theory*. *Multilingua*, 31, 199–229.

Bednarek, M. (2013, September). *What happened and who dunnit?* Exploring questions in contemporary US crime drama: From *Breaking Bad* to *The Wire*. Paper presented at the Symposium on Crime in a Post-CSI Mediascape, Oxford Brookes University, UK.

Bednarek, M. (2014a). 'Who are you and why are you following us?' Wh-questions and communicative context in television dialogue. In J. Flowerdew, ed., *Discourse in Context*. London: Bloomsbury Academic, pp. 49–70.

Bednarek, M. (2014b). 'And they all look just the same'? – A quantitative survey of television title sequences. *Visual Communication*, 13(2), 125–45.

Bednarek, M. (2014c). The television title sequence: A visual analysis of *Flight of the Conchords*. In E. Djonov and S. Zhao, eds., *Critical Multimodal Studies of Popular Culture*. London: Routledge, pp. 36–54.

Bednarek, M. (2014d). Involvement in Australian talkback radio: A corpus linguistic investigation. *Australian Journal of Linguistics*, **34**(1), 4–23.

Bednarek, M. (2015a). Corpus-assisted multimodal discourse analysis of television and film narratives. In P. Baker and T. McEnery, eds., *Corpora and Discourse Studies*. Basingstoke: Palgrave Macmillan, pp. 63–87.

Bednarek, M. (2015b). 'Wicked' women in contemporary pop culture: 'Bad' language and gender in *Weeds*, *Nurse Jackie* and *Saving Grace*. *Text & Talk*, **35**(4), 431–51.

Bednarek, M. (2015c). 'What we contrarians already know': Individual and communal aspects of attitudinal identity. In M. Charles, N. Groom, and S. John, eds., *Corpora, Grammar and Discourse. In Honour of Susan Hunston*. Amsterdam: John Benjamins, pp. 257–81.

Bednarek, M. (2015d). An overview of the linguistics of screenwriting and its interdisciplinary connections, with special focus on dialogue in episodic television. *Journal of Screenwriting*, **6**(2), 221–38.

Bednarek, M. (2017a). (Re-)circulating popular television: Audience engagement and corporate practices. In J. Mortensen, N. Coupland, and J. Thøgersen, eds., *Style, Mediation and Change: Sociolinguistic Perspectives on Talking Media*. Oxford: Oxford University Press, pp. 115–40.

Bednarek, M. (2017b). The role of dialogue in fiction. In M. Locher and A. H. Jucker, eds., *Pragmatics of Fiction*. Berlin: de Gruyter Mouton, pp. 129–58.

Bednarek, M. (2017c). Fandom. In C. R. Hoffmann and W. Bublitz, eds., *Pragmatics of Social Media*. Berlin: de Gruyter Mouton, pp. 545–72.

Bednarek, M. (2018). *Guide to the Sydney Corpus of Television Dialogue (SydTV)*. Available at www.syd-tv.com.

Bednarek, M. (in press a). On the usefulness of the Sydney Corpus of Television Dialogue (SydTV) as a reference point for corpus linguistic and stylistic analyses of TV series. In C. Hoffmann and M. Kirner-Ludwig, eds., *Telecinematic Stylistics*. London: Bloomsbury Academic.

Bednarek, M. (in press b). The multifunctionality of swear/taboo words in television series. In J. L. Mackenzie and L. Alba-Juez, eds., *Emotion in Discourse*. Amsterdam: John Benjamins.

Bednarek, M. & Caple, H. (2014). Why do news values matter? Towards a new methodological framework for analyzing news discourse in Critical Discourse Analysis and beyond. *Discourse & Society*, **25**(2), 135–58.

Bednarek, M. & Caple, H. (2017a). *The Discourse of News Values: How News Organizations Create Newsworthiness*. New York: Oxford University Press.

Bednarek, M. & Caple, H. (2017b). Introducing a new topology for (multimodal) discourse analysis. In P. Chappell and J. S. Knox, eds., *Transforming Contexts. Papers from the 44th International Systemic Functional Congress*. Wollongong: 44th ISFC Organizing Committee. Available at www.isfc2017conference.com/copy-of-sfl-lct, 8 August 2017.

Bednarek, M. & Zago, R. (2018). Bibliography of linguistic research on fictional (narrative, scripted) television series and films/movies, version 2 (February 2018). Available at http://unipv.academia.edu/RaffaeleZago/Bibliography.

Beers Fägersten, K. (ed.). (2016). *Watching TV with a Linguist*. Syracuse, NY: Syracuse University Press.

Bell, A. (2016). 'An evil version of our accent': Language ideologies and the neighbouring other. In J. Thøgersen, N. Coupland, and J. Mortensen, eds., *Style, Media and Language Ideologies*. Oslo: Novus Press, pp. 235–58.

Bennett, T. (2014). *The Official Companion to the Documentary Showrunners: The Art of Running a TV Show*, Kindle edn. London: Titan.

Berber Sardinha, T. & Veirano Pinto, M. (2017). American television and off-screen registers: A corpus-based comparison. *Corpora*, **12**(1), 85–114.

Berber Sardinha, T. & Veirano Pinto, M. (in press). Dimensions of register variation across American television registers. *International Journal of Corpus Linguistics*.

Biber, D., Johansson, S., Leech, G., Conrad, S. & Finegan, E. (1999). *Longman Grammar of Spoken and Written English*. London: Longman.

Biber, D., Reppen, R., Schnur, E. & Ghanem, R. (2016). On the (non)utility of Juilland's D to measure lexical dispersion in large corpora. *International Journal of Corpus Linguistics*, **21**(4), 439–64.

Bleichenbacher, L. (2008). *Multilingualism in the Movies: Hollywood Characters and Their Language Choices*. Tübingen: Francke.

Bleichenbacher, L. (2012). Linguicism in Hollywood movies? Representations of, and audience reactions to multilingualism in mainstream movie dialogues. *Multilingualism*, **31**, 155–76.

Bonsignori, V. & Bruti, S. (2014). Across lingua-cultures: Introductions and wishes in subtitled TV series. In B. Garzelli and M. Baldo, eds., *Subtitling and Intercultural Communication: European Languages and Beyond*. Pisa: ETS, pp. 77–100.

Brezina, V., McEnery, T. & Wattam, S. (2015). Collocations in context: A new perspective on collocation networks. *International Journal of Corpus Linguistics*, **20**(2), 139–73.

Brock, A. (2011). Bumcivilian: Systemic aspects of humorous communication in comedies. In R. Piazza, M. Bednarek, and F. Rossi, eds., *Telecinematic Discourse: Approaches to the Language of Films and Television Series*. Amsterdam: John Benjamins, pp. 263–80.

Brock, A. (2015). Participation frameworks and participation in televised sitcom, candid camera and stand-up comedy. In M. Dynel and J. Chovanec, eds., *Participation in Public and Social Media Interactions*. Amsterdam: John Benjamins, pp. 27–47.

Brock, A. (2016). The borders of humorous intent – The case of TV comedies. *Journal of Pragmatics*, **95**, 58–66.

Bruti, S. & Vignozzi, G. (2016a). Voices from the Anglo-Saxon world: Accents, dialects across film genres. *Status Quaestionis*, **11**, 43–72.

Bruti, S. & Vignozzi, G. (2016b). Routines as social pleasantries in period dramas: A corpus linguistic analysis. In R. Ferrari and S. Bruti, eds., *A Language of One's Own: Idiolectal English*. Bologna: I libri di Emil, pp. 207–39.

Bubel, C. (2006). The linguistic construction of character relations in TV drama: Doing friendship in *Sex and the City*. Doctoral thesis, Saarland University.

Bubel, C. (2008). Film audiences as overhearers. *Journal of Pragmatics*, **40**, 55–71.

Bubel, C. (2011). Relationship impression formation: How viewers know people on the screen are friends. In R. Piazza, M. Bednarek, and F. Rossi, eds., *Telecinematic Discourse: Approaches to the Language of Films and Television Series*. Amsterdam: John Benjamins, pp. 225–48.

Bubel, C. & Spitz, A. (2006). 'One of the last vestiges of gender bias': The characterization of women through the telling of dirty jokes in *Ally McBeal*. *Humor*, **19**(1), 71–104.

Bublitz, W. (1992). Transferred negation and modality. *Journal of Pragmatics*, **18**, 551–77.

Bucholtz, M. (2011). Race and the re-embodied voice in Hollywood film. *Language and Communication*, **31**, 255–65.

Bucholtz, M. & Lopez, Q. (2011). Performing blackness, forming whiteness: Linguistic minstrelsy in Hollywood film. *Journal of Sociolinguistics*, **15**(5), 680–706.

Bull, S. (2007). *Elephant Bucks: An Inside Guide to Writing for TV Sitcoms*, Kindle edn. Studio City, CA: Michael Wiese Productions.

Buscombe, E. (2013). 'They will speak in our language': Indian speech in Western movies. In J. Jaeckle, ed., *Film Dialogue*. London: Wallflower Press, pp. 157–71.

Bybee, J. (2015). *Language Change*. Cambridge: Cambridge University Press.

Chambers, J. K. (2012). Global features of English vernaculars. In R. Hickey, ed., *Areal Features of the Anglophone World*. Berlin: Walter de Gruyter, pp. 261–76.

Chambers, J. & Chambers, D. (2013a). Writing the on-air half-hour comedy spec: The story and outline. In L. Venis, ed., *Inside the Room: Writing Television with the Pros at UCLA Extension Writers' Program*, Kindle edn. New York: Penguin, pp. 97–122.

Chambers, J. & Chambers, D. (2013b). Writing the on-air half-hour comedy spec: The script. In L. Venis, ed., *Inside the Room: Writing Television with the Pros at UCLA Extension Writers' Program*, Kindle edn. New York: Penguin, pp. 123–50.

Chatman, S. (1978). *Story and Discourse: Narrative Structure in Fiction and Film*. Ithaca, NY: Cornell University Press.

Chen, Y.-H. & Baker, P. (2010). Lexical bundles in L1 and L2 academic writing. *Language Learning & Technology*, **14**(2), 30–49.

Chotiner, I. (2015, 12 August). Everything is not *The Wire*. *Slate*. Available at www.slate.com/articles/arts/culturebox/2015/08/david_simon_interview_the_wire_creator_on_his_new_series_freddie_gray_ta.html, 7 December 2016.

Chung, H. S. (2013). From 'me so horny' to 'I'm so ronery': Asian images and yellow voices in American cinema. In J. Jaeckle, ed., *Film Dialogue*. London: Wallflower Press, pp. 172–91.

Clift, R. (2016). *Conversation Analysis*. Cambridge: Cambridge University Press.

Cook, M. (2014). *Write to TV: Out of Your Head and onto the Screen*, 2nd edn. Kindle edn. New York: Focal Press.

Cotter, C. & Damaso, J. (2007). Online dictionaries as emergent archives of contemporary usage and collaborative codification. *Queen Mary's Occasional Papers Advancing Linguistics* (OPAL), **9**, 1–10.

Coupland, N. (2007). *Style: Language Variation and Identity*. Cambridge: Cambridge University Press.

Coupland, N. (2010). Language, ideology, media and social change. In K. Junod and D. Maillat, eds., *Performing the Self*. Tübingen: Gunter Narr, pp. 127–151.

Coupland, N. (2016). Dialect dissonance: The mediation of indexical incoherence. In J. Thøgersen, N. Coupland, and J. Mortensen, eds., *Style, Media and Language Ideologies*. Oslo: Novus Press, pp. 259–85.

Coupland, N., Thøgersen, J. & Mortensen, J. (2016). Introduction: Style, media and language ideologies. In J. Thøgersen, N. Coupland, and J. Mortensen, eds., *Style, Media and Language Ideologies*. Oslo: Novus Press, pp. 11–49.

Csomay, E. & Petrović, M. (2012). 'Yes, your Honor!': A corpus-based study of technical vocabulary in discipline-related movies and TV shows. *System*, **40**(2), 305–15.

Culpeper, J. (2001). *Language and Characterisation: People in Plays and Other Texts*. Harlow: Longman.

Culpeper, J. (2009). Keyness: Words, parts-of-speech and semantic categories in the character-talk of Shakespeare's *Romeo and Juliet*. *International Journal of Corpus Linguistics*, **14**(1), 29–59.

Culpeper, J. & Kytö, M. (2010). *Early Modern English Dialogues: Spoken Interaction as Writing*. Cambridge: Cambridge University Press.

Curzan, A. (2014). *Fixing English: Prescriptivism and Language History*. Cambridge: Cambridge University Press.

Daille, B. (1995). Combined Approach for Terminology Extraction: Lexical Statistics and Linguistic Filtering, *UCREL Technical Papers* 15. Department of Linguistics, Lancaster University.

Davies, M. (2008–). *The Corpus of Contemporary American English: 520 million Words, 1990–Present*. Available at http://corpus.byu.edu/coca/.

Davies, M. (2009). The 385+ million word Corpus of Contemporary American English (1990–2008+): Design, architecture, and linguistic insights. *International Journal of Corpus Linguistics*, **14**(2), 159–90.

Davies, M. (2010). The Corpus of Contemporary American English as the first reliable monitor corpus of English. *Literary and Linguistic Computing*, **25**(4), 447–64.

Davies, M. (2012). *Corpus of American Soap operas*. Available at http://corpus.byu.edu/soap/.

Davies, M. (2013). *Corpus of Global Web-Based English: 1.9 billion words from Speakers in 20 Countries*. Available at http://corpus.byu.edu/glowbe/.

Davies, M. (2015). Introducing the 1.9 billion word Global Web-based English corpus (GloWbE). *21st Century Text*. Available at https://21centurytext .wordpress.com/feature-article/, 1 April 2016.

Davies, M. (n.d. a). Comment on 'spoken transcripts'. Available at http://corpus .byu.edu/coca/, 10 February 2016.

Davies, M. (n.d. b). Comparing the Corpus of American Soap Operas, COCA, and the BNC. Available at http://corpus.byu.edu/soap/overview_detailed.asp, 24 March 2016.

Davies, M. (n.d. c). Corpus of Contemporary American English. Available at http://corpus.byu.edu/coca/, 13 April 2016.

Davies, M. & Fuchs, R. (2015). Expanding horizons in the study of World Englishes with the 1.9 billion word Global Web-based English corpus (GloWbE). *English World-Wide*, 36(1), 1–28.

Deshors, S. C., Götz, S. & Laporte, S. (eds.). (2016a). Linguistic innovations: Rethinking linguistic creativity in non-native Englishes [Special issue]. *International Journal of Learner Corpus Research*, 2(2).

Deshors, S. C., Götz, S. & Laporte, S. (2016b). Linguistic innovations in EFL and ESL. Rethinking the linguistic creativity of non-native English speakers. *International Journal of Learner Corpus Research*, 2(2), 131–50.

Dewaele, J.-M. (2004). The emotional force of swearwords and taboo words in the speech of multilinguals. *Journal of Multilingual and Multicultural Development*, 25(2–3), 204–22.

Dewaele, J.-M. (2005). Investigating the psychological and the emotional dimensions in instructed language learning: Obstacles and possibilities. *The Modern Language Journal* 89(3), 367–80.

Dewaele, J.-M. (2016a). Thirty shades of offensiveness: L1 and LX English users' understanding, perception and self-reported use of negative emotion-laden words. *Journal of Pragmatics*, 94, 112–27.

Dewaele, J.-M. (2016b). Self-reported frequency of swearing in English: Do situational, psychological and sociobiographical variables have similar effects on first and foreign language users? *Journal of Multilingual and Multicultural Development*, 38(4), 330–345.

Dewaele, J.-M. (2017). Why the dichotomy 'L1 versus LX user' is better than 'native versus non-native speaker'. *Applied Linguistics*, 1–6. Advance Access, https://doi.org/10.1093/applin/amw055.

Díaz Cintas, J. (2009). Introduction – Audiovisual translation: An overview of its potential. In J. Díaz Cintas, ed., *New Trends in Audiovisual Translation*. Bristol: Multilingual Matters, pp. 1–20.

Dose, S. (2013). Flipping the script: A Corpus of American Television Series (CATS) for corpus-based language learning and teaching. *VariEng. Studies in Variation, Contacts and Change in English 13 (Corpus Linguistics and Variation in English: Focus on Non-Native Englishes)*. Available at www.helsinki .fi/varieng/series/volumes/13/dose/, 15 February 2017.

Douglas, P. (2011). *Writing the TV Drama Series: How to Succeed as a Professional Writer in TV*, 3rd edn. Studio City, CA: Michael Wiese Productions.

Du Bois, J. W. (1991). Transcription design principles for spoken discourse research. *Pragmatics*, 1(1), 71–106.

Du Bois, J. W., Schuetze-Coburn, S., Cumming, S. & Paolino, D. (1993). Outline of discourse transcription. In J. A. Edwards and M. D. Lampert, eds., *Talking Data: Transcription and Coding in Discourse Research*. Hillsdale, NJ: Lawrence Erlbaum, pp. 45–87.

Dunn, A. (2005). The genres of television. In H. Fulton, R. Huisman, J. Murphet, and A. Dunn, eds., *Narrative and Media*. Cambridge: Cambridge University Press, pp. 125–39.

Dunne, P. (2007). Inside American television drama: Quality is not what is produced, but what it produces. In J. McCabe and K. Akass, eds., *Quality TV: Contemporary American Television and Beyond*. London: I. B. Tauris, pp. 98–110.

Dynel, M. (2011). 'I'll be there for you!' On participation-based sitcom humour. In M. Dynel, ed., *The Pragmatics of Humour across Discourse Domains*. Amsterdam: John Benjamins, pp. 311–33.

Dynel, M. (2012). Setting our House in order: The workings of impoliteness in multi-party film discourse. *Journal of Politeness Research*, 8, 161–94.

Dynel, M. (2015). Impoliteness in the service of verisimilitude in film interaction. In M. Dynel and J. Chovanec, eds., *Participation in Public and Social Media Interactions*. Amsterdam: John Benjamins, pp. 157–82.

Dynel, M. (2016). With or without intentions: Accountability and (un)intentional humour in film talk. *Journal of Pragmatics*, 95, 67–78.

Eble, C. (2004). Slang. In E. Finegan and J. R. Rickford, eds., *Language in the USA: Themes for the Twenty-First Century*. Cambridge: Cambridge University Press, pp. 375–86.

Eckert, P. (2004). Adolescent language. In E. Finegan and J. R. Rickford, eds., *Language in the USA: Themes for the Twenty-First Century*. Cambridge: Cambridge University Press, pp. 361–74.

Edley, N. & Litosseliti, L. (2010). Contemplating interviews and focus groups. In L. Litosseliti, ed., *Research Methods in Linguistics*. London: Continuum, pp. 155–79.

Egbert, J. (2018, February). Frequency is overrated: Using text dispersion to measure word importance. Paper presented at the University of Birmingham, UK. Abstract available at www.birmingham.ac.uk/research/activity/corpus/events/2018/frequency-is-overrated.aspx, 3 March 2018.

Egbert, J. & Biber, D. (in press). Incorporating text dispersion into keyword analysis.

Elliott, N. (2000). Rhoticity in the accents of American film actors: A sociolinguistic study. In R. Dal Vera, ed., *Essays on Voice and Speech: Standard Speech and Other Contemporary Issues in Professional Voice and Speech Training*. New York: Applause, pp. 103–30.

Epstein, A. (2006). *Crafty TV Writing: Thinking Inside the Box*, Kindle edn. New York: Henry Holt.

Finer, A. & Pearlman, D. (2004). *Starting Your Television Writing Career: The Warner Bros. Television Writers Workshop Guide*. Syracuse, NY: Syracuse University Press.

Finegan, E. (2004). American English and its distinctiveness. In E. Finegan and J. R. Rickford, eds., *Language in the USA: Themes for the Twenty-First Century*. Cambridge: Cambridge University Press, pp. 18–38.

Flowerdew, L. (2005). An integration of corpus-based and genre-based approaches to text analysis in EAP/ESP: Countering criticisms against corpus-based methodologies. *English for Specific Purposes*, 24, 321–32.

Flowerdew, L. (2009). Applying corpus linguistics to pedagogy: A critical evaluation. *International Journal of Corpus Linguistics*, 14(3), 393–417.

Fludernik, M. (2009). *An Introduction to Narratology*. London: Routledge.

Forchini, P. (2012). *Movie Language Revisited: Evidence from Multi-Dimensional Analysis and Corpora*. Bern: Peter Lang.

Freddi, M. (2009). The phraseology of contemporary filmic speech: Formulaic language and translation. In M. Freddi and M. Pavesi, eds., *Analysing Audiovisual Dialogue: Linguistic and Translational Insights*. Bologna: CLUEB, pp. 101–23.

Gibson, A. & Bell, A. (2010). Performing Pasifika English in New Zealand: The case of *bro'Town*. *English World-Wide*, 31, 231–51.

Gieve, S. & Norton, J. (2007). Dealing with linguistic difference in encounters with Others on British television. In S. Johnson and A. Ensslin, eds., *Language in the Media: Representations, Identities, Ideologies*. London: Continuum, pp. 188–210.

Goffman, E. (1976). Replies and responses. *Language in Society*, 5, 257–313.

Goffman, E. (1979). Footing. *Semiotica*, 25, 1–29.

Goggin, J. (2014). 'Is it true blondes have more fun?' *Mad Men* and the mechanics of serialization. In R. Allen and T. van den Berg, eds., *Serialization in Popular Culture*. New York: Routledge, pp. 80–90.

Goldberg, L. & Rabkin, W. (2003). *Successful Television Writing*, Kindle edn. Hoboken, NJ: John Wiley.

Gramley, S. E. (2012). Vocabulary. In R. Hickey, ed., *Areal Features of the Anglophone World*. Berlin: Walter de Gruyter, pp. 439–62.

Grant, L. E. (1996). Teaching conversation using a television soap. *Prospect*, 11 (3), 60–71.

Green, L. J. (2002). *African American English: A Linguistic Introduction*, Cambridge: Cambridge University Press.

Green, L. J. (2004). African American English. In E. Finegan and J. R. Rickford, eds., *Language in the USA: Themes for the Twenty-First Century*. Cambridge: Cambridge University Press, pp. 76–91.

Gregoriou, C. (2012). 'Times like these, I wish there was a real Dexter': Unpacking serial murder ideologies and metaphors from TV's *Dexter* internet forum. *Language and Literature*, 21, 274–85.

Gregory, M. (1967). Aspects of varieties differentiation. *Journal of Linguistics*, 3 (2), 177–98.

Gries, S. Th. (2006). Some proposals towards a more rigorous corpus linguistics. *Zeitschrift für Anglistik und Amerikanistik*, 54(2), 191–202.

Grieve, J., Nini, A. & Guo, D. (2017). Analyzing lexical emergence in American English online. *English Language and Linguistics*, 21, 99–127.

Hanf, A. (2015). Resourcing authentic language in television series. In D. Nunan and J. C. Richards, eds., *Language Learning beyond the Classroom*. London: Routledge, pp. 138–48.

Hardie, A. (2014). Log ratio – an informal introduction. Available at http://cass .lancs.ac.uk/?p=1133, 16 June 2016.

Hassler-Forest, D. (2014). *The Walking Dead*: Quality television, transmedia serialization and zombies. In R. Allen and T. van den Berg, eds., *Serialization in Popular Culture*. New York: Routledge, pp. 91–105.

Heyd, T. (2010). How you guys doin'? Staged orality and emerging plural address in the television series *Friends*. *American Speech*, 85(1), 33–66.

Hickey, R. (2012). Standard English and standards of English. In R. Hickey, ed., *Standards of English: Codified Varieties around the World*. Cambridge: Cambridge University Press, pp. 1–33.

Hills, M. (2002). *Fan Cultures*. New York: Routledge.

Hohenhaus, P. (2004). Identical constituent compounding – A corpus-based study. *Folia Linguistica*, 38(3–4), 297–331.

Huang, Y. (2015). Lexical cloning in English: A neo-Gricean lexical pragmatic analysis. *Journal of Pragmatics*, 86, 80–5.

Hundt, M. & Mair, C. (1999). 'Agile' and 'uptight' genres: The corpus-based approach to language change in progress. *International Journal of Corpus Linguistics*, 4, 221–42.

Hunston, S. (2002). *Corpora and Applied Linguistics*, Cambridge: Cambridge University Press.

Hunston, S. (2013). Review of: McEnery, T. and Hardie, A. 2012. *Corpus Linguistics: Method, Theory and Practice*. *International Journal of Corpus Linguistics*, 18(2), 290–4.

Hyland, K. (2000). *Disciplinary Discourses: Social Interactions in Academic Writing*. New York: Longman.

Hyland, K. (2010). Researching writing. In B. Paltridge and A. Phakiti, eds., *Continuum Companion to Research Methods in Applied Linguistics*. London: Continuum, pp. 191–20.

Isaacs, D. (2013). Sitcom master class: Creating comedy through character. In L. Venis, ed., *Inside the Room: Writing Television with the Pros at UCLA Extension Writers' Program*, Kindle edn. New York: Penguin, pp. 174–91.

Jaeckle, J. (2013). Introduction: A brief primer for film dialogue study. In J. Jaeckle, ed., *Film Dialogue*. London: Wallflower Press, pp. 1–16.

Jakobson, R. (1960). Closing statement: Linguistics and poetics. In T. Sebeok, ed., *Style in Language*. Cambridge, MA: MIT Press, pp. 350–77.

Jaworski, A. (2007). Language in the media: Authenticity and othering. In S. Johnson and A. Ensslin, eds., *Language in the Media: Representations, Identities, Ideologies*. London: Continuum, pp. 271–80.

Jenkins, H. (1992). *Textual Poachers: Television Fans and Participatory Culture.* New York: Routledge.

Juilland, A., Brodin, D. & Davidovitch, C. (1970). *Frequency Dictionary of French Words.* The Hague: Mouton.

Kilgarriff, A., Baisa, V., Bušta, J., Jakubíček, M., Kovář, V., Michelfeit, J., Rychlý, P. & Suchomel, V. (2014). The Sketch Engine: Ten years on. *Lexicography,* 1(1), 7–36.

Koester, A. (2010). Building small specialised corpora. In A. O'Keeffe and M. McCarthy, eds., *The Routledge Handbook of Corpus Linguistics.* London: Routledge, pp. 66–79.

Kozloff, S. (2000). *Overhearing Film Dialogue.* Berkeley: University of California Press.

Kress, G. & van Leeuwen, T. (2006). *Reading Images: The Grammar of Visual Design,* 2nd edn. London: Routledge.

Kretzschmar, W. A. & Meyer, C. F. (2012). The idea of Standard American English. In R. Hickey, ed., *Standards of English: Codified Varieties around the World.* Cambridge: Cambridge University Press, pp. 139–58.

Lambrou, M. (2014). Stylistics, conversation analysis and the cooperative principle. In M. Burke, ed., *The Routledge Handbook of Stylistics.* Oxon: Routledge, pp. 136–54.

Landau, N. (2014). *The TV Showrunner's Roadmap: 21 Navigational Tips for Screenwriters to Create and Sustain a Hit TV Series,* Kindle edn. New York: Focal Press.

Lavery, D. & Burkhead, C. (eds.). (2011). *Joss Whedon: Conversations.* Jackson: University Press of Mississippi.

Lawson, M. (2007). Mark Lawson talks to David Chase. In J. McCabe and K. Akass, eds., *Quality TV: Contemporary American Television and Beyond.* London: I. B. Tauris, pp. 185–220.

Lin, P. M. S. & Siyanova-Chanturia, A. (2015). Internet television for L2 vocabulary learning. In D. Nunan and J. C. Richards, eds., *Language Learning beyond the Classroom.* London: Routledge, pp. 149–58.

Lippi-Green, R. (1997). *English with an Accent: Language, Ideology and Discrimination in the United States.* London: Routledge.

Lippi-Green, R. (2012). *English with an Accent: Language, Ideology and Discrimination in the United States,* 2nd edn. New York: Routledge.

Lopez, Q. & Bucholtz, M. (2017). 'How my hair look?' Linguistic authenticity and racialized gender and sexuality on *The Wire. Journal of Language and Sexuality,* 6(1), 1–29.

Luginbühl, M. (2015). Media linguistics: On mediality and culturality. *10 Plus 1: Living Linguistics,* 1, 9–26.

Lutzky, U. & Kehoe, A. (2016). Your blog is (the) shit: A corpus linguistic approach to the identification of swearing in computer mediated communication. *International Journal of Corpus Linguistics,* 21(2), 165–91.

Macdonald, I. W. (2016, July). Synthesis based on dogma 2016 survey of 101 US sources. Unpublished manuscript distributed via the Screenwriting Research

Network's electronic mailing list. www.jiscmail.ac.uk/cgi-bin/webadmin?A0= SCREENWRITING-RESEARCH-NETWORK.

MacIntyre, D. (2016). Dialogue: Credibility versus realism in fictional speech. In V. Sotirova, ed., *The Bloomsbury Companion to Stylistics*. London: Bloomsbury Academic, pp. 430–43.

Mair, C. (2006). Tracking ongoing grammatical change and recent diversification in present-day standard English: The complementary role of small and large corpora. In A. Renouf and A. Kehoe, eds., *The Changing Face of Corpus Linguistics: Papers from the 24th International Conference on English Language Research on Computerized Corpora* (ICAME 24). Amsterdam: Rodopi, pp. 355–76.

Mair, C. (2013). The world system of Englishes: Accounting for the transnational importance of mobile and mediated vernaculars. *English World-Wide*, 34(3), 253–78.

Mandala, S. (2007). Solidarity and the Scoobies: An analysis of the -y suffix in the television series *Buffy the Vampire Slayer*. *Language and Literature*, 16(1), 53–73.

Mandala, S. (2008). Representing the future: Chinese and codeswitching in *Firefly*. In R. V. Wilcox and T. R. Cochran, eds., *Investigating Firefly and Serenity: Science Fiction on the Frontier*. London: I. B. Tauris, pp. 31–40.

Mandala, S. (2011). *Star Trek: Voyager*'s Seven of Nine: A case study of language and character in a televisual text. In R. Piazza, M. Bednarek, and F. Rossi, eds., *Telecinematic Discourse: Approaches to the Language of Films and Television Series*. Amsterdam: John Benjamins, pp. 205–23.

Martin, J. R. & Matthiessen, C. M. I. M. (1991). Systemic typology and topology. In F. Christie, ed., *Literacy in Social Processes*. Darwin: Centre for Studies in Language in Education, NT University, pp. 345–83.

Martin, J. R. & White, P. R. R. (2005). *The Language of Evaluation: Appraisal in English*. Basingstoke: Palgrave Macmillan.

McCabe, J. & Akass, K. (eds.). (2007). *Quality TV: Contemporary American Television and Beyond*. London: I. B. Tauris.

McEnery, A., Baker, J. P. & Hardie, A. (2000). Assessing claims about language use with corpus data – Swearing and abuse. In J. M. Kirk, ed., *Corpora Galore: Analyses and Techniques in Describing English*. Amsterdam: Rodopi, pp. 44–55.

McEnery, T. & Hardie, A. (2012). *Corpus Linguistics: Method, Theory and Practice*. Cambridge: Cambridge University Press.

McMillan, J. B. (1980). Infixing and interposing in English. *American Speech*, 55, 163–183.

Meek, B. A. (2006). And the Injun goes 'how!': Representations of American Indian English in white public space. *Language in Society*, 35(1), 93–128.

Messerli, T. C. (2016). Extradiegetic and character laughter as markers of humorous intentions in the sitcom *2 Broke Girls*. *Journal of Pragmatics*, 95, 79–92.

Mitchell, J. G. (2015). Ain't no *Bones* about it: Dialect discrimination in primetime. In P. Donaher and S. Katz, eds., *Ain'thology: The History and Life of a Taboo Word*. Cambridge: Cambridge Scholars Publishing, pp. 298–322.

Mittell, J. (2015). *Complex TV: The Poetics of Contemporary Television Story-telling*. New York: New York University Press.

Mittmann, B. (2006). With a little help from Friends (and others): Lexico-pragmatic characteristics of original and dubbed film dialogue. In C. Houswitschka, G. Knappe, and A. Müller, eds., *Anglistentag 2005, Bamberg – Proceedings*. Trier: WVT, pp. 573–85.

Mukherjee, J. (2015). Response to Davies and Fuchs. *English World-Wide*, 36(1), 34–37.

Murray, T. E. & Simon, B. L. (2008). Colloquial American English: Grammatical features. In E. W. Schneider, ed., *Varieties of English*, vol. 2: *The Americans and the Caribbean*. Berlin: Mouton de Gruyter, pp. 401–27.

Nation, I. S. P. & Waring, R. (1997). Vocabulary size, text coverage, and word lists. In N. Schmitt and M. McCarthy, eds., *Vocabulary: Description, Acquisition and Pedagogy*. Cambridge: Cambridge University Press, pp. 6–19.

Newman, M. (2014). *New York City English*. Boston: Walter de Grutyer.

Oakes, M. (1998). *Statistics for Corpus Linguistics*. Edinburgh: Edinburgh University Press.

O'Keeffe, A., McCarthy, M. & Carter, R. (2007). *From Corpus to Classroom: Language Use and Language Teaching*. Cambridge: Cambridge University Press.

Osimk-Teasdale, R. (2013). Applying existing tagging practices to VOICE. In M. Huber and J. Mukherjee, eds., *VariEng: Studies in Variation, Contacts and Change in English 13 (Corpus Linguistics and Variation in English: Focus on Non-Native Englishes)*. Available at www.helsinki.fi/varieng/series/volumes/13/osimk-teasdale/, 9 March 2016.

Oxford Dictionaries. (2012a). Seven words that gained fame on TV shows. Blog post. Available at http://blog.oxforddictionaries.com/2012/11/words-that-gained-fame-on-tv-shows/, 17 March 2016.

Oxford Dictionaries. (2012b). The language of Buffy Speak. Blog post. Available at http://blog.oxforddictionaries.com/2012/08/buffy-the-vampire-slayer/, 8 February 2017.

Paltridge, B., Thomas, A. & Liu, J. (2011). Genre, performance and *Sex and the City*. In R. Piazza, M. Bednarek and F. Rossi, eds., *Telecinematic Discourse: Approaches to the Language of Films and Television Series*. Amsterdam: John Benjamins, pp. 249–62.

Pearson, R. E. (2007a). Anatomising Gilbert Grissom: The structure and function of the televisual character. In M. Allen, ed., *Reading CSI: Crime TV under the Microscope*. London: I. B. Tauris, pp. 39–56.

Pearson, R. E. (2007b). *Lost* in transition: From post-network to post-television. In J. McCabe and K. Akass, eds., *Quality TV: Contemporary American Television and Beyond*. London: I. B. Tauris, pp. 239–56.

Penfield, J. & Ornstein-Galicia, J. L. (1985). *Chicano English: An Ethnic Contact Dialect*. Amsterdam: John Benjamins.

Peters, P. (2015). Response to Davies and Fuchs. *English World-Wide*, 36(1), 41–4.

Petersen, L. N. (2014). *Sherlock* fan talk: Mediatized talk on Tumblr. *Northern Lights*, 12(1), 87–104.

Petrucci, P. (2012). The translation of cinematic discourse and the question of character equivalence in *Talk to Me*. *Multilingua*, **31**, 231–51.

Pfister, M. (1988). *The Theory and Analysis of Drama*. Cambridge: Cambridge University Press.

Piazza, R., Bednarek, M. & Rossi, F. (eds.). (2011). *Telecinematic Discourse: Approaches to the Language of Films and Television Series*. Amsterdam: John Benjamins.

Pitzl, M.-L., Breiteneder, A. & Klimpfinger, T. (2008). A world of words: Processes of lexical innovation in VOICE. *Vienna English Working Papers (VIEWS)*, **17**(2), 21–46.

Price, J. (2015). 'Oh Jesus Christ!' The use of bad language in contemporary American television series. Honours thesis, University of Sydney.

Priggé, S. (2005). *Created by . . . Inside the Minds of TV's Top Show Creators*. Los Angeles, CA: Silman-James Press.

Prince, G. (2003). *A Dictionary of Narratology*, revised edn. Lincoln: University of Nebraska Press.

Quaglio, P. (2008). Television dialogue and natural conversation: Linguistic similarities and functional differences. In A. Ädel and R. Reppen, eds., *Corpora and Discourse: The Challenges of Different Settings*. Amsterdam: John Benjamins, pp. 189–210.

Quaglio, P. (2009). *Television Dialogue: The Sitcom* Friends *vs. Natural Conversation*, Amsterdam: John Benjamins.

Queen, R. (2004). 'Du hast jar keene Ahnung': African American English dubbed into German. *Journal of Sociolinguistics*, **8**(4), 515–37.

Queen, R. (2012). The days of our lives: Language, gender and affluence on a daytime television drama. *Gender and Language*, **6**(1), 153–80.

Queen, R. (2013). Working with performed language: Movies, television, and music. In C. Mallison, B. Childs, and G. van Herk, eds., *Data Collection in Sociolinguistics: Methods and Applications*. New York: Routledge, pp. 217–27.

Queen, R. (2015). *Vox Popular: The Surprising Life of Language in the Media*. Malden, MA: Wiley-Blackwell.

Rasinger, S. M. (2010). Quantitative methods: Concepts, frameworks and issues. In L. Litosseliti, ed., *Research Methods in Linguistics*. London: Continuum, pp. 49–67.

Raymond, C. W. (2013). Gender and sexuality in animated television sitcom interaction. *Discourse & Communication*, **7**(2), 199–220.

Redvall, E. N. (2013). *Writing and Producing Television Drama in Denmark: From* The Kingdom *to* The Killing. Basingstoke: Palgrave Macmillan.

Renouf, A. (2007). Tracing lexical productivity and creativity in the British media: 'The Chavs and the Chav-Nots'. In J. Munat, ed., *Lexical Creativity, Texts and Contexts*. Amsterdam: John Benjamins, pp. 61–89.

Rey, J. M. (2001). Changing gender roles in popular culture: Dialogue in *Star Trek* episodes from 1966 to 1993. In D. Biber and S. Conrad, eds., *Variation in English: Multi-Dimensional Studies*. London: Longman, pp. 138–56.

Richardson, K. (2006). The dark arts of good people: How popular culture negotiates 'spin' in NBC's *The West Wing*. *Journal of Sociolinguistics*, 10(1), 52–69.

Richardson, K. (2010a). *Television Dramatic Dialogue: A Sociolinguistic Study*. Oxford: Oxford University Press.

Richardson, K. (2010b). Multimodality and the study of popular drama. *Language and Literature*, 19(4), 378–95.

Rimmon-Kenan, S. (2002). *Narrative Fiction: Contemporary Poetics*, 2nd edn. London: Routledge.

Sandler, E. (2007). *The TV Writer's Workbook: A Creative Approach to Television Scripts*, Kindle edn. New York: Bantam Dell.

Scannell, P. (ed.). (1991). *Broadcast Talk*. London: Sage.

Scott, M. (2017a). WordSmith Tools (Version 7). Computer software. Stroud: Lexical Analysis Software.

Scott, M. (2017b). *WordSmith Tools Help*. Stroud: Lexical Analysis Software.

Scott, M. & Tribble, C. (2006). *Textual Patterns: Key Words and Corpus Analysis in Language Education*. Amsterdam: John Benjamins.

Scripted Series Report (2010/11). 2010/11 season. *Médiamétrie*. Available at www.mediametrie.com/eurodatatv/.

Short, M. (1981). Discourse analysis and the analysis of drama. *Applied Linguistics*, 2(2), 180–201.

Short, M. (2014). Analyzing dialogue. In P. Stockwell and S. Whiteley, eds., *The Cambridge Handbook of Stylistics*. Cambridge: Cambridge University Press, pp. 344–59.

Sinclair, J. M. (2005). Corpus and text: Basic principles. In M. Wynne, ed., *Developing Linguistic Corpora: A Guide to Good Practice*. Oxford: Oxbow Books/Arts and Humanities Data Service, pp. 1–16.

Smith, E. S. (2009). *Writing Television Sitcoms*, 2nd edn. Kindle edn. New York: Perigee.

Squires, L. & Iorio, J. (2014). Tweets in the news: Legitimizing medium, standardizing form. In J. Androutsopoulos, ed., *Mediatization and Sociolinguistic Change*. Berlin: De Gruyter, pp. 331–60.

Squires, L. & Queen, R. (2011). Media clips collection: Creation and application for the linguistics classroom. *American Speech*, 86(2), 220–34.

Starfield, S. (2010). Ethnographies. In B. Paltridge and A. Phakiti, eds., *Continuum Companion to Research Methods in Applied Linguistics*. London: Continuum, pp. 50–65.

Stokoe, E. (2008). Dispreferred actions and other interactional breaches as devices for occasioning audience laughter in television 'sitcoms'. *Social Semiotics*, 18(3), 289–307.

Stuart-Smith, J. (2011). The view from the couch: Changing perspectives on the role of the television in changing language ideologies and use. In T. Kristiansen and N. Coupland, eds., *Standard Languages and Language Standards in a Changing Europe*. Oslo: Novus, pp. 223–39.

Stuart-Smith, J. (2016). Bridging the gap(s): The role of style in language change linked to the broadcast media. In J. Thøgersen, N. Coupland, and J. Mortensen, eds., *Style, Media and Language Ideologies*. Oslo: Novus Press, pp. 51–84.

Stubbs, M. & Barth, I. (2003). Using recurrent phrases as text-type discriminators: A quantitative method and some findings. *Functions of Language*, **10** (1), 61–104.

Sunderland, J. (2010). Research questions in linguistics. In L. Litosseliti, ed., *Research Methods in Linguistics*. London: Continuum, pp. 9–28.

Szmrecsanyi, B. & Anderwald, L. (2018). Corpus-based approaches to dialect study. In C. Boberg, J. Nerbonne, and D. Watt, eds., *The Handbook of Dialectology*. Hoboken, NJ: Wiley-Blackwell, pp. 300–313.

Tagliamonte, S. & Roberts, C. (2005). So weird; so cool; so innovative: The use of intensifiers in the television series *Friends*. *American Speech*, **80**(3), 280–300.

Taylor, C. J. (2004). The language of film: Corpora and statistics in the search for authenticity. *Notting Hill* (1998) – A case study. *Miscelánea*, **30**, 71–86.

Taylor, C. (2013). Searching for similarity using corpus-assisted discourse studies. *Corpora*, **8**(1), 81–113.

Thompson, K. (2003). *Storytelling in Film and Television*, Cambridge, MA: Harvard University Press.

Toolan, M. (2001). *Narrative: A Critical Linguistic Introduction*, 2nd edn. London: Routledge.

Toolan, M. (2009). *Narrative Progression in the Short Story: A Corpus Stylistic Approach*. Amsterdam: John Benjamins.

Toolan, M. (2011). 'I don't know what they're saying half the time, but I'm hooked on the series': Incomprehensible dialogue and integrated multimodal characterisation in *The Wire*. In R. Piazza, M. Bednarek, and F. Rossi, eds., *Telecinematic Discourse: Approaches to the Language of Films and Television Series*. Amsterdam: John Benjamins, pp. 161–83.

Toolan, M. (2014). Stylistics and film. In M. Burke, ed., *The Routledge Handbook of Stylistics*. Oxon: Routledge, pp. 455–70.

Trotta, J. & Blyahher, O. (2011). *Game done changed*: A look at selected AAVE features in the TV series *The Wire*. *Moderna Spark*, **105**(1), 15–42.

Trudgill, P. (1999). Standard English: What it isn't. In T. Bex and R. J. Watts, eds., *Standard English: The Widening Debate*. London: Routledge, pp. 117–28.

Urios-Aparisi, E. & Wagner, M. M. (2011). Prosody of humor in *Sex and the City*. *Pragmatics & Cognition*, **19**(3), 507–29.

Valdeón, R. A. (2011). Dysfluencies in simulated English dialogue and their neutralization in dubbed Spanish. *Perspectives*, **19**(3), 221–32.

Valentini, C. (2013). Phrasal verbs in Italian dubbed dialogues: A multimedia corpus-based study. *Perspectives: Studies in Translatology*, **21**(4), 543–62.

van Leeuwen, T. (1996). Moving English: The visual language of film. In S. Goodman and D. Graddol, eds., *Redesigning English: New Texts, New Identities*. London: Routledge, pp. 81–105.

van Leeuwen, T. (2005). *Introducing Social Semiotics*. London: Routledge.

van Leeuwen, T. (2011). *The Language of Colour: An Introduction*. London: Routledge.

Venis, L. (ed.). (2013). *Inside the Room: Writing TV with the PROS at UCLA Extension Writers' Program*, Kindle edn. New York: Penguin.

Vorhaus, J. (2012). *The Little Book of Sitcom*, Kindle edn. CreateSpace Independent Publishing Platform.

Wagner, E. (2010). Survey research. In B. Paltridge and A. Phakiti, eds., *Continuum Companion to Research Methods in Applied Linguistics*. London: Continuum, pp. 22–38.

Wagner, S. (2012). Pronominal systems. In R. Hickey, ed., *Areal Features of the Anglophone World*. Berlin: Walter de Gruyter, pp. 379–409.

Walshe, S. (2011). 'Normal people like us don't use that type of language. Remember this is the real world.' The language of *Father Ted*: Representations of Irish English in a fictional world. *Sociolinguistic Studies*, 5(1): 127–48.

Webb, S. (2015). Extensive viewing: Language learning through watching television. In D. Nunan and J. C. Richards, eds., *Language Learning beyond the Classroom*. New York: Routledge, pp. 159–68.

Webb, S. & Rodgers, M. P. H. (2009). Vocabulary demands of television programs. *Language Learning*, 59(2), 335–66.

Widawski, M. (2015). *African American Slang: A Linguistic Description*. Cambridge: Cambridge University Press.

White House. (2015). President Obama Interviews the Creator of *The Wire* David Simon. Available at https://medium.com/@WhiteHouse/president-obama-interviews-the-creator-of-the-wire-david-simon-40fb7bd29b18.

Wildfeuer, J. (2014). *Film Discourse Interpretation: Towards a New Paradigm for Multimodal Film Analysis*. London: Routledge.

Wirth, J. & Melvoin, J. (eds.). (2004). *Writing for Episodic TV: From Freelance to Showrunner*. Los Angeles, CA: Writers Guild of America, West. Available at www.writersguildtheater.org/content/default.aspx?id=156, 24 April 2017.

Witten, M. (2013). Revising one-hour drama specs and pilots. In L. Venis, ed., *Inside the Room: Writing Television with the Pros at UCLA Extension Writers' Program*, Kindle edn. New York: Penguin, pp. 73–92.

Wodak, R. (2009). *The Discourse of Politics in Action*. Basingstoke: Palgrave Macmillan.

Wolfram, W. (2008). Urban African American Vernacular English: Morphology and syntax. In E. W. Schneider, ed., *Varieties of English*, vol. 2: *The Americas and the Caribbean*. Berlin: Mouton de Gruyter, pp. 510–33.

Wolfram, W. & Schilling-Estes, N. (2006). *American English*, 2nd edn. Malden, MA: Blackwell.

Woodrow, L. (2010). Researching motivation. In B. Paltridge and A. Phakiti, eds., *Continuum Companion to Research Methods in Applied Linguistics*. London: Continuum, pp. 301–17.

Woods, F. (2008). Generation gap? Mothers, daughters and music. In R. Calvin, ed., Gilmore Girls *and the Politics of Identity: Essays on Family and Feminism in the Television Series*. Jefferson, NC: McFarland, pp. 127–42.

Woolley, S. W. (2013). Speech that silences, silences that speak: 'That's so gay,' 'that's so ghetto,' and safe space in high school. *Journal of Language and Sexuality*, 2(2), 292–319.

Xiao, Z. & McEnery, T. (2005). Two approaches to genre analysis: Three genres in modern American English. *Journal of English Linguistics*, **33**(1), 62–82.

Zago, R. (2015). 'That's none of your business, Sy': The pragmatics of vocatives in film dialogue. In M. Dynel and Chovanec, J. eds., *Participation in Public and Social Media Interactions*. Amsterdam: John Benjamins, pp. 183–207.

Zago, R. (2016). *From Originals to Remake: Colloquiality in English Film Dialogue over Time*. Rome: Bonanno Editore.

Index of TV Series

General Index

accents, 24, 25, 27, 39, 91, 117, 214, 228
act structure, 9
actors
  authenticity, 214
  authorship, 14
  changing the script, 14, 123, 182, 213, 238
  characters, 10
  opportunities for star turns, 63–4, 144
affect. *See* expressivity
African American Vernacular English (AAVE), 26, 50, 169, 180
ain't, 25, 95, 157, 164, 169–77, 242
allegory, 36, 67
alliteration. *See* literary devices
allusion. *See* intertextuality
animation. *See* Disney
apologising, 26, 41, 102, 127, 132, 160
applied linguistics, 4, 5, 17, 113, 245, 248
argument. *See* conflict; disagreement markers
aside. *See* narration
audience. *See also* audience design; authenticity; dramatic irony; functional approach to television series; German university students; language change; socialisation
  characters, 10–11, 49
  community building, 61
  dialogue functions, 22
  discourses, 28
  immersion, 20
  international, 3–4, 219–20
  in linguistics, 218
  moral messages, 67
  non-standard language, 23, 25, 201
  overhearers, 15
audience design, 15, 16, 19, 25, 36, 153, 176, 177, 201, 241, 242

authenticity, 19–23, 70–3, 76, 137, 210, 213, 214, 225–31; *see also* naturalism; realism
authorship, 12–14, 16

bazinga, 74, 202, 231
be like, 29, 230
beat, 9; *see also* scene
broadcast television, 7, 85, 191, 215; *see also* network television
business models, 6, 11, 249

cable television, 7, 11, 85, 157, 191
camera shots, 39, 40, 76; *see also* multimodality
catchphrase, 74, 76, 212, 229
character. *See* characterisation
characterisation. *See also* actors; indexicality
  actor, 11
  age, 47, 50, 62, 183
  anchorage, 36, 47–8, 49, 77, 135, 136, 159, 186
  biographies, 46, 48–9, 161
  character diffusion, 99–100, 174–5
  class, 46, 161, 168, 169, 175
  development, 10, 264
  dialogue cues, 10–11, 26, 49, 51, 201
  education, 169, 170, 175
  ethnicity, 24, 50, 169, 175, 214
  expressive character identity, 10, 49, 50, 191
  gender, 28, 29, 69–70, 137–40, 162, 168, 170, 174
  indexicality, 18, 26, 49, 174, 175, 180, 181–2, 198
  LGBTQI, 66, 160–1
  linguistic bundles/clustering, 26, 49–50, 174, 177, 248

297